Food Supply Chain Management

DISCARD

Food Supply Chain Management

Issues for the hospitality and retail sectors

Edited by
**Jane F. Eastham, Liz Sharples and
Stephen D. Ball**

OXFORD AUCKLAND BOSTON JOHANNESBURG MELBOURNE NEW DELHI

Butterworth-Heinemann
Linacre House, Jordan Hill, Oxford OX2 8DP
225 Wildwood Avenue, Woburn, MA 01801-2041
A division of Reed Educational and Professional Publishing Ltd

R̵ A member of the Reed Elsevier plc group

First published 2001

British Library Cataloguing in Publication Data
Food supply chain management: issues for the hospitality and
retail sectors
1. Business logistics 2. Food industry and trade
I. Eastham, Jane F. II. Sharples, Liz III. Ball, Stephen D.
664'.0687

ISBN 0 7506 4762 0

For information on all Butterworth-Heinemann
publications visit our website at www.bh.com

Typeset by Florence Production, Stoodleigh, Devon
Printed and bound in Great Britain by MPG Books Ltd, Bodmin, Cornw

Contents

Contributors

Stephen Allen is a management consultant currently working in the food sector. His career to date spans 15 years in the strategic consultancy role but has included international CEO roles in different sectors (Pharmaceuticals and Construction, Heavy Equipment), in the USA, South East Asia and Central and Western Europe. A move into the food sector some three years ago involved looking at the issues facing the fresh produce sector and the wholesale markets. His work has particularly focused on facilitating business change on the basis of supply chain principles.

Nicholas Alexander is Professor of Service Management in the School of Retail and Financial Services at the University of Ulster. Previously he was Professor of Retail Management at Bournemouth University and Coca-Cola Lecturer in Retailing at the University of Edinburgh. His main research interests are international retailing and retail financial services. He has published numerous books and articles on retail management. He is editor of *The Service Industrial Journal*.

Stephen D. Ball is Reader in Hospitality Management at Sheffield Hallam University and visiting Research Fellow at Manchester Metropolitan University. He has considerable operational, management, consultancy and lecturing experience within the hospitality industry and has tutored on management development programmes for national and international organizations. He was editor and chief contributor to the Jordans Survey, Britain's Fast Food Industry, and he recently collated and compiled information for the British Hospitality Association's British Hospitality: Trends and Statistics 2000 Report.

Colin G. Bamford is Professor of Transport and Logistics at the University of Huddersfield, West Yorkshire. His interest in transport issues orginated in the early 1970s when he was one of Ken

Gwilliam's researchers at the University of Leeds. At Huddersfield he has been responsible for the development of a pioneering suite of undergraduate courses in transport and logistics management, More recently, he has been involved in setting up a new distance-learning training programme for logistics managers in Hungary. He has written articles and supervised research on a variety of supply chain management topics and published textbooks in the field of transport economics.

David Barling is a Senior Lecturer at the Centre for Food Policy at the Wolfson Institute of Health Sciences, Thames Valley University in London. He is programme leader for the MA in Food Policy, the first taught MA of its kind. David has researched the regulation of GM food since the early 1990s and has published in a number of journals. He was lead author of a policy assessment of GM foods, entitled 'The social aspects of food biotechnology: a European view', published in *Environmental Toxicology and Pharmacology* in 1999.

Sean Beer is an agriculturalist with considerable practical experience, but for the past twelve years the focus of his work has been in education. He is currently Senior Lecturer in Agriculture at the Centre for Land Based Studies at Bournemouth University. Current research and consultancy interests include retailing and the food supply chain, marketing and cooperation in agriculture, small family farms, the producer/consumer relationship, and hill and upland farming. He has been awarded both a Rotary Foundation Scholarship and a Winston Churchill Fellowship. He was recently made a Nuffield Scholar and is a regular commentator on rural, food and environmental matters on radio and television.

Anthony J. Berry is Professor of Management Control at Sheffield Hallam University. His research interests cover supply chains and he has managed a number of consultancy projects in risk and control. He previously spent 14 years in the UK and US aircraft industry and 25 years at Manchester Business School. He is joint editor of the *Leadership and Organizational Development Journal*.

Michael A. Bourlakis is a Lecturer in Food Marketing in the Department of Agricultural Economics and Food Marketing, University of Newcastle-upon-Tyne. He graduated in Business Administration at the Department of Business Administration, Athens University of Economics and Business, Greece and obtained his MBA degree in 1995 from the Department of Business Studies, University of Edinburgh. Michael worked as a sales manager for the largest dairy company in Greece, and as a research associate at the Management Centre, University of

Leicester and at the Oxford Institute of Retail Management, Templeton College, University of Oxford. His current teaching and research interests include logistics and supply chain management, food marketing, European food retailing and retail strategy.

Paul D. Cousins is a Lecturer at the University of Bath, a post he has held (amongst others) since 1993. Paul began his working life with Westland Helicopters Ltd, Yeovil, Somerset, where he was employed as chief buyer. He has had further experience as a contractant negotiator for Sikovsky Aircrafts, USA and AT Kearney consultants. In 1993 he won, along with Richard Lamming, a research grant to develop a methodology for assessing supplier/buyer relationships in a project known as the 'RAP project'. Thereon followed other key research projects in supply chain management, including ESSCMO, Environmentally Sound Supply Chain Management. Paul has written extensively in this area, including academic texts and papers.

John Cullen is Professor of Management Accounting at Sheffield Hallam University. He worked in senior financial and commercial roles in the manufacturing industry before entering into higher education. He has written books, with other colleagues, on the management of financial resources and the consequences of inter-firm supply chains for management accounting. He has also published numerous articles in both academic and professional journals. He is the Head of the Centre for Supply Chain Accounting Research, which is based at Sheffield Hallam University. His current research interests are in the areas of supply chain accounting, management control and developing management accounting systems in the health service.

Rachel Duffy is a PhD student at Imperial College Wye, University of London. Her PhD focused on food supply chain issues.

Jane F. Eastham is a Senior Lecturer in Food Management at Sheffield Hallam University. The daughter of an archaeologist who was interested in eating patterns of Palaeolithic man, she developed an early interest in food, sources of food and food consumption. After a number of years in the hospitality sector, she moved into higher education, in 1990, to teach food and hospitality students at Sheffield Hallam University. Her research interests include supply/demand issues for the hospitality industry, supply chain management, total quality management and the role of independents in new concept development. She has been involved in a number of consultancy projects across the fresh produce sectors.

Andrew Fearne is a Senior Lecturer in Food Industry Management at Wye College, University of London. The son of a pig farmer in the South East of England, he is a graduate from Kingston, and Newcastle-upon-Tyne Universities. His main research interests are supply chain management, consumer behaviour and market research. He is editor of *Supply Chain Management*, an international journal which addresses both practical and research issues concerned with the linkages in the food supply chain, from the primary producer to the consumer.

Matthew Gorton is a Lecturer in the Department of Agricultural Economics and Food Marketing, University of Newcastle-upon-Tyne. His research considers the evolution of agri-food systems in Central and Eastern Europe.

Ferenc Z. Guba is a PhD research student at the Budapest University of Economic Sciences. His research focuses on agri-food industry restructuring and his thesis considers transfers and inefficiencies along Hungarian food supply chains.

Lynette Harris is Director of HR Professional Development at the Nottingham Trent University's Business School. Prior to joining the university in 1988 Lynette was a personnel director and has worked as a personnel practitioner in both the public and private sectors. Lynette is the joint editor of *Strategic Human Resourcing: Principles, Perspectives and Practice* (1999: Financial Times/Pitman Publishing), an active researcher on contemporary issues in human resource management and the author of articles in both academic and practitioner journals. Lynette is a member of the IPD's Membership and Education Committee, serves on its Quality Assurance panel and is policy adviser to the Derbyshire and Nottingham Branch.

David Hughes is Sainsbury Professor at Wye College, University of London, a post he has held since September 1991. David has over twenty years' experience in the fields of agribusiness management and food marketing and is a frequent speaker at major national and international conferences on global food industry issues. He has published extensively in areas of food supply chain.

Tim Knowles is Senior Lecturer in Hospitality Management at Sheffield Hallam University. His PhD in the field of Food Safety applied to the European Hotel Industry was awarded from the University of Luton. He is consultant editor of Croner CCH Food Hygiene Manual and is on the Editorial Board of the *International Journal of Wine Marketing*. He has some 85 publications to his name, including books, chapters in books and refereed articles in internationally recognized journals. In addition, he has lectured extensively abroad for organizations such as the World Tourism Organization, British Council, Cyprus Government, Chilean Government and the European Commission.

Herbert Kotzab is an Assistant Professor of International Supply Chain Management in the Department of Operations Management at the Copenhagen Business School. He received a Master of Business Administration in Marketing and Management and a doctorate degree from the Vienna University of Economics and Business Administration. His research focuses on the critical success factors of retail logistics systems and the application of new information technology for supply chain management. He has lectured and offered executive education programmes in close cooperation with the Budapest University of Economic Sciences, the J.L. Kellogg Graduate School of Management and INSEAD. In 1998, he was visiting scholar at the Centre for Transportation Studies at the Massachusetts Institute of Technology.

Kevin Nield has worked in a wide variety of positions within the catering and retail industries. His specialist subject areas are the economic and financial aspects of international hospitality management and quality management. He has written a number of papers on the subject of quality management and has given presentations at international conferences, in particular on work conducted in Romania. Kevin is the member of the editorial advisory committee for *Hospitality* magazine and is a member of the Council for Hospitality Management's teaching, learning and assessment committee. Kevin has undertaken consultancies for small, medium and large-scale concerns in the hospitality industry in areas such as market research, facilities development, menu design and costing.

Rayka Presbury has 21 years' experience in hospitality management and has held management roles at the Sydney Marriott, Southern Cross Hotel and Holiday Inn Menzies. She has run Customer Service and Banquet Sales courses for a number of five star hotels, including the Cebel, the Wentworth, Quay West and the Carlton Crest Hotels. Rayka is currently enrolled as a M.Comm. (Hons) student and her research interests are in the area of customer service, employee relations and empowerment.

Terry Robinson is Reader in Marketing and the leader of the marketing section at the University of Teesside. He has published extensively in the areas of relationship marketing, the internationalization of retailing and retailing in the newly emergent states of central and Eastern Europe. He has taught in many countries in Central and Eastern Europe and given research papers in conferences around the world.

William Seal is Professor of Management Accounting in the Department of Accounting, Finance and Management at the University of Essex. He has published extensively in accounting and management control systems. His research interests range from accounting in post-socialist Europe, management accounting and autopoietic systems theory and management accounting in supply chains.

Liz Sharples has a wide experience of the hospitality industry with a background in hotel management and university catering. Her teaching and research interests relate to the management of food in hospitality operations, environmental issues and the inter-relationships between food, wine and tourism. Her publications have focused on vegetarianism, environmental impact of the food supply and wine tourism. She has acted as consultant to several national organizations advising on concept development, hospitality operations and the implementation of healthy eating programmes.

Denis R. Towill is presently Director of the Logistics Systems Dynamics Group, Cardiff University. He holds a Doctor of Science Degree from the University of Birmingham, is a Fellow of the Royal Academy of Engineering, and a distinguished overseas scientist in Eta Kapa Nu. He has served as chairman of the management division, Institution of Electrical Engineers, and been a member of the Royal Academy of Engineering Construction Sector Panel and Management of Technology Panel. Professor Towill has wide industrial and academic experience in the areas of engineering management, logistics and manufacturing systems. He has also been selected to receive the Andersen Consulting Award for the best paper published in the *International Journal of Logistics Management.*

Jennifer A. Wade is a Senior Lecturer in Hospitality Management at Sheffield Hallam University. Jennifer has researched and published on the hospitality industry and environmentalism for more than a decade. Jennifer is a member of the HCIMA Environmental Working Group.

Kathryn Webster is a Lecturer in the School of Service Management at the University of Brighton. Her areas of research include food and health policy, and environmental management in the hospitality industry. Her book *Environmental Management in the Hospitality Industry* was published by Cassell in 2000.

Foreword

Of all the commercial sectors that espouse the concept of supply chains, the two that are addressed in this book can perhaps claim the most legitimacy.

First, the very concept derives much of its logic from the fundamental principle of the food chain. A study of the passage of matter from earth to earth through every living organism on the planet, taking the many forms of mass and energy, has much to teach us about supply – not least its cyclical nature and fragility.

Second, the business of retailing has always been a genuine chain of events – getting the goods to market. In some chains the perishability of produce drives urgency and the search for efficiency, creating in its wake social institutions ranging from the early hours kept by fruit and vegetable markets to the annual dash to bring Beaujolais Nouveau to Britain. In others, the ability to delay supply has long been a source of commercial power – make it hard to get and the customers will beat a path to your door.

These historic and basic features of food and retailing have always been critical to people and organizations engaged in these sectors. The advent of electronic trading and genetic engineering may be seen as revolutionary but they are perhaps no more profound than, say, the invention of the refrigerator or pasteurization. The sheer scale of connectivity in modern supply networks, however, means that impacts are felt very quickly in many sectors – and become widespread, internationally, almost immediately.

A colleague of mine recently commented that in developing personalized marketing and home proficiency in home delivery of groceries, Tesco have finally mastered the services provided for centuries by the corner shop! Perhaps nothing is really new.

The concepts of inter-organizational strategic supply relationships, supply mapping and dynamics, international operations and so on, covered in this book, are clearly of central importance to managing this dynamic and fragile part of human endeavour.

How might collaboration be combined with competition between buyer and seller? How can large-scale logistics be reconciled with Victorian infrastructure? Are people going to stay at home and buy their groceries by computer: what will happen to shops? Will all hotels and restaurants look the same, eventually?

These chapters provide many valuable perspectives on these questions and many more, dealing with the management challenges associated with supply chains in the food industry and the retail and hospitality sectors. I commend the editors in their choice of authors.

Richard Lamming
CIPS Professor of Purchasing and Supply Management
Director: Centre for Research in Strategic Purchasing and Supply
School of Management
University of Bath UK

Preface

This book takes as its theme food supply chain management. Supply chains and their management are relatively new, yet important, emerging, fields of interest. Both are fast becoming pivotal to business success and survival. This is as much a truism for those sectors involved with food as it is for all other industrial sectors. This book concentrates upon the application of supply chain management to the food retail and hospitality sectors – both of which are large and significant.

This text is believed to be the first of its kind and has come about from a longstanding personal interest in supply chain management. This interest has brought me into contact with colleagues from Innovative Supply Chain and Networks (ISCAN), and the research body attached – the Research Development and Dissemination Unit (REDDIS), some of whose members have contributed to this book. A further consequence of my interest in the management of supply chains has been the development of a much needed unit in food supply chain management for final year undergraduates at Sheffield Hallam University. This book will be of help to them in their studies.

It is intended that the book be used on a variety of business and management courses at undergraduate and postgraduate level, but, in particular it has been designed to meet the needs of final year undergraduates on Food and Hospitality Management programmes. Postgraduate Management students, particularly those on conversion masters, will also benefit. The book is also relevant for managers who are active in the food industry.

The principal aim of the book is to enable readers to make the transition between operations management and the more holistic approach of supply chain management. With the assistance of a number of experts from across traditional functional areas, who have in common a focus on the 'business' of managing across businesses, the intention is to analyse the food supply chain and issues of managing according to cross organizational management principles.

The text emphasizes these ideas through a series of case studies drawn from the hospitality and retail sectors. Given the sensitivity of businesses to the disclosure of their activities in this area, some of the names of the organizations have been changed.

Supply chain management is a new business practice and has been stimulated by the growth of global markets and the diversity of market needs. It has arisen from individual business sectors, like the catering and food retail sectors, as a means of managing the increased complexity within the marketplace. In post-industrial society businesses have moved away from vertical integration strategies towards concentrating on core competencies in order to reduce costs and add value. Supply chain management is thus a response to two main factors; the management of outsourced non-core activities and, given the diversity of consumer markets, the recognition of the synergistic value of collaboration, in terms of market access, information, technological developments and innovation.

The recent fuel crisis in the UK and other Western European countries demonstrated the significance of supply chains and their management. In Autumn 2000, hauliers, farmers and other interested bodies reeked havoc on the supply structure of these countries. The failure to maintain supplies of fuel from UK refineries and depots to retailers and consumers resulted in a restricted movement of raw materials, finished goods and people. Such action raises complex issues relating to, on the one hand, the interconnectivity of the supply structures and of businesses, and, on the other, the implications of managing a business operation when the action of one part of the supply chain has a major impact on another.

If the ingredient of 'quality' is then added, it can be demonstrated that the success of a business revolves around its ability to coordinate key suppliers and suppliers of suppliers, in line with customer needs and expectations. A firm's success is linked to the strengths of its weakest supply chain partner.

So what is supply chain management? Responses vary, even from the contributors to this book. Paraphrasing Lummas and Vokurka (1999), we as editors define supply chain management as the:

> Coordination and integration of all activities in delivering a product from its initial primary source through to the consumer into a seamless process, thereby linking all partners in the chain internal and external to the organization. External linkages can be both horizontal and vertical.

Issues about managing across organizational boundaries are different from those of just internal functions (Harland *et al.*, 1999) Whilst this could imply that there is a need to move purchasing out of the realms of a clerical activity into a strategic function, there is an argument that all operational functions likewise need to become strategic in function.

This book has three main objectives:

1. to examine the development of food supply chain management related to the hospitality and retail industries;

2. to explore issues for operational management;

3. to present a range of expert perspectives relating to food supply chain management and to the hospitality and retail sectors.

To reflect these, the text is divided into three sections:

Part 1 – Supply Chain Management

Part 2 – Management of the Supply Chain

Part 3 – Supply Chain Perspectives.

In Part 1 we examine the nature of the food supply chain and the development of supply chain management in the food sectors. Authors explore the function of food in society in the food supply chain, the nature of supply chain management in principle and practice, and broader issues such as social responsibility. It is worth noting that the term 'food' has been taken to refer to both food and drink. The contributors in this section include Sean Beer, Kathryn Webster, Andrew Fearne, David Hughes, Rachel Duffy, Colin Bamford and Jenny Wade, all of whom are specialists in their fields.

Part 2 is designed to confront the issues for operational management in the management across organizational boundaries. Paul Cousins, Denis Towill, Lynette Harris, Tony Berry, John Cullen, William Seal and Terry Robinson confront issues such as stages of emergence of long term relationships and the importance of trust and commitment. The key to this section is in recognizing the implications of changing from traditional adversarial relationships to those of collaboration. Problems of changing culture, practice and mindsets appear critical to business success. In this section all authors are actively involved in research in their respective operational areas and are drawing ideas from a whole range of industries, including food.

Part 3 is a group of diverse perspectives offered by experts in their fields including, Nick Alexander, Kevin Nield, David Barling, Tim Knowles, Herbert Kotzab, Rayka Presbury, Matthew Gorton, Ference Guba, Michael Bourlakis, Sean Beer and Steve Allen. This section is divided into three parts – Internationalization, in both the hospitality and retail sectors, Contemporary Issues and Insights into the Future.

In the International section we note, with interest, the diverse market penetration strategies of the retail and hospitality sectors as they move towards international status.

In other instances authors have conflicting perspectives. For example, in the Kotzab discussion on ECR (Efficient Consumer Response) in Europe, he suggests that Category Management has enhanced the grocer's ability to meet consumer needs – a distinct variance to Allen's proposition that Category Management and the de-listing process will, in effect, reduce the number of small and medium-sized suppliers, produce choice, and thus negatively impact on the retailers' ability to meet customer needs. These highlight current debates such as the relative value of regional as against global commerce. The implications of the legislative process on the compatibility of food safety policy in European hotels, and comparisons between ECR in the US with the development of ECR in the EU and their respective impact on the supply chains.

Finally, on a personal note, my co-editors and I would like to acknowledge the contributions from all the authors, and proffer our thanks for both their enthusiastic support and their patience on receipt of more feedback than anticipated.

Jane F. Eastham
Sheffield 2001

References

Harland C.M., Lamming R.C. and Cousins P.D (1999) Developing the concept of supply strategy. *International Journal of Operations and Production Management*, 19 (7), pp. 650–73.

ummas R.R. and Vokurka R.J. (1999) Defining supply chain management: a historical perspective and practical guide. *International Management and Data Systems*, 99 (1), pp. 11–17.

The Supply Chain

The catering and food retail industries: a contextual insight

Jane F. Eastham, Stephen D. Ball and Liz Sharples

Key objectives

- To define the catering and the food and drink retail industries

- To explain the blurring between the two industries

- To identify similarities and differences between the two industries

- To provide an overview of the size, scale, structures and operating formats of the catering and the food and drink retail industries

- To identify and discuss the key issues that have affected the food and drinks supply chain related to the catering and the food and drink retail industries

Introduction

Put simply, consumers have two basic options when purchasing and consuming food and drink. One is to eat and drink outside the home in a hospitality operation. The other is to purchase food and drink from food retailers, which is fresh or partially prepared, for consumption in or away from the home, but outside a hospitality operation. This basic distinction conceals many exceptions such as: the purchase of ready meals from delicatessens, takeaway meals from fish and chip shops, Chinese, Indian or other takeaways, hot pies or filled sandwiches from a baker's shop or garage forecourt. The boundary between catering and food and drink retail is therefore fuzzy and the division between the two industries is becoming increasingly blurred as a result of technological developments and the activities of operators. These factors are explained further below. This chapter takes the stance that because of this blurring, issues facing the food supply chain of each of these industries, cannot be considered independently. This stance underpins the rationale for the consideration of these industries jointly throughout this book.

The purpose of this chapter is to provide the contextual backdrop for the rest of the book. The UK scene is emphasized in particular. However, given the global nature of both industries reference will also be made to the international perspective.

Defining the catering and food and drink retail industries

Ideally in order to examine food and drink supply chain management, in the context of the catering and food retail industries, the constituents and boundaries of each need first to be defined. Unfortunately, this is less than straightforward, as there are no single, universally accepted definitions or interpretations for either of these industries.

Inconsistencies particularly lie in the classification of subsectors and their constituents. Different sources such as government agencies, market intelligence consultants and other experts use different criteria. Jones (1996), for example, uses a sectoral classification for the foodservice/catering industry in order to focus on the customer's needs and how the industry responds operationally to these needs. Market intelligence agencies reporting on the retail sector, may variously classify according to store size, customer usage, and ownership. This leads to inconsistencies in data provided.

Retail defined

Market pressures and changing life styles have brought about new formats. In the 1970s food retail establishments could be divided into multiples, co-operatives (Co-ops) and independents.

Changes in shopping patterns and preferred retail formats and the emergent dominance of the major retailers in the market-place, have resulted in the appearance of, on the one hand, new retail formats e.g. convenience stores, and on the other, the diversification of non-food retailers into the food retail sector. As major retailers have moved into other retail sectors as a means of increasing market share, other retail sectors such as petrol stations and licence retailers, have adapted to supply the growing convenience market. Food retail can be now classified according to usage. Shopper surveys (Mintel 1999a) demonstrate a clear increase in secondary shopping activity. Whilst the main weekly shop may still be conducted at an out of town or edge of town location, increasingly there is a demand for local en-route units. Likewise, treats may be purchased from specialist producers or vendors. At its simplest this means that we can identify three venue types: major shopping venues, secondary shopping venues or convenience, and specialist shops. Main weekly shops tend to be carried out at multiple retailers, particularly the Big Four, i.e. Sainsbury, Tesco, Asda and Safeway, although a smaller proportion of consumers utilize discounters, e.g. Netto. Secondary shopping takes place at convenience retailers, which are constituted of a wide range of formats including forecourts, Co-ops, symbol groups and licensed retailers.

Catering defined

In contrast, the catering industry is simply considered to cover all undertakings concerned with the provision of prepared food and drink ready for consumption away from home. It also includes establishments that provide a take-away and/or delivery service where the food and/or drink are prepared within the establishment but consumed elsewhere. Yet, likewise, convenience stores, major retailers and independent retailers increasingly provide a similar service.

The industry can be characterised by its diversity comprising many types of food and beverage outlets in a range of different sectors. It is possible to distinguish the different types of outlets in various ways. For instance, distinctions can be made according to: size, core products (menu items sold), branded or unbranded. Catering can be also classified according to whether catering is the main activity of the undertaking as, for example, in a privately owned restaurant, and those where it is a secondary activity as, for example is the case of catering in a school.

Traditionally catering activity has been divided into either that associated with 'profit' markets or 'cost' markets. The former includes such profit-orientated establishments as restaurants, fast-food chain outlets, cafes/takeaways, pubs, leisure and travel catering outlets while the latter includes catering outlets for business, education and health care. This system of classification may have its shortcomings; recent developments have blurred the division between profit- and cost-orientated establishments, for example, some hospital catering is now carried out by profit centred contract caterers. It is generally understood, however, that in the main most establishments fall into one of these categories and it is this system that is used by most market research organizations.

Separate or overlapping industries?

The distinctions between catering and food and drink retailing are becoming blurred for a variety of reasons.

Changes in food processing and packaging (Lawson 1987) ● ● ●

Take sandwiches for example. The advent of vacuum packaging has enabled these to be sold in food retail outlets as well as in hospitality operations. Corporate high street retailers such as Boots and Marks & Spencer have dominated the sandwich market. The purchase of commercially prepared meals for consumption at home, or away from the home, which minimize the need for preparation, are a key contributory factor towards the blurring of catering and food and drink retailing. Technomic, a USA consultancy firm, relates this blurring to the desire for convenience (see Figure 1.1).

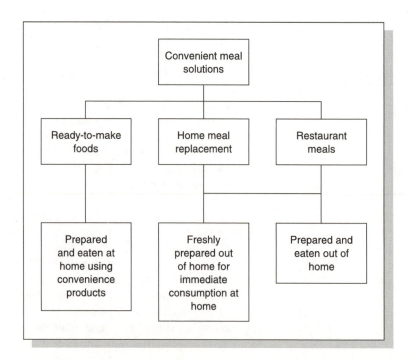

Figure 1.1
Blurring definitions – the growth of 'convenience' (Technomic 1997, cited in Haines and Turner, 1998)

The operator • • •

Often organizations may be considered hospitality entities, e.g. quick service restaurants or public houses but their operators call themselves retailers.

The location • • •

Some retailers are located adjacent to hospitality operations thus offering themselves as alternative sources of food for immediate consumption.

An overlap of interests • • •

This has led to an increased investment by retail, hotel and leisure groups in setting up their own foodservice operations either independently or through agreements with established restaurant chains. Retailers have become increasingly aware that their revenues can grow through foodservice as a result of retaining shoppers on site for longer and attracting more customers and the relatively higher margins on foodservice products *vis-à-vis* food retail items. Similarly, hotel and leisure groups have used foodservice to extend their product mix for customer benefit and enhance their overall margins.

Conglomerate activity • • •

Certain companies have interests in both food/drink retailing and catering. Whitbread plc, for example, operates, amongst others, First Quench, which is a prominent name in High Street drinks retailing with retail brands such as Thresher, and restaurant brands such as Beefeater and Pizza Hut.

The diversification of retailers, leisure groups and others into catering and the growth of home meal replacement has contributed to the blurring and has led the Henley Centre to state that 'The dividing line between catering and food retailing is getting thinner. How, for instance, should sandwich bars, home delivery pizza and sandwich bars from convenience stores be defined?' (Haines and Turner 1998).

Size, significance and growth of the UK catering industry

Catering, or what is increasingly being called foodservice, forms a substantial part of the British hospitality industry and, as such, it can be regarded as an industry in its own right. However, it is important to note that independents continue to hold the predominant market share – 66% of sales and 71% of outlets – and are particularly prevalent in less central urban and rural locations (Eastham and Johnston 1998).

Today, the UK catering industry generates large revenues for its providers and is a valuable contributor to government income, economic growth, the balance of payments and employment. The precise numbers employed in 'catering' occupations are unknown but in 1998 of the 1.88 million total hospitality employees, 1 263 000 were employed in specialist hospitality businesses, i.e. hotels, restaurants, pubs, clubs and bars, contract catering or were self-employed, while the remainder were employed in hospitality services, e.g. health care and services (HtF, 1999). It is estimated that about 75% of hospitality employees are employed in the provision of food and drink away from home and that around 70% are part-time employees.

In 1999, the UK catering industry grew compared with the previous year and 1995 in terms of food sales, meals consumed and food purchases, even though the total number of outlets declined marginally (see Tables 1.1 and 1.2). The profit sector,

	1995	1998	1999
Outlets	301 619	297 872	296 541
Profit sector meals (m)	5351	5820	5853
Cost sector meals (m)	3132	3145	3123
Total meals (m)	8483	8965	8976
Food purchases (£bn)	8.3	8.7	8.7
Food sales (£bn)	21.2	22.5	22.6

Source: Foodservice Intelligence
NB Prices are expressed in constant 1999 prices

Table 1.1
UK catering industry, 1995, 1998 and 1999

Hotels	60 949
Restaurants	15 954
Fast food	2221
Cafes and takeaways	29 270
Pubs	54 723
Travel	1359
Leisure	48 523
Subtotal for profit sector	212 999
Business and industry	20 683
Health care	25 075
Education	34 429
Ministry of Defence	3355
Subtotal for cost sector	83 543
Overall total	296 541

Source: Foodservice Intelligence

Table 1.2
Number of outlets in the profit and cost sectors, 1999

which represented almost three-quarters of all catering outlets in 1999, accounted for this decline, with cafes and takeaways and public houses being mainly responsible. Some profit sectors did, however, increase their numbers of outlets, most notably the fast-food, leisure catering sectors and hotels (BHA 2000). In the cost sector the number of health care catering outlets especially increased, while outlets in business and industry decreased. Table 1.1 shows the outlet numbers in 1999. Over 8900 million meals were served from UK catering outlets in 1999, with the majority from the profit sector. This showed an increase from 1995. While those served from profit sector outlets increased, those from the cost sector declined slightly.

In 1999 the value of food purchases in the profit sector accounted for over 82% of all food purchases within the catering industry (see Table 1.3). From 1995 to 1999, at constant prices, the value of purchases in the profit sector increased by nearly 7% while those in the cost sector declined by 5%. In 1999, food sales in the profit sector accounted for 93% of total food sales. Yet in comparison to the retail sector the range of products purchased by each operating unit is relatively small. A pizzeria outlet may stock a total of 60 SKUs (stock keeping units) as opposed to 25 000 SKUs found within a major supermarket chain, 600–800 SKUs held by discount stores, and 100–500 SKUs held by specialist retailers.

	1995	1999
Hotels	1579	1667
Restaurants	1081	1137
Fast food	606	684
Cafes and take-aways	1018	959
Pubs	1580	1878
Travel	319	357
Leisure	516	574
Business and industry	527	513
Health care	525	500
Education	517	469
Ministry of Defence	86	84
Total	8354	8741

Prices are expressed in constant 1999 prices.
Source: Foodservice Intelligence

Table 1.3
Value of food purchases (£m), 1995 and 1999

Three hundred and forty-seven companies with branded food-service units have been identified by the Hotel and Catering Research Centre (HCRC) (2000). In 1999 they operated 713 brands with 22 859 units. Table 1.4 shows that Scottish and Newcastle Retail is the leading operator with seven other brewers/pub retailers. The 20 leading UK foodservice operators in 1999 represented nearly 62% of all the branded foodservice units. However, the industry is fragmented and no operator dominates. Table 1.5 shows that the three largest UK foodservice brands are pub retailers.

Size, significance and growth of the UK retail sector

The grocery retail sector is a significant area of economic activity in the UK. It employs more than 950 000 people and it has a current value of £9.6 billion (IGD 2000). The UK grocery sector is the third largest in the European Union. However, the projected market size for the year 2005 has been given (IGD 2000) at £112 billion, representing a continuation of the slow-down in market growth that began in the 1990s.

Retail formats

Supermarkets

During the second half of the twentieth century, UK food retail formats have changed significantly. The supermarket, which first emerged in the USA in 1930, arrived in Europe after the Second World War, and now has become the major form of food retailing across the UK and Northern Europe. In the UK the top four food retailers hold 45% of the market share (see details in Tables 1.6 and 1.7). The supermarket, in its current form, carries 20 000–25 000 SKUs, half of which are own brand, produced by the manufacturers to retailer specifications.

From the 1980s, larger stores were developed in areas of town, or on the edge of towns, and are linked to major road infrastructures. This promoted access and encouraged still further the trend of one-stop, weekly shopping. During this period retailers sought to achieve greater efficiencies through retailer controlled regional distribution centres (RDCs). RDCs receive, and consolidate produce from a whole range of suppliers, before delivery to stores. Although many of the distribution centres are composite (Marchant 1999), i.e. receive all ranges of produce – ambient, chilled, frozen etc. – this is not always the case. In addition, there are variations relating the degree of contracting out. This appears to vary according to the scale of investment. 'Smaller companies, with one or two depots, tended to run their own operation whereas the majors had a mix of in-house and contracting out . . .' (Marchant 1999). Centralization has the additional advantage of increasing their purchasing power and changing the power balance in the supply chain in their favour (Harvey 2000).

Operator	Units in 1999	% mkt share
Scottish and Newcastle Retail	1978	8.2
Whitbread Inns	1832	7.6
Allied Domecq Restaurants & Bars	1534	6.4
Greggs plc	1057	4.4
McDonald's Restaurants	851	3.5
Wolverhampton and Dudley Brewery plc	825	3.4
Whitbread Restaurants	769	3.2
Greenalls Pub Division	656	2.7
Bass Leisure Retail	615	2.6
Allied Domecq Inns	598	2.5
Granada Little Chef and Travelodge	470	2.0
Burger King (UK)	460	1.9
Tricon International	400	1.7
Pizza Hut (UK)	389	1.6
Greene King plc	355	1.5
City Centre Restaurants	303	1.0
JD Wetherspoon	295	1.2
Rank Hovis	281	1.2
Wimpy International Ltd	270	1.1
Tesco	232	1.0

Source: HCRC 1999

Table 1.4
The leading UK foodservice operators by number of units, 1999

Brand	units in 1999	% mkt share
Scottish and Newcastle Mgd Pub Estate	1331	5.5
Allied Domecq Mgd Pub Estate	1137	4.7
Whitbread Inns Mgd Pub Estate	1077	4.5
McDonald's	850	3.5
Greenalls Mgd Pub Estate	594	2.5
Greggs	536	2.2
Wolverhampton & Dudley Mgd Pub Estate	528	2.2
Burger King	460	1.9
KFC	400	1.7
Little Chef	400	1.7
Brewer's Fayre	394	1.6
Pizza Hut	389	1.6
Big Steak	366	1.5
Strollers	300	1.3
Wetherspoon's	295	1.2
Wimpy	270	1.1
Three Cooks	268	1.1
Beefeater	253	1.1
Mr Q's	247	1.0
Tesco Coffee Shops	232	1.0

Source: HCRC 1999

Table 1.5
The leading UK foodservice brands by units, 1999

Retail format	Sales (£)	Number of outlets	Major players
Main weekly shop			
Hypermarkets, superstores, supermarkets	69.8bn[a]	4078	Tesco, Asda, Sainsbury, Safeway, Iceland, Morrisons, M&S, Somerfield, Waitrose
Discount stores	815m	1373	Aldi, Netto, Lidl, Kwiksave
Secondary shopping			
Convenience stores	19.2bn	56 473	
Petrol station forecourts	3168m	10 061	Esso, Elf, BP, Texaco[b]
Convenience multiples	2171	2715	Alldays, T&S stores, one-stop community stores
Co-ops	972m	1236 (48 groups)	CWS, CRTG, CRS (Co-operative) United Northwest
Symbol groups	4000m	6961	Spar, Londis, Costcutter
Independents – non-affiliated licensed retailers	8861m	35 500 (63%)	First Quench, Paris, Unwins

[a]IGD 2000
[b]Some of these are joint ventures
Source: Extracted from Beard *et al.* 1999; IGD 2000

Table 1.6 Retail formats

Main players	£ billion (1998/99)	Market share 1998	Number of stores 1/1/99
Tesco[a]	15.835	15.6	593
Asda[a]	8.178	8.7	223
Sainsbury[a]	12.100	12.6	410
Safeways[a]	7.511	7.7	471
Somerfield/KwikSave		3.8 + 3.4	1421
Morrisons	2.552	2.6	95
Iceland		1.8	755
Marks & Spencer	3 170	3.1	294
Waitrose	1.638	1.9	117
Total	67 bn	61.2%	

[a]Tesco, Asda, Sainsbury and Safeway hold 45% (Mintel 2000).
Source: Data are extracted from two key sources: Mintel (2000) and Beard *et al.* (1999). Discrepancies in the figures are due to the times at which company reports are published

Table 1.7
Breakdown of major players in the main weekly shop sectors

Discount stores • • •

Discount stores arrived in the UK in 1959. Kwiksave offered a product range of around 800 items at discounted prices. Kwiksave has subsequently extended its product range to 3000 lines, but there has been a new influx of 'hard' discount stores, which began in 1990 when Aldi, a German discount store, opened in the UK, closely followed by Netto and Lidl. These offer a limited range of 600–800 product lines. Whilst Aldi represent 30% of the market in Germany, they have proved less successful in the UK.

Convenience sector

Whilst convenience stores remain relatively new in the UK, the format is gradually replacing a whole series of store formats. Stores which have previously traded as small grocers (i.e. symbols and Co-ops), CTNs (confectioners, tobacconists and newsagents), petrol forecourt shops and off licences, have broadened their product range as a means of replacing turnover lost to the multiples. The format of convenience stores looks to continue changing. Bread and milk are currently the most frequently purchased items from convenience stores (Mintel 1999b). Changes in demographics and the increases in single person households, who have less need for superstore trolley shopping (Mintel 1999b) is driving convenience stores more towards ready meals and meal solutions, e.g. Spar (Beard *et al.* 1999).

New formats

Farmers' markets

In response to the continued decline in income, due to the changes in the EU's Common Agricultural Policy, the high rate of the pound sterling, increases in imports and the purchasing decisions of large multiples and manufacturers (Stewart 1999), farmers have sought an alternative route to the consumer. Farm shops have long been evident within the UK countryside, however outlets are dispersed and are not easily accessible (Lohmann and Foster 1997).

The first UK farmers' market opened in Bath in 1997. In 1999 there were 36 farmers' markets being held regularly across the UK (Stewart 1999) and at the time of writing there are over 200 (MAFF 2000). Farmers have been reported to say that the development of farmers' markets not only enables them to retain a greater proportion of added value but also offers consumers greater certainty as to the origins of the produce purchased (Stewart 1999). This is increasingly important in days where consumer sensibilities are very much heightened as the result of scares such as *E. coli*, BSE and GM foods.

Home shopping – e-commerce and e-markets

The emergence of home delivery or more precisely home shopping is a recent 'grocery' retail stratagem. In many respects this is not a new idea. Grocers in local communities traditionally offered consumers a delivery service. Brown and white goods retailers such as Comet, Currys, MFI offer a free or minimal charge delivery service to all consumers. Furthermore, organizations such as Grattans and Empire (catalogue retailers) offer home delivery to all customers.

With the advent of the Internet, home delivery has become an alternative marketplace to a whole range of retail formats. The Internet has been used by small bakers such as 'Bothams' at Whitby to extend both area and times of sales outside their physical locational constraints. The small convenience store chain T&S have recently linked up with Littlewoods to offer a home delivery service. The big four – Asda, Sainsbury, Tesco and Safeway – have all invested in this market.

However, not all systems are based on the Internet. Asda, Iceland and Safeway are limited to phone/fax ordering. There are other restrictions such as minimum order levels and areas of delivery, e.g. Asda restrict delivery to the London area only for a minimum order of £50 (Anon 1999). Whilst there is some dispute as to the long-term value of home shopping (Terbeek 1996; Morganosky and Cude 2000; Småros and Holström 2000), many appear to consider that there is a strong likelihood that the trends towards markets found in the US market will be shortly reflected within the UK (Pratt, 2000).

Required supply procedures of the grocery retail and catering sector

In an earlier section we explored the breakdown of sharp distinctions between the nature of the product and service offered by the retail and catering sectors, a change primarily instigated by the diversification strategies employed by the food retailers, competing in a mature market.

When comparing the two industries, however, it is evident that whilst there is less differentiation between the retail and catering sectors on the demand side, there are distinctly different supply structures and conditions of supply developing. Traditionally, within the two sectors there were:

a. strong similarities in sources of supply

b. similar sourcing strategies

c. similar procurement procedures.

Food traditionally passed through the same intermediaries of farmers, manufacturers and/or wholesalers who delivered locally to the food outlets or operated as 'cash and carrys'. Multiples retailers, including to some extent symbol groups and Co-ops, have by-passed these supply routes and operate either partially, or totally, their own logistics systems.

Similarly, centralized purchasing departments have emerged within the catering sector. Organizations such as Granada employ the distribution and stockist facilities of catering supply companies, e.g. 3663 (see Chapter 3) but, as yet, have not moved to the contracted or in-house distribution systems favoured by the retailer. Single-branded catering operations such as McDonald's and Dominos (see Towill, Chapter 8) have, however, developed central distribution businesses. This suggests that organizations feel that in circumstances, where they are operating multiple brands, savings are not necessarily found through operating centralized contracted/inhouse distribution systems. An exception can be found in the Whitbread in-house system, a system that reputedly could restrict the flexibility of sourcing, required for a multi-product, multi-brand operation, particularly as regards new brand development. In essence, irrespective of size, the diversity of 'Branded' establishments and the large number of widely dispersed catering outlets operated by any one organization, have resulted in a continued reliance on the wholesaling sector.

However there is a more recent supply initiative, the development of which could be interesting to observe. Recent reports in trade magazines (Carmichael 2000) have indicated that home delivery services initiated by retailers to serve consumer markets have now been opened up to supply the catering sector. This builds upon an existing trend, where small-scale catering organizations find considerable savings (e.g. time and money) by sourcing through supermarkets rather than from traditional catering sources of supply.

Own labels and ranges of product formula

The manufacture of own label products, and organizational specific product formula, is generic across retail, catering supply companies, wholesalers and catering organizations. However, manufacturers find that product sizes, and the requisite product formulae, vary across sectors (Eastham 2000). A multi-brand catering organization may require a greater range of formula and packaging than its retail equivalent; each formula and packaging being integral to the specific brand operated. The top three UK catering operators have 46 fascias/brands across 10 000 outlets, an average of 200 outlets (Backman 2000) per fascia, each potentially requiring distinctive formula.

Price negotiation

Opportunities for price negotiation with independent operators, either retail or catering, are limited. Much is dependent on volume sold and the promotional activities of the wholesale sector (Eastham, 2000). Multiple retailers, wholesaler/catering supply companies and multiple catering organizations negotiate through their central purchasing department with manufacturers, growers and importers on price, quality and volume. Discounts are obtained on volume, and described as 'over rider discounts' reimbursed to head office.

Contracts with multiple caterers, e.g. Granada, are more complicated. Caterers will negotiate with manufacturers, price and quantities for products, but will be supplied through the catering supply company and/or wholesaler, usually on a cost-plus basis. This means that the initial price paid by the caterer will be the same as the price paid normally by the catering supply company. The manufacturer will refund the difference between the initial price and the negotiated price to the caterer subsequently, this is known as a 'confidential rebate'.

Supply chain costs and technological systems

Retail

- In the 1980s improvements in the distribution systems within retail in the 1980s brought about large efficiency gains to this sector (Marchant 1999).

- In the 1990s incremental reductions to the cost of supplying food were also generated through the development of technological systems such as EPoS, EDI, EFTPoS, inventory management schemes designed to manage stock from regional distribution centres (RDCs) more effectively.

- Automatic ordering systems such as sales based order (SBO), SABRE and SM111 are now prevalent. Tesco orders 97% of lines through SBO (IGD 1998).

- Self-scanning systems also appeared in the multiple sector in the 1990s.

- The penetration of EPoS, EDI to the independent and convenience retail sectors remains marginal, recent figures (IGD 2000) indicate that only 46% of symbol group stores have EPoS. Wholesalers and buying groups are starting to promote such systems, offering funding to members (e.g. Londis, Bestway) to install equipment.

- Co-ops have introduced technology such as EPoS and EFTPoS more rapidly.

- Late 1990s–2000 category management and ECR are becoming standard within the multiple retail sectors. This involves greater sharing of information between retailer and manufacturer.

- The twenty-first century – the next stage will be e-markets and e-commerce (Heathcote 2000).

Catering ● ● ●

- EPoS is now prevalent within the hospitality sector.

- EFTPoS is emerging, particularly within pub chains and restaurant sectors.

- Technology remains little advanced with the exception of large operators, there is considerable resistance to EDI, sales based ordering systems. Primary reasons for this relate to the structure of the catering sector. The sector is still dominated by independents, for which the cost of EDI, EPoS/EFTPoS is prohibitive.

- Procurement procedures in large catering organizations are becoming more advanced but still lag behind the retail sector.

- EFR (Efficient Foodservice Response), launched in the USA in 1994, is being piloted in the UK supported by key players in the manufacturing, catering supply and catering sectors.

- Contract caterers have tended to lead the way, installing inventory systems as early as the 1970/80s.

Further factors

Catering is seen to be a far more complex market than its retail counterpart. Caterers are seen by their suppliers to be more cost sensitive (Eastham 2000). Supply volumes are significantly lower, outlets dispersed, forecasting techniques particularly underdeveloped, formula range greater, and orders are predominantly made by telephone. Catering, by its nature, takes place in small units, the customer cannot be herded into a parallel consumer experience as in retail (with certain mass consumer exceptions). Even so, it would be incorrect to suggest that the supply requirements required by each sub-sector of the catering industry are identical. Independents and 'undisciplined multiples' (i.e. smaller hotel chains) (Haines and Turner 1998) require a wide range of produce, whilst 'disciplined' (i.e. larger hotels, pub and pub restaurant chains) require a more limited static range of produce. However, they do require suppliers to offer some flexibility in the range offered and can negotiate flexible drop sizes. The key concerns of the cost sector are ' price' and more recently with changes in legislation, traceability.

Conclusion

As a backdrop to the text this chapter provides an insight into the issues of supplying both the retail and catering industries. The structure of each industry is defined and explored along with their respective issues for supply. As discussed previously, the level of differentiation between the two industries is more marked at the supply side than at the demand side, where distinct blurring is taking place between the catering and retail sectors.

There is some question as to whether this state of affairs will continue given the growth of multiples within the catering sector. The development of centralized distribution systems operated in the food retail sector may yet emerge within the catering sector, although the development of catering supply companies suggests that this is problematic. The adoption of technological systems such as EPoS, EFTPoS and sales based order systems has been relatively slow. Much of this would appear to be due to the continued predominance of independents within the catering sector. With the growth of multiple catering organizations within the catering industry, the low level of technology may be redressed.

Therefore, whilst it is important to recognize that the boundary between catering and food retail is distinctly fuzzy in relation to the product they serve and technological developments, they do remain distinct industries.

References

Anon (1999) Who offers what? A guide to home shopping. *The Grocer* 11 September, p. 19.

Backman P. (2000) 'The next decade for food service', IGD Conference – The Future of Food Service, 19 April 2000.

Beard J., Gordon D., Spillow L. *et al.* (1999) Grocery retailing, *The Market Review* (IGD), pp. 16, 18, 36 (section 1 plus section 3.6 p. 171).

BHA (2000) *British Hospitality: Trends and Statistics.* London: British Hospitality Association.

Carmichael M. (2000) Catering for all tastes, *The Grocer*, 18 November, pp. 40–2.

Eastham J.F. (2000) Unpublished research on the perceptions of suppliers of the operating constraints regarding supply for the retail and catering industries.

Eastham J.F. and Johnston S. (1998) 'The independent catering market within Yorkshire and the Humber', Report 2 – Fresh Produce Wholesale and Independent Catering, ISCAN July 1998, unpublished.

Haines D. and Turner D. (1998) *Catering 1998, Surveying the Supply Chain*, Institute of Grocery Distribution.

Harvey M. (2000) Innovation and competition in UK supermarkets. *Supply Chain Management: an International Journal*, (1), pp. 15–21.

HCRC (2000) *The UK Food Service Brands Directory.* Huddersfield: Hotel and Catering Research Centre.

Heathcote P. (2000) 'Responding to the challenge of e-business', IGD Conference – The Future of Food Service, 19 April 2000.

HtF (1999) *Key Facts and Figures*. London: Hospitality Training Foundation.

IGD (1998) *Grocery Wholesaling*. Institute of Grocery Distribution.

IGD (2000) *Grocery Retailing*. Institute of Grocery Distribution.

Jones P. (1996) *Introduction to Hospitality Operations*. London, Cassell, p. 117.

Lawson F. (1987) *Restaurants, Clubs and Bars*. London: Architectural Press.

Lohmann U. and Foster C. (1997). From 'niche' to 'mainstream' – strategies for marketing organic food in Germany and the UK. *British Food Journal*, 99 (8), pp. 275–82.

MAFF (2000) Farmers' markets – good for British agriculture and the food chain. News Release, 25 May; www.Maff.gov.uk/inf/newrel/2000/000525b.htm.

Marchant C. (1999) *Retail Logistics*. IGD Business Publications, pp. 3–6.

Mintel (1999a) Consumer shopping. *Food Retailing*, 23 June (Mintel International).

Mintel (1999b) The convenience shopper. *Convenience Retailing*, April (Mintel International)

Mintel (2000) *Food Retailing*, August (Mintel International)

Morganosky M.A. and Cude B.J. (2000) Consumer response to online grocery shopping. *International Journal of Retail and Distribution Management*, 28 (1), pp. 17–26.

Pratt R. (2000) 'The implications of the information revolution', IGD Conference – The Future of Food Service, 19 May.

Småros J. and Holmström J. (2000) Viewpoint: reaching the consumer through e-grocery VMI, *International Journal of Retail and Distribution Management*, 28 (2), pp. 51–61.

Stewart J. (1999) Gamekeepers turn poachers, *The Grocer*, 15 May, p. 44.

Terbeek G.A. (1996) 1996 and beyond: the value of value. *Progressive Grocer*, December, pp. 91–5.

Activities

1. Using appropriate information, identify and define all sub-sectors of the retail and catering sectors illustrated within this chapter.

2. For a defined geographical area, establish the number and type of catering, and food and drink, operations. Try to classify these. What are the issues in tackling this activity?

3. Visit two to three different local supermarkets. Observe whether they have any catering operations. For those that do identify specific characteristics of both their retail and catering operations. Do they have anything in common and if so what? Should each be treated separately? Are they clearly members of different industries?

4. For each of the following:

- an independent catering operation
- a branded catering operation
- an independent food and drink retail operation
- a branded food and drink retail operation

attempt to discover: the annual turnover of each, the number of suppliers each has and the criteria for selecting these suppliers. Are there any noticeable commonalties or differences?

CHAPTER 2

Food and society

Sean Beer

Key objectives

The objectives of this chapter are for readers:

- To understand how our food supply chain has developed

- To develop a model that will help to put food into context within any given situation

- To develop an appreciation of some of the dynamics of our food supply chain and the influence of those who sell food and those who consume it

Introduction

Food is central to life. If you remove everything that plays a part in sustaining life, the last things that you consider are air, food and water. Therefore food, as fuel, underpins all that we do. Above and beyond this biological need, food also permeates all aspects of our culture and society; these social patterns of food production and consumption are sometimes known as the 'social appetite' (Germov and Williams 1999). Our relationships revolve around food. Our pursuit of a mate, the basis of family life (although some would argue that family life and the role of food within it are both in decline) and our business deals, all involve it. The study of food is in itself a truly vast subject. This chapter aims to help readers understand how our food supply chain has developed. It will go on to develop a model that will help them put food into context within any given situation. And finally, it will help the reader develop an appreciation of some of the dynamics of our food supply chain and the influence of those that sell food and those that consume it. It is not meant to be a fully comprehensive overview of food and culture but an entrée to aspects of food and how it affects our lives.

Given the vastness of food as a subject area, it is unlikely that one single academic approach can ever do it justice. What is needed is a truly interdisciplinary holistic approach. Consider, for example, the current discussions surrounding the technology of genetic modification. Despite all of the media coverage and fierce debate, how much do we really know and understand about genetic modification (GM)? The question is do we understand and trust the science and do we trust those that control it? What will be the effect of this technology on society? One way or the other many consider that the revolution in biotechnology will overshadow that in Information Technology. And how do we examine it? Traditional academic approaches are reductionist, that is, they try to break down everything into small subjects. What we need are interdisciplinary ways of working, looking at systems from a new perspective. There are not many people who think in this way.

What is food: modern and post-modern definitions of food quality

Genetic modification asks fundamental questions of us in terms of what food is, and what good food is. A food is generally defined as a substance taken into the body to maintain life. Yet it is, of course, much more than this. Increasingly society is obsessed with quality; people talk about good quality and bad quality but the reality is that quality is all about a given specification at a given price. Yet what goes into that specification? In many ways the actual concept of food quality is still developing.

There have been trade classifications for a long time, but these have often been very limited and addressed only specific dimensions of the quality concept. A new concept of food quality is now emerging. For sake of argument we could call this a post-modern view of food quality. (For early reviews see Kilkenny 1994; Lowman and McClelland 1994; Ritchie and Leat 1994.)

The traditional view of food quality was based on appearance, technical quality and biological quality (see Wood *et al.* 1994 amongst others.) Thus, you expected your food to look good, to taste good and to do you good, or, at least, no direct harm. Recently this definition has extended to look at factors relating to cultural, environmental and ethical values. Cannon (1990) highlights biological, sensual, nutritional and environmental factors. Woodward *et al.* (1990) categorize the major components of food quality as being authentic, sensual, biological, nutritional and ethical (see also Foster and Macrae, 1992). All these must exist within a social, political and economic environment, and reflect society's increasing interest in the environment, animal welfare and culture. This change in the concept of food quality is illustrated in Figure 2.1 taken from Beer (1998).

It is not easy to merge social, psychological, environmental and ethical considerations into the quality framework. When does the food stop and when does the eating experience begin? Many of these more qualitative traits give rise to a blurring of quality definitions. However, it is against these criteria that food quality must 'supposedly' now be measured. The word 'supposedly' is used because just as the term 'post-modern' is an 'educated middle class' expression that most people do not know the meaning of, so many of the new ideas of food quality are equally foreign. Social and psychological factors are probably quite strong. Thus, we are what we eat, but also, we eat what we are. In other words, our patterns of consumption reflect who we are, and who we want to be. Consuming a pie at a football match maybe what you have always done or it may be a way of accessing the trendy football culture that is a new middle-class aspiration. The same applies to the restaurant with the £100

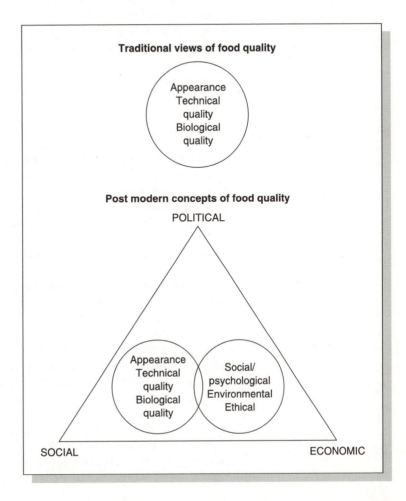

Figure 2.1
The changing view of food quality (Beer 1998)

per person dinner price tag: is this good food in a fantastic setting or conspicuous consumption and social climbing?

Ethical and environmental considerations are also things to think about. In the UK, there is a very vocal consumer lobby keen on animal welfare and the environment, that petitions for restrictive laws and legislation. But, in general, people go out and buy the cheapest food they can, often from abroad, thereby exporting the ethical problems along with rural jobs. This at a time when, in real terms, food has seldom, if ever, been so cheap. If consumers really are so ethical why do they consume so little organic food, free range eggs and food from fair trade labels? When it comes down to it, a possible 10% of people will pay an extra 10% for some additional social/psychological, environmental or ethical dimension. (Good reviews of food and ethics can be found by Adams *et al.* 1991; Mepham 1996 and Strong 1996.)

So where does all this this leave us? Food is a vast subject that needs an interdisciplinary approach if we are to get to grips with it. To give us a start there is quite a useful analytical framework in terms of the commonly used PESTE analysis. This views things from a Political, Economic, Social, Technological and Environmental series of perspectives, and will allow us to look again at food. But first the chapter examines how the food supply chain has developed, the relationship between food and the economy and the globalization of the food economy.

Evolution of the food supply chain

The food supply chain is not a static entity and has evolved over time. It has developed from the hunter–gatherers through primitive agriculture to developed agricultural economies. Gradually, agricultural revolutions took place with the evolution of scientific agriculture, then industrial agriculture, and now towards genetic agriculture. As this process evolved, so more intermediaries stepped into the chain between producer and consumer. Figure 2.2 illustrates this.

As mentioned before, initially there was a direct link between food producer and consumer (Time period 1 in Figure 2.2). Here, those who grew the food, then sold it direct on a local basis. Subsequently, with increasing urbanization (period 2) small retailers developed in the towns. Some of these then developed into large retailers and a dual track system was formed (period 3). With increasing concentration, this is increasingly favouring the large retailers. Vertical and horizontal integration followed. Vertical integration where organizations along the chain join together to facilitate supply. Retailers developing supplier contracts would be an example of this. Horizontal integration involves organizations at a given level getting together. Trade organizations would be an example of this. (Obviously this is

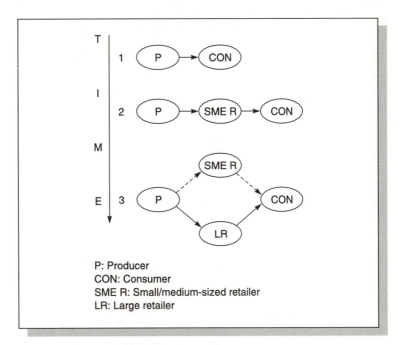

P: Producer
CON: Consumer
SME R: Small/medium-sized retailer
LR: Large retailer

Figure 2.2
Various stages in the
evolution of the food
supply chain

looked at further in the book, but also see Bawcutt 1997, Dussage and Garette 1999, Hughes 1994, King and Phumpiu 1996, O'Keeffe 1997, Spedding 1989 and Tarrant 1996.)

Farmers in the UK are increasingly going back to the first model and supplying the consumer direct. Farmers' markets are an example of this. Indeed it has been estimated that about 200 farmers' markets are now generating an extra £65 million in sales for the agricultural industry (Brown 2000.) The Internet may also provide opportunities for consumers to purchase direct, with better communication about the producer, information on the product and product authenticity as key elements of added value. This is fuelled increasingly by perceived inequalities of return in food supply chains (see Beer 1999).

Relationship between food and the economy

The food industry is a major economic player. In the UK food makes a significant contribution to the Gross National Product directly, and also indirectly, through the service industries. Estimates of output are very variable and tend to be dated; however, in 1996 home farm output was estimated at about £8 billion (MAFF 1997). Food imports (raw and processed) for 1996 were estimated at £14.8 billion (Howitt 1998a). At the same time, output from the catering industry was estimated at £40.7 billion (Howitt 1998b) and the retail industry at £76.3 billion (Howitt 1998a). On one hand this represents a significant industry. Globally, this situation needs to be set in context. Wal-Mart, the

United States based retailer, had sales in the accounting year ending 31 January 1998 of US$ 118 billion (Wal-Mart 1998), some £82 billion at current exchange rates – a global phenomenon in a truly global industry.

The economic relationship between food cost and the food consumer is a complex one. First, between the farm gate and the consumer there is often a long chain, in which value is added and profits taken. The relative returns are difficult to assess. There are suspicions that retailers may be making excessive profits. This has given rise to a Competition Commission inquiry into food retailing. The reality is a complex situation, and needs careful analysis. However figures like those in Table 2.1 have fuelled the debate and more work, openness and honesty is required in this area.

The other important point to bear in mind is that consumers, who tend to look upon food as fuel, pursue cheap food. This has an on-going effect within the economy, in that food costs increasingly less in real terms. The percentage of average 'total income' spent across all households on food in the UK has declined from 33% in 1957 to 13.75% in 1986 to 10.6% in 1997 (Holroyd 1997.) This is an example of Engel's law (see Burk 1962, Tangermann 1986). Engel's law indicates that with increased personal income, the proportion of income spent on food declines.

It is possible that food expenditure will increase in the future but food share of total expenditure will decline (Cranfield et al. 1998). The reality is a genuine downward pressure on food commodity prices in real terms. Thus, UK farm gate prices for wheat (tonne), lamb (per lamb) and milk (litre) were £93, £38 and 16p in 1987 and over the next 12 years this changed, by, on average, –2%, 0% and +1.6% per year, respectively (Nix 1987, 1999). This has a pressurizing effect on the food supply chain in that by no stretch of the imagination does this keep up with inflation.

Commodity	Average percentage change in farm gate prices	Average percentage change in retail prices
Milling wheat (bread)	–33%	+0.5%
Lamb	–36%	–4%
Beef	–35%	–4%
Pork	–57%	–23%
Milk	–22%	+1%
Eggs	–36%	–3%
Chicken	–26%	–3%

Source: Knight Frank, 1999

Table 2.1
Farm gate prices versus retail prices, September 1996 to September 1998

There is a final point in all of this. Not all the costs of food production are accounted for. Environmental costs associated with the transport of food have already been alluded to, but there are a whole host of other add-on costs. Redman (1996) has tried to identify some of these simply for the primary producer in his report 'The Hidden Costs of Industrial Agriculture'. In this he looks at a series of case studies such a BSE, soil erosion, the cost of removing pesticides from drinking water and the cost of pesticides to human health. It makes an interesting point to start off discussion. These costs all represent costs of food production but they are externalized, i.e. you do not pay for them when you pay for your food. Thus, you do not see them. This penalizes producers of, say, organic food as it is supposed that organic food is more expensive. A true comparison, however, reveals that the normal food prices do not include all of the hidden costs.

Globalization of the food economy

We are now looking at a global food supply chain. We can buy the best foods from all over the world. We eat glorious food and partake of food cultures that originate thousands of miles from home. I can go out this evening and eat Italian or Indonesian, or with the help of a cookbook or, aided by a celebrity chef from the television, I can go to the supermarket, buy the food and cook the meal myself. This represents a fantastic opportunity to be innovative in terms of food. We can develop new products by using a whole range of cultural backgrounds and food producers. It also represents an enormous market for products and services. This global dimension has challenges associated with dealing with, and operating in, new situations, cultures and countries.

There is, however, a downside. Increasingly large multinational companies dominate the global economy. The classical Friedman (1962) business paradigm states that the first duty of every business is to its shareholders. There are, however, a whole series of other stakeholders involved in any business. How multinational companies relate to these stakeholders is open to debate. David Korten's book *When Corporations Rule the World* (1995) provides a fascinating insight into this whole area and draws some rather disturbing conclusions. Power can corrupt and globalization is not necessarily to our benefit.

There are also environmental implications. It may only cost 20p to ship a kilogram of meat from New Zealand but there are associated environmental costs. It has been estimated that the contents of the average shopping trolley has travelled 4000 miles before it reaches you at home. What is the cost of this environmental impact? As long as there is comparatively cheap oil, the actual cost is not felt. For consumers and those involved in the food industry, other costs can be put out of our mind and effectively ignored until our group social conscience recognizes it and forces us to address the issues through legislation.

There are also other issues relating to world trade. Simply, the distribution of food is a cause for concern. While the Western world has a surfeit of food many people in developing countries are starving. (See commentators such as Brown and Kane 1995.)

Indeed 24 000 people a day die from hunger or hunger-related illness: 75% are children (http://www.thehungersite.com). It can be argued that purchasing decisions in the developed world kill people in the third world, and in the developed world obesity increases and along with it obesity-related disease. This whole issue is tied up with third world debt. Third world countries need hard currencies to pay off the debt and so produce cash crops, often at the expense of feeding their own populations, to sell to consumers in developed countries. This can be viewed as a modern-day slavery (see http://www.oxfam.org.uk and http://www.tearfund.org, Brown and Kane 1995 and Whit 1999).

The globalization juggernaut is launched. Many argue that this is progress and a lack of acceptance reflects the philosophy of the luddite, and anyway, it is not desirable nor possible to turn the clock back. In many ways this is the case. But the protests at the recent World Trade Organization (WTO) discussions in Seattle would seem to indicate that there is a different viewpoint, and an increasing number of people, including some of those involved in the negotiations themselves, are sympathetic to it.

STEEP or PESTE analysis of food as a model

So how do we look at food and society? A STEEP or PESTE model which looks at things from a Social, Technological, Environmental, Economic and Political perspectives is a good starting point. What does this involve? One way to do this is to go through the different areas using an example, in this case the meat lamb.

Social

The sociological analysis of food can be complex. Willis (1995) uses a model based on historical, structural, cultural, critical, dimensions to a product/situation. This is imposed onto whatever you want to examine. Thus, for our lamb, we might do the following:

- *Historical*, the evolution of lamb in different cultures, the role of lamb versus mutton and lambs for meat as opposed to wool.

- *Structural*, how the economy and government regulations seek to control the structure of the industry.

- *Cultural,* different cultural relations to the product, for example Christians and Jews have a religious connection with lamb. For Jews, it is the feast of the Passover and much more and for Christians, Jesus was the Lamb of God. Both cultures are linked through it.

- *Critical,* how over-grazing of sheep in the uplands may cause environmental damage to heather moorland.

Sociological study of food obviously involves a whole host of different areas and overlaps with many others. Germov and Williams, *A Sociology of Food and Nutrition* (1999) provides a fascinating starting point for such a study. They look at the subject in terms of McDonaldization (standardization), social differentiation (consumption and identity) and self-rationalization (nutrition, food and the body). Other authors such as Harris 1985, Schwartz 1986, Mennell *et al.* 1992, Whit 1995, McIntosh 1996, Ritzer 1996 and Warde 1997) also give a real insight into this area of food sociology.

Technological

Food as technology and the technology of producing food is the basis and the process of the food industry. Thinking about the lamb, the genetic makeup of the animal, and how it is fed will influence how fat the meat is. Alternatively we could genetically engineer the lamb to produce leaner meat. Once we have that meat, how do we go about processing it to add value before it is consumed? There are many ways of reducing the fat from direct trimming, to fat removal during cooking. One of the problems with the fat is that it is here, that much of the flavour resides. Breeding leaner animals has resulted in much blander tasting meat, a lesson that livestock producers and consumers are learning to their cost.

Economic

The economic question is often the most important as cynically money can often help ease other areas. When we look at the humble lamb one question might be who benefits from its death, financially. Recently this question has been much in the news given declining farm gate prices and 'stable' prices at the retail end of the market. Some commentators have tried to analyse this but it is difficult, as the figures below show (see Table 2.2).

Environmental

Food production and the environment are inherently linked, as it is through the exploitation of our environment that we eat. Lamb production is quite good in that, on the whole, it utilizes grass as a food, something that humans cannot readily eat. Other systems of production rely on cereals, which we could consume directly ourselves. Passing them through another animal merely wastes resources and adds to pollution. The sheep industry is not without its problems though, as previously indicated with regard to overgrazing in the uplands. (Food and the environment is another vast area. To get a better insight to the downside, try Carson 1965, Harvey 1998; Body 1982, 1984, 1987, is more balanced; Clunies-Ross and Hildyard 1992 is interesting.)

Political

Within Europe and the world, the lamb is one of the ultimate symbols of food politics. The political game of food production personified in the Common Agricultural Policy often revolves around the lamb. There are subsidies, quotas, inspectors, trade wars and millions of pounds tied to the little woolly characters that originally gave Britain its head start in international trade through wool. Globally, they still exert their power, forming the central point of many arguments within the WTO, particularly with countries such as New Zealand and Australia.

Contrasting views of the modern consumer

The food consumer exists in a complicated socio-economic/environmental/political/technological melting pot. The same can be said for all connected with the food industry. Between the 'plough' and the 'plate', or 'the seed and the soul', lie innumerable intermediaries with their own agendas. These agendas, along with those of the consumer, form a milieu or possibly a mêlée that we might call popular food culture. The consumer is, however, central to this process.

If we look at consumer behaviour in a holistic way we can see the consumer as the one that consumes, and also as a player within food culture. There are many good accounts of consumer behaviour (see East 1990, Engel et al. 1990, Gabriel and Lang 1996). The way in which they behave is complex, but can be and needs to be understood. Engel et al. (1990) outline four principles that underline consumer behaviour.

1. The consumer is sovereign.

2. Consumer motivation and behaviour can be understood through research.

3. Consumer behaviour can be influenced.

4. Consumer influence is socially legitimate.

In short, the consumer is king, but can be manipulated. The consumer therefore has power to consume in such a way that

Year	Market price (£)	Abattoir/wholesale costs (£)	Retailer costs	Total cost (£) (A)	Total cost with added retail costs[b] (£) (B)	Retail price MLC (C)	Retail price Telegraph (D)	% return for retailer on cost (A) retail price (C)	% return for retailer on cost (A) retail price (D)	% return for retailer on cost (B) retail price (C)	% return for retailer on cost (B) retail price (D)
1997	42.4	1.4	16.7	60.5	68.8	62.8	87.0	3.7	17.4	-9.5	7.9
1998	36.0	5	16.7	57.7	66.0	62.8	87.0	8.1	20.6	-5.0	11.1
1997[a]	42.8	1.4	16.7	60.9	69.2	62.8	87.0	3.0	17.0	-10.1	7.4
1998[a]	29.8	5	16.7	51.5	59.8	62.8	87.0	18.0	28.0	4.8	18.2

[a]Figures calculated using lamb prices from *Farmers Weekly* average for November of each year.
[b]Additional retail costs put forward by British Retail Consortium of £8.26 per lamb
MLC: Meat and Livestock Commission.
Source: Beer 1999, based on data from Johnston 1998 (all basic figures unless stated otherwise) and *Farmers Weekly* 1998

Table 2.2
Percentage returns on sheep meat for a retailer given a range of cost scenarios

fulfils their own agendas and value systems, but may be manipulated to fulfil those of others. If we are dealing with businesses perceived as being 'ethical businesses' this needs to be done 'fairly'. Engel *et al.* (1990) qualify their fourth principle by saying that 'the key to social legitimacy is a guarantee that the consumer retains complete and unimpeded freedom throughout the process. This freedom is manifested when nothing induces the consumer to act in ways that would be regretted and even disavowed after more careful reflection.' A significant statement.

In the end complex questions arise. What do consumers want? Whom do they trust? What is the role of industry, is it to shape or respond? There is good evidence to suggest that consumers want cheaper, innovative, timesaving, safe products. Some may want something with some sort of other added value in terms of culture and the environment, but few will pay for it. In terms of trust, increasingly it would seem that we trust no one and need everything backed up with a quality assurance scheme from plough to plate, at least in the retail sector that is. And what is the role of industry? If we are market orientated, then it should be one of responding to the needs of our customers. The reality is that responding and shaping are bedfellows in the modern food industry and to say anything else, is to ignore the truth.

Conclusions

This chapter set out to look at food and society. An enormous subject, in fact something that enters every area of our lives. As such, the chapter was not designed to be a fully comprehensive account but a taster of a rich subject. The references provide a resource to plunder for further information.

You should now have a better understanding of how our food supply chain has developed, a model that will help put food into context within any given situation, and an appreciation of some of the dynamics of our food supply chain. You should also have an insight into the influences of both the people selling the food and the consumer who buys it.

The best way to learn about the food industry is to get involved. It is amazing the number of people involved in the food and hospitality industry who have no clue as to where their food comes from and who never cook!

The reality is that, as food consumers, we will probably get the food that we deserve – whatever that might be!

References

Adams R., Curruthers J. and Fisher C. (1991) *Shopping for a Better World: A Quick and Easy Guide to Responsible Shopping*. London: Kogan Page. (2000 edn published by the Council for Economic Priorities.)

Bawcutt D.E. (1997) Agricultural marketing in a highly competitive and customer responsive total UK food chain. *Agricultural Progress*, 72, pp. 75–88.

Beardsworth A. and Keil T. (1997) *Sociology on the Menu*. London: Routledge.

Beer S.C. (1997) BSE a systems analysis: lessons to be learnt. In *Proceedings of the International Conference on Agriculture and Nutrition*, Tufts University, pp. 35–46.

Beer S. (1998) Cultural tokenism? An investigation into the nature of food quality assurance schemes with specific reference to the meat production sector. In *Proceedings of the Second International Conference on Culinary Arts and Sciences, Global and National Perspectives* (ed. J.S.A. Edwards), Worshipful Company of Cooks Centre for Culinary Research, Bournemouth University, pp. 225–36.

Beer S. (1999) What has happened to the integrity of our food supply chain? Moves towards an ethical framework for food retailing in the United Kingdom. Proceedings of the 10th International Conference on Research in the Distributive Trades, pp. 47–56.

Body R. (1982) *Agriculture: the Triumph and the Shame*. London: Temple Smith.

Body R. (1984) *Farming in the Clouds*. London: Temple Smith.

Body R. (1987) *Red or Green for Farmers (and the Rest of Us)*. Broadleys Publishing Company.

Brown D. (2000) Market revival gives a £65m boost to farmers. *Daily Telegraph*, 25 May, p. 14.

Brown L.R. and Kane H. (1995) *Full House*. London: Earthscan Publications.

Burk M.C. (1962) Ramifications of the relationships beween income and food. *Journal of Farm Economics*, XLIV, 1 February.

Cannon G. (1990) Food policy and definitions of food quality, in L. Woodward, S. Stolton and N. Dudley (eds), *Food Quality: Concepts and Methodology*. Elm Farm Research Centre.

Carson R. (1965) *Silent Spring*. Harmondsworth: Penguin.

Clunies-Ross T. and Hildyard N. (1992) *The Politics of Industrial Agriculture*. London: Earthscan.

Cranfield J.A.L., Hertel T.W., Ealse J.S. and Preckel V. (1998) Changes in the structure of global food demand. Staff paper 98–5, Department of Agricultural Economics, Purdue University.

Dussauge P. and Garrette B. (1999) *Co-operative Strategy. Competing Successfully through Strategic Alliances*. Chichester: John Wiley & Sons.

East R. (1990) *Changing Consumer Behaviour*. London: Cassell.

Engel J.F., Blackwell R.D. and Miniard P.W. (1990) *Consumer Behaviour*, 6th edn. Hinsdale, IL: The Dryden Press.

Farmers Weekly (1998) Market reports, 4, 11, 18 and 25 November 1998.

Foster A. and Macrae S (1992) Food quality. What does it mean? In National Consumer Council, *Your Food, Whose Choice?* London: HMSO.

Friedman M. (1962) *Capitalism and Freedom.* Chicago: University of Chicago Press.

Gabriel Y. and Lang T (1996) *The Unmanageable Consumer, Contemporary Consumption and Its Fragmentation.* London: Sage Publications.

Germov J. and Williams L. (1999) *A Sociology of Food and Nutrition. The Social Appetite.* Oxford: Oxford University Press.

Harris M. (1985) *Good to Eat. Riddles of Food and Culture.* London: Allen and Unwin.

Harvey G. (1998) *The Killing of the Countryside.* London: Jonathon Cape.

Holroyd P.H. (1997) The changing food chain. *Journal of the Royal Agricultural Society of England*, 158, pp. 87–96.

Howitt S. (ed.) (1998a) *UK Food Sector 1998 Marketing Review.* Hampton, Middx: Keynote.

Howitt S. (ed.) (1998b) *UK Catering Market 1998 Marketing Review.* Hampton, Middx: Keynote.

Hughes D. (1994) *Breaking with Tradition. Building Partnerships and Alliances in the European Food Industry.* Ashford, Kent: Wye College Press.

Johnston P. (1998) Farm gate prices are falling: so who gets the biggest slice of the Sunday joint? *Daily Telegraph*, 15 November, pp. 15–16.

Kilkenny B. (1994) Quality in the marketing of meat. In *Quality Meat and Milk from Grassland Systems*. Reading: British Grassland Society.

King R.P. and Phumpiu P.F. (1996) Reengineering the food supply chain: the ECR initiative in the grocery industry. *American Journal of Agricultural Economics*, 78, pp. 1181–6.

Knight Frank (1999) Cited by F. Fulford, While farmers face disaster and farm gate prices continue to drop, supermarkets glean the profits. *The Field*, January, pp. 31–32.

Korten D.C. (1995) *When Corporations Rule the World.* London: Earthscan.

Lowman B.G. and McClelland T.H. (1994) An overview of quality assurance schemes. In *Quality Meat and Milk from Grassland Systems*. Reading: British Grassland Society.

MAFF (1997) *UK Food and Farming in Figures.* London: Government Statistical Service.

McIntosh W.A. (1996) *Sociologies of Food and Nutrition.* London: Plenum Press.

Menell S., Murcott A. and van Otterloo A.H. (1992) *The Sociology of Food: Eating, Diet and Culture.* London: Sage Publications.

Mepham B. (1996) *Food Ethics.* London: Routledge.

Nix J. (1987) *Farm Management Pocket Book.* London: Wye College.

Nix J. (1999) *Farm Management Pocket Book.* London: Wye College.

O'Keeffe M. (1997) Supply chain management. *Agricultural Science*, 10 (3), pp. 29–32.

Redman M. (1996) *Industrial Agriculture: Counting the Cost.* Bristol: Soil Association.

Ritchie C.A. and Leat P.M.K. (1994) A supermarket view of marketing quality meat and milk. In *Quality Meat and Milk from Grassland Systems*. Reading: British Grassland Society.

Ritzer G. (1996) *The McDonaldization of Society*, 2nd edn. London: Pine Forge Press.

Schwartz H. (1986) *Never Satisfied: A Cultural History of Diets, Fantasies and Fat*. New York: The Free Press.

Soucie W.G. (1997) Efficient consumer response meets the industrialization of agriculture. *Agribusiness*, 13 (3), pp. 349–55.

Spedding C.R.W. (1989) The food chain: forging links, in *The Human Food Chain*. Amsterdam: Elsevier Applied Science.

Stainer L., Gully A. and Stainer A. (1998) The UK food supply chain – an ethical perspective. *Business Ethics: A European Review*, 7 (4), pp. 205–11.

Strong C. (1996) Features contributing to the growth of ethical consumerism – a preliminary investigation. *Marketing Intelligence and Planning*, 14 (5), pp. 5–13.

Tangermann S. (1986) Economic factors affecting food choice, in R. Ritson, L. Gofton and J. McKenzie (eds), *The Food Consumer*. Chichester: John Wiley & Sons, pp. 61–8.

Tarrant S. (1996) Partnership in the food chain – the role of support players. *Food Science and Technology Today*, 10 (1), pp. 35–8.

Warde A. (1997) *Consumption Food and Taste*. London: Sage Publications.

Wal-Mart (1998) Wal-Mart 1998 Annual Shareholder Report, Bentonville, Arkansas.

Whit W.C. (1995) *Food and Society. A Sociological Approach*. New York: General Hall.

Whit W.C. (1999) World hunger. In J. Germov and L. Williams (eds), *A Sociology of Food and Nutrition. The Social Appetite*. Oxford: Oxford University Press.

Willis E. (1995) *The Sociological Quest*, 2nd edn. Sydney: Allen and Unwin.

Woodward L., Stolton S. and Dudley N. (1990) *Food Quality Concepts and Methodology*. Elm Farm Research Centre.

Wood J.D., Enser M. and Fisher A.V. (1994) Meat quality definitions and factors affecting it. In *Quality Meat and Milk from Grassland Systems*. Reading: British Grassland Society.

Activities

1. For any given food product, outline its journey from plough to plate and evaluate the added financial value at each stage. What relationship does this have to profit and return on capital for each member of the chain?

2. Start a collection of supermarket food magazines. Identify and analyse the messages that they are trying to put across with regard to food.

Questions

1. Outline your image of the food supply chain in 30 years' time.

2. Can consumers have their cake and eat it?

3. What duty of care does the food industry owe to its stake-holders?

The scope and structure of the food supply chain

Kathryn Webster

Key objectives

- To define the term 'supply chain'
- To define the term supply chain management
- To identify the various sectors of the food supply chain in the UK
- To discuss the issues for each sector, at each stage in the food supply chain

Introduction

The value of spending on food and drink in the UK, whether on food designed to be eaten in the home, or away from home, has increased substantially year on year. People's disposable incomes are rising, and one consequence of this is their ability to spend relatively more on sophisticated styles of eating. This increased 'spend' is reflected in the industries which provide this food at increased profitability; and with this comes increased complexity. The customer is now more demanding, and no longer relies on 'seasonal' foods. It is now possible, in fact, to purchase foods from every corner of the globe, at any time of the year, generally at an affordable price. We are used to being able to shop seven days a week, and in most urban areas of the UK, 24 hours a day. The consumer does not expect to see empty shelves at any time. When eating out, the UK customer has a very wide choice of eating experiences: take-aways, bistros, restaurants and coffee shops offering cuisine from all over the world, and this trend has been replicated by the major supermarkets who offer packaged takeaway meals to challenge the traditional outlets. This chapter explores how organizations meet these challenges, identifies the issues at every stage, and considers how the use of partnerships is harnessed to achieve this. In the first instance, it is necessary to examine some terminology, and to define exactly what is meant by the term 'supply chain'.

Definition of the food supply chain

The food and drink supply chain has been a linear relationship involving the primary producers, or farmers, the manufacturers or processors who 'fabricate' the food for the table, and the retailers who gather a range of such products and sell them to the consumer. Food supplies have traditionally been sourced not only from within the UK, but widely from all parts of the world. Indeed the UK was the traditional market for its colonies until it joined the European Economic Community in 1973. Figure 3.1 shows that the UK continues to import a substantial quantity of its food.

The food and drink supply chain can be sub-divided into a number of sectors. Agriculture, horticulture, fisheries and aquaculture are the 'primary producers', the manufacturers who process the food into products ready for the table or further cooking, together with the packaging companies, are an intermediate stage, and the wholesalers, retailers and caterers are the end stages of the supply chain. At each stage in the chain the food is passed into a new ownership and 'value' is added to allow for the costs of the journey, and also to provide a small margin of profit.

In 1999, excluding imports and exports, the entire food chain was worth £56 billion, contributing towards 8% of the UK's GDP, and it employed 3.3 million people (12% of the workforce). It provided 6% of the country's total exports, worth £9 billion (MAFF 1999a).

Figure 3.1 shows how the food chain in the UK starts, as in any country, with the primary producers, the farmers and the fishing industry. In 1999 the farming sector was worth £8.2 billion, and the UK fishing sector landing fish, into the UK, £0.4567 billion. Note that the country imported raw and processed foods to the value of £16.9 billion.

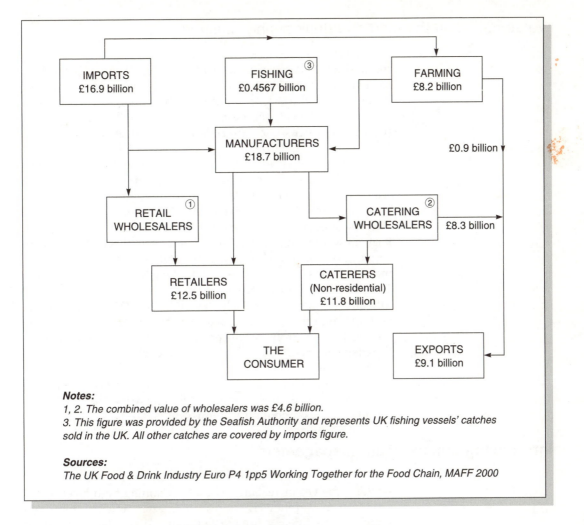

Figure 3.1 The food and drink supply chain in the UK

After harvest, or slaughter, or upon landing in port, the raw materials are sent to the manufacturers for some style of processing. This will range from milling grain into flour, malting of grain for alcohol production, grading, trimming and packing of vegetables, to a variety of processes ending in cooking and packing. This sector was worth £18.7 billion in 1999.

Processed products are then either sent directly to the retailers, or to wholesalers for distribution to the smaller retailers, or in the case of catering, to specialist wholesalers for onward sale to caterers. In each case the consumer is the final customer.

We also can see from Figure 3.1 that, although the UK imported £16.9 billion worth of raw and processed foods, there were exports to the value of £9.1 billion in 1999. International trade is a significant factor at all stages of the UK's food chain.

'Value added' in the food and drink supply chain

At each stage in the food chain 'value' is added: this means that the additional costs of processing, packaging and distribution, together with profits, are added on. The costs of unwanted or waste products are also covered at these stages. For example, in the case of beef, the costs of disposal of the 'fifth quarter' (hide, offal, carcass etc.) are covered by their incorporation into the selling price. There is a general 'rule of thumb' that only 15% of the final retail cost of any product will reflect the cost of the original agricultural raw material, the balance reflecting 'value added' at various stages, and representing the degree of processing that it has received (MAFF 1999a).

In the summer of 1998, there were accusations that at market, farmers were being paid a pittance for their sheep, whereas the cost of lamb in the shops was prohibitively expensive. Supermarket chains were accused of making unfair profits (Anon 1998, Gannaway 1998). However, research commissioned by the Ministry of Agriculture, Fisheries and Food (MAFF) suggested that although meat price changes are transmitted equally along the food chain, from producer to retailer, there tends to be a time lag for such 'adjustments' to work their way through the supply chain, which can result in unfair price comparisons. Further investigations by the 'Competition Commission' in 2000 supported these findings and found that there had been no unfair profiteering (Competition Commission 2000).

Introducing supply chain management

'Older' business practices involved managing the problem of stocking shelves or restaurants by maintaining high levels of all products: in warehouses, stores, in freezers and on storeroom shelves. This meant buying enough goods, far enough in advance, to ensure that supply was seldom jeopardized by shortages of goods, ingredients or menu items. Tougher competition has demanded shorter 'product life cycles' and made such an approach increasingly expensive. Today 'service-driven systems' are replacing these old 'inventory-driven systems'. This type of system is 'pulled' by customer demand rather than being 'pushed' by a supply system. The system, pioneered by the retail industry, has been copied over the past decade by the catering wholesaling and other manufacturing sectors, in order to maintain a competitive edge. It has involved heavy investment in technology and often a change in attitude toward the customer – indeed a complete culture change.

Supply chain management is a concept that is used increasingly to replace traditional fragmented management approaches to the buying, storing and moving of goods. Companies have tended, in the past, to move and store goods in a disparate way, using different departments and different managers. The supplier would transport the goods to the purchaser, who would then handle all internal transport and storage. But there would be separate transport or distribution departments to handle transportation to the ultimate customer. Supply chain management deals with the same issues, throughout the chain, from their source to the customer, but is concerned with ensuring quality, continuity of supply, the control of costs, customer service, and the increase of profits. In essence, supply chain management is managing flows across departments, sites and often companies, for which a high degree of management integration is needed.

The supply chain

Agriculture and associated trades

In 1999, the agricultural industry accounted for gross 'value added' of £8.2 billion, equivalent to 1.2% of the UK's GDP. This sector's contribution to the country's GDP is one of the lowest in the world, and reflects the UK's 'post-industrial' economy. The sector only produced 53% of the total food that the country consumes, the balance being imported (MAFF 1999a). It is important to note that this is balanced by the fact that the UK exported £851 million of unprocessed food (i.e. raw materials) in 1999, being the equivalent of 0.5% of the country's total exports.

The agricultural sector itself is diverse, ranging from small scale to large scale businesses. Tenant farmers to owners, managed farms to family-run businesses, some of these being full-time operations, but increasingly the smaller farms are characterized by being run on a part-time basis. Some farms are mixed, others are cereal based, some are virtual monocultures and yet others are accredited organic production systems. There were in total about 450 000 registered agricultural businesses in the UK in 1999, of which 300 000 were classified as 'minor'.

Some 150 000 farms were registered for VAT, which implies an individual turnover of more than £52 000 (as of 6 April 2000). Of this number, 2800 had a turnover of £31 million or more, and 300 had a turnover of £5 million or more (1999 figures).

Despite such diversity, there are many things which the farmers have in common. The sector has been reduced to being a very small player in the UK food chain over the past 50 years, and as such, has limited power to determine what is grown. As a consequence, farmers are forced to make commercial decisions based upon pressures from their suppliers, from their purchasers, and also as a result of national and international policies such as the Common Agricultural Policy (CAP). It used to be custom and practice for farmers to sell their produce to a wholesaler, who in turn would sell the products on to a range of manufacturers and retailers. Figure 3.2 provides four examples of a particularly complex chain, that of red meat.

A Farmers → Auctioneers → Abattoirs → Processors and manufacturers → Retailers → the Consumer

B Farmers → Auctioneers → Abattoirs → Retailers → the Consumer

C Farmers → Auctioneers → Abattoirs → Processors and manufacturers → Caterers → the Consumer

D Farmers → Auctioneers → Abattoirs → Processors and manufacturers → Independent butcher → the Consumer

Figure 3.2 Four alternative models of the beef supply chain

However, a number of recent initiatives have led to a more direct relationship between the primary producers and the end user, or the farmers and the retailers. These include 'contract farming', 'farmers' markets', and the advent of 'box schemes'.

Contract farming

This is a development whereby the farmer signs an agreement to supply a food processor or retailer with a specific crop. The 'contract' will specify the variety of crop to be grown, when it is to be planted, when and with what agro-chemicals it is to be sprayed, when it is to be harvested and so on. Although farmers have a guaranteed market, if the crops do not appear at the right time, or to the required standard, the buyer can reject them. In addition, if the produce is not selling well the buyer can reserve the right to reduce the purchasing price or even reject the crop. Like the CAP, this system encourages another form of high dependency – this time upon the purchaser's business skills. Such an imbalance, maybe even an abuse, of economic power has been criticized as being potentially dangerous to the agricultural and horticultural industries (Seth and Randall 1999). Indeed Tansey and Worsley (1995) suggest that farmers are now 'out-workers in an industrialized food production system'.

Farmers' markets

These are a late 1990s development in which farmers responded to the economic pressures on their businesses by creating a way in which local produce could be sold directly by the farmer to the consumer. These markets provide an outlet for food that has had minimal processing (fruit and vegetables), or where processing has taken place on the farm (cheese manufacture), or where the primary processor (abattoir) can return the product to the farmer to sell (cuts of meat). The number of these markets is expanding rapidly. In England, MAFF reported a figure of between 50 and 60 operating on a regular basis in 1999 (MAFF 1999a); by 2000 this had increased to over 200 (MAFF 2000).

Box schemes • • •

This is a development – exclusive to the organic sector – where farms or co-operatives pack a 'box' with seasonal vegetables, fruit, eggs and even bread and deliver them to a collection point for the customer to collect. These have increasingly grown in popularity in urban areas. They are successful in as much as they bypass the retailer whose organic produce can be as much as 50% more expensive.

'Niche markets' in agriculture • • •

Another development has been the growth of 'niche markets' for specific produce; examples include the Jersey Royal potato, Scottish beef and Welsh lamb. These are premium products which are strongly marketed.

Issues for the agricultural communities

The emergence of co-operatives • • •

Co-operatives have long been present in France as a means through which small farmers may access markets. In the UK, co-operatives are beginning to emerge in response to the increasing demands placed by retailers on the farming communities. Farmers, through their joint investment in marketing, breeding programmes and consumer research are now able to more effectively compete within the marketplace. An example of this is Kentish Garden. Kentish Garden is a fruit growers co-operative comprising 53 members which had a turnover of £31 million in 1999. This has been a result of joint initiatives, e.g. marketing, breeding, consumer research and the commissioning Research and Development. The co-operative now supplies soft fruit to all the major supermarkets and also to caterers. Outside the English growing season it packs imported fruit so that it can maintain a year-round supply to its major customers. Kentish Garden receives EU and MAFF assistance as a 'producer organization' for work on improving growing techniques, the introduction of new varieties, consumer research and improved planning and logistics.

Food safety • • •

The introduction of the Food Safety Act of 1990 which makes the retailer legally responsible for all aspects of the food they sell, coupled with public concerns over the mishandling of the BSE crisis, and increasing interest in animal welfare, has led food retailers to restrict their range of suppliers. They now choose suppliers on the basis of consistency of the quality of the meat and its traceability back to the farm (Hobbs 1996). Long term supply relationships with a few suppliers, in order to minimize their costs of monitoring, is now much more the norm. This system, known as 'vertical co-ordination', will typically comprise a grouping of a retailer, a processor and a limited number of farmers.

Traceability • • •

Assured British Meat (ABM) is a food industry initiative to improve consumer confidence in beef, lamb and pork by the establishment of a safety assurance framework for the entire supply chain. Sector-specific standards cover the manufacture of feed, on-farm production, transport, livestock markets, abattoirs, caterers, butchers, manufacturers and retailers. All members of the scheme are subjected to rigorous independent inspection to ensure that they adhere to these standards; the standards combining current legislation and industry good practice. Since September 2000 sheep also comply with the tagging system already applied to cattle.

Food and drink manufacturing

Figure 3.1 shows how in 1999 in the UK this sector accounted for gross 'value added' of £19 billion, equivalent to 2.6% of GDP. Exports were worth £8.3 billion; £2.8 billion of this was alcohol – 75% being Scotch Whisky (MAFF 1999a). The sector is highly concentrated; in 1999 only 8000 businesses were classified as food and drink manufacturers, of these, the largest ten food manufacturers accounted for 21% of the industry's turnover. Indeed there is a global trend towards this concentration of market power and the internationalization of both manufacturers and customers. Familiar international names include Procter and Gamble, Nestlé, Unilever and Kelloggs.

Case study – Unilever

Unilever is a massive multinational company, whose world-wide sales in 1999 reached £27.3 billion. It was formed as the result of the merger of Dutch and British companies in the 1920s. Unilever's Food product categories include:

- Culinary products (e.g. cooking sauces, mustards)
- Frozen foods (e.g. fish fingers, frozen peas)
- Ice cream
- Tea-based beverages (e.g. instant tea and iced tea)
- Spreads and cooking products (e.g. margarine and oils).

In 1999 the company made 27 acquisitions, and a survey of company press releases for the first half of 2000 indicates a similar pattern. The company acquired:

- Grupo Cressida in March – Honduras-based: doubled Unilever's presence in Central America.

- Ben & Jerry's Homemade in May for $326 million.

- SlimFast Food Companies for US$ 2.3 billion in May.

- Best Foods for $24.3 billion in June.

The company sold:

- Schoten meat factory to the Dutch Struik Food Group in May.

Such massive interests inevitably create problems for competing companies, which is illustrated by the following example. Unilever was investigated by the Competition Commission for maintaining a monopoly against public interest as a result of the activities of its Birds Eye Walls subsidiary. As a result of this, the Commission recommended a ban on exclusive supply agreements with retailers (FT 2000). All the major manufacturers of ices, which include Nestlé and Mars, will be similarly affected.

The reasons for the trend towards concentration via mergers and acquisitions owes much to the belief that large scale production is essential for global competitiveness, particularly in the European Single Market. In addition, in the 1980s, UK growth was funded by easy access to loans as a result of the liberalization of the UK financial sector by the Financial Services Act 1986, which also fuelled the consumer boom and hence demand for products. By 1994, 13 of the top 20 European food companies were based in the UK. These included Unilever, Grand Metropolitan, Eridania, Allied Domecq, Guinness, Hillsdown, Dalgety, Bass, Tate and Lyle, Cadbury Schweppes, Booker and United Biscuits.

Statistical analysis of the manufacturing sector

The activities of food and drink processors and manufacturers are divided into the following groups according to the Standard Industrial Classification system (SIC) (EuroPA 1995):

- Oils and fats

- Slaughtering of animals and production of meat and by-products

- Preparation of milk and milk products

- Processing of fruit and vegetables

- Fish processing

- Grain milling

- Bread, biscuits and flour confectionery

- Sugar and sugar by-products

- Ice cream, cocoa, chocolate and sugar confectionery

- Animal feeding stuffs (this should really be in the agricultural sector)

- Starch and miscellaneous foods

- Spirit distilling and compounding
- Wines, cider and perry
- Brewing and malting
- Soft drinks.

The food processing groups can be further sub-divided into first- and second-stage groups. First-stage groups are those which produce undifferentiated products, which are then sold on to intermediate producers. These include grain milling, sugar and sugar by-products, animal feeding stuffs, and organic oils and fats. Second-stage processors are those whose products are differentiated and which are sold to final-stage manufacturers who 'finish' the manufacturing process.

Value is 'added' at these various stages in the supply chain by the preparation of a range of dishes or ingredients for retail sale; farm products are processed, and new food concepts are developed. Originally preservers of food, the manufacturers are now continuous production lines. Interestingly, despite the trend towards concentration, the market is becoming increasingly segmented. Important new market 'niche' sectors have developed over the past 20 years, including cook–freeze, cook–chill, regional, ethnic, vegetarian and organic foods; examples of other niche products include 'fun' foods, i.e. foods containing minimal or 'non' nutrients such as olestra, 'lite' foods, status foods like bottled water, and 'functional foods' such as Benecol or the Aviva range, and diet meals.

Research shows that people in 'Western' societies consume less food every decade, as the result of increasingly sedentary life styles (MAFF 1999b), and that despite this increasing numbers of people are becoming overweight or obese (DOH 1992). So it is clear that as total food consumption is unlikely to grow in these Western societies, the continuous development of new product lines with 'added value' is the only way that this sector can 'grow'.

Supplier–retailer collaboration

Although this section is concerned with the role of the food processors in the food chain, the increasingly close nature of their working relationships with the major food retailing companies, in the UK, means that it is necessary briefly to examine the relationship at this stage. Hogarth-Scott (1999) identifies three differing types of retailer–supplier relationship which characterize today's environment:

1. Partnership between retailer and strong branded supplier, usually a market leader in which power is well balanced.

2. Own brand/private label relationship. These are important producers for the retailer and there is a very close working relationship. This relationship can be seen as a 'joint venture'.

3. Retailer relationships with 'secondary brand' manufacturers. The supplier is dependent upon the retailer which leads to a compliant relationship by the latter.

Today it is the major UK retailers who decide which manufacturers they deal with, and which of their brands they offer for sale; in other words, they control the manufacturer's 'access' to the consumer. This changed relationship means that the manufacturer must agree to terms set by the retailers in order to ensure that their products are not 'de-listed', and that they are displayed in the best shelf positions. In today's market, 'branded' merchandise is a weakened product.

Like the multi-nationals, the major food retailers have also been accused of anti-competitive practices such as demanding 'over-riders' from the manufacturers. These are discounts demanded by the retailer from the manufacturer against volume sales over a year, but which are not passed on to the consumer. Manufacturers are also charged higher prices for special positioning of their products.

Another allegation of unfair competition by the retailers is the marketing of 'look-alikes'. In 1994 there were a series of challenges to Coca-Cola by Sainsbury, Tesco and Virgin who marketed their own brands of cola product in very similar packaging at much reduced prices. The retailers were able to provide premium positions in store for these products.

There is some evidence to indicate that the success of 'own label' products by the major retailers has led to a decline in market concentration of the manufacturers. Retailers tend to use small and medium-sized firms to produce their own label products, as this enables them to closely control production and supply, with a view to ensuring quality and availability. However this state may be redressed with the advent of ECR (Efficient Consumer Response) and Category Management (see Chapters 4 and 5).

Wholesaling

This sector accounts for gross value added of £4.6 billion. The sector is divided into three broad categories: 'delivered', 'cash and carry' and 'food service' (catering supply). Included in these categories are commission agents, commodity brokers and wholesalers who trade on behalf of others, as well as those who trade on their own account. In 1999 approximately 17 000 businesses were classified as food and drink wholesalers; although only a few large companies dominate the 'delivered' and 'cash and carry' categories. 'Foodservice', which supplies the caterer, is much more diverse, with many specialist operators embracing a complex range of activities. Overall, the largest ten firms account for 17% of the wholesale sector's turnover. In addition, the few independent convenience stores have formed their own buying groups to protect their interests; names like Spar and Londis are familiar.

Traditionally, retail wholesalers would purchase in bulk from a wide range of manufacturers, and then sell these products on to the retailers. However, as the retailers have become more efficient in their own logistical operations, this role has declined substantially. Manufacturers now deliver directly to retailers rather than to 'middle men'. In contrast, the 'foodservice' side, delivering to caterers, has expanded in the wake of the growth of eating out in the UK.

We should note that, unlike retail wholesalers, catering wholesalers combine a range of functions including primary manufacture as well as distribution. Larger companies also offer a full service to their clients, including business advice, supply of equipment, large and small, and also nutritional and legal advice. Many of these companies are also characterized by their international and multi-divisional natures. The following company profiles indicate the range and variety of activities that some of the major players in this sector undertake.

Case study – Booker Cash and Carry

In April 1999 Booker sold off its food service business to Bidvest SA. As Booker Cash and Carry, the company operates 176 branches in the UK. It is the country's largest cash and carry operation, with over 35% of market share. In the late 1990s Booker acquired its competitor, the Nurdin and Peacock Cash and Carry chain, and substantially invested in a new central distribution project, known as Heartland. With sales of £3.4 billion, it is the key link between independent retailers, caterers and the manufacturing sector, its customer base comprising over 100 000 retailers and 300 000 caterers. It is a major purchaser of major manufacturing brands including Cadbury, Walkers Crisps, Coca-Cola and Mars, with significant buying power. The company also has its own strong private label brands for the caterer, retailer and licensed trade. In 1998 the company also introduced a

delivery service worth £400 million in its first year.

Collaboration with suppliers
Booker has initiated 'category partnerships' with a number of leading, branded suppliers. Typically, these initiatives involve signing up to common goals, implementing agreed action plans, and then carrying out stringent evaluation of the outcomes. The aim of these and other branded supplier initiatives is to generate more profit throughout the supply chain; pilot schemes have proved encouraging, with all parties seeing more profit.

Own label ranges
In 1998 Booker's range of private labels accounted for over 14% of sales. These lines providing increased profit margins for both the wholesaler and the customer. For instance, there are over 200 Happy Shopper

lines for the independent retailer, Chef's Larder is Booker's own-brand for caterers, and Malt House Vintners is Booker's own label for the licensed trade.

Booker Foodservice

This company is a leading distributor of frozen, chilled and ambient food for caterers. Sold off from the main Booker cash and carry company in 1999, it was acquired by the South African Bidvest Group. The company trades under its own name as well as owning a range of famous names such

as Lovell and Christmas, Fitch and Sons, Kearley and Tonge, Allinson, Bluecrest, Kinloch, Snowden and Bridge, United Yeast, Ross, Young and Pullman Foods.

Booker Foodservice itself supplies all the major food brands as well as their Coronet, Ashcroft & Moreton and own label products. The range of up to 15 000 lines includes frozen and chilled foods, groceries, cleaning materials, disposables and other non-food products. It also stocks light catering equipment and utensils.

Case study – Brake Brothers

This company is another major supplier to the catering trade. In 2000 its pre-tax profits were £35.5 million, an 18% increase over 1998. Its turnover had increased by 28% during that year, to £970 million. Like most major companies, it has built itself by the judicious purchasing of a range of other companies which have been 'off loaded' by others, to give it a balanced, but specialist portfolio. Current divisions of the Brake Brothers chain include Brake France, Larderfresh, Puritan Maid, Country Choice and Foodservice.

Brake Bros Foodservice supplies over 1000 frozen lines to the catering industry in the UK. Country Choice supplies bakery and branded frozen products to the independent bakery and retail sectors. It also offers technical support, advice on equipment, product range, bakery techniques, merchandising, added value and profit generating ideas. Puritan Maid offers a multi-temperature

logistics service delivering ambient, chilled and frozen foods to large multiple caterers who need tight central controls to ensure consistency throughout their branded outlets nation-wide. Larderfresh provides fine foods with an emphasis on fresh chilled products. Brake France is the supplier in France.

Watson & Philip offers grocery and chilled products to the catering trade; products include its own brand Orchard Farm food range and Catercare non-food and cleaning products.

A Taste of Italy is Brake Brothers' specialist importer and distributor of products to the Italian restaurant sector. Twin Chef Foods is the Group's manufacturing division, specializing in product development and innovation, both in the Brake Brand and bespoke for major caterers. M&J Seafoods is a specialist supplier of seafoods.

The competitive nature of the catering wholesaling sector reflects the activities of the major caterers themselves. The following example serves to illustrate the complex inter-relationships and challenges of the hospitality industry.

The pub chain Wetherspoon has plans to expand to 800 outlets by 2005. In the spring of 2000 Brake Brothers' Puritan Maid won a three-year contract worth £30 million annually to supply the chain. At the same time Granada terminated its £50 million contract with Puritan Maid. Although this contract involved the supply of over 2000 lines, the 'drop size' delivered to each outlet at Wetherspoons will equal that delivered to Granada. The smaller number of lines, coupled with a similar size 'drop', should make for better profit margins than the Granada business had offered.

Wetherspoon was previously supplied by Holroyd Meek, part of Booker Foodservice. Holroyd Meek is gaining the Granada business that Brake Brothers are losing, which it can combine with its sales to Burger King (owned by Granada).

In concluding this section, we should note that, like the food manufacturers who supply the retail trade, the catering wholesalers and product suppliers also see that innovation is the key to increased profitability, especially with their own label ranges. Brake Brothers has been disappointed with the performance of their own manufacturing division, Twin Chef Foods, and see the development of new products as the way to improve this. In the same way, Booker Foodservice plans to introduce a new quality own label range for caterers in 2000 to take the place of Booker Cash and Carry's 'Chef's Larder' range. Branding and differentiation are just as much key tools for success in this sector as in the retail sector.

Food and drink retailers

The food and drink retail sector accounted for gross 'value added' of £12.5 billion in 1999. About 60 000 businesses (with 90 000 outlets) were classified as mainly or specialized food and drink retailers. The industry is highly concentrated. The proportion of independent grocers fell from just over half in 1961 to one-third of this in 1978, and by 1999 the largest ten food retail companies accounted for 62% of the industry's turnover (MAFF 1999a). Today four major companies dominate the sector: Tesco, Sainsbury, Asda (owned by the US company Wal-Mart) and Safeway. Smaller players include Somerfield, Waitrose, Morrisons and the Co-op. The UK 'multiple grocers' make two or three times the operating profit of their European counterparts: up to 8%, compared with 2% in EU states and 1% in Australia. Large stores can stock between 20 000 and 30 000 lines, and have many hundreds of suppliers (IGD 1998).

This chapter has already discussed the fact that the economic 'balance of power' has shifted from manufacturers and processors to the retailers over the past 20–30 years. Like the manufacturers, the food retail sector can only 'grow' by selling more 'added value products', by increasing their market share and/or by diversification. Whilst the development of IT, as a means of increasing the efficiency of logistic systems, has contributed to the changes in market structure, other factors include the increasing concern, by both consumers and legislators, about food safety, traceability and quality. To facilitate this, many of the supermarkets directly obtain their food products from 'preferred suppliers' which in turn have groups of 'designated producers' supplying them to a particular specification. One drawback of this type of collaboration is that if company A is collaborating with company B, and company C with company D, then it might not be possible for company A to be able to work with company D. In this way, the collaboration is restricted to a few key players, and companies are very rigidly tied in with each other (Hogarth-Scott 1999).

The collaborative nature of the UK supply chain is probably the most sophisticated in the world, although it is important to note that the UK's grocery retailing environment is very different from that of other countries, where the market is far more segmented, and the sales mixes are very different. For instance, the UK sells twice as much frozen food and far fewer perishables than any other country in Europe (IGD 2000). In addition, people shop less often than their European neighbours, preferring to make weekly 'big shops' instead of daily visits; this requires a sophisticated supply chain able to provide volume supplies at a rapid speed. As a result of such differences, savings in the UK retail sector, which are reflected in profits, are typically between 0.5% and 2% of retail sales over comparable turnover in Europe (IGD 2000).

Discount retailers

There are some sectors of the UK retail market where collaboration between the manufacturer and the retailer is inappropriate. In the discount sector the drive for low prices overrides consistency of supply, and many suppliers are 'de-listed'. Manufacturers that are prepared to collaborate with the discount sector are limited (Walker 1994).

Caterers

In 1999 the UK non-residential catering sector accounted for gross 'value added' of over £9.1 billion (MAFF 1999a). Caterers are the single largest employers in the food system. In 1999 approximately 90 000 businesses (with 250 000 outlets) were classified as caterers; indeed concentration in this sector is very low – the largest ten firms accounting for only 21% of the sector's turnover (MAFF 1999a). Low concentration means that this sector is characterized by the variety of its outlets, which include fast-food outlets, self-service cafeterias, motorway service stations, restaurants, bistros, cafes, ethnic restaurants of every style, hotels of all classes, motels and so forth.

However, there are a few large companies which do dominate the sector, mirroring the complexity of some of the companies in the retail, foodservice and wholesaling sectors. The major players include Granada, whose catering interests include hotel chains, a road service division and catering contracting, the international company Sodexho, which owns a range of familiar catering contractors such as Gardner Merchant and Ring and Brymer, and pub chains such as Bass and Whitbread. For trading purposes each 'division' is self-sufficient and is responsible for its own supply chain.

Given the variety of catering outlets, the issues in terms of supply chain management are disparate. Certain major companies own their own supply and manufacturing divisions (see section on wholesaling), whereas the smaller outlets will source their produce from the wholesalers who specialize in catering for the hospitality industry. In many cases, these are different names but they are owned by the same parent company. However, the issues of quality, consistency of supply, traceability and price remain as important for this sector as for any other in the food industries.

Conclusion

This chapter has examined a number of the challenges which face the food and drink supply chain today. These include:

- Globalization of markets.

- An acute emphasis on food safety, so the utilization of 'tools' such as 'due diligence', HACCP, and 'traceability', assurance schemes and so on are present at all stages of the supply chain.

- Greater customer choice and market segmentation.

- Diversification in the rural economy: farmers are increasingly squeezed in a cost/price wedge that demands higher production and greater technological inputs, and results in either larger holdings or part-time farming.

- A major shift in power relationships over the past 30 years between the manufacturers and the retailers.

References

Anon (1998) Manufacturers split over multiple power. *The Grocer*, 8 August, p. 4.

Competition Commission (2000) Supermarkets – a report on the supply of groceries from multiple stores in the UK, CM44842 10/10/2000 (www. Opengov.uk).

Dobson P., Waterson M. and Chu A. (1998) *The Welfare Consequences of the Exercise of Buyer Power*. Paper No. 16. London: Office of Fair Trading

DOH (1992) *The Health of the Nation*. London: HMSO.

EuroPA (1995) *The UK Food and Drink Industry: A Sector by Sector Economic and Statistical Analysis*. Cambridge: EuroPA and Associates.

FT (2000) Kellogg set to eat its words. *Financial Times*, 25 February.

Gannaway B. (1998) The OFT's new stamping ground. *The Grocer*, 8 August, pp. 26–7.

Hogarth-Scott S. (1999) Retailer–supplier partnerships: hostages to fortune or the way forward for the millennium? *British Food Journal*, 101 (9), pp. 668–82.

Hobbs J. (1996) A transaction cost analysis of quality, traceability and animal welfare issues in UK beef retailing. *British Food Journal*, 98 (6), pp. 16–26.

IGD (1998) *Efficient Consumer Response. An Industry Response.* Institute of Grocery Distribution.

IGD (2000) *European Grocery Retailing 2000: A Practical Guide.* Institute of Grocery Distribution.

MAFF (1999a) *Working Together for the Food Chain.* Views from the Food Chain Group. London: Ministry of Agriculture, Fisheries and Food.

MAFF (1999b) *The National Food Survey.* London: Ministry of Agriculture, Fisheries and Food.

MAFF (2000) Farmers' markets – good for British agriculture and the food chain. News Release, 25 May; www.Maff.gov.uk/inf/newrel/2000/000525b.htm

Seth A. and Randall G. (1999) *The Grocers: The Rise and Rise of Supermarket Chains*. London: Kogan Page

Tansey G. and Worsley T. (1995) *The Food System: a Guide*. London: Earthscan.

Walker M. (1994) Supplier–retailer collaboration in European grocery distribution. *Logistics Information Management*, 7 (6), pp. 23–7.

Activities

1 (a) Visit a supermarket and calculate the selling price of a whole lamb. You will need to refer to a text that shows all the cuts from the carcass first. Which of these cuts are to be found within the supermarket? Consider how the butcher may use the missing parts.

(b) Carry out the same exercise at a local independent butcher.

(c) Find out:

   (i) the cost of the whole lamb to the farmer (a copy of *Farmers' Weekly* may help you)

   (ii) the value of the whole carcass to the caterer (prices are published in *Caterer and Hotelkeeper*)

(iii) calculate the difference in the value of that lamb to the farmer and the cost to the consumer.

(d) What steps in the food chain may account for this price difference?

(e) How can the independent butcher or the supermarket justify the prices that they charge?

2 Visit a number of websites for large foodservice companies:

(a) Identify the range of innovations that they are offering.

(b) Is this 'value added'?

(c) What are the advantages for the caterer in using these products?

(d) To what extent are the innovations reflected in those of competitor foodservice companies?

Questions

1. '. . . buyer power may be socially detrimental where it under-mines the long term viability of suppliers and their willingness to commit to new product and process investments' (Dobson, Waterson and Chu 1998). Discuss this statement.

2. A number of companies in both the foodservice and food retailing sectors now consider their prime objective to be 'customer satisfaction'. Why should this concept be the current 'buzzword' of the business?

Concepts of collaboration: supply chain management in a global food industry

Andrew Fearne, David Hughes and Rachel Duffy

Key objectives

- To examine the process of globalization and the emergence of food retailers as the dominant force in the food supply chain

- To explore the strategic response of the food manufacturing sector

- To explore the theoretical constructs of supply chain management

Introduction

Less than a decade ago, the days of the giant conglomerate seemed over; they were too big, too complacent and too inflexible. However, the US economy has grown fast since 1992, with many big organizations becoming flatter, less bureaucratic and hierarchical in structure. The big corporation of the twenty-first century looks like being a loose alliance, a confederation of small entities, held together by knowledge and competencies, shared values and integrated missions. The edges of these amorphous organizations will become fuzzier, but their control, through patents and contractual agreements seems likely to grow. The knowledge economy requires 'big science' and only big corporations with big Research and Development budgets look likely to be able to afford it. Of course, the human brain cannot continue to accommodate an exponential growth of knowledge and the 300-year-old explosion of knowledge was flattening off by the 1960s. It is these diminishing returns to Research and Development that means the future belongs to the big corporation with deep pockets.

This chapter is concerned with the battle for supremacy in a food industry in which competition is played out on a global field, with fewer, larger, global players battling for market share. The stalemate which results from global retailers confronting global manufacturers has been broken by the introduction of Efficient Consumer Response (ECR) and the realization that co-operation between trading partners is more effective than confrontation. Traditional inter-firm competition is being superseded by competition between supply chains, as retailers and manufacturers alike seek competitive advantage through strategic supply chain partnerships.

The globalization of grocery retailing

The latter half of the twentieth century, in both Europe and North America, has seen the emergence of the supermarket as the dominant grocery retail form. The reasons why supermarkets have come to dominate food retailing are not hard to find. The search for convenience in food shopping and consumption coupled to car ownership, led to the birth of the supermarket. As incomes rose and shoppers sought both convenience and new tastes and stimulation, supermarkets were able to expand the products offered. The invention of the bar code allowed a store to manage thousands of items and their prices, and led to 'just-in-time' store replenishment and the ability to carry tens of thousands of individual items. Computer-operated depots and logistical systems integrated store replenishment with consumer demand in a single electronic system. The superstore was born.

The expansion of retailers across European borders has been one characteristic of structural change in industry in general and the food industry in particular (Table 4.1). Starting slowly in the 1970s, retail firms sought to extend their market territories within Europe. The pace of expansion accelerated in the 1980s and 1990s; with over half of post-Second World War retail firm moves within Europe being initiated during the 1990s.

The 1980s were a decade of 'border hopping'. Firms from many sectors expanded into adjacent markets – fashion retailers were most active in the first half, followed by the French grocery hypermarket companies (e.g. Carrefour) expanding into Spain, Italy and Greece and German hard discount chains (e.g. Aldi) moving into adjacent countries in the second half. Cross-border alliances between non-competing national grocery retail firms were initiated with the intent of enhancing purchasing power and developing new product sourcing opportunities, for example, the European Retail Alliance/Associated Marketing Services.

In Europe and led by grocery retailers, the 'border hopping' accelerated during the 1990s, despite the economic recession early in the decade. With the end of the 'Cold War', German

	Pre-1980s	1980s	1990s
Percentage of cross border retail moves	11	34	55
Top 5 Destinations	Belgium France Austria Netherlands Switzerland	Belgium Spain Germany UK Netherlands	UK Spain Germany France Czech Rep.
Top 5 Initiators	UK Germany France Netherlands Sweden	France UK Germany Outside Europe Italy	UK France Germany Outside Europe Netherlands
Most active sectors	Fashion/footwear Grocery	Fashion/footwear Grocery Health/beauty	Grocery Fashion/footwear Health/beauty Household

Source: Oxford Institute of Retail Management and James Lang Wooton (1997) *Shopping for New Markets: Retailers Expansion Across Europe's Borders.* Oxford Institute of Retail Management, Templeton College, University of Oxford. November, 1997

Table 4.1
Retailers' expansion across European borders, pre-1980s to 1997

and other Northern European retailers expanded into Eastern and Central European countries. Firms from Germany (e.g. Tengelmann), France (e.g. Carrefour), Belgium (e.g. Delhaize Le Lion) and the Netherlands (e.g. Royal Ahold) have taken a global perspective on trading. The major UK retailers have had less of an international presence – Sainsbury in the USA, Tesco faltering in Northern France and, then, acquiring retail businesses in Eastern Europe and Thailand.

At the end of the twentieth century there are three grocery retail firms – Wal-Mart, Carrefour and Royal Ahold – who have strikingly similar global aspirations. For example, Royal Ahold's mission statement is 'to grow quickly and profitably to become the world's leading supermarket company', a statement that is strikingly similar to that espoused by the other two major international players.

Supermarketing retail strategy

The genesis of the supermarket era – the emergence of the self-service grocery store – is attributed to retail developments in the USA. The first supermarket was opened in 1930 (King Kullen) by Michael Cullen, a New York merchant and, numerous supermarkets then emerged at varying speeds in the years immediately following the Second World War, as the major form of food retailing right across North America and Northern Europe. The principal merchandising model that emerged and was adopted by major supermarket chains can, for shorthand, be labelled the 'American model'. The model can be characterized as having a wide range of branded goods, a narrower range of much cheaper own label/store brand products, with the promotional focus on price discounts, 'specials' etc. and the stores leased, not owned, by the supermarket chain.

From the American model emerged two alternates. First, German 'hard' discount chains. These are secondary small stores with a limited, largely low-price, product offer, with store/own label brands. These stores offer minimum in-store service. The second is the UK retailing model – out of town, company-owned super stores with a far greater product range. As much as half of their products may be own label/store brand items, positioned to compete with national brands on an equal and slight price discount basis. There is a strong emphasis on premium quality, chilled, almost exclusively own label value-added food products. Company staff work closely with manufacturers of the own label products and new product development is prolific (e.g. Sainsbury and Tesco each launch around 1500 new own label products per annum). The overall offer to the customer is value driven.

Arguably, the UK model can be seen as merely a variant of the 'American' model, with particular emphasis placed on premium own label and fresh foods. Certainly it has delivered higher margins to British grocery retailers (double or even triple the net profit margins of other countries). Its proponents argue that the UK shopper is well satisfied. Yet British shoppers do also have the opportunity to patronize price-driven retail formats. For example, European hard discounters have a place, although a modest one, in the UK grocery market.

The focus on price competition and average quality, rather than service and/or high quality, that is characteristic of most Northern European and North American food retailers, is a self-reinforcing merchandising strategy that encourages periodic price wars. Typically a retailer will respond to declining sales by reducing prices. It is important to note that a drop in sales tends to be linked to a decline in numbers of shoppers rather than a reduction in average spend, thus the aim of a price reduction is to attract customers back into the store. When retailers are operating at relatively low net profitability levels (i.e. 1–2%), a small downturn in sales for the retailer is translated into a disproportionately high decline in net profitability (Table 4.2). In the example given, a sales decline by a modest 2% and, in the short term, the retailer has little flexibility in cutting costs. Some minor adjustments can be made, for example, by reducing the usage of part-time staff to push variable costs down.

A high decline in net profitability to retailers operating on a low net margin is crucial as it has a disproportionate negative impact on return on equity (ROE). A modest increase in sales boosts net margin sharply and, in turn, this has a very attractive impact on ROE. From the example (Table 4.3), a 0.1% decline in net margin for the French or USA retailer translates into a tenfold decline in ROE, i.e. the ROE falls by a full percentage point. The UK retailer, operating at much more attractive levels

	$000	$000
Sales	100	98
COGS	80	78.4
Gross margin	20	19.6
Fixed costs	13.3	13.3
Variable costs	5.7	5.6
Net profit ($000)	1.0	0.7
Net margin (Net profit/Sales)%	1.0	0.71

A 2% decline in sales translates into a 29% decline in net margin

COGS: Cost of Goods Sold.
Source: Hughes and Ray 1999

Table 4.2
The impact of a sales decline on retail net margins: a hypothetical example

of net profit margin, has substantially more latitude should there be a short term dip in sales. In the example given, a 0.1% decline in net margin translates into a threefold decline, 0.3%, in ROE – reason for considerable concern, but not for mass panic and the slashing of product prices across the board.

Interestingly, the ROE of French/American grocery chains are not substantially different to those earned by the 'high margin' UK retailers and thus has equal attraction for shareholders. However, there is a fundamental difference between the two models in the means by which an similar ROE is achieved, as seen in Table 4.3.

In the American model it is the leverage (i.e. assets divided by shareholder equity), that drives the return on shareholder funds (ROE). The 'American' model retailers invest little in the physical stores, preferring to lease rather than purchase. The financial trump card in this form of retailing is to maximize the extent to which the business can be run on supplier credit (i.e. through gaining extended terms of payment) thereby, maximizing leverage.

In the UK, the major retailers are 'blue chip' quoted, public companies, with strong balance sheets reflecting their investment in the, now very scarce, out of town sites for superstores and the bricks and mortar of the stores themselves. This high level of capitalization reduces leverage and identifies that UK retailers are in two businesses, namely grocery retailing and property development and investment.

There are three principal implications of the 'American' retail model focus on price, with service being an ancillary concern.

1. There is consistent pressure within the supermarket business – from board level to store department manager – to reduce

$$ROE = \frac{Net\ Profit}{Sales} \times \frac{Sales}{Assets} \times \frac{Assets}{Shareholder\ Equity}$$

Return on Equity | Net Margin | Asset Turnover | Leverage

Northern Europe/North American retailer
ROE = 1.6 × 2.0 × 4.9 = 16
0.1% decline/increase translates to **±1.0%** change in ROE

UK retailer
ROE = 6.1 × 1.4 × 2.1 = 18
0.1% decline/increase translates to a **±0.3%** change in ROE

Source: Adapted from Wileman and Jary 1997

Table 4.3 The impact of a decline in net margins on ROE for grocery retailers

in-store labour and to minimize head office staffing costs, with a net impact of:

(a) reducing the quality of the shopping experience for the customer,

(b) allowing head office staff less time to develop effective commercial relationships with their suppliers and shoppers.

2. The totally price-driven model has the effect of fostering an ethos of constant confrontation between retailers and their suppliers – manufacturers, distributors, growers etc.

3. The transfer of income from manufacturers to retailers – in the form of 'street money' such as slotting fees (overriders etc.) increases the comparative advantage of large versus small manufacturers through raising entry barriers to the food industry.

An almost exclusive focus on price, rather than other product attributes and supplier services, ensures that supplier–retailer relationships are, characteristically, confrontational and, in most cases, dominated by the retailer. Further, the merchandising tactic of using 'specials' has convinced shoppers that they should only buy when many products are 'on offer'. This creates significant inefficiencies in the supply chain; for example, creating 'spikes' in demand for products with the consequential requirement for suppliers and retailers to build up huge inventories in anticipation of abnormal demand. The combination of a frustrated shopper and a 'bullied' supplier will serve to accelerate the demise of traditional supermarket retailing as it exists in the late-1990s. Clearly, there are supermarket firms to whom this does not apply (e.g. some American examples of best retailing practice would include Wegman's, H.E. Butt, Hannaford Bros.). However, for many, the final decade of the twentieth century may have been the supermarkets' halcyon period of domination in many markets in Northern Europe and North America.

The competitive threat for retailers is increasing as new routes to the shopper and consumer emerge. Traditional supermarkets have struggled to maintain market share in the face of increasing competition from growth sectors such as food service, warehouse clubs, gas station/forecourt 'mini-supermarket' outlets and the much-publicized, although still incipient, home delivery options using the Internet, telephone etc. As shown in Tables 4.2 and 4.3, a relatively small decline in sales for some supermarket companies, which can result from this competitive pressure can have a draconian impact on net profit margin and ROE.

The flurry of supermarket chain acquisition and merger activity in the latter part of the 1990s in Northern Europe and North America is testament to this as the more aggressive firms seek to consume their competitors and generate scale efficiencies in purchasing, logistics and promotion etc.

Changing retailer behaviour

Successful retailers now recognize that it is their customers who are their greatest assets, not their stores. Thus, a race has been initiated to establish loyalty programmes that will bind customers to specific stores through their lifetime, a cultural shift for retailers who, in history, were fixated on maximizing transactions and traffic, irrespective of relative profitability of types of customers. Clearly, the current loyalty schemes represent the first tentative steps of retailers learning how to cope with the mountain of data that is generated through the bar codes on every product and every till. In many cases, the schemes are no more than discount programmes that benefit shoppers who may, or may not be, profitable for the retailer in question. They have been beneficial in attracting trip loyalty rather than higher trip spend and spend is clearly the next target. The future emphasis will be a move from 'one to many' mass marketing towards 'one to one' mass customization.

The implementation of Category Management, as part of the global ECR initiatives, provides a scientific boost to the business of retailing as it relies on comprehensive analyses of store- and market-level data for making a wide range of strategic and tactical decisions. Further, it requires the retailer to appraise its relationships with key suppliers and to move away from confrontation and towards co-operation. This, in itself, is a cultural *volte face* that many will fail to attain. When retail buyers have been trained through the years to gain maximum leverage from their suppliers ('bullying' in many cases) and to consider all retail sales data as confidential, simply re-labelling the buyer as a category manager will not be sufficient to change the nature of the commercial relationship. Yet, Category Management is not 'rocket science'! In the final analysis, it is simply getting the basics of retailing right, namely listing the consumer relevant SKUs (stock keeping units); having them in-store at the right time; merchandising the display cabinet/shelfspace efficiently and effectively; providing effective promotional support; and ensuring price competitiveness on products that are price sensitive. In short, it is a matter of understanding the shopper and generating shopper and consumer enthusiasm for each product category and for the store overall.

Thus, to survive in the twenty-first century, traditional supermarkets must change radically. In essence, they must use IT and transformed staff to recreate the customer–retailer relationship that was characteristic of the very best specialist retailer businesses in the early twentieth century. Radical changes will come quickly. AC Nielsen Europe surveyed 300 leading European grocery retailer executives and asked them about the changes they expected to see in their sector in the first decade of the next century. Responses to four of the key questions are instructive:

- What percentage of today's food retailers will be in existence in 2005? *63% said less than 50%*.

- Who will own most of the stores in 2005? *65% said large international/global retailers*.

- If you were **not** in the food business, would you invest 50% of your personal wealth in food retailing, today? *52% said **definitely not.***

- By what date will consumer-direct sales represent 20% or more of food 'retail' volume? *20% said by 2005 and 48% said by 2010.*

If changes in the retail sector occur of the expected magnitude and at the expected pace, then, there will be substantial reverberation throughout the food industry. In the next section the consequences of such radical change for manufacturers are explored in more detail.

Food manufacturing – the clash of the Titans

In this section, the focus is placed on the larger scale manufacturing companies – fast moving consumer goods (FMCG) companies – such as Unilever, Kraft Jacob Suchard, Nestlé – and particular account is taken of their evolving relationships with major national and international retailers. First, structural changes in food and beverage manufacturing are addressed. Factors that stimulate international expansion of FMCG firms into global markets are reviewed. Briefly, the relative performance of food manufacturing firms is assessed and initiatives that major FMCG firms can undertake to improve their commercial position *vis-à-vis* large scale and often global retailers are discussed.

Structural changes in international food manufacturing

In the food industries of the developed world, the balance of power has shifted over the past 30 years or so to favour food retailers. This has been particularly marked in Northern Europe where national grocery markets are characterized by relatively high levels of retail concentration. This is in contrast to the USA, where retail concentration has been relatively low at the national market level, but often high at the regional/state level.

In the early 1970s FMCG companies had field sales forces roaming the land and taking orders from individual shops. Promotions were local in orientation. In subsequent decades, the retail landscape became, increasingly, structured with supermarket chains consolidating and the trade focus shifting to negotiations between retail head office and manufacturers. In the low growth 1990s, margins have been under pressure for most parties and the emphasis has shifted to capturing supply chain efficiencies to compensate for low growth. In the next decade, retailers will seek to reduce their supply bases and concentrate on building partnerships with preferred suppliers. Joint business planning will be initiated to build consumer demand and to reduce logistics costs and improve supply chain management efficiencies.

While the globalization of retailing is a relatively recent phenomenon, food manufacturing has been international in character for decades and, if not dominated, at least led by firms with their headquarters in the USA. The instigator of the convenience food revolution, the USA, accounts for about one-quarter of the industrialized world's total processed food production. American firms comprise the majority of both the top 10 and top 30 global food and beverage manufacturers. The UK is the next most frequently listed, followed by Japan and France (Table 4.4).

Since the 1970s, the nominal value of total world trade in processed food has increased at an average annual rate of about 10.5%. This figure understates the importance of globalization in the food industry, however, as it does not take into account the trans-national activities of food processing firms. For example: in 1994 sales from foreign affiliates of US processed food firms exceeded $100 billion, more than four times the total value of US exports of processed foods. Most of these sales were in foreign markets; only about 2% were shipped to the USA.

The EU food manufacturing sector is highly fragmented, although sales are dominated by companies with more than 100 employees. In 1992, there were 256 000 food manufacturing firms each employing less than 20 people and accounting for 15% of sector turnover, whilst 4500 firms with 100+ employees accounted for 70% of sales turnover. Across-EU comparisons of change in the size distribution of enterprises in the food and drink manufacturing sector from 1980 to 1992 are difficult. However, the various pressures that we expected to promote concentration in the industry and lead to convergence of food industry structures across Europe, appear to have had little impact during the 1980s. In the USA, food manufacturing is much more concentrated: 16 000 registered food manufacturing firms in 1995, with the top 50 companies accounting for an estimated 50% of total sector output.

Modest although concentration may have been during the 1980s, the pace of structural change seemed to pick up during the 1990s. The early 1990s saw substantial polarization taking place in the European food manufacturing sector. In 1991, the three largest companies, Philip Morris, Nestlé and Unilever, posted European food sales of ECU 48.5 billion, out of a total

Rank	Company	HQ base	Food sales ($ billion)	Total sales ($ billion)
1	Nestlé	Switzerland	45.4	47.6
2	Philip Morris	USA	31.9	72.1
3	Unilever	UK/Holland	24.2	48.5
4	Conagra	USA	24.0	24.0
5	Cargill	USA	21.0	56.0
6	PepsiCo	USA	20.9	20.9
7	Coca-Cola	USA	18.9	18.9
8	Diageo	UK	18.8	20.2
9	Mars	USA	14.0	14.0
10	Danone	France	14.0	14.8
11	ADM	USA	13.9	13.9
12	IBP	USA	13.3	13.3
13	Anheuser-Busch	USA	12.8	12.8
14	Kirin	Japan	10.9	10.9
15	Sara Lee	USA	10.4	17.9
16	Eridania Béghin-Say	France	9.6	10.7
17	H.J. Heinz	USA	9.4	9.4
18	Asahi Breweries	Japan	9.1	9.5
19	RJR Nabisco	USA	8.7	17.1
20	Best Foods	USA	8.4	8.4
21	Suntory	Japan	8.1	8.1
22	Campbell's Soup	USA	8.0	8.0
23	Seagram	Canada	7.0	12.6
24	Kellogg	USA	6.8	6.8
25	ABF	UK	6.8	8.5
26	Cadbury Schweppes	UK	6.8	6.8
27	Heineken	Holland	6.8	6.8
28	Tate & Lyle	UK	6.4	7.6
29	Tyson Foods	USA	6.4	6.4
30	General Mills	USA	6.3	6.3

Table 4.4
The top thirty food manufacturing firms, ranked by food sales, 1997

Source: Cooke T. (1998) Leading food and drinks groups. In*: Trends in the Global Food Industry, 1998.* Seymour-Cooke Food Research International, London, UK

European food sales of ECU 135 billion from the top 50 companies, i.e. 36% of total. By the early part of the 1990s, the major sub-sectors of the European food manufacturing sector showed a relatively high degree of three firm concentrations in most EU countries (Table 4.5). With the exception of pasta in the UK (a relatively under-developed market in European terms), the top three manufacturers accounted for more than 50% of output in the pasta, coffee, biscuit, chocolate confectionery, ice cream and mineral water product areas. Within the selected NACE codes, the leading manufacturers are, typically, multi-national firms with a strong European presence at the least and, generally, a global presence (Table 4.6).

	Pasta	Coffee	% of total supply Biscuits	Choc. confect.	Ice cream	Mineral water
UK	27	78	70	79	58	50
France	58	64	50	51	56	76
Germany	57	63	50	51	88	24
Italy	52	67	67	50	80	34

These formed by independent wholesale operators in order to improve trading terms with suppliers and offer their members, through the power of bulk buying, significant price benefits. The main distinguishing feature compared to symbol groups is that it allows members to trade under their own name, facia or group identity.

Source: Fearne A. (1996) *The Impact and Effectiveness of the Internal Market Programme on the Processed Foods Sector.* Food Industry Management Group, Wye College, University of London, January

Table 4.5
Three firm concentration ratios for selected food product categories, 1991

417 Pasta	423 Tea/Coffee	419 Biscuits	421 Confectionery	421 Ice Cream
Barilla	Douwe Egberts[a]	Bahlsens Keksfabrik	Cadbury	Unilever
Danone	Jacobs Suchard[b]	Campbell	Ferrero	Scholler
RHM	Nestlé	Danone	Suchard[b]	Nestlé
Nestlé	Unilever	United Biscuits	Mars	Mars
Heinz		RJR Nabisco	Nestlé	Grand Met.

424 Spirits	427 Beer	428 Soft Drinks	428 Mineral Water
Allied Domecq	Anheuser Busch	Coca-Cola	Nestlé
Grand Met.	Bass	Pepsi-Cola	Danone
Seagram	Danone	CCSB[c]	San Benedetto
Guinness	Fosters	Bass	San Pellegrino
Heineken			

[a] Sara Lee
[b] Phillip Morris
[c] Coca-Cola Schweppes (Cadbury) Beverages
Source: As Table 4.5

Table 4.6 Major manufacturers of selected food product categories (by NACE code) in the early 1990s

In the early 1990s, merger and acquisition (M&A) activities of major food manufacturing and beverage companies in Europe was intense, accounting for close to two-thirds of all M&A activity in the global food industry and, largely, cross-border in nature as companies *within* the EU 'jockeyed' for commercial position. By mid-decade, the global M&A activity remained at high levels, but the proportion accounted for by EU firms had declined. Within Europe the M&A activity was undertaken by the major FMCG firms. Western European and US firms have dominated M&A activity during the 1990s, accounting for 70%

of total M&As in 1996 (Table 4.7). Globally, most M&As are cross-border and, often, for non-EU and non-US firms, involve purchases of mergers with firms in adjacent countries. American firms accounted for around one-third of all M&As in the mid-1990s, followed by firms from the UK, France, Canada and Germany (Table 4.8). M&As are spread out over the food industry by product category, although they are particularly noticeable in the alcoholic and soft drink sectors (20% of global total) and the dairy sector.

Just as retailers have established horizontal, cross-border alliances with each other in Europe, Northern Hemisphere-based food manufacturers have undertaken similar initiatives. In the

Region	1994	1995	1996	Percentage cross-border in 1996	Percentage of total M&A in 1996
Western Europe	214	262	202	49	38
Central/Eastern Europe	29	38	35	86	7
North America	143	158	168	22	32
Latin America/Caribbean	33	42	52	92	10
Asia/Pacific	47	44	48	85	9
Africa/Middle East	17	15	23	74	4
Total	483	559	528	51	100

Source: Cooke T. (1994, 1998) Mergers & Acquisitions world-wide. Seymour-Cooke Food Research International, London

Table 4.7 Food industry mergers and acquisitions, by major regions, 1994–6

HQ location of lead firm	Percentage of total M&As 1994	1996
USA	32	35
UK	20	14
France	6	10
Canada	7	6
Germany	7	5
Italy	4	4
Spain	5	4
Netherlands	4	4
Poland	2	3
Australia	3	3
Others	10	12
Total	100	100

Source: As Table 4.7

Table 4.8
Mergers and acquisitions by headquarters location of lead firm, 1994 and 1996

early 1990s, Nestlé and Coca-Cola formed the Coca-Cola–Nestlé Refreshment Co. to develop ready-to-drink tea and coffee markets outside Japan. Unilever linked up with Pepsi-Cola to develop tea-based drinks and Danone to market frozen yoghurt products. Most active has been General Mills, from the USA, linking with Nestlé to form Cereal Partners World-wide, Pepsico, to focus on the European snack market and Best Foods to launch desserts and baking mixes in eight Latin American countries.

The three most commonly cited reasons for forming alliances are: to gain access to a market and/or a distribution system, to exploit complementary technology and to reduce time taken for innovation. Alliances are, likely, to be a sustaining feature of the food manufacturing scene.

Increasingly competitive environment in food manufacturing

Food manufacturers view the emergence of a relatively few, very large global retailers with some trepidation. The major FMCG food manufacturers have first hand experience in dealing with major national retailers in the mature market regions of Northern Europe and North America and, more recently, it has been a struggle.

From a period of market dominance in the 1950s and early 1960s, manufacturers have come under increasing commercial pressure from major retail chains who, now, are expanding aggressively on a global basis. In their home markets, food companies have learnt that strong brands and market leadership is critical to fending off the challenge of retailer own label products. This is particularly the case for premium own label products such as those offered by Sainsbury in the UK, Safeway Select in the USA and President's Choice of Loblaw's in Canada. Even in the USA where own label sales were slow to become established, they are forecast now to increase at three times the rate of nationally branded grocery products.

The launch of the Europe currency programme at the beginning of 1999 has served to compound the challenges for the multinational FMCG companies and, is a harbinger of what is to come when the global retailers elect to source globally and, seek a single net price from their major suppliers. Manufacturer selling prices for FMCG products have varied significantly across the European Union as manufacturers have sought to exploit their bargaining position by country reflecting, in the past, that retailing was on a national basis. Cross-border mergers have 'Europeanized' the market. With the introduction of the Euro and removal of exchange rate risk, price differentials between markets will become more transparent. For example, German retailers may wish to quiz Coca-Cola on the rationale for the 100% price differential between Germany and Spain for a 1.5 litre bottle of Coke! The French food retailer, Promodès, operates in France, Belgium, Italy, Spain and Portugal and, indubitably, will be demanding one price and the very lowest price from Coca-Cola for all its companies in Europe.

Combating the competitive threat from global retailers: FMCG initiatives

There are a range of responses that FMCG companies can consider as mechanisms to combat the growing competitive threat from increasingly powerful global retailers:

- Innovate
- Cost leadership (cost consciousness)
- Diversify sectors within existing geographical markets
- Explore new distribution channels
- Seek to develop long term partnerships with those retailers who will lead the industry in the future.

The emergence of supply chain management as a source of competitive advantage and, the growing emphasis on the development of strategic supply chain partnerships within the global food industry, is a relatively recent phenomenon. It is also one of the challenges which retailers, food manufacturers, farmers and all the other intermediaries in the food supply chain find particularly difficult to tackle. This chapter now moves on to discuss the principles of supply chain management and the key requirements for the development of strategic supply chain partnerships in the global food industry.

Supply chain partnerships for a global food industry

It is commonplace today for strategic writers to argue that competition is dead (Moore 1996), or that co-operation rather than competition is the way forward (Brandenburger and Nalebuff 1996). At the operational level there has also been a plethora of writing about more collaborative relationship management and procurement, and logistical effectiveness and efficiency, that draws on this experience. The work by Bhote (1989), Carlisle and Parker (1989), Christopher (1992, 1997), Gattorna and Walters (1996), Harrison (1993), Hines (1994), Houlihan (1988), Kay (1993), Lamming (1993), Lewis, (1990), Sako (1992) and Saunders (1994) all falls into this category.

The basic argument of this writing is that business success will be derived from companies managing the enhancement of the total performance of the supply chain, so that it can deliver improved value to customers. Thus waste is normally seen as the major enemy and closer and long term working relationships, even partnerships, with suppliers at all levels in the chain are recommended in order to deliver exceptional value to customers. Companies are, therefore, instructed to construct ever more efficient and responsive supply chains because it will no longer be company competing with company, but supply chain competing against supply chain.

The development of collaborative marketing ventures in the global agri-food chain is a response to the economic pressures that are driving the evolution of the chain and encouraging greater vertical and horizontal co-ordination. To some, such vertical and horizontal collaborative ventures ('linkages', 'alliances', 'value added chains' or 'partnerships') are seen as a compromise in market organization between the extremes of open market trading and complete vertical integration. To others, they offer an alternative less rigid way of co-ordinating the market.

Christopher (1992) has defined the supply chain as a network of organizations that are involved through upstream and downstream linkages in the different processes and activities that produce value in the form of products and services in the hands of the ultimate consumer. Thus, a supply chain consists of a number of businesses through which, information concerning demand flows upstream, from the marketplace, and ultimately to the raw material supplier. Material flows downstream, ending up as the particular physical product satisfying end-customer needs.

Cox (1999) argues strongly that the supply chain concept has both a strategic as well as an operational importance. Thus, he regards the supply chain as having two dimensions. The first can be referred to as *the operational supply chain*; the second can be referred to as *the entrepreneurial supply chain*.

The *operational supply chain* refers to the series of primary and support supply chains that have to be constructed to provide the inputs and outputs that deliver products and services to the customers of any company. All companies have operational supply chains and these supply chains are normally unique to the company creating them. They have choices about the input and output supply chains that they create operationally, and about when they position strategically to provide a particular product and service within a specific primary supply chain.

This notion of companies positioning strategically within a primary supply chain is an under-developed aspect of thinking in business strategy. It is true that Porter (1980) was well aware of the importance of buyer–seller relationships in the development of his famous Five Forces Model. However, Cox argues, that strategic management thinking has systematically underestimated the importance of these types of vertical business-to-business relationships as the basis for a proper understanding of entrepreneurial action and, sustainable business success.

Furthermore, it is clear that supply chain thinking can provide a significant insight into the conduct of business strategy and that it is not merely an operational tool or technique.

In recent years, the idea of companies focusing on their core competencies has been much-promulgated (Hamel and Prahalad 1990). Indeed, one could say that it has been the dominant thinking in strategic management in the 1990s. The core competence paradigm is based on companies understanding what internal skills and resources they should own and control through internal contracts, in order to sustain their business success. It is also based on the understanding that the key strategic decision within the company, the entrepreneurial make–buy decision, is always a supply chain management one.

When companies decide to become involved in any supply chain they have to make decisions about how they will control and manage the primary supply chain itself. They face decisions about where they should position in the chain. At one extreme they can decide to vertically integrate the whole chain, from raw materials to end customer, or they can decide to own only one or two of the resources that exist in the chain.

It is clear that in an ideal world companies ought to position strategically to own those supply chain resources that are difficult to imitate and around which they can build defensible barriers to market entry. Only by possessing supply chain resources, that have a low propensity for contestation, is it possible for superior performance to be achieved by companies over the long term. It follows, therefore, that companies ideally must only outsource those supply chain resources that are highly contested and which have low barriers to market entry. In this way it is likely that if the company also understands how to limit its dependency on suppliers, and how continuously to monitor any threats to its own supply chain position from suppliers that the company will be able to maximize its ability to appropriate value for itself.

This is what is meant by strategic, or entrepreneurial, supply chain thinking. It is a way of thinking that recognizes that, for whatever is produced for customers; it will always require the construction of an entrepreneurially defined generic supply chain. Within this chain there will be resources around which there is a variable scope for contestation and market closure. Historically, strategy has tended to concentrate on horizontal competitive rivalries around particular supply chain resources, rather than on knowing entrepreneurially where to position to own and control particular resources, within a specific supply chain, in order to appropriate the maximum share of value for oneself.

In practice, the concept of supply chain management is relatively new, first appearing in the 1980s and emanating from the Japanese motor industry (Womack, Jones and Roos 1990).

The Japanese management philosophy 'Kaizen', which means continual improvement, is at the core of supply chain management. The Japanese were the first to recognize that in increasingly competitive markets, continual improvement, however it is measured in a business context, is increasingly difficult to achieve when business organizations work in a vacuum. The paramount importance of meeting consumer needs more quickly, more effectively and more efficiently, led them to share their strategic vision with their suppliers and their distributors and invited members of their respective supply chains to contribute to the process of making the Japanese motor industry the 'best in class'.

Following the success enjoyed by the Japanese motor industry during the late 1980s and early 1990s, manufacturers worldwide began to view their supply chains as an important source of competitive advantage. Initially, the emphasis was on logistics and the reduction of lead-times and inventory levels, reducing uncertainty and making better use of production capacity and hitherto under-utilized resources. Thus, efficiency was the key driver at the outset. More recently, the emphasis has moved towards innovation and the creation of value added in the supply chain. New product development and improved customer service is a key motive for supply chain management in the new millennium, embracing new technology and capitalizing on the information revolution which has been created by the Internet.

The food industry has been slow to emulate the success of the motor industry and it is only in recent years that supply chain management has made its way onto the boardroom agendas of the world's leading food manufacturers. Progress has been particularly slow upstream, where a distinct lack of trust between trading partners has made the task more difficult and the process longer. O'Keeffe (1998) identifies four key characteristics in the agri-food sector that have historically impeded the process of trust-building at the grow-processor interface:

- In commodity markets the sum of value created is fixed and the major issue is how it is divided among channel participants. This is a win–lose game and leads to adversarial relationships.

- Auction systems and regulated markets isolate farmers from the rest of the food system and farmers do not gain any insight into their customers and why they act the way they do. Likewise processors have not needed, or had the opportunity to, develop relationships with growers.

- Supply chain management does not remove the volatile nature of prices and supply, both quantity and quality, characteristic of agriculture. Price volatility puts pressure on the relationship.

- Interdependence is difficult to achieve owing to size imbalance between processors and farmers.

However, the launch of the Efficient Consumer Response (ECR) initiative, initially in the US grocery industry and later throughout Europe, represented a paradigm shift in the operation of the food supply chain, with adversarial trading relationships being replaced by co-operation and co-ordination, facilitated by a willingness to exchange information of both strategic and operational importance. As a result, the world's leading food manufacturers are shaving days off production lead times, weeks off inventory levels and months off New Product Development (NPD) cycles. They are delivering a more effectively managed range of carefully targeted products and services to increasingly diverse groups of consumers, at substantially lower costs. The commodity sectors have still a long way to catch up, but it is evident that throughout the global food industry supply chain management is here to stay and likely to remain a key point of focus for the leading players in the future. For further insights into the topic of ECR, the reader is directed to Kotzab's perspective in Part 3 of the book.

The principles of supply chain management

What is most striking about the principles of supply chain management is that they are extremely simple, yet implementation invariably proves problematic. The following definitions demonstrate the scale and scope of supply chain management from a functional, process and business philosophy perspective.

Supply chain management is

> the process of planning, implementing and controlling the efficient, cost-effective flow and storage of raw materials, in-process inventory, finished goods and related information from point-of-origin to point of final consumption for the purpose of conforming to customer requirements. (Council of Logistics Management, *What Is It All About?*, Oak Brook, IL, 1986)

> the integration of business processes from end user through original suppliers that provides products, services and information that add value for customers. (The International Centre for Competitive Excellence 1994)

> working *together* in *all* activities of the firm: Planning (strategic and tactical), Operations (purchasing, manufacturing, sales, marketing, distribution, NPD), Human Resource Management, Monitoring & Control (feedback). (Fearne A. (1996) Editorial, *International Journal of Supply Chain Management*, vol. 1 no. 2)

In simple terms, supply chain management is concerned with the sharing of information, in order to:

- Save time (markets across the world are becoming increasingly dynamic and product life cycles are getting shorter).

- Reduce costs (manufacturing, inventory, distribution and waste).

- Increase effectiveness (accurate targeting of consumer needs and wants).

- Add value (innovation in new product development and customer service remains the only sustainable source of competitive advantage, difficult to achieve and most difficult to emulate).

In practice, implementing supply chain management is complicated by the fact that it requires a fundamental change in the way firms operate. It is not merely a case of doing something better, it requires strategic managers to have an open mind towards the alternative ways of getting things done (e.g. the 'make or buy' decision) and effective mechanisms for communicating strategic objectives to operational staff, who live in fear of rationalization and outsourcing. It also requires strategic managers to re-visit the question of core competence and competitive advantage from the perspective of the entire supply chain not merely from where they are positioned. The problem here is that this represents a major threat to the status quo, existing authority relationships, responsibilities and the balance of power, within and between firms operating in the supply chain.

Figure 4.1 illustrates the basic structure of the food supply chain, which combines the 'push' of value added material flow, from the breeding of genetic stock downstream right through to retail, with the 'pull' of information from the final consumer upstream right through to the production of raw materials.

The supply chain comprises functions (what people and organizations do), such as those depicted in Figure 4.1 and processes (the way in which things get done), which link the functions and translate the information flow into value added activity, throughout the supply chain.

The focus of supply chain management is explicitly on processes. Finding the most effective and efficient way of adding value, with the aim of generating cross-functional solutions to the many complex problems associated with meeting consumer requirements effectively and at minimal cost. Cross-functionality may occur within an organization (e.g. sales, marketing, logistics and production combining to reduce inventory levels, whilst maintaining customer service levels), or, between organizations (e.g. third party logistics, production planning and growers

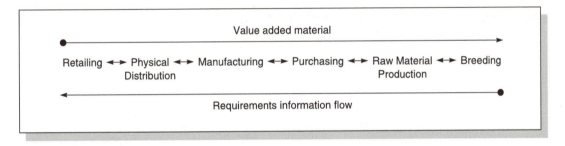

Figure 4.1 Basic structure of the food supply chain

combining to manage raw material supplies in a way that optimizes short term storage and the utilization of vehicle and processing capacity). This is dependent on who does what and how, the fundamental questions that supply chain management aims to address.

As far as the food processing supply chain is concerned, the functions are known to all and not open to question. The *production* of raw materials for processing requires *breeding, production, storage* and *distribution*, the *procurement* of other inputs and the management of a number of discrete 'production functions'. Agricultural commodities are subject to *grading* and *storage* will be necessary for some, as will *further preparation* for certain markets. The *procurement* of raw materials is undertaken in tandem with the *scheduling* of various production processes (continuous rather than discrete) within the processing plant. Finished products are then *stored* and *distributed* to retail distribution centres, where *consolidation* takes place prior to *distribution* to retail stores. *Merchandising* and *marketing* activities complete the process from the selection of genetic stock to the purchase of the finished product.

However, whilst most of the functions necessary for the transformation of raw materials into finished food products are universally accepted, the way in which they are undertaken, individually and in combination, are not. There is no consensus regarding the most effective and efficient way of combining these functions to secure competitive advantage.

What is quite clear is that in order for any process to be completed efficiently there needs to be effective communication between and within all organizations involved. In theory, market forces and the dynamics of competition will force the discovery or adoption of 'the one best way', as failure to do so will, other things being equal, result in loss of market share. However, sharing information poses a real threat to independence, particularly when those involved lack mutual trust and have a tendency to behave opportunistically, with a short term planning horizon – a real challenge for supply chain management.

Theoretical perspectives on supply chain partnerships

'A move from the traditional perspective'

Traditionally the marketing literature has viewed exchange between buyers and sellers as taking place on an ad hoc basis in the competitive marketplace. Firms who wished to avoid the market could do so by backwards or forwards integration. Based on these traditional views of exchange, exchange is conceptualized as existing on a continuum with pure market transactions at one end and hierarchical within firm transactions at the other. In-between these two extremes Williamson (1979) suggested that the market mechanism could be modified through some kind of formal or informal contractual arrangement between the parties involved.

Traditionally, channel relationships have tended to be towards the transactional end of this spectrum (Dawson and Shaw 1987). Relationships at this end of the spectrum are assumed to be inherently arm's length and adversarial (Carlisle and Parker 1989; Ellram 1991; Heide and Stump 1995). In this type of transactional relationship the primary goal of buyers is to minimize the price of purchased goods and services. Spekman (1988) argues that this is done by having a large number of suppliers who can be played off against each other to gain price concessions while still ensuring a continuity of supply. This model of buyer–seller relationships centres on homogeneity of supplies and substitutability of suppliers and as such does little to engender long term co-ordination or co-operation between buyer and supplier. Therefore, the traditional adversarial model is a classic case of win–lose, with both buyers and sellers spending considerable amounts of time searching for ways to capture some of the other party's margin.

The movement away from the traditional model was driven by the competitive pressures of the mid-1970s, such as the oil crisis and the onset of global competition (Lamming 1993). These pressures exposed the weaknesses of the traditional model, which was not able to respond quickly or efficiently to the need to reduce costs or improve quality due to the nature of the dealings between buyers and suppliers. Under this model, costs could only be reduced by squeezing suppliers' prices, this left them unable to invest in the systems needed to ensure the quality control required by manufacturers. Thus, for example, in the motor industry, where supply chain partnerships originated, Western companies, such as General Motors, engaging in traditional adversarial relationships found themselves losing market share to Japanese manufacturers such as Honda and Toyota who could produce cars of higher quality and at lower cost (Webster 1992; Lamming 1993).

Buyer–seller relationships in Japan involve partnerships with fewer, larger and more talented suppliers who are the sole sources of supply for varying components (Turnbull *et al.* 1993). These partnerships are based on co-operation, a full exchange of information and a commitment to improve quality and reduce price. However, one of the key distinguishing features of these relationships is that cost reductions and quality improvements are made by working together. Although suppliers still have to be highly competitive, under partnership arrangements cost reductions are achieved through co-operation rather than confrontation. They state that bargaining is not based on price *per se* but on how to reach the target price while maintaining a reasonable level of profit for the supplier. Therefore, the focus of these relationships is on mutual benefit and as a result trust and collaboration replace mistrust and antagonism.

This pattern of co-operation was virtually unknown in the adversarial sourcing systems of US manufacturers, and other researchers suggest that it was these co-operative partnerships that were giving Japanese competitors, in numerous industries a competitive advantage against their Western competitors. There is therefore recognition that adversarial arm's length purchasing relationships have historically robbed firms of the opportunity to gain a competitive edge.

Supply chain partnerships have thus emerged as a panacea for improving a firm's competitiveness. Literature suggests that there have been widespread moves to emulate Japanese manufacturing practices, particularly in the automotive industry (Hamel *et al.* 1989; Landeros and Monczka 1989; Turnbull *et al.* 1993; Heide and Stump 1995; Mudambi and Schrunder 1996). However, while most partnership activity may have started in the car industry, the movement towards closer relationships is seen to be a general trend that has been reported by numerous researchers, in response to each industry's own set of competitive pressures. It is clear that supply chain partnerships are emerging at a pace in the food industry, driven by private incentives to secure market growth, gain market share, improve margins and increase efficiency. Public pressure for transparency, traceability and 'due diligence' throughout the food supply chain has also played a role.

In discussing the movement towards relationships of a more co-operative nature, Spekman (1988) states that co-operative relationships seek to establish open lines of communication, nurture and sustain longer relationships between trading partners, and develop mechanisms to solve differences, such that the trading relationship is maintained, to the mutual benefit of buyer and seller. He adds that philosophically such a model can only be built if trust and co-operation exist. Galt and Dale (1991) also suggest that emerging long term supplier relationships require substantial changes in terms of behaviour and attitude. They state that these new types of relationships must be based on common aims, trust, co-operation, mutual dependency and a joint problem-solving approach. This is in line with Lyons *et al.* (1989), who argue that the new order of buyer–supplier relationships are characterized by cross-functional teams and team decision making, longer term contracts and increased interdependence. The main motivation for developing supply chain partnerships is to gain competitive advantage. Successful companies today are those who have developed and are implementing a supply chain philosophy and that organizations who continue to operate adversarial relationships with suppliers and customers are eroding their competitive advantage. The adoption of a supply chain philosophy will increasingly become a critical success factor as market demands of globalization, customer expectations and satisfaction and technology drive the requirement to co-operate.

Hobbs (1996) suggests that supply chain management can be viewed as a continuum of vertical integration. At one extreme lie spot markets, where goods are exchanged between multiple buyers and sellers in the current time period, with price as the sole determinant of the final transaction. In other words, other aspects of the transaction are non-negotiable. The buyer either accepts the product in its current form, or does not purchase it. Examples of spot markets are auction markets, stock markets and most consumer good purchases (e.g. purchases of food in a supermarket). In a spot market transaction, management of the supply chain, in any formal sense, is entirely absent. At the other end of the vertical co-ordination spectrum lies full vertical integration, where products move between various stages of the production–processing–distribution chain as a result of within-firm managerial orders, rather than, at the direction of prices.

In between the two extremes of spot market transactions and vertically integrated firms lie a myriad of alternative ways of co-ordinating economic activity, from strategic alliances and formal written contracts, to vertical integration. These represent different degrees of supply chain management; some more formal than others. A strategic alliance is an agreement mutually entered into by two independent firms to serve a common strategic objective. It is often more flexible than a contract or full vertical integration. Central to the success of a strategic alliance are trust between firms and a strategy that is to the mutual benefit of all the participants. For example, a meat processor might reach an agreement with a group of pig producers to obtain finished pigs of a certain quality, providing producers with a list of acceptable breeders. A meat processor might also introduce a high quality packaged pork product jointly developed with a major retailer under a strategic alliance (Sporleder 1992).

Under a contract, a firm usually devolves control over various aspects of the supply chain, i.e. marketing and/or production of its product, to a buyer. Contracts can be classified into three broad groups (Mighell and Jones 1963):

1. Market specification contracts represent an agreement by a buyer to provide a market for a seller's output. The seller transfers some risk and the decisions over when the product is sold and how it is marketed to the buyer. Control over the production process, however, remains with the seller.

2. A production-management contract gives more control to the buyer than a market-specification contract. The buyer participates in production management through inspecting production processes and specifying input usage.

3. Even more control rests with the buyer, in the case of resource-providing contracts, in which the buyer provides a market outlet for the product, supervises its production and supplies key inputs. Often, the buyer may own the product, with the seller paid according to the volume of output. This is the closest contractual arrangement to full vertical integration. For example, a feedstuffs manufacturer might contract with pig producers, supplying feedstuffs, overseeing production methods and marketing the finished pigs.

Quasi-vertical integration ● ● ●

This refers to a relationship between buyers and sellers that involves a long term contractual obligation where both parties invest resources in the relationship. It differs from full vertical integration because the arrangement ceases at the end of an agreed period of time and the firms remain independent of one another. A joint venture is one example of quasi-integration. Participants share the costs, risks, profits and losses of the venture. Franchises and licences are other examples of quasi-vertical integration.

Tapered vertical integration ● ● ●

This occurs when a firm obtains a proportion of its inputs through backward integration with a supplier. For example, a beef processing firm integrated backwards into beef production could obtain a proportion of its beef supplies from its own farms with the remainder procured from auction markets or direct from beef producers. Alternatively, a firm could transfer a proportion of output forward through its own distribution network, with the remainder sold on the open market.

Full vertical integration ● ● ●

This occurs when one firm carries out two or more consecutive stages of the production–distribution chain. A firm can be integrated forwards (downstream) into distribution or retail functions or backwards (upstream) into supply functions.

Horizontally integrated networks ● ● ●

Whilst not specified as part of the Mighell and Jones model, horizontally integrated networks refer to the relationship between businesses serving similar markets, often serving different markets or locations. Businesses who combine forces more readily access new markets, develop new products and share purchasing functions, thereby increasing cost and resource efficiencies.

Levels of interdependence ● ● ●

An alternative way of viewing supply chain partnerships is proposed by Lorange and Roos (1993), who choose to focus on the degree of interdependency between trading partners. At one extreme lie informal co-operative ventures, low on inter-dependency and easy to get out of, while at the other extreme we find mergers and acquisitions, where the parties are highly inter-dependent and the relationship is very difficult to reverse. In between we find formal co-operative ventures, strategic alliances, joint ventures and joint ownership, representing alternative forms of partnership arrangement with increasing levels of inter-dependence.

The main motivation for partnering is to gain competitive advantage (Mohr and Spekman 1994). For example, Ellram (1994) states that successful companies today are those who have developed and are implementing a supply chain philosophy, and that organizations who continue to operate adversarial relationships with suppliers and customers are eroding their competitive advantage. Ellram also argues that the adoption of a supply chain philosophy will increasingly become a critical success factor as market demands of globalization, customer expectations and satisfaction, and technology drive the requirement to co-operate.

Numerous other researchers also suggest that the creation of closer relationships can help to improve a firm's competitive position and create benefits that are not possible using traditional arm's length (Spekman 1988; Lyons et al. 1989; Ellram 1991; Munday 1992). Indeed, the number of companies entering into or exploring customer/supplier alliances pays testimony to the extent of the perceived benefits involved. Yet, the quantification of the benefits remains elusive to academic researchers.

The potential advantages of partnering from a customer perspective are:

1. easier management of a reduced supply base;

2. less time searching for new suppliers and tendering;

3. increased mutual dependence creates greater stability and loyalty and may increase supplier attention and service in areas such as lead time reliability, greater attention to common problems and priority in times of scarcity;

4. allows for joint planning and information sharing based on mutual trust and benefit;

5. better quality following from involvement of supplier in design;

6. reduced inventory levels;

7. more stable supply prices (Ellram 1991, 1994).

The general impression of new buyer–supplier relationships is that manufacturing firms accrue significant advantages while their suppliers face significant disadvantages. Referring to interviews with purchasing managers from firms in a variety of industrial manufacturing industries, Lyons, Krachenberg and Henke (1989) suggest that both parties gain and lose something from the new arrangements. They suggest that buyers can benefit from:

1. reduced costs and improved quality;

2. reduced complexity and cost of buying;

3. enhanced support relationships.

On the other hand, the disadvantages to buyers were identified as:

1. increased dependence;

2. the challenge of a new negotiating style;

3. less supplier competition;

4. new sources of added costs,

5. implementation of new reward structure;

6. new and potentially risky channel interactions.

As the degree of partnership increases, the buying firm typically enjoys significantly increased short term productivity improvements and long term strategic advantages. The short term benefits, such as reduced downtime and rework, speedier throughput time and inventory reductions, are strongly related to the extent of the supplier partnership. The longer term benefits, such as reduced cost structure, product sales gains and improved product quality, show an even stronger relationship with the degree of partnership formed.

Suppliers also benefit from adopting a strategy of maintaining long term relationships with their customers compared to employing a transactional approach to servicing customers. Supplier firms in long term relationships are able to achieve a higher level of sales growth, compared to suppliers that use a transactional approach to servicing customers.

Furthermore, they achieve higher profitability by differentially reducing their discretionary expenses and they are able to reduce inventory holding and control costs through more efficient inventory utilization over time. However, firms in long term relationships often face lower gross margins over time, suggesting that supplier firms are forced to reduce prices to a greater extent than the reduction in costs, through more efficient inventory utilization.

While the majority of researchers have attempted to identify the benefits of supply chain partnerships and the reasons why they are expected to develop further, a number of researchers warn against the doctrine that partnerships are universally desirable. For example, although collaborative partnerships have been widely suggested as a source of competitive advantage they may not be appropriate for every trading relationship (Spekman and Salmond 1992). When parties recognize that the current state of their business requires no more than a minimal commitment they should agree not to collaborate, since non-collaborators can enjoy a very long and profitable trading relationship. Similarly, it is unwise to assume that all trading relationships should warrant equal attention. In some instances, establishing close ties may be more costly than beneficial and in other instances, a potentially important relationship may be managed poorly and a strategic opportunity lost to competitors. Thus, not all trading relationships should be collaborative and, as Spekman, Kamauff and Myhr (1998) stress, it is acceptable to engage in arm's length transactions provided that such behaviour is appropriate.

Researchers generally suggest that the degree to which a partnership can be developed will depend on the nature of the product market (Jackson 1985; Hughes 1996; Spekman 1988; Spekman and Johnston 1986; Spekman and Salmond 1992) and the nature of the power-dependence relationship (Kearney 1994; Frazier 1983; Kumar et al. 1995; Frazier and Antia 1995; Spekman et al. 1998). For example, while a more co-operative approach is evident, a number of purchasing decisions involve buying commodity-like goods and for these goods a more adversarial approach might be more appropriate. Collaborative relationships are not likely to be suitable for commodity purchases (even in high volume) and low value added goods. Partners involved in the purchase of these type of products may be linked through an inventory management system but the linkages may not pervade any other aspects of their business. Similarly, the extent of collaboration will be related to which industry they operate in and as such the type of product that is produced. For commodity products, long term contracts and 'just-in-time' inventory programmes may generally represent the extent of potential collaboration.

Efficient Consumer Response and the role of the 'Category Captain'

Effective supply chain management requires trading partners to share long term strategic objectives, develop mutual trust and work together to identify the most efficient and effective way of reaching their objectives. The emergence of Efficient Consumer Responses (ECR) in the US grocery industry in the early 1990s and its subsequent adoption in Western Europe, gave the process of developing effective supply chain partnerships a major boost (see Chapter 5 and Part 2).

The fundamental principle of ECR is that through partnership within the global food supply chain, significant cost reduction (efficiencies) and improved performance (effectiveness) can be achieved through a better allocation of shelf space in the retail store, fewer wasteful promotions and new product introductions and more efficient physical replenishment. The key to the achievement of these goals is shared information, in particular, information on sales gathered at the checkout and transferred directly to suppliers through Electronic Data Interchange (EDI). Using this shared information, manufacturers and retailers can create more consumer value through the supply chain. Specifically, it is suggested that benefits can be accrued in four key areas: New Product Development; Promotions; Category Management; and Product Replenishment (see Table 4.9).

Whilst ECR brings many potential benefits to both suppliers and retailers, in terms of improvements in efficiency and effectiveness, the biggest opportunity it presents is to enable real supply chain collaboration. By sharing information it enables

Efficient new product introductions	Efficient promotions	Efficient range and assortment	Efficient product replenishment
Improve success rate	Improve consumer targeting	Match to consumer and shopper needs	Improve on-shelf availability
Reduce time to market		Reduce duplication	Reduce costs
Improve return on investment	Improve return on investment	Improve return on space	Reduce inventory
Improve quality and reduce costs	Co-operation across the supply chain		

Source: Adapted from Christopher M. (1992) *Logistics and Supply Chain Management*. London: Pitman Publishing

Table 4.9 The four pillars of ECR

supply chains effectively to become *demand chains* and in so doing to deliver enhanced customer value. For decades, food retailers (buyers) and manufacturers (sellers) have acted more as adversaries than as partners. Even though commercial realities will prevail so that individual entities in the supply chain will still seek competitive advantage, there now exists a framework in which they can co-operate not only to 'grow the cake' but to decide how it will be divided.

Within the ECR paradigm, the concept and practice of Category Management (CM) has created the position of 'Category Captain'. Retailers may select a 'Category Captain' to work with retail staff to create a plan for the entire category, including competitors' brands and private label brands. The CM planning process often leads to a reduction in the number of SKUs being carried by the retailer. As a result, it takes significant objectivity for the Category Captain to resist the temptation to make a case for de-listing its competitors and maximizing shelf space for its company's own brands.

The retailers' expectations of 'Category Captains' in FMCG product categories are at a higher level than those who are in the fresh food categories – characterized by smaller-scale companies operating on lower margins, with less resources to invest in category research. Overall, however, the more forward-thinking retailers seek, at a minimum, the following from their preferred suppliers and 'Category Captains'.

- Increasingly, complete electronic integration is becoming a requirement and, fortunately, as the cost of IT equipment declines, EDI is becoming financially feasible for smaller-scale companies.

- Sharing a comprehensive range of information directed at improving existing and building future business.

- As identified in the previous section, retailers seek suppliers who show excellence in innovation, in NPD, but also in supply chain management, finance, etc.

- Suppliers who understand the role and structure of the category and who can assist the retailer in forecasting its future development.

- Suppliers who show sufficient commitment to each key customer that they are willing to develop customer-specific products and services.

- Suppliers who have the objectivity and knowledge to develop jointly a strategy for mutual business growth.

Forging successful partnerships between historic adversaries – retailers and manufacturers – is a challenge that stands or falls on both parties committing to the idea, communicating the purpose within their respective organizations and between themselves, and showing continuity of effort (the longer the partnership survives, the more likely it is to last, as the two parties and, particularly, the supplier gains the self-confidence to point out problems). In Table 4.10 the major factors that influence successful establishment and sustained operations of partnerships and alliances are identified. Each of the twenty factors are of significance, but, three that should be reiterated are: clear benefits (although, not necessarily equal benefits) for each partner; partners should share the same long term objectives; and aim for leadership in quality as it makes it difficult for others to follow.

1. Clear benefits for all partnership and alliance members
2. Business proposition underpinning the partnership that makes long term commercial sense
3. Focus on specific partnerships, products and markets
4. Build upon successful partnerships
5. Apply lessons learnt from the partnership to gain benefits in other business areas
6. Partners/alliance members should have a good strategic fit
7. The commercial relationship should be based on interdependence
8. Companies have similar corporate values and the same commercial ethos
9. Mutual trust and respect
10. Aim high on quality – make it difficult for others to follow
11. For junior partners: pick a senior partner with a long-term commercial future
12. Build relationships and communication links between all levels of the two businesses
13. Gain full endorsement of the venture by the most senior management and strong personal commitment of all staff
14. Members should hold a common view on the long-term objectives of the partnership
15. Partnership members should hold a common view of what the final consumer wants
16. Raise the veil of secrecy and focus on sharing information required to make the partnership a success
17. Investment in physical plant and, for horizontal partnerships, joint investment by members builds commitment to the venture
18. Build flexible organizations that meet the specific needs of each partnership
19. Fix problems as they arise – delays only serve to disrupt
20. To ensure success, partnerships require their fair share of commercial good fortune

Source: Hughes and Ray (1994)

Table 4.10
Major factors that influence successful establishment and sustained operations of supply chain partnerships

Conclusions

In the 1950s, manufacturers were the pivotal point between many raw material suppliers and the myriad of small shops that comprise the independent grocery trade. In Europe and North America the major retailers have taken over the captaincy. In increasingly concentrated, mature, slow-growth markets, major supermarket companies seek means to differentiate themselves from the competition. One such way is to build unique supply chains – with exclusive commitment from chain members, manufacturers and farmers and an exclusive range of products. The premium private label product programs of UK retailers are addressing exactly this issue; building a product offer that is not directly comparable and, hopefully, discernibly better than immediate competitors. Each retailer wishes to corral the 'best' suppliers and, in turn, the 'best' raw material producers in their respective supply chains and deny access to these 'best' members to the competition.

What is emerging is the antithesis of neo-classical perfect competition, indeed, it is supply chain-based competition. The food industry is not unique in this regard; indeed, co-operation rather than confrontation in the supply chains has underpinned the substantial productivity improvements that have been characteristic of the motor car industry, for example. Members of specific supply chains share a common commercial interest, i.e. increasing the market share and profitability of their supply chain. In supply chains where the relationships between the channel captain and other members is adversarial, then, this mutuality of interest collapses. Unfortunately, in many countries, the retailers – as 'Category Captains – are oriented predominately towards controlling the supply chain and to doing so through threatening behaviour and engendering fear; the threat of de-listing and the fear of being de-listed.

Successful supply chains will be those that embrace the notion of the 'learning chain'. In his seminal work on building learning organizations, Peter Senge (1990) identified that 'over the long run, superior performance depends on superior learning'. Further, 'Leaders engaged in building learning organizations . . . [should seek] to change the way businesses operate . . . From a conviction that their efforts will produce more productive organizations, capable of achieving higher levels of organizational success and personal satisfaction than more traditional organizations'. Senge identifies three critical areas of skills for establishing a learning organization, namely building shared vision, challenging conventional wisdom and current practice without inducing defensiveness and engaging in systems thinking. These three skills are directly relevant to building a 'learning chain'. Unfortunately, they are not skills that are abundantly evident or, indeed, available in the skill set of many senior retail category managers as we enter a new century.

References

Bhote K.R. (1989) *Strategic Supply Management*. New York: Amacom.

Brandenburger A.M. and Nalebuff B.J. (1996) *Co-opetiton*. New York: Doubleday.

Carlisle J. and Parker R. (1989) *Beyond Negotiation*. Chichester: Wiley.

Christopher M. (1992) *Logistics and Supply Chain Management*. London: Pitman.

Cox A. (1999) Power, value and supply chain management. *International Journal of Supply Chain Management*, 4 (4), pp. 167–75.

Dawson J.A and Shaw S.A. (1987) Management of the retailer–supplier interface. *Management Research News*, 10 (3).

Ellram L.M. (1991) Supply chain management: the industrial organizational perspective. *International Journal of Physical Distribution and Logistics Management*, 21 (1), pp. 13–22.

Ellram L.M. (1994) A taxonomy of total cost of ownership models, *Journal of Business Logistics*, 15 (1), pp. 171–91.

Frazier G.(1983) On the measurement of interfirm power in channels of distribution. *Journal of Marketing Research* (May), pp. 158–66.

Frazier G. and Antia K. (1995) Exchange relationships and Interfirm power in channels of distribution. *Journal of the Academy of Marketing Science*, 23 (4), pp. 321–6.

Galt J.D.A and Dale B.G. (1991) Supplier development: a British Case study. *International Journal of Purchasing and Materials Management*, 27 (1), pp. 16–22.

Gattorna J.L. and Walters D.W. (1996) *Managing the Supply Chain*. Basingstoke: Macmillan.

Hamel G., Doz Y. and Prahalad C. (1989) Collaborate with your competitors – and win. *Harvard Business Review*, Jan–Feb, pp. 133–4.

Hamel G. and Prahalad C.K. (1990) The core competence of the corporation. *Harvard Business Review*, May–June, p. 79.

Harrison A. (1993) *Just-in-time Manufacturing in Perspective*. London: Prentice Hall.

Heide J.B. and Stump R.L. (1995) Performance implications of buyer–supplier relationships, industrial markets: a transaction cost explanation. *Journal of Business Research*, 32, pp. 57–66.

Hines P. (1994) *Creating World Class Suppliers*. London: Pitman.

Hobbs J. (1996) A transaction cost approach to supply chain management. *International Journal of Supply Chain Management*, 1 (2), pp. 15–27.

Houlihan J. (1988) Exploiting the industrial supply chain, in J. Mortimer (ed.), *Logistics in Manufacturing*. London: IFS Publications.

Hughes D. (1996) Reversing market trends: the challenge for the UK fresh fruit sector. *British Food Journal*, 98 (9), pp. 19–25.

Hughes D. and Ray D. (1994) Factors determining success in partnerships and alliances. In Hughes D. (ed.), *Breaking with Tradition: Building Partnerships & Alliances in the European Food Industry*. Ashford, Kent: Wye College Press, University of London, ch. 10.

Hughes D. and Ray D. (1999) *The Global Food Industry in the 21st Century*. Food Industry Management, Wye College, University of London.

Jackson B. (1985) Build customer relationships that last. *Harvard Business Review*, Nov–Dec, pp. 120–8.

Kay J. (1993) *Foundations of Corporate Success. Oxford*: Oxford University Press.

Kearney A.T. (1994) *Partnership or Power Play?* London: AT Kearney.

Kumar N., Scheer L.K. and Steenkamp E.M. (1995) The effects of perceived interdependence on dealer attitudes. *Journal of Marketing Research*, xxxii, pp. 348–56.

Lamming R. (1993) *Beyond Partnership*. New York: Prentice Hall.

Landeros R. and Monczka R.M. (1989) Co-operative buyer/ seller partnerships and a firm's competitive posture. *Journal of Purchasing and Materials Management*, 25 (4), pp. 9–17.

Lewis, J.D. (1990) *Partnerships for Profit*. New York: Free Press.

Lorange P. and Roos J. (1993) *Strategic Alliances: Formation, Implementation and Evolution*. Oxford: Blackwell Business.

Lyons T.F., Krachenberg A.R. and Henke J.W. (1989) Mixed motive marriages: what's next for buyer–supplier relations? *Sloan Management Review*, 31 (3), pp. 29–30.

Mighell R.L. and Jones L.A. (1963) *Vertical Co-ordination in Agriculture*, USDA ERS-19, Washington DC.

Mohr J. and Spekman R. (1994) Characteristics of partnership success: partnership attributes, communication behaviour and conflict techniques. *Strategic Management Journal*, 15, pp. 135–52.

Moore, J.F. (1996) *The Death of Competition*. New York: Harper Collins.

Mudambi R. and Schrumber C. (1996) Progress towards buyer–supplier partnerships – evidence from small and medium sized manufacturing firms, *European Journal of Purchasing and Supply Management*, vol. 2/3, pp. 119–27.

Munday M. (1992) Buyer–supplier partnerships and cost data disclosure. *Management Accounting*, June.

O'Keeffe M. (1998) Establishing supply chain partnerships: lessons from Australian agribusiness. *International Journal of Supply Chain Management*, 3 (1), pp. 5–9.

Porter M. (1980) *Competitive Strategy*. New York: The Free Press, ch. 2, pp. 34–46.

Sako M. (1992) *Prices, Quality and Trust*. Cambridge: CUP.

Saunders M. (1994) *Strategic Purchasing and Supply Chain Management*. London: Pitman.

Senge P.M. (1990) The leader's new work: building learning organizations. *Sloan Management Review*, 7 (Autumn).

Spekman R.E. (1988) Strategic supplier selection, towards an understanding of longer buyer–seller relations. *Business Horizons*, 31 (4), pp. 24–36.

Spekman R. and Johnston V. (1986) Relationship management: managing the selling and the buying interface. *Journal of Business Research*, 14, pp. 519–31.

Spekman R and Salmond D. (1992) A working consensus to collaborate. In *A Field Study of Manufacturing-Supplier Dyads*. Cambridge, Massachusetts: Marketing Science Institute.

Spekman R.E., Kamauff J.W. and Myhr N. (1998) An empirical investigation into supply chain management: perspective on partnerships. *International Journal of Physical Distribution and Logistics Management*, 28 (8), pp. 630–50.

Sporleder T.L. (1992) Managerial economics of vertically co-ordinated agricultural firms. *American Journal of Agricultural Economics*, 74 (5), pp. 1226–31.

Turnbull P. Delbridge R., Oliver N. and Wilkinson B. (1993) Winners and losers – the tiering of component suppliers in the UK automotive industry. *Journal of General Management*, 19 (1), pp. 48–63.

Webster F. (1992) The changing role of marketing in the corporation. *Journal of Marketing*, 56 (October), pp. 1–17.

Wileman A. and Jary M. (1997) *Retail Power Plays, From Trading to Brand Leadership*. London: Macmillan Business Press.

Williamson O.E. (1979) Transaction cost economies: the governance of contractual relations. *Journal of Law and Economics*, 22, pp. 232–62.

Womack J.P, Jones D.T. and Roos D. (1990) *The Machine That Changed the World*. New York: Rawson Associates.

Questions

1. Identify the key motivations for the emergence of supply chain management.

2. What is supply chain management?

3. Identify the key characteristics of the following forms of organizational integration

   (a) Full vertical integration

   (b) Quasi-vertical integration

   (c) Tapered vertical integration

   (d) Horizontal integration

4. Identify the changes to operations resulting from the implementation of a supply chain management strategy. What may be the key barriers to implementation?

Current practice: inter-firm relationships in the food and drinks supply chain

Colin Bamford

Key objectives

This chapter will provide an understanding of recent developments in supply chain management and their application to the food supply chain. More particularly, it aims to look at:

- The development of vertical and horizontal integration within the retail and catering supply chain. The discussion particularly focuses upon the nature of supply partnerships in the retail sector (quasi-vertical integration/vertically integrated networks) and buying groups and marketing consortium in the retail and catering sectors (horizontally integrated networks)

- The relevance of an integrated approach to supply chain management and the benefits that this can provide for food and drinks manufacturers. These benefits include those of a better service level and cost savings which can result from the application of Efficient Customer Response (ECR) and Efficient Foodservice Response strategies

- The ways in which major food retailers have exerted and imposed their own control over food and drinks manufacturers in the supply chain. The costs and benefits are discussed with particular emphasis on the challenges posed for these producers and manufacturers

- The arguments for contracting out the supply chain management function to specialist third party operators and in turn, why manufacturers who retain an in-house distribution function should continuously review whether this is appropriate for their future well-being and business development

- The external regulatory, environmental and political pressures, which have to be addressed by food and drink manufacturers and their significance in determining how supply changes are controlled and managed

- The scope for strategic alliances and supply partnerships, in particular between retailers and producers and within the context of a future food retail market, which will see the continued increase in home delivery services

- The continued emergence of horizontal partnerships within the catering and retail sectors.

Introduction

We all need food and drink! Yet the way in which our food and drinks move through the food chain is not recognized or understood by supermarket shoppers and licensed house customers. In some respects this is not surprising. After all, what they want is the right product, at the right time, at the right place, in the right condition and, significantly, at the right cost. How it gets there is of no particular relevance to them except when the supply chain fails to provide what they are wanting.

The customer is the last point in the food chain, whether as a retail/catering consumer, or, as a bulk trade purchaser. When the supply chain malfunctions and customer expectations are not met, the impact on business well-being can be very damaging. The most regular causes of complaint are in the case of 'stock outs', or products reaching customers in a damaged state, or where operational delays have meant that products arrive at their point of sale in a poor condition. These can be nightmare scenarios for food producers, processors and manufacturers.

Public concern over food hazards cannot be overlooked or underestimated. When health hazards occur, the first reaction may be to blame the manufacturer or supplier. In some cases this is justified; in most cases though the fault has occurred at some stage in the supply chain, once those products have left the manufacturer, en route to their point of sale. This ever-increasing public concern and awareness makes it particularly relevant for all food and drinks manufacturers constantly to monitor and evaluate their supply chain management practices.

As identified in Chapter 4, collaborative relationships designed to generate a more efficient and effective provision of products to the consumer may be found in various structural forms. Two distinct forms are horizontal or vertical partnerships. The form chosen will, to some extent, depend on the relative size and purchasing power of the businesses involved. In sectors dominated by larger multiples (e.g. the retail sector) quasi-vertical integration – supplier– buyer relations – are more apparent. Small and medium-sized enterprises, or even smaller non-market leaders may opt to increase market penetration through horizontal integration – supply chain networks.

Quasi-vertical integration within the supply chain

All food and drinks businesses have a supply chain. Figure 5.1 shows a typical traditional supply chain for a food manufacturer (DTI 1995). At first glance it looks complex and with the following characteristics:

1. A large number of businesses act as 'participants' in the sense that they provide a service or input into the supply chain, for example, as suppliers of raw ingredients, processed ingredients, packaging, transport, warehousing or wholesaling of the final product.

2. Many intermediate stages are involved and as a consequence, the production and sale of the final product requires the smooth flow of information between these participants for the supply chain to function smoothly.

3. It is inevitable that lead times are often quite long, with service levels and targets leaving much to be desired.

4. Costs tend to be higher than the optimum; each participant acting as a profit centre and with their own business objectives.

For the manufacturer faced with this situation, it is highly likely that from an organizational standpoint the supply chain is managed on a conventional line management basis. This approach splits the operation into identifiable watertight compartments whereby:

- buying is handled by the purchasing department
- sales forecasting and promotion by the marketing department
- inventory is managed by a stock control unit
- transport and warehousing by a distribution department
- sales and customer accounts by a sales team
- invoicing and credit control by the accounts team

and so on. In short, it is a recipe for confusion and misunderstanding which, if unchecked, could have a detrimental effect on the business.

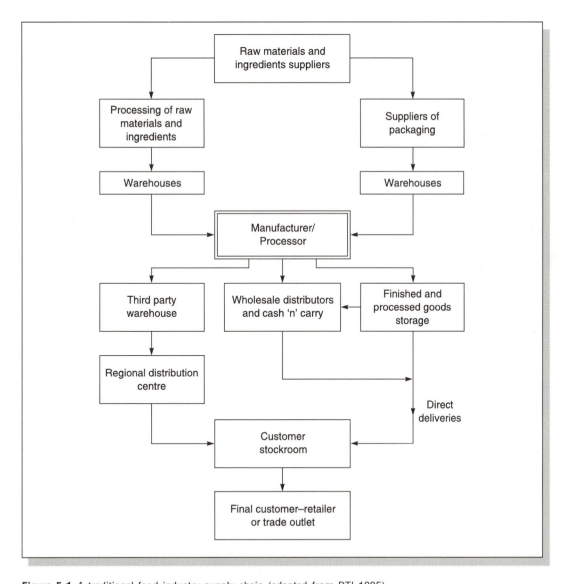

Figure 5.1 A traditional food industry supply chain (adapted from DTI 1995)

The supply chain management approach in business is designed to replace these line management operations, by providing for the strategic management of the supply chain, in order to a take costs out and give businesses a competitive edge. In many respects, as Figure 5.2 shows, it can be regarded as an umbrella management technique, pulling under a single function the many aspects which make up a business's supply chain (Bamford 1999a).

The outcome is that the supply chain represented in Figure 5.1 can be re-drawn. This is shown in Figure 5.3, where the approach shown has been driven by two very significant influences. These are:

1. The need for food and drink manufacturers to be in control of their supply chains, particularly where their main customers are large multiple food retailers. If this is impractical, then as the figure shows, the next best alternative is to enter into partnership with such retail customers.

2. The need to integrate the flow of information in the business into one all-embracing information management system. A particularly good illustration of this has been the way in which Electronic Point of Sale (EPoS) systems, now used by all major retailers, have provided the means for this integration to come about. Through this, up to the minute data can freely flow to all participants in the supply chain.

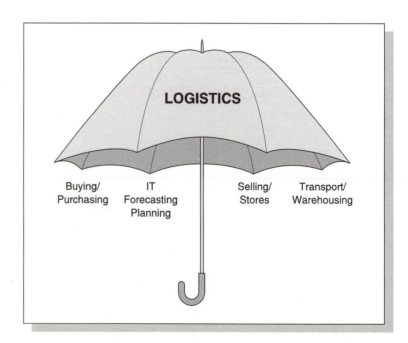

Figure 5.2
Logistics – an umbrella management technique

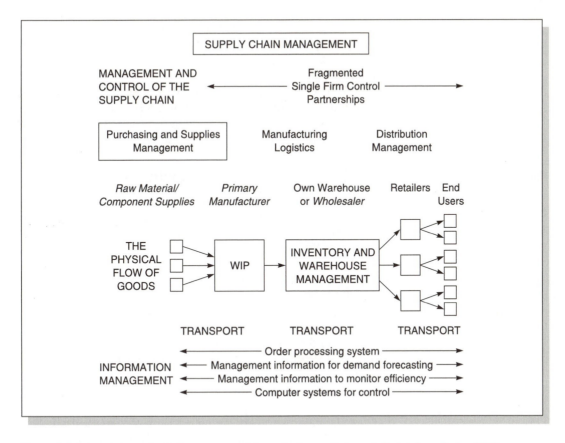

Figure 5.3 Integrated supply chain management for a food manufacturer (adapted from Taylor 1997)

This approach, found within the retail sector, is entirely consistent with the strategy of Efficient Consumer Response (ECR), which aims to take costs out of the supply chain and provide improved value for customers. The concept, which, like many supply chain strategies, originated in the USA, has been co-ordinated in the UK by an industry steering group, which has a particular focus on the grocery market and of course, includes many types of food and drink product.

ECR can be applied to both sides of the market. On the demand side, it seeks to establish the requirements of customers and to respond effectively and efficiently to their wishes and demands. For example, this might involve better product ranges, customer promotions and new product introductions, all of which have particular relevance in the food industry. On the supply side, ECR is designed to improve the flow of products through the supply chain, as previously suggested. To achieve this, supply chains need to be leaner, responsive and more efficient but with no losses in the service levels which are provided. Accurate information is therefore essential to its realization.

ECR is not an easy concept for companies to embrace, particularly if they have been successful. It requires a major cultural change away from a 'them and us' attitude to one of partnership, whereby the mutual benefits of co-operation are clearly recognized. Companies must also co-operate whilst competing but with the common objective of taking costs out of their supply chains. ECR will not go away – when it has a lower profile, this will be indicative that it has become good business practice.

Retailer power and control in the food supply chain

Looking back to Figure 5.3, at first sight, the power of the main food retailers could be under-estimated, especially when mapping out the supply chain from a manufacturer's standpoint. To think in these terms would be a great error of judgement, as over the last ten or fifteen years the major food retailers have exerted tremendous control over the food supply chain (Fernie 1999). Table 5.1 shows, in a crude way, the extent to which they control the UK grocery market at the present time. The 'Big Six', i.e. the four in Table 5.1 plus Somerfield and Marks & Spencer, control over 70% of sales in a fiercely competitive market (IGD 1999). In structural terms, the market displays many of the characteristics of an oligopoly, but in terms of behaviour, price competition is undoubtedly prevalent as the main players battle for market share.

Over the past four years, Tesco has replaced Sainsbury in pole position. The former's image of 'stack it high and sell it cheap' has been replaced by a growing reputation for quality products at a fair price to the customer. Fundamental to Tesco's business success has been its success in developing effective supply chain management practices. In contrast, Sainsbury and Marks & Spencer have lost market positions for various reasons, one of which has been recognized deficiencies in their supply chains (Wheatley 1999). In many respects, therefore, it is supply chains that compete and, if properly organized, will give retailers a competitive edge in their markets. Whilst similar trends have been predicted for the catering sectors this is relatively under-developed due to level of maturity of the sector.

All of the main grocery retailers have restructured their own supply chains on a centralized basis, which involves suppliers delivering direct to the retailer's own dedicated regional distribution centre. From the retailer's perspective, this produces important benefits, which include

- ECR, with improved stock availability
- the better and more efficient use of warehouse space
- reduced distribution costs
- supplier discounts for bulk deliveries

as well as being in full control of their supply chains. Centralization in this market is now virtually at 100% saturation, with stock levels having fallen by an estimated 16% since 1996 (IGD 1999).

The food supply chain is further controlled by the major retailers in other ways such as the ever-increasing number of own label products, store loyalty cards, in-store promotions and more recently, home delivery services. It is easy to see why even the largest food and drink manufacturers have been forced into complying with the stringent demands of their retail customers. In some respects, it is a clear example of a partnership but where the power, influence and control of the respective partners is by no means equal.

Market forecasts clearly indicate that these trends will continue. The home delivery sector especially is expected to grow substantially over the next few years. Following Iceland's lead, the major grocery retailers are moving into this in a positive yet selective way, as Internet shopping becomes more commonplace. Further developments in the supply chain are inevitable, the most likely outcome being that of dedicated structures being further refined to meet an ever-increasing consumer demand.

Recent development in the catering sector

Supply strategies and the development of quasi-vertical integration/vertically integrated networks throughout the food-service supply chain is less well advanced than its retail counterpart. There are, however, recent developments, which look set to reverse this trend.

Efficient Foodservice Response – the emergence of multiple players

EFR (Efficient Foodservice Response) is currently being heavily promoted through the Institute of Grocery Distribution (IGD). The term, interestingly, is different to its equivalent in retail. In 1994 the International Foodservice Manufacturers Association (IFMA) and the International Foodservice Distributors Association (IFDA) instigated the evaluation of the ECR with respect to the foodservice sector. From their initial endeavour,

Total value of market		£80 billion
% turnover	Tesco	19.6%
	Sainsbury	17.4%
	Asda	11.2%
	Safeway	9.4%
Source: Institute of Grocery Distribution, 1999		

Table 5.1
The UK grocery market in 1999

representatives from the foodservice manufacturers, brokers, distributors, catering organizations and key industry trade associations produced a report that stated that the foodservice sector differed sufficiently that a total adoption of ECR was not appropriate.

The group identified five key strategies:

- Equitable alliances
- Supply chain demand forecasting
- Electronic commerce
- Logistics optimization
- Foodservice Category Management.

In the UK EFR began to emerge as a recognizable term around the mid/to late 1990s. The IGD report (Haines and Turner 1998) provided evidence to suggest that foodservice organizations were aware of the term and recognized its importance. In 1999 a working group comprised of key foodservice groups and suppliers to that sector was progressed by the IGD (IGD 2000). Key players included: Allied Domecq Leisure, Bass Leisure Retail, Best Foods UK Ltd, Brake Bros Foodservice Ltd, Cearns and Brown, Nestlé UK Ltd, Cuisine Foodservice, DBC Foodservice, E3 United Kingdom Ltd, RHM Food service, Mckey Food service Ltd, Premier Poultry, Procter and Gamble Ltd, Tetley GB Limited, Tricon Restaurant Service, Van Den Bergh, W&P Foodservice Limited, Whitbread.

Key problems identified for the catering sector relate to issues of low tech, fragmented distribution and lack of good forecasting techniques. In the foodservice sector there is limited communication between suppliers, a lack of IT standard, highly distrustful business relationships and complex product ranges.

The initial stages of the EFR pilot involved some key players – Whitbread W&P, Cearns and Brown, Brake Bros, 3663, P&G, New Zealand Milk and RHM. The pilot focused on the development of systems prevalent in the retail sector: Category Management, back-hauling, consolidation and cross docking, with a view to facilitate the process of streamlining.

Estimations of cost savings cannot be given at this stage due to the relatively underdeveloped nature of the UK catering sector in comparison with the US market (Haines and Turner 1998).

Contracting out – an obvious partnership

The market for distribution services in the UK has experienced considerable growth since the early 1980s, following the privatization of the National Freight Company and the sale of other smaller companies to new owners. Growth in catering supply occurred later in the 1990s with the emergence of catering supply companies who hold a dual role of distribution and wholesale. Overall market growth has been broadly in line with the rate of growth of the economy, but this masks what has undoubtedly been the success story, namely the unprecedented and sustained growth in demand for third party logistics services. The emergence of specialist contractors such as Exel, Wincanton Logistics, Christian Salvesen and the Tibbett and Britten Group has undoubtedly been one of the major business successes in this period. Such companies have emerged, not only as powerful logistics operators, but also as major industrial forces in the service sector as a whole (Bamford 1999b). Interestingly one of the major catering companies, Whitbreads, has recently run counter to this trend and changed from contracted distribution through Exel to in-house logistics services. Their reasons for this decision related primarily to the difficulties they had experienced in the management of the diversity of their product portfolio within a contracted distribution system.

None the less, food and drink companies, along with major retailers, are now amongst the most important customers of such operators. This is hardly surprising in view of the range of supply chain management services on offer to clients. The services include:

- transporting finished products from factories to the point of sale

- the holding and management of stock in warehouses

- 'just-in-time' methods of stock control and inventory forecasting

- sophisticated information management systems

- packaging and labelling

- supplier collections.

As the market has grown and become more sophisticated so it has also become segmented. Alongside the major operators, smaller companies have established niche market positions as specialists in fresh food and vegetable distribution, in frozen and chilled distribution and drinks distribution. Table 5.2 shows some of these, the services they provide and the nature of collaborative links. It is evident that in many cases they are involved in vertical and horizontal partnerships.

The basic arguments as to why food and drink businesses should enter into a partnership with one or more of the companies shown in Table 5.2 are well documented (Walters 1993). These arguments have particular relevance in the food and drinks sector, with the possible exception of secondary

Company	Temperature-controlled services			
	Chilled	Frozen	Dedicated[b]	Shared-user[c]
Associated Cold Stores & Transport		✔	✔	✔
Baylis Distribution	✔		✔	✔
Bibby Distribution	✔		✔	✔
BOC Distribution Services	✔		✔	
Christian Salvesen	✔	✔	✔	✔
Eddie Stobart	✔	✔	✔	✔
Exel	✔	✔	✔	✔
Fiege Merlin	✔	✔	✔	✔
Fowler Welch	✔	✔		✔
Frigoscandia Distribution	✔	✔	✔	✔
Fullers Logistics Group	✔	✔	✔	✔
Gregory Distribution	✔	✔	✔	✔
Grocery Logistics	✔	✔	✔	✔
Hays Distribution Services	✔	✔	✔	✔
Initial Transport Services	✔	✔	✔	✔
Langdons	✔	✔	✔	✔
Lloyd Fraser Holdings	✔	✔	✔	✔
NFT Distribution	✔	✔	✔	✔
Taylor Barnard Group	✔		✔	✔
TDG	✔	✔	✔	
Tibbett and Britten Group	✔	✔	✔	✔
UCI Logistics	✔		✔	✔
Wincanton Logistics	✔	✔	✔	✔

[a]Excludes ambient food and drinks operators.
[b]Normally contracted.
[c]Where the operator consolidates and transport loads for more than one customer in the same warehouse or on the same vehicle.
Source: Distribution Business, January 2000

Table 5.2 Specialist contract operators[a] in the food and drinks market in 2000

distribution in the brewing industry where own operation remains strong. They include:

1. The customer is able to focus on their core business, for example food processing, food manufacturing or drinks retailing. This is a very important reason for contracting out since supply chain management operations from a strategic standpoint are non-core activities for such businesses. For some types of food activity, say involving home deliveries, distribution is clearly part of the core business. If contracting out gives any business a competitive edge, it should be seriously evaluated.

2. Capital investment in non-productive assets can be reduced. Valuable business capital can be tied up in vehicles and

storage facilities when it might well be better employed in developing the core business. The downside of divesting though, is that annual costs will be higher, although many contractors will be able to share the benefits of economies of scale with their customers.

3. Better budgeting control. Costs are known and budgets can be prepared once the terms of a contract have been signed. Operating the supply chain is therefore no longer 'a step into the unknown' that it can be for many businesses.

4. Leading edge IT systems can be provided and used by the contractor.

5. Labour relations problems are transferred from the customer to the contractor.

6. Operational efficiency will improve – the expertise of the contractor will bring significant benefits in supply chain management performance.

For some types of food and drink operation though the retention of in-house distribution is seen as essential for business well-being. This particularly occurs where customer service and the effective management of customer service levels, is an important objective. A particularly good example is in the case of van sales, but in any operation where there is immediate interface with the customer, own operation remains strong. Customer interface and communications are rightly seen as an integral part of the core business.

There are other reasons why food and drinks businesses may wish to persist with their own distribution arrangements. Cost is an obvious one but, in addition, it does allow the business to retain greater control over their supply chains. Especially where the product life is short or demand is irregular and volatile, this is an important consideration. So, for some businesses, the supply chain is considered as so vital to their business well-being that they remain unwilling to move from their traditional in-house operation.

Notwithstanding, the growth in the use of third party contractors has simultaneously resulted in the development of partnerships between themselves and their customers. These partnerships are designed to promote quick response, take costs out of the supply chain and provide mutually beneficial outcomes. Open-book accounting, with agreed profit levels, is now commonplace. Such partnerships become strained and under threat when the terms of the contract and the performance levels stipulated in it, are not realized. This more so than any other reason tends to be why companies switch from one provider to another.

Customer	Contractor	Details
Allied Bakeries	TNT Logistics	Geographical extension of existing contract to north of England
Apetito	TDG Novacold	Storage of Waldens Premier range of ready meals
Avebury Taverns	Exel Tradeteam	Centralized distribution for licensed houses
Avon Foods	Taylor Barnard	National food distribution
Birds Eye Walls	Christian Salvesen	Long term vegetable processing and cold storage
Direct Wine	Business Express	Home delivery of wine
Fresh Fruit Services	Salvesen Logistics	Capespan (South Africa) fruit distribution
Häagen Dazs Café	Hays Food Logistics	National distribution
KFC	Hays Food Logistics	National distribution
Mackie's	TDG Novacold	Ice cream distribution
Manor Bakeries	Christian Salvesen	National distribution
Nisa – Today's	Bibby distribution	National wines and spirits distribution
Signatory Whisky	Business Express	National distribution
Southern Wine Brands	McGregory Cory	National distribution
W T Maynard	TDG Novacold	Cold storage

Source: Distribution, December 1999

Table 5.3 Selected food and drinks contracts completed in 1999

Table 5.3 shows some typical examples of partnerships between food and drinks companies and supply chain management providers. It indicates a diversity of customer across the full range of food and drinks services. It also shows that would-be customers have a wide choice of potential contractor, all of whom (except for Business Express, a home delivery specialist) were also shown in Table 5.2.

Future prospects for the further development of such partnerships in the food and drinks industries remain good. They do, of course, depend on the state of the food and drinks market, certain sectors of which are heavily dependent upon the state of the economy. Recent forecasts point clearly to an 8–10% increase over the next few years. For food and drinks manufacturers, there is little purpose in resisting the erosion of the rationale behind the retention of an in-house operation (Pellow 1998). There is much more to be gained by the business as a whole by improving the core skill of food and drinks manufacturing and processing.

Contracting out the strategic purchasing function

In recent years within the catering sector, there has emerged a trend for outsourcing the purchasing/supply function. These developments have emerged as solutions both to the fragmented nature of (a) the catering sector, (b) the supply base.

Independent negotiants • • •

This development is particularly evident within the branded restaurant sector. Bitz and Pizza, a brand owned by Out of Town Restaurants, a Sheffield based company, currently uses the services of Michael Weaving Associates. Certain hotel groups/hotels are linked to Ivan Schenkman. These 'negotiants' operate as independent central purchasing departments taking a percentage of the savings made through collective increased purchasing power. Although there is limited research into this area, it would appear (Eastham 2000) that the contracting out of the purchasing is largely a practice of small catering and hotel chains. In essence, they are similar to strategies employed to reduce costs inherent in buying groups such as Landmark and Strategic Alliances. An example of this is EMS (see later sections). They represent horizontal collaboration in reality, however the collaboration between caterers is incidental rather than by design.

Outsourced RDCs or umbrella organizations • • •

Organizations such as NCB and IDC (Independent Dairy Company) have an essential role in linking the larger scale hotel and catering organizations to smaller scale suppliers. Emerging in fresh produce, NCB, originally an abbreviation for National Catering Butchers, focused on meat. They initiated their role as a central link point for caterers, marketers and managers of depots providing local supply to catering outlets. NCB have more recently expanded to be a single sourcer to caterers for all fresh produce. IDC, primarily play a similar role in dairy produce, but are looking to expand into a whole range of chilled food.

Horizontally integrated networks

Horizontally integrated networks are made up of businesses serving similar markets, often in different locations, may combine forces in order to increase cost and resource efficiencies. These networks have materialized in both the retail and catering sectors in the form of:

• Buying groups
• Symbol groups
• Co-ops
• Purchasing/marketing alliances
• Strategic alliances
• Umbrella organizations.

The retail sector

Buying groups • • •

Buying groups were formed by independent wholesale operators to improve trading terms with suppliers (Mintel 1999). They offer their members significant price benefits achieved through the power of bulk buying. They are described as 'voluntary non-profit organizations'. In certain cases, e.g. NISA, membership is not limited to wholesalers but also includes retailers. They offer a number of services: negotiation of overriding discounts, promotional programmes, provision of own label ranges and the dissemination of information and advice (Marchant 1999). There are three main buying groups in the UK: NISA which today has 306 depots, Landmark with 84 depots and Lekkerland UK with 11 depots (Mintel 1999).

Symbol groups • • •

At one stage there was a clear distinction between buying groups and symbol groups. Until recently, buying groups did not market their fascia and allowed members to trade under their own (Mintel 1999). Increasingly, buying groups and indeed members of buying groups, are taking a stronger position in the symbol sub-sector, e.g. Today and Bestway.

A symbol group is formed when a wholesale firm enters into an arrangement with independent retailers. The terms of the agreement mean that, in return for discounts and other advantages, e.g. centralized accounting, software for instore computing systems, etc. retailers agree to specific terms including a given volume of goods each week and an annual fee for membership. The exact nature of these terms vary between symbol. Spar is the largest symbol group in the UK, considered the most elite and charging the highest fees. It also operates alongside Landmark with whom it shares overrider agreements with Makro. Other good examples are Londis, Costcutter and Key Lekkerland.

Co-ops • • •

The Co-operative Movement began in Rochdale in England in 1844 to protect consumers against unfair trading practices through sharing profits with customers. In essence, the principles under which Co-ops operate have changed little over the 157 years, They are based on voluntary and open membership, democratic control, limited interest given to shareholders and, based on the purchases made by members, a pro-rata distribution of profits. The number of Co-ops has declined over time. In 1998 there were 68 separate societies, by 1999 (IGD 1999) these had been reduced to 48 with 1236 outlets. However, the movement has also evolved horizontal linkages. The CWS (Co-operative Wholesale Society), the largest co-operative group, also operates a buying group, CRTG (Co-operative Retail Trading Group). A major 'competitor', CRS (Co-operative Retail Society – Co-operative Society) gained membership to the CRTG in 1999; other smaller Co-ops are also members, to the extent that the CRTG accounts for 90% of co-operative sales.

Strategic alliances ● ● ●

A strategic alliance is a horizontal co-operation between retailers who could often be seen as competitors. They can be loose or tight alliances (McGoldrick *et al.* 1995) Such alliances had traditionally appealed to the SMEs (e.g. Co-ops) within the sector. However, recent years have seen the involvement of major players, in such groups, as a means of either expanding or consolidating their current national position. First emerging in 1989, they are, in the main, international alliances that form together and create a central secretariat for the purpose of co-ordinating operational activities. Buying, branding, expertise exchange and product marketing are just some of the activities (Robinson and Clarke-Hill 1994). They are an alternative to the process of concentration among the grocery retail multiples and a point of contact for multi-national manufacturers (Beard *et al.* 1999).

The catering sector

Purchasing and marketing alliances in hotels ● ● ●

In the hotel sector there has been a long tradition of alliances. Best Western established a marketing consortium for independent motels in the US in 1946. It subsequently expanded world

	Details	Members
European Marketing Distribution	Alternative process of concentration amongst grocery retail multiples – acts as a point of contact for multi-national manufacturers	Leclerc, Markant Handels, Euromadis Iberica, Uniarme, ZEV, Supervib, Nisa Today's, Unil, Musgrave, Dagab, Syntrade
Associated Marketing Services	Founding members were Ahold, Safeway and Casino. Aims to create synergy agreements with around 50 core suppliers which represented a reduction of 800~% of supply base	Ahold, Safeway, Casino, Edeka, ICA, K-group, Mercadona, Hakon, Superquinn, JMR

Table 5.4 The two largest international strategic alliances

wide and offers a wide range of services including education and training, a central reservation system (telephone and website) and a purchasing alliance. Members range from 4-star hotels to roadside motels. Other alliances such as Relais Chateau and Grandes Etapes are smaller in nature but operate in a similar manner. Members' benefits include lower purchasing and marketing costs.

While hotel consortia are the most common approach, the range of alliances between hotels is much more widespread than might be presumed. Agreements vary; in some circumstances purchasing is an informal arrangement between individual hotels located in proximity to each other. These alliances may take the form of hoteliers guaranteeing the use of only one grocery wholesaler, on the basis that, the wholesaler agrees to provide a worthwhile discount.

Whilst alliances are evident within the independent hotel sector, they are limited within other commercial food service operations. In contrast, in the cost sector they are a well-established entity. Organizations such as Yorkshire Purchasing Organization (YPO) and SNUPI (the Scottish and Northern University Purchasing Initiative, defined as serving the Scottish and Northern England universities and colleges and incorporating Midland University Catering) play a key role in the central purchasing of educational and governmental institutions.

Internet initiatives

Small and medium-sized enterprises

The Internet could be argued to have equal value for SMEs as for large enterprises. This is particularly so since location and market access are no longer issues. In the following we examine an example of how a network of SMEs have used the Internet to extend their market.

Case study 1 – Club Chef Direct

The recently launched Club Chef Direct, an offshoot of Heritage Fine Foods is designed to provide the 'discerning' consumer with fine food within the home. Heritage Fine Foods, a company providing custom-prepared foods to top restaurants in the UK, has operated for the last ten years. They operate through a website www.clubchefdirect.co.uk, providing consumers with all they need to provide a 'top chef' dinner party in their home. For a membership fee of £100, plus the cost of the meal, consumers, on request, are provided with the menu, illustrated recipe cards, boxes of ingredients for each dish. All the consumer needs to do is prepare the food, cook, serve and eat. Chefs who have provided their recipes to the scheme include Michel Roux, Pierre Koffmann and Rick Stein (Bateman 2000).

Case study 2 – Yorkshire Pantry

Within the UK there are a number of food and drink networks; designed to promote the food industry and particularly SMEs within a region. One such organization is Yorkshire Pantry, a network of farmers, manufacturers, retailers and caterers. As with all food and drink networks within the UK, this initiative is designed to redress the impact of globalization on the Yorkshire food industry. Yorkshire Pantry is administered by North Yorkshire Country Council, but steered by the 150 or so members. It aims to address issues of managerial/technical expertise and promote the development of customer bases for Yorkshire produce. Much of its value lies in the networking, information sharing and sales opportunities provided through events such as health and hygiene training sessions and produce shows.

In the mid 1990s one of the members, Mike Jarman at 'Bothams', began to develop an Internet site in order to extend his customer base. Bothams is a bakery based in Whitby, a seaside town in North Yorkshire. The business had already extended to include several bakery shops and teashops within Whitby and the surrounding area. Yet the decline of the seaside resort and the shorter duration of the season had presented particular difficulties in retaining good qualified staff. Mike Jarman saw the Internet as a means of extending the season and retaining his staff over the winter period.

Through his example and guidance many other members also established sites, enabling them to reach markets worldwide. For many this represented a joint opportunity. Relationships developed through networking naturally led to supply partnerships between for example, jam manufacturers and teashops, tea suppliers and bakers. The progression towards the production of joint products for export, i.e. hampers, was inevitable.

Larger scale Internet commerce – e-markets

The development of e-markets, where buyers are connected through a website, is considered by many consultants to be very much the direction in which businesses will go (i.e. Druid). In the case below one such e-market is illustrated.

Case study 3 – Efdex.com

Efdex is a fresh produce e-market. It says that it provides a 'low cost network that connects buyers and sellers so that they can communicate and trade efficiently'. Founded by Tim Carron-Brown, Efdex was launched on a trial basis on 17 January 2000. The company has three main addresses dealing with Europe, the US and East Asia (Singapore) as separate markets. It is expected that businesses joining this service will span the whole food sector and include: hotels, restaurants, caterers, public bars, takeaways, retailers, manufacturers and farmers/growers. It offers buyers and sellers a range of services:

- Up to date news stories, from press, television and radio broadcasts categorized according to business sector.

- Information on legislation.

- Banks of information on suppliers and buyers.

- Facilities for ordering direct through the Internet.

The e-market site is expected to create greater efficiencies in a number of ways:

- Enhance current supplier/buyer relationships.

- Reduction of administration costs associated with purchasing and sales.

- Greater information:

  (a) suppliers on other market prices and potential customers

  (b) buyers on the respective availability and price of items across suppliers.

Conclusion

The main theme of this chapter is that of partnership, that is, the business relationships between food and drinks manufacturers and other businesses involved in the food supply chain. These partnerships are between

- Manufacturers and their raw materials providers.

- Manufacturers and their customers.

- Manufacturers and their supply chain management service providers.

- Wholesalers and their customers.

- Caterers and caterers.

- Wholesalers and wholesalers.

- Retailers and retailers.

In terms of power and control, the dominance of the major food and drinks retailers cannot be ignored. Fifteen to twenty years ago, it was manufacturers who controlled their supply chains. This is no longer the case with the retailers very firmly in control. In a market likely to be increasingly responsive to more home deliveries and Internet shopping, the retailer's control is likely to be undiminished. It is also inevitable that retailers will continue to rationalize their number of suppliers and continue to search for non-UK sourcing opportunities. It is apparent that similar trends may emerge in the catering sector.

The power of the retailers over the food chain does however present problems, as the on-going investigation by the Competition Commission has indicated. In addition, certain parts of their market are being challenged by 'discounters' such as Lidl, Netto and Aldi from the rest of the EU. This in turn presents challenges for UK manufacturers as these retailers tend to source many food products, processed as well as fresh, from outside the UK. Such developments provide for a very challenging future business environment for our food and drinks manufacturers.

References

Bamford C.G. (1999a) Logistics. *Business Review*, April, pp. 24–5.

Bamford C.G. (1999b) The internationalization of logistics in the UK. In Waters D. (ed.), *Global Logistics and Distribution Planning*. London: Kogan Page, ch. 21.

Bateman M. (2000) Special deliveries. *The Independent on Sunday*, 6 August, pp. 24–5.

Beard J., Gordon D., Spillard L., Walton J. and Webb S. (1999) Grocery retailing 1999. *The Market Review*, May, pp. 72, section 1.

Department of Trade and Industry (DTI) (1995) *Logistics and Supply Chain Management*. London: DTI.

Eastham J.F. (2000) Unpublished research on suppliers' perception of constraints regarding supply to the retail and catering industry.

Fernie J. (1999) Retail logistics. In Waters D. (ed.), *Global Logistics and Distribution Planning*. London: Kogan Page, ch. 16.

Haines D. and Turner D. (1998) *Catering 1998, Surveying the Supply Chain*. London: Institute of Grocery Distribution.

IGD (1999) *Retailer Profiles*. London: Institute of Grocery Distribution.

IGD (2000) The Future of Foodservice. Executive Briefing, conference proceedings 19 April 2000.

Marchant C. (1999) *Retail Logistics*. London: IGD Business Publications.

McGoldrick P.J. and Davis G. (1995) *International Retailing, Trends and Strategies*. London: Pitman, pp. 135–9.

Mintel (1999) *Wholesaling and Cash and Carry*, 2 October (Mintel International).

Pellow M. (1998) Food logistics – an irresistible force in the supply chain. *Distribution Business*, Issue 6, p. 18.

Robinson T.M. and Clarke-Hill C.M. (1994) Competitive advantage through strategic retail alliances: a European Perspective. Presented at Recent Advances in Retailing and Service Science Conference, University of Alberta, Canada, May 1994. Cited in Goldrick P.J. and Davis G. (1995) *International Retailing, Trends and Strategies*. London: Pitman, pp. 135–9.

Taylor D.H. (1997) *Global Cases in Supply Chain Management*. Thompson Business Publications.

Walters P.J. (1993) *In or Out? The Contract Distribution Dilemma*. Distribution Dynamics.

Wheatley M. (1999) The salvation of St Michael. *Logistics Europe*, June, pp. 14–20.

Activities

1. For a food and drinks manufacturer of your choice and using Figures 5.1 and 5.3 as a guide, produce a diagrammatic representation of their supply chain. How does your representation differ from Figures 5.1 and 5.3? Why is this?

2. Using the Internet and corporate publicity, investigate how three of the large third party supply chain management operators market themselves to potential clients. Use this evidence to prepare a short marketing presentation to a client who is a producer of chilled food products for the multiple grocery market.

3. Using Table 5.2 of this chapter as a model identify similar characteristics for two or three catering supply companies. You may like to use information sources such as the Internet and unstructured telephone interviews.

Questions

1. Discuss the effects on food and drinks manufacturers of the increased control of major retailers on the food chain.

2. Evaluate the arguments why

   (a) a food manufacturer

   (b) a producer of alcoholic drinks

   should form a supply chain partnership with a third party logistics contractor.

3. Comment upon the ways in which food and drinks manufacturers are likely to have to respond to the increase in demand for home shopping.

Stakeholders, ethics and social responsibility in the food supply chain

Jennifer A. Wade

Key objectives

This chapter examines the wider role of food and hospitality organizations by analysing their broader responsibility with regard to food supply in society. These areas of responsibility include how organizations manage utilities and production methods, the characteristics of the food purchased and their relationships with their stakeholders. The key objectives of this chapter are:

- To explain what is meant by ethical business practice and social responsibility

- To identify the key stakeholders of food and hospitality organizations and comment on how they may influence the ethics of the organization

- To explore the demand for 'ethical food'

- To determine the characteristics of 'ethical food'

- To analyse the implications for retail food and hospitality organizations

Introduction

Corporate social responsibility (CSR) is not a twentieth-century phenomenon. In 1844, the 'Rochdale Pioneers' opened a co-operative shop to sell wholesome food at fair prices at a time when the adulteration of food was common (Co-op 2000). In 1800, Robert Owen began the set up of the model village and factory of New Lanark in Scotland (Cannon 1994). This philanthropist ensured his workers received education, health care and comfortable homes. There may have been a touch of paternalism in Victorian 'model' institutions but there was a genuine concern that 'the lot' of the worker should be improved. As the values of society changed, legislation was introduced that forced organizations to become more responsible in the way they operated. Today, companies operate in an environment where many aspects are controlled by government policy and legislation. This provides a baseline for conduct.

It could be argued that, high standards of conduct are essential to a sound reputation, and, the value of a reputation is realized when conduct is compromised. An example of this is the pensions fund scam initiated by the late Robert Maxwell. The public reaction was profound, as their expectations of good conduct (as well as legal regulations) had been slighted. For many, the standards of society had been snubbed.

Fritzsche (1997) defines business ethics as 'the process of evaluating decisions, either pre or post, with respect to the standards of the society's culture'. What are 'good' decisions and what are bad ones? What standards are the right ones? Although organizations are usually legal entities in their own right and can negotiate contracts and so on, it is the people in organizations who have values and morals, act out behaviour and make judgements within and on behalf of, the organization. Therefore, business ethics is about relationships, relationships between organizational members themselves, and, with the organization's stakeholders. To understand these relationships it is necessary to analyse the wider impact of an organization and the contribution it makes to the community. As the ripples from a stone thrown into a pond, expand across the surface of the water so the impact of any organization spreads across its community and environment. To comprehend the significance of this impact, those with an interest or 'stake' in the organization must be identified. Webley (1992) lists the stakeholders as the 'shareholders, employees, customers, suppliers and society'. Stakeholders are not just those with a financial stake in the organization, it seems that everyone (society) has a 'stake' in an organization.

Corporate business ethics and social responsibility

Webley (1992) also comments:

> there has been a measurable increase in both company awareness of ethical issues and public disquiet about standards of business practice.

McDonald and Nijhof (1999, p. 134) suggest an organizational framework of ethics has three levels. First, a macro or political level that stems from industry power bases, legislation and market mechanisms, that ensure organizations do not act in a morally reprehensible way. This is certainly true of hospitality and retail food organizations which must meet their legal responsibilities for the supply of safe food. The second level is the 'meso' level that concentrates on the ethics of the organization itself, arising from the norms and values of that organization. The Co-op Bank, for instance, trades according to an ethical policy, first issued in 1992. The policy covers human rights, environmental issues and social involvement. The policy defines with whom the bank will, and will not, establish commercial relationships. For example, the bank will not invest in armament manufacturers but positively supports organizations that promote the fair trade concept. The third level of ethics is the 'micro' level that represents how the individuals behave within and on behalf of their organization.

At the macro level, the ethical performance of an organization will be controlled, to some extent, by external forces such as government legislation and industry codes of practice. Any internal attempt (meso level) to establish a code of ethics must reflect the macro factors and the norms and values of the organization. An internal ethical policy must then seek to influence and, be reflected in, the behaviour of the organization's members, especially its decision makers. If there is conflict between what the individual thinks is ethical and what the organization purports to consider ethical, then it will become increasingly difficult for decision makers to act responsibly (McDonald and Nijhof 1999).

In poor trading periods for example, organizations can delay the payments of invoices to facilitate their own cash flow. In the short term the purchaser benefits but, to the detriment of their supplier. In the longer term, however, the organization may put at risk the supply of resources that they need. Alternative sources of supply could be found but short term financial advantage may again endanger long term supply continuity and put the supplier stakeholder at risk.

Stakeholders all have their own priorities. Webley (1992) comments that a company must 'seek to keep responsibilities in balance'. Relationships with each of the stakeholders need to be conducted in such a way that each of their particular needs are met without compromising the needs of the others. Organizations need to ensure that the relevant information is available for each stakeholder. For example, environmental health officers will require information about standards of hygiene management whilst shareholders will require honest statistics on financial performance.

Organizations must also be able to prove ethical performance and this requires some definition or interpretation of its ethics into standards that can be verified. The source of these standards will vary, some may be external, such as the hygiene standards required by environmental health officers, while others will be internal, for instance, the declared relationship an organization has with its suppliers.

Organizations can choose to operate to an externally generated set of standards that interpret ethical principles or develop their own. The advantage of using an external standard is that it may be widely recognized and will therefore have more credence in the wider community. In the past two decades many organizations have identified the need to become 'environmentally responsible'. External verification can lead to accreditation for standards such as the International Standards Organization (ISO) 14000 series. This allows an organization to operate a prescribed environmental quality management system and verify their environmental good practice. The environmental performance standards they have to define, monitor and attain may include: energy management, water conservation, emissions control, waste management, staff training, use of transport, health and safety standards and purchasing policy. Staff need training in how to save energy and purchasing specifications should ensure 'least energy' consumption for electrical goods, or biodegradable contents in cleaning chemicals.

Organizations can join a host of special interest or trade bodies that will verify their adherence to a given code of practice or set of guidelines that promote particular ethical standards. These include 'sustainable' tourism accreditation schemes such as Greenglobe, registration for organic food supply with UK Organic Register of Food Standards (UKROFS), or becoming a member of the Ethical Trade Initiative (ETI).

Consumer issues

Supermarkets have enormous purchasing power and influence on what food is sold and produced. This is a complex, sophisticated market with supply chains that criss-cross the globe. The demand for fresh food, often seen as more nutritious and healthier, means that sources must be found that can plug seasonal gaps in the home market. Interest in new ingredients leads to a rapidly escalated demand and new sources of the produce have to be established. Tiger prawns, for example, are now a common ingredient. They are now farmed in artificial ponds, on tropical coastlines and in 1995, 27% of total world production came from Thailand. Since then, factory farms have spread to South America and other parts of Asia. Research (Christian Aid 1996) has revealed that this farming has caused 'social and environmental damage'. This includes the destruction of mangrove forests and the salination of local water and soil, leading to contaminated water for human consumption, and reduced crop growth. The pollution may lead to sites being abandoned and the need for new ones. Christian Aid calls for supermarkets (and, by implication, caterers as well) to encourage importers and supermarkets to be more responsible and to ensure their demands are sustainable.

Ethical consumerism allows the consumer to influence the food chain, by purchasing goods based on critieria additional to price and quality. This forces the food retailer or caterer to look at their source of supply. There is an 'ethical' consumer movement, as evidenced by the Ethical Consumer Research Association (ECRA). They publish a magazine, the *Ethical Consumer*, which gives '*Which?*-style' reports on consumer goods and the companies behind them. They describe ethical consumerism as 'in its truest sense it means without harm or exploitation of humans, animals and the environment' (ECRA 2000). They suggest various tactics to pressurize shops to stock more ethical food. One tactic they suggest is the 'positive purchasing' of fair trade goods, organic food and 'cruelty free' food.

Case study 1 – the Fairtrade mark

The Fairtrade Foundation in the UK was set up by charities well known for their beliefs and 'ethics', including CAFOD, Oxfam, Traidcraft and Christian Aid. The Foundation also belongs to an international body called the Fairtrade Labelling Organizations International (FLO). The Foundation exists to 'improve the position of poor and marginalized producers in the developing world, by encouraging industry and consumers to support fairer trade'. The Fairtrade mark products include coffee, loose tea and tea bags, chocolate, cocoa, honey and in some countries, orange juice and even wine.

The Foundation commissioned a MORI poll in March 1999 to survey consumer demand for ethical goods. They found that overall 11% of the general public recognized the Fairtrade mark: in the AB socio-economic group this rose to 15% and to 20% of those with higher education qualifications. Some 12% of the general public associated the Fairtrade mark with a better deal for third world suppliers and 3% of the population were committed to buying Fairtrade goods. The Fairtrade consumer profile is someone who is well educated, over 55 years, from the professional classes, in full-time work.

This information helps the caterer or food retailer to focus on which customers will appreciate the supply of Fairtrade mark food (coffee and tea in particular). There is a Fairtrade Catering Directory on www.Fairtrade.org.uk/Catering.htm, and although the produce list is limited it does provide a starting point for the ethically minded purchasing manager.

(*Source:* The Fairtrade Foundation on www.fairtrade.org.uk, 26 November 1999)

A series of food crises over the past decade has highlighted to consumers that the issue of how food is produced can be as significant as the taste or the price. The media exposure of a series of food related health scares experienced in the UK, including the 1988 salmonella outbreak in eggs, the 1989 outbreak of listeria found soft cheeses, the BSE controversy starting in 1988, the 1996–7 *E. coli* 125 outbreaks, the disputed effects of food additives, the safety of irradiated food and the debate around genetically modified food, has compounded consumer awareness. This is in addition to the demand for 'healthy eating' and concerns over food allergies and animal welfare. Consumers are now sensitized to food issues. Organizations such as McDonald's have responded by making information available to their customers, For example, McDonald's (2000) comment on their animal welfare policy, declaring that:

> McDonald's cares about the treatment of animals . . . McDonald's believes that the humane treatment of animals is an integral part of our world class supplier system. Therefore we buy all our beef . . . from suppliers who maintain the highest standards and share McDonald's commitment to animal welfare.

They also make available, information on the content of their products, for those with food allergies.

The characteristics of the food are becoming so important that consumers demand more information about how and where food is grown and how it is processed. The labelling of food has become much more sophisticated as consumers' rights are enforced and consumers are given the information they need to make choices. Humphries (1998) reports on a CWS 1997 'label' survey that found that whilst 89% of consumers believed the law protected them, consumers were also realistic and accepted a 'degree of creative licence'. However, words such as 'traditional' and 'natural' were found to be confusing, so if consumers are to make 'real' choices the information must be clear and trustworthy. Some words and standards have a legal status. For example, UK grown organic food labelling is controlled by the UKROFS who allow organizations such as the Soil Association and the Organic Farmers and Growers Ltd to verify and certify organic growers and suppliers. Only permitted labels are allowed on food supplied as 'organic'. The European Commission has adopted a European Union logo to label organically produced foodstuffs. The logo will act as a guarantee for all European consumers and will be useful for importers. The logo can only be used on agricultural crop products and on foodstuffs containing 95% organic ingredients. The products must have been submitted to the inspection system throughout the entire production and preparation process including processing, packaging and labelling (EU 2000). Other descriptions have some legal recognition, for instance the 'Freedom Food' label means animals are reared in conditions prescribed by the Royal Society for the Prevention of Cruelty to Animals (RSPCA), but the words 'traditional' or 'heritage' have no legal status.

Under the Food Labelling Regulations 1996, since September 1999, catering establishments in the UK must provide information for their customers on the use of genetically modified soya and maize in the food on their menus. This conforms to the principle that 'the public has a right to know'. Customers can be told by staff which dish contains GM ingredients or it can be written on the menu for each individual dish. A general statement or disclaimer is not permitted. Relying on staff to tell customers could be problematic in an industry where staff turnover is significant, the training implications are onerous. For the purchasing manager it means that they must read the contents specification thoroughly and must have confidence in their suppliers' labels.

Ethical food

Towards a definition

Consumers have sought to reduce health risks, environmental risks and the perceived risks of GMOs (Kerr 1999) by buying food they perceive to be safer and healthier. Organic food is seen to be 'more natural' as its production avoids the use of artificial herbicides and pesticides, fertilizers and genetically modified seed.

Expenditure on organic food has doubled in three years and the Soil Association believes that by 2001 it will account for 7–8% of the total food market in the UK (CateringNet 2000). Ethical food however is more than organic food, not all organic food would fulfil the criteria of ethical food. It may not have been traded 'fairly' or could have compromised food security. The food supply chain traces food from source to consumption and there will be factors at each stage that will determine the ethicality of the produce.

Any definition of 'ethical' will be defined by the priorities of the stakeholder. To a vegan consumer the eating of any animal produce is unethical but, to an omnivorous consumer, albeit with high ethical principles, meat may be perfectly acceptable, as long as it comes from an animal that is reared in a natural way and has not been 'factory farmed'. The characteristics of 'ethical' food will embrace all parts of the food chain from production methods to consumption and overarching these are political and management issues. Figure 6.1 summarizes these.

The impact of society in general and of government legislation has already been alluded to and, in the following sections other factors will be considered.

Management issues

From a management perspective CSR means that organizations must deal with suppliers, customers and their own members ethically. They will not trade with organizations who exploit workers and do not pay minimum wages, or companies with unethical investment sources, or compromise the health and safety of their workers.

Environmental policy implementation has already been established as a prerequisite for an ethical organization and this quote from one of the world's most successful fast food restaurant chains emphasizes this. McDonald's declare, 'We realize we are a business leader, we must be an environmental leader' (McDonald's 2000). Organizations must introduce policies that demonstrate a commitment to more than dealing in ethical food and introduce policies that address the ethical management of all resources.

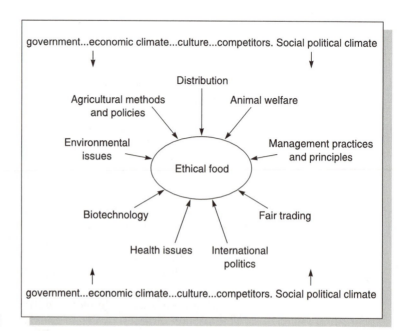

Figure 6.1
Characteristics of ethical food

Case study 2 – the Ethical Trading Initiative

The Fairtrade Foundation also helped to set up the ETI, an initiative to help organizations develop a shared approach to sourcing policies. Their 'base code' covers labour relations, working conditions, working hours and discrimination. They claim supermarkets such as Asda, Tesco, Sainsbury, the Co-op and Somerfield as members (ETI 1999). With these members they hope to set up an initiative with Costa Rica banana growers, associated government departments and NGOs to audit the labour conditions of the growers to establish whether they are of an 'acceptable international level'. The supermarkets can then give their customers the assurance that the bananas they buy have not been to the detriment of a third world economy. As the 'ethical' consumer movement grows so these labels will give 'value added' to the products and the organizations who use them. The labelling also demonstrates to any stakeholder the ethical purchasing policy of the organization.

On 17 January 2000 Fairtrade bananas were on sale in the UK in Co-op stores for the first time, at £1.30 per kilo as against 99p per kilo for conventional bananas.

(Source: ETI (1999a)
http://www.eti.org.uk/about/
basecpde.shtml; ETI (1999b)
http://www.eti.org.uk/resources/
costarica01.shtml accessed 26 January 2000)

Socio-political issues

Local suppliers may be unable to meet fully the demands of a market now used to buying 'out of season' produce all the year round. However, by searching for supplies in other world regions a business may be compromising the food security of that region. Food security (Committee for World Food Security 1996) requires 'the right of everyone to have access to safe and nutritious food, consistent with the right to adequate nutrition and fundamental right of everyone to be free from hunger'. It is argued that in some regions, in order to supply other world regions with out of season supplies, agriculture is directed towards export cash crops, rather than producing staple foodstuffs to feed the local population, thus compromising local food security (Paxton 1994). Put simply, food security means that each area of the world should be able to feed itself adequately. Potentially, this means that disaster in one region will not compromise the nutrition of the population in another area. This is an emotive subject and the economics complex, but it raises the question that 'where food comes from' can be an ethical consideration. For many managers the supply chain only starts with their wholesaler. To buy produce, that does not compromise the food security of a region, would demand informed and co-operative partnerships between suppliers and businesses. The implication is that to adopt a policy that incorporates food security could restrict the produce available, increase costs and restrict what can be offered to the consumer at any one time. Food security is also as much about fair pricing as nutrition (see Fairtrade case study).

Agricultural issues

Concerns over the long term impact of GMOs range from religious objections (playing God!) to possible allergic and toxic reactions to their impact on the biodiversity of the countryside. Over time, such technological innovations may become more acceptable but the issue is that when consumers are worried about an ingredient it will influence their choice of food in the supermarket and, on the menu. Consumer uncertainty and wariness has so far been more evident in Europe than in North America. The EU want all GMO imported produce labelled whereas the USA, do not think this is necessary (Bunting 1999).

Case study 3 – the soya bean

The UK imports around 2 000 000 tonnes of soya beans a year. It is cheaper to import than to grow high protein feed alternatives at home for meat production. Over half the soya is used for food processing and it is found in many of the familiar foods we purchase every week, from biscuits to sausages to instant desserts to meat pies. Soya imported from the USA and Argentina may be genetically modified (for instance the Round-up Soya Bean developed by Monsanto), and although there are no known health risks there has been much media interest in 'Frankenstein foods'. There are concerns about the toxic potential and allergy properties of these foods. Many supermarkets now declare that their own brands are 'GMO free' and thus seek alternative sources. There have been international trade power struggles taking place as the companies try to ensure a global market for their expensively developed GMO seed.

(*Source:* Sustain (1999)
www.sustainweb.org/foodfact/soya.htm)

Organic farmers are particularly concerned about potential cross pollination by GM crops and organic crops. If organic crops are contaminated they can no longer be certified organic and the farmer loses valuable revenue. The UK produces insufficient organic food and about 70% of organic food for retail sale in the UK is imported (Sustain 1999). It is therefore important to increase the land available in the UK for organic production. This will help to safeguard supply, decrease the cost of organic produce and make it more affordable to consumers and the cost conscious catering market sectors, in particular the 'not for profit' sectors such as education, health and residential institutions. An increase will also contribute to environmental improvement (such as increasing biodiversity, minimizing water pollution by artificial fertilizers). The UK Government is looking to increase land under organic production by offering incentives.

It is argued that although organic yields are sometimes lower than conventional agricultural methods, the reintroduction of 'set aside' land and the reduction in costs of treating polluted water would make organic production economically viable.

There will always be a balance between organic and conventional methods but the demand for food that is seen to be healthier, safer, and grown in a more environmentally responsible way, is growing. Market forces may yet prove irresistible.

Distribution issues

The 'Food Miles Report' (Paxton 1994) identifies the environmental costs of importing or transporting food over long distances. The report states that pollutants and climate change gases are released into the atmosphere as fossil fuels are used for production, transportation and packaging. The report also proposes that a hierarchy of purchasing priorities should be established. This hierarchy, although indicating that food *can* be sourced locally, regionally, or nationally, stresses the benefits that can be gained if food is purchased from local or regional suppliers in order to minimize transportation pollution and energy consumption. The key is to buy local produce where possible. Fresh food is preferable as there are no energy costs required for processing or long term storage, although there is transport pollution from intercontinental distribution.

The Food Miles Report (Paxton 1994) recognizes that packaging is needed to protect food in transit and storage. Therefore, a reduction in packaging is not a viable concept, as this would lead to damaged products that would in turn have implications for food safety, quality and cost. Paxton states that the issue of food packaging must be addressed from a recycling and reuse policy incorporated into purchasing practices, for instance buying in bulk rather than pre-packaged individual portions.

Conclusions – implications for the food retail and hospitality industries

Ethics must be interpreted into standards and standards into good practice. This must be demonstrable to convince stakeholders. Evidence of good practice could include:

- A food purchasing policy based on fair trade principles.
- An environmental policy.
- A consumer code of good practice.
- Open and honest codes of conduct in accounting, marketing, public relations and human resources.

A catering organization could demonstrate an 'ethical menu' by purchasing local, fresh, seasonal food and buying fairly traded food. More than 20 suppliers in the UK supply Fairtrade coffee and teas to the catering industry (Fairtrade 2001). Retail food outlets could respond in a similar manner. This is not practicable for all industry sectors, especially fast food, but a start is to review the food purchased in the light of the issues discussed in this chapter. Realistically, all organizations must look at the price of food and while organic food remains at a premium its use will not be economic for cost conscious market sectors. Customer choice is related to their disposable income and it is only the value driven 'ethical' consumer who will put the ethicality of food as a top priority while prices compare unfavourably with conventional food. Changes in agricultural policy to support conversion to organic production and improved animal welfare may facilitate price reductions. There is a view that conventional food is unrealistically priced, as Brenman (2000) comments:

> The higher prices often charged for organic food actually represent the true cost of healthy food production. Consumers are applying indirectly for industrialized farming though higher water bills (to remove nitrates and pesticides) and precious tax revenues spent on the BSE disaster (£4.5 billion) . . .

If agricultural policy changes and conventional food is not subsidised, as inferred by the quote, the price comparison between organic and conventional food could be less dramatic. For the food retailer and caterer the adoption of an ethical policy means more effort has to be put into sourcing and purchasing. Evidence has to be available of the 'life story' of the produce.

The constraints to ethical food supply are:

- the need for the purchasing hierarchy (as implied by the Food Miles concept);

- the restrictions imposed by seasonal nature and perishability of fresh produce;

- the need for skilled staff and frequent changes in produce range or menus;

- the premium pricing of organic food and the willingness of consumers to pay this.

At one end of the spectrum is conventional factory farmed food and at the other fairly traded organic food. It is likely that all parts of the spectrum will be represented for some time to come but, that, in developed post-modernist economies, there will be an increased demand for 'ethical' food, whose characteristics will be determined by the particular priorities of the individual consumer. It is likely that there will be more organic food available which will satisfy the needs for most consumers but the other issues identified in this chapter may also develop a higher, and thus more influential, profile. Both consumers and professionals will have to be more informed and discriminating.

References

Brenman S. (2000) Organic food for everyone at a fair price. Soil Association Press Release on www.soilassociation.org; accessed 26 January.

Bunting M.(1999) The battle over trade; what the talks mean to you. *Guardian*, 26 November, p. 16.

Cannon T. (1994) *Corporate Responsibility*. London: Pitman.

CateringNet (2000) News – Organic food demand doubles. www.cateringnet.co.uk/monthly/month05599/news06059901.htm; accessed 10 February.

Christian Aid (1996) *The Global Supermarket – Britain's Biggest Shops and Food from the Third World*. Christian Aid.

Committee on World Food Security (1996) Rome Declaration on World Food Security and World Food Summit Plan of Action, approved by the committee at the conclusion of its 22nd Session on 31 October 1996, FAO Conference Resolution 2/95, Food and Agriculture Organization of the United Nations, Rome, http://www.fao.org/wfs/policy/english/96-3eng.htm.

Co-op (2000) Co-operative Union – outline of the Co-operative Movement. www.co-op.co.uk; accessed 7 January.

ECRA (2000) Ethical consumerism – what is it? www.ethical-consumer.org/whatsethcons.htm; accessed 7 February.

ETI (1999) http://www.eti.org.uk/resources/costariaO1.shtml; accessed 26 January 2000.

European Union (20009) 'EU approval for logo on organic food' on www.organicinfo.ndirect.co.uk/news/1999/19991222.htm; accessed 7 February.

Fairtrade (2001) www.fairtrade.org.uk/catering.htm; accessed 12 March 2001.

Fritzsche D.J. (1997) *Business Ethics: a Global and Managerial Perspective*. New York, McGraw-Hill.

Humphries C. (1998) A code of practice for food labelling. *Nutrition and Food Science*, 98 (4), pp. 193–7.

Kerr W.A. (1999) Genetically modified organisms, consumer scepticism and trade law. *Supply Chain Magazine*, 4 (2), pp. 67–74.

Mcdonald G. and Nijhof A. (1999) Beyond codes of ethics: an integrated framework for stimulating responsible behaviour in organizations. *Leadership and Organizational Development Journal*, 20 (3).

McDonald's (2000) McDonald's FAQs on http://www.mcdonalds.com/corporate/info/faq/faq.html; accessed 10 February.

Paxton A. (1994) *The Food Miles Report: The Dangers of Long Distance Transport*. London: Safe Alliance.

Sustain (1999) European indicators. www.sustainweb.org/indicators,fir3.htm; accessed 26 January 2000.

Webley S. (1992) *Business Ethics and Company Codes*. London: Institute of Business Ethics.

Activities

- Carry out a survey of two different groups, for example teenagers and mothers with young children, to establish if they buy food that is organic, GMO free, or has a 'Fairtrade' logo. Compare the results and identify the differences.

- Visit a local supermarket and a local greengrocer to find out what organic supplies they carry, and compare the prices. Also, establish if there are any specialist organic suppliers locally and compare their prices to the other suppliers. Establish what implications the price comparison has for local consumers.

- Design an organic restaurant and see whether you can source all the ingredients from local suppliers or shops.

Questions

- Does 'ethical food' mean expensive food?

- Is it inevitable that consumers will want increasing variety and choice all the year round?

- Will social responsibility values influence the real choice of consumers and diners in the future?

PART 2

The Management of the Supply Chain

Strategic supply and the management of relationships

Paul D. Cousins

Key objectives

It is clear from the literature written on purchasing and from a range of personal research with a large number of companies, across different industrial sectors, that purchasing is developing from a predominantly service/clerical, tactical function towards an integrated strategic process. This chapter will examine the reasons for this change and explore the benefits and problems that various firms have experienced with this transition. This chapter introduces a model to help students think about analysing the strategic nature of supply within firms.

After reading the chapter students should be able:

- To understand the difference between purchasing and supply management

- To have an understanding of the different relationship typologies that fit with each strategy

- To understand the integrated nature of supply management

- To appreciate the difficulties with operating such a strategic approach

Introduction: a new strategic focus

Traditionally, purchasing has long been thought of as being responsible for the management of a firm's inputs, i.e. raw materials, services and sub-assemblies into the organization. This is generally illustrated in most operations management textbooks by using a simple input–transformation–output model (see Figure 7.1).

Purchasing's role was to buy these goods and services from approved sources of supply. The skill of the buyer was seen in obtaining a good 'deal' whilst maintaining the required levels of quality and delivery performance; but this view of purchasing as a clerical service department is rapidly changing.

Purchasing in today's organizations is often viewed as a dynamic high profile role with a professional career path (Cousins 1992). Firms are no longer simply focusing on the acquisition of goods and services into the organization. Their focus is now much more strategic and holistic, taking a view of the entire supply process. There is a major distinction to be drawn between the purchasing, which is the organization and acquisition of goods and services and the supply process, which permeates the entire organization, as opposed to stopping when the goods are received. Managing supply strategically focuses on understanding and manipulating which resources are held within the firm and which are moved outside of the boundaries of the firm. These strategic approaches are often known as Outsourcing or Supply Delegation strategies.

> **Definition**
> Purchasing is the acquisition of inputs into the firm. Strategic supply is the management of inputs and the transformation process, which includes the structuring of the supply activity of the firm.

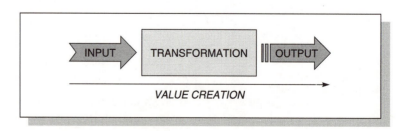

Figure 7.1
Input–output model

Strategic supply will also develop and implement a variety of supply structure approaches that are designed to sustain the competitive position of the firm, such as improving cycle times, reducing time-to-market and the acquisition of new technology into the firm. For example, many firms in a variety of industries have decided that they are no longer assemblers, rather they are design houses. For example, the automotive, aerospace and retail industries have all moved towards this delegated sourcing structure. These include Rover, Rolls-Royce, Westland Helicopters and, in the food sector, Marks & Spencer. This strategy involves allocating the build responsibility to a 'first tier' supplier.

Telfer Foods – sandwiches for Marks & Spencer plc

Marks & Spencer (M&S), a major global retailer, has close collaborative links with suppliers and indeed suppliers of suppliers. This is particularly evident in the areas of food produce. Marks & Spencer offer a number of formats in food retail including grocery sales, deli-counters, coffee shops and the still growing market of sandwiches. In busy locations it has upgraded its provision of lunch time snacks with the development of sandwich shops, featuring a wide choice of filled rolls and sandwiches.

In 1980, M&S started a range of 'to go' sandwiches which, in the early years, were produced in-house, with bought-in fillings. In one store in Croydon a team of seven were required to make 500 sandwiches in less than four hours every day. As the demand grew, Marks & Spencer looked to outsource sandwich production.

One of their sources was Telfer Foods Terranova, now a subsidiary to UNIQ, formally known as Unigate. Whilst the origins of Telfer foods date back to 1926 as 'Ticky Foods', a producer of meat pies, Telfer Foods diversified into sandwich related products in 1981. In 1989 the company disposed of the meat pie side of the business and moved into a new purpose-built building, used totally for the production of sandwiches. In 1996 the company began to supply part foods to M&S. Their position with M&S has been further consolidated through the successful development of Deli fillers, a standardized fresh sandwich fill concept. By 1998 they were solely supplying to M&S and now operate a £40 million concern.

This level of commitment is reflected in the M&S strategy. Telfer Foods is one of three suppliers of sandwiches to M&S, along with Gunstones, a part of Northern Foods and Heinz. M&S draws upon the particular strengths of each company, whilst creating the opportunities for each to continue to meet the M&S standards, through providing additional purchasing power, the inspection of second tier supplier premises and market research.

Telfer Foods currently operate two production plants: Sandwiches and Delicatessen. They supply M&S with five product types: tortilla wraps, fish sandwiches, meat sandwiches and one-third of the M&S Healthy Choice range. They also supply platters for corporate entertainment into the four distinct categories within M&S. These operate under the 'to go' banner which emerged from their original sandwich filling business. In 1996, they moved into Party Foods and have expanded into coffee shops and delicatessens in line with M&S developments.

Each area of the M&S business is managed as a category with designated category teams who include technologists, buyers and merchandisers to ensure the continual upgrading of their products. These teams work extremely closely with 500/600 designated first and second tier suppliers.

New product development

It is evident that the M&S approach to new product development is keenly focused on the increase of efficiencies within the supply chain. In traditional scenarios, whilst first tier suppliers had a significant role in new product development, briefs were often vague or non-existent. Market research and analysis was very much in the hands of the first tier suppliers. Products would be developed with little information provided as to the customers long term strategies, resulting in the rejection of a high proportion of protocol products. Today nine-tenths of new product development projects are based on a clear brief provided by M&S. This results in a significant reduction in the number of products rejected, and, thus clear cost savings for the first tier suppliers and the supply chain as a whole.

Trust and long term relationships

The understanding of their mutual operating constraints is key to the relationship between Telfer Foods and M&S. In traditional adversarial relationships suppliers often had little understanding about what was expected of them and likewise were unaware of the operating constraints that the purchaser was working under.

This is not the case with Telfer Foods and M&S. Telfer indicate that M&S are very keen that new products should not be developed which would result in continual cuts in supplier margins as they see this as not being conducive to long term relationships. Telfer likewise understand M&S margins and therefore are clear regarding acceptable ingredient cost parameters, which further eliminates unnecessary costs of a new product development. Over the past year to 18 months Telfer and M&S have worked towards a greater understanding. The development of a team 'Away-Day' in which information and criticisms are shared, builds up further understanding between the parties.

The first tier supplier becomes responsible for the delivery of a complete assembly such as a gearbox, wing, suit or sandwich! It is the responsibility of supply to decide how the sourcing should be delegated and to work internally to make sure that the required knowledge is passed to the supplier to enable the delivery of the completed assembly. Figure 7.2 illustrates this sourcing process.

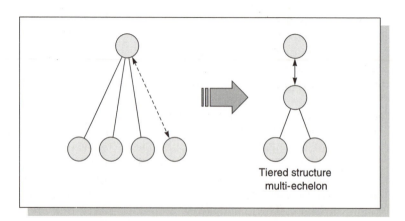

Figure 7.2
Delegated sourcing strategies

Strategic supply management is concerned not only with the efficient management of inputs into the firm, but also the transition and management process of goods and services through the organization; its aim is to make the firm more competitive. This involves not only purchasing goods and services at competitive prices, but also focusing on cost reduction techniques, improving cycle times and reducing time-to-market.

None the less, as companies attempt to shed old habits and begin to view procurement as a strategic resource, from which competitive advantages may be gained, there remains a good deal of corporate baggage to shed. More importantly there is a new mind-set to be instilled both in procurement and across the firm. Barriers to the development of long term interdependent relationships generally relate to the continued existence of opportunist approaches by buyers within the food sector as in others (Cousins and Spekman 2000); seeing short-term price cuts against long term cost reductions. The traditional model of price driven procurement, however, is hard to change. Change it must if procurement is to take its rightful place among the influencers of corporate strategy.

Pressures for change

Whilst it is clear that purchasing is changing from a clerical function to a strategic process, it is important to understand why this change has taken place. This is because it is the drivers for change that will affect how strategy is formulated and implemented.

Purchasing has had a range of pressures upon it that have forced it to change. A simple PEST (Political, Economic, Social and Technological) model can be used to illustrate this point.

Political pressures have caused changes in both the focus of supply, i.e. the move from price to cost focus and the structure of industries, i.e. government policy on privatization of public services. These major policy changes have meant that within certain industrial economic sectors, the focus of the organization as a whole, has had to change. Generally this has been away from defining the 'best' specification possible towards finding the lowest cost solution. For example, defence spending reductions, combined with a policy change away from sourcing, not only from domestic manufacturers, caused a massive shock wave throughout the industry. Aerospace had to move away from its traditional 'cost plus' focus and concentrate on 'value-for-money', i.e. move towards a cost focused approach.

It is important to recognize that cost and price are not used interchangeably here. Price refers to the process of driving down the quoted price of a good. This will often have the net effect of reducing the supplier's margin. Cost is a more sophisticated approach, which focuses on understanding the entire cost of the product (including process) and then jointly finding ways to reduce this (see Chapter 11).

Further policy changes, such as privatization, moved public sector services into the private sector, where the pressures of competition and cost competitiveness are much higher.

Economic pressures also forced organizations to examine the way that they managed supply. Recessions and depressions, plus competition on a global, as opposed to domestic, level, i.e. global village, meant that increased costs could not be passed onto the final consumer. These costs had to either be absorbed, resulting in lower profits, or passed back, which often meant that suppliers would go out of business or otherwise these costs had to be eliminated. This era of the late 1980s and early 1990s, spurned the development of concepts such as lean manufacturing and lean supply management. The focus with all of these approaches was primarily on improving efficiency and reducing waste, both within the organization and, within the firm's supply chain, thus resulting in overall cost reductions to the firm.

Social pressures have also forced purchasing to change. If purchasing wanted to develop it would need to utilize professional and well-qualified personnel. In order to attract these types of people into the area it would need to present a professional profile similar to that of finance or marketing. Purchasing's main problem was that it was not seen as 'sexy'. This view is now beginning to change as purchasing achieves higher strategic status within the organization. In addition, purchasing now has a professionally chartered institute, as does marketing, finance etc. All of these elements help in the raising of the profile of purchasing. Further social pressure on the firm by other stakeholders, to save money, and therefore jobs, was exerted by trade union groups and various pressure groups both within and external to the firms.

Finally, the development of new and innovative technologies has meant that purchasing can communicate and involve a much wider range of the organization in the supply process. For example, it is now possible, via the Internet to allow anyone to purchase (authorized budget holders) against an E-Catalogue. Purchase cards (credit cards for managers) are also revolutionizing the way that we do business. In addition to technologies that facilitate the purchasing process, firms are also requiring improved times-to-market of their own products. This can only be achieved if the supply structure is able to deliver quality suppliers that can work with the buyer (black box engineering) as opposed to the specification.

Figure 7.3 illustrates the PEST analysis, showing the forces of change on purchasing that have acted as a catalyst to move it from a clerical function to a strategic process.

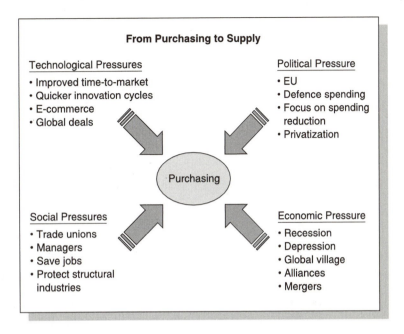

Figure 7.3
Pressures for change

In summary, the need to be increasingly competitive, flexible and efficient has been exacerbated by the global village phenomenon, with domestic firms having to benchmark with the best in the world.

The evolution from purchasing to supply management

It was clear in the late 1980s that inefficiencies in production and the management of supply could not be passed onto the customer in the form of increased prices. Firms had to absorb these costs (usually within their own margin), or find ways of migrating or reducing these costs through efficiency savings. Organizations realized that if they were going to manage them efficiently they had to manage the inputs into the organization. As consulting companies constantly remind firms savings of 10–20% are not uncommon with a focused strategic sourcing initiative. Strategic sourcing bookings for one large consulting company in 1998 amounted to $750 million (Kearney 1999).

'Strategic sourcing is big business!' (Lopez 1993). The realization that with managing supply strategically firms can save huge amounts of money (typically a 1% cost saving by purchasing equates to a 10% increase in sales), has led firms to begin to invest in this area of management. The creation of strategic purchasing departments has given purchasing a 'new lease of life'. They are no longer seen as a clerical function, rather a strategic business process. This rise to fame is not without a price. There is a distinct difference between purchasing implementing strategies and purchasing being strategic.

> As Ellram and Carr (1994) succinctly put it: '. . . it is critical to understand that there is a difference between purchasing strategy and purchasing performing as a strategic function. When purchasing is viewed as a strategic function, it is included as a key decision maker and participant in the firm's strategic planning process . . .'

Case study – Bass plc

Bass plc is an international hospitality and leisure group with a strong focus on brands. Bass traditionally was one of the major players in the brewing sector, with a substantial estate of managed and tenanted public houses whose wet sales were largely internally sourced. In their compliance with the 1989 MMC report, there was some considerable consolidation of their managed estate. In the long run, however, as with other UK brewers their strategy was to define the organization, invest into the hospitality sector and redraw their interest from the brewing sector. Bass plc finally sold the last of their brewing division to Interbrew in 1999. Interests in the catering business are largely concentrated in Bass Leisure Retail, including the 550 outlets acquired from Allied Domecq at the end of 1999. Bass Leisure retail was formed in 1998 from Bass Taverns and selected brands from Bass Leisure.

With a portfolio of 30 000 branded and unbranded pubs and restaurants and leisure venues, it is a key player within the UK hospitality sector and an active player in the promotion of the pub catering sector. Whilst Bass traditionally specialized in unbranded pubs they are emerging as active players in a number of market sectors. Growth for the main has been through acquisition of existing brands. Bass Leisure brands include Vintage Pubs, Toby Carverys, Harvester, All Bar One, It's A Scream, Edwards, O'Neills, Browns, Barcoast, Dave and Busters and Hollywood Bowls, with a broad format range from traditional pubs, stylistic restaurants, student bars, bars for young professionals and ten pin bowling alleys.

In the event of the organizations shift towards the hospitality catering sector, Bass have been innovative in their sourcing. Supply, traditionally a key area of activity within Bass became a strategic function once the repositioning of the organization had taken place. The issues of establishing brand identities and purchasing efficiencies, given the dispersion of Bass outlets, became key to an organization functioning in the highly competitive marketplace of hospitality. In the late 1990s a supply chain management role and department were established with the aim of developing single sourcing strategies.

The evolution of purchasing from a clerical function to a strategic process is well noted in the literature. However, the way that we think about the management of supply has also changed. The unit of analysis of how we think about supply is important and has also changed in both complexity and strategic nature. Figure 7.4 shows a model (Harland, Lamming *et al.* 1999) that is helpful in illustrating how supply thinking has changed.

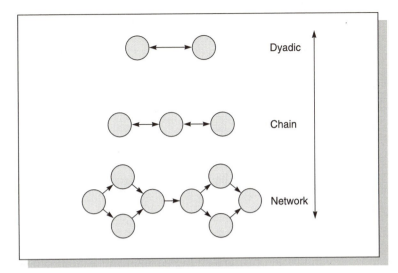

Figure 7.4
Supply structure (model taken from Harland, Lamming *et al.* 1999)

Initially, academics and practitioners concentrated on the dyadic linkage. The dyad refers to the relationship between the buyer and supplier, i.e. two. This thinking was extended in the late 1980s to thinking of supply as a chain or pipeline. This added increased complexity to the study of supply management as it took into account the buyer, supplier and final customer relationships. The final stage in the evolution of this thinking is viewing supply structure as a network. This involves examining the inter-relationships across an entire industry sector, where frequently buyer and supplier roles can be reversed several times throughout the network structure. The Industrial Marketing and Purchasing (IMP) Group first conducted the pioneering work for this type of thinking.

The IMP's work has been succinctly summarized by Ford (1990). He explains that the work of the IMP can be traced to two distinct areas: inter-organizational theory and the new institutional economic theory.

Ford (1990, p. 11) explains: '... [the] relationship between buyer and seller is frequently long term, close and involving a complex pattern of interaction between and within each company. The marketer's and buyer's task in this case may have more to do with maintaining these relationships than with making a straightforward sale or purchase ...'

The IMP group went on to develop the 'interaction' model (Hakansson, 1982) that conceptually indicates the effect of relationships within the context of the entire network system.

Writers within the IMP group clearly recognize the importance of business relationships and it is their view that the entire system needs to be considered in a holistic and systematic way, mapping the various relationships and types of relationships in a *pseudo* mathematical manner. Whilst this process is indeed very useful in determining the type and quantity of relationships within a given network, the measurement and management of the process is again ignored.

The work of the IMP has had a growing effect on how academics view relationship strategy by indicating that relationships between firms are highly complex and inter-related through many levels of the supply hierarchy.

How can we manage supply strategically?

The management of the supply chain is an extremely difficult task as it relies heavily on cross-functional co-operation. As previously suggested, the buying firm will often not consider the ramifications of managing the entire supply chain and its interfaces, i.e. the supplier/buyer, buyer/customer and internal buyer/buyer linkages.

The first question to ask is what is the difference between implementing a strategy and acting strategically? Authors have been writing on the development of purchasing from a tactically focused service role to a strategic process since the early 1970s. Table 7.1 summarizes some of the main literature in the field.

The topic of strategic supply has been developed by a great many authors, some thinking conceptually and others using empirical research methods to measure the development process. There have also been several tools and frameworks developed to measure the strategic extent of purchasing itself. Reck and Long in 1988 developed a four-phase positioning tool (see Table 7.2). They categorized the level of purchasing capability ranging from 'passive' through to 'integrative', they also went on to produce a more detailed benchmarking mechanism to allow firms to position themselves and to see what needed to be done, in order to extend and develop their current position.

For supply to be strategic, it needs to be clearly understood what pressures are on the organization and how it will react to these pressures. The key question here is how can supply design the supply structure to meet the competitive needs and demands that face the firm. These issues go far beyond the purchasing of goods and materials; they embody the entire process of inputs and then the translation of those inputs into outputs. In other words, supply will be involved in developing outsourcing strategies, examining the amount and types of suppliers, moving towards delegated supplier tier and/or the development of supplier associations.

Author	Type of study	Description of study and findings
Farmer (1973)	Empirical	Linking of purchasing to the strategic mechanism of the firm
Caddick and Dale (1987)	Empirical – case study	Purchasing must develop strategies and link purchasing and corporate strategy
Spekman (1989)	Conceptual	Purchasing needs to be integrated into corporate strategy. First, purchasing must think and develop strategically
Browning *et al.* (1983)	Conceptual	Purchasing is linked to corporate strategy because it supports corporate strategy in terms of monitoring and interpreting supply trends, identifying ways to support strategy and developing supply options
Burt and Soukup (1985)	Conceptual	Purchasing can have an impact on achieving success in new product development if purchasing is involved early in the new product development process
Landeros and Monczki (1989)	Empirical – interviews	Purchasing can support the firm's strategic positioning using co-operative buyer-seller relationships
Ellram (1994)	Empirical	Level of strategic competence of supply
Saunders (1994)	Conceptual	Purchasing is no longer a service function. A discussion of practical approaches for strategic purchasing
MacBeth and Ferguson (1994)	Empirical – case study	Strategic relationship assessment and implementation. Development of internal and external relationships
Burt and Doyle (1994)	Conceptual	Purchasing should become part of the *keiretsu* culture. Implementation of the Japanese *keiretsu* approach to the supply chain activities of firms
Hines (1994)	Empirical – case study and interview	Strategic rationalization of the supply chain – Particularly concerned with the development and application of Japanese supplier association management techniques on UK supply chains
Nishiguchi (1994)	Empirical – case study and interview	Study of Japanese co-ordination of the supply chain for competitive advantage

Table 7.1 Key authors on the development of supply strategy

STAGE I	In the **passive stage,** purchasing normally begins as a reactor to requests from the other departments. Many of purchasing's legitimate activities are handled by other functions outside of purchasing
STAGE II	In the **independent stage**, purchasing departments spend considerable time attempting to professionalize the purchasing function by introducing such things as computerized information systems, formalized supplier programmes and communication links with the technical function
STAGE III	In the **supportive stage**, top management views purchasing departments as essential business functions. Purchasing is expected to support and strengthen the firm's competitive advantage by providing timely information to all departments in the firm about potential changes in the price and availability of materials, which may impact the firm's strategic goals
STAGE IV	In the **integrative stage**, the firm's competitive success rests significantly on the capabilities of the purchasing department's personnel. Purchasing's role within the firm changes from facilitator to functional peer. This development process must be implemented and guided by management over a period of time

Table 7.2
Reck and Long's strategic positioning tool

The issue then is about strategic alignment. It is essential for the functions within the firm to have a clear understanding of the value process within the organization, how this is being communicated and utilized. The concept of strategic alignment makes common sense to most people. The problem comes when trying to apply it in practice. As the level of information that the purchasing function receives will depend on the level of strategic maturity that it is viewed as having within the organization.

The strategic alignment model (see Figure 7.5) shows how important it is to align strategies. However, it is also equally important to develop these approaches by aligning both the performance measurement systems and the skills and competencies of the individuals involved within procurement. As the model argues you are only as good as the bottom box, i.e. the skills and competencies of the individuals within your organization.

The development of a strategic positioning model

In *Improving Purchase Performance* (1992), Syson suggested that the most fundamental factor to influence the purchasing strategy is the focus of the department. He believes it is from this starting point that the manager can then begin to evaluate the purchasing

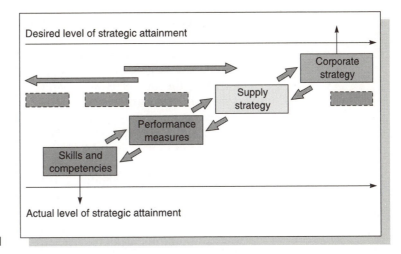

Figure 7.5
The strategic alignment model

department. Similar to Reck and Long's development stages, Syson believes that by having a different organizational view (or focus), the purchasing department will develop according to criticality of materials and the attitude of top management towards purchasing (see Figure 7.6 for stages of development).

Syson suggests that the role of purchasing is changing due to the changing business environment. With the move from large-scale production to differentiation becoming the principal competitive thrust, must the purchasing department be moulded according to the strategy of the business?

It is important to note that such strategic changes also cause distinct managerial problems. As Quinn *et al.* (1998) note, strategic movements take place in a step by step manner or, as they term it, 'logical incrementalism'. These stages take a good deal of time and must be managed carefully. It is therefore vitally important, when considering the implementation of any new strategy, that the internal infrastructure is firmly in place. This concerns both the internal resources, such as the correctly

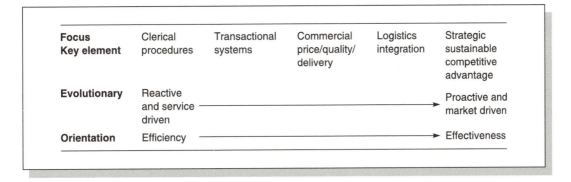

Figure 7.6 Purchase focus (Syson 1992, xi)

qualified personnel and also the relevant management systems and philosophies.

This thinking led Cousins to develop the four-phase approach to supply strategy formulation, as seen in Figure 7.5. The objective of the model is a firm must have alignment of the four main mechanisms, that is: Corporate Strategy, Supply Strategy, Performance Measures (both internal and external) and finally Skill and Competence Sets. Without alignment, firms will not manage to effect any change.

The principal driver in the model is the level of skills and competencies of the individuals. If the appropriate skills are not in place the organization will not be able to move forward. In turn, these must be motivated with the appropriate measurement systems, which should align with the supply and corporate strategies. While this sounds conceptually very simple, the reality of the situation is that a great many purchasing functions have little perception of the overall corporate strategy, little to no development of supply strategy, unitary performance measures and a haphazard approach to skill and competence development. With these findings in mind, this research project went on to generate a strategic transition model for the development of purchasing.

The strategic transition model

The transition model was based on research with ten of the Supply Chain Development Programme's sponsor companies. These companies were chosen from a wide range of sectors covering utilities, public sector, retail, engineering and chemicals. A series of focus groups and individual interview sessions was organized. The purpose of these was to support the findings from the literature, test, iterate and validate the transition model so that a usable and realistic framework could be developed. Figure 7.7 shows the overview of the transition model, which consists of five phases.

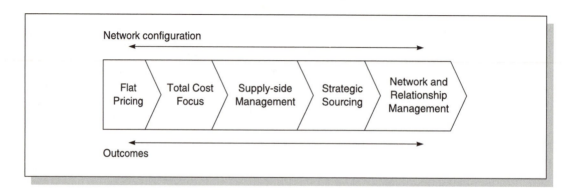

Figure 7.7 The transition model

The model shows the movement from a purchasing focus on 'Flat Pricing' at one extreme towards 'Network and Relationship Management' at the other end of the spectrum. The research clearly indicated that there were five distinct phases: Flat Pricing, Total Cost Focus, Supply-side Management, Strategic Sourcing and Network and Relationship Management. Each of these phases has a given output and set of characteristics that defines it. There were also nine key elements involved in purchasing strategy: Key Objectives, Supply Mechanism, Supply Structure, Strategic Approach, Why Fails, Key Issues, Network Structure, Performance Measurement and Purchasing's Perception within the organization (see Table 7.3).

The factors were then mapped against the overall 'transition model'. This produced a matrix, which allows firms to see their relative positioning; the matrix is shown in Table 7.4.

Factor	Definition
Key Objectives	Refers to the main goal of the purchasing functions, i.e. price reduction, cost improvement, relationship development etc.
Supply Mechanism	Shows how the purchasing function uses its position within the supply chain to achieve the key objectives, such as price leverage, cost transparency, benchmarking etc.
Supply Structure	Refers to the structure of the supply market, for example is it multi-sourced, single sourced, dominant supplier, buyer's market etc?
Strategic Approach	This is the focus of the purchasing organization, is it predominantly short-term, fire-fighting and tactical or longer term, proactive and strategic
Why Fails	This category was placed in the model as respondents felt that in order to move on to the next phase they needed to understand why their current approach was not sustainable. Reasons for failure could be the focus of the approach was more on price than on cost, less on quality than on service and so on
Key Issues	Refers to common problem areas realized with these strategies, such as skill base requirements, resource development, technology infrastructure etc.
Network Structure	This category was used to show the type of interfaces that are most prevalent, i.e. buyer–supplier, one-way, or two-way, customer–supplier–customer or indeed, network structure
Relationship Type	Refers to the dominant relationships within the model such as traditional/adversarial through to long term, close collaborative
Performance Measurement	This is a key characteristic; it is essential to have the correct measurement systems in place. Measurement systems refer to internal as well as external measures
Purchasing's Organization Perception	The final characteristic refers to how the rest of the firm sees purchasing. This is an extremely important factor and one which will directly influence the way in purchasing can and does interact with the rest of the firm. The higher the perception within the organization, the greater the resource allocation and ability to effect change within the firm

Table 7.3 Purchasing assessment factors

Stages of excellence	Stage 1	Stage 2	Stage 3	Stage 4	Stage 5
Approach:	Flat Pricing	Total Cost Focus	Supply-side Management	Strategic Sourcing	Network and Relationship Management
Description:	Adversarial Tactical Focus on price Transactional	Focus on total cost Distant relationship with suppliers	Focus on supply service package Develop closer relationships with suppliers	Co-operative Strategic focus on supply Commitment to single/ few suppliers	Focus on supply, demand and mutual development Total commitment
Key Objectives:	Contain price	Contain cost over total product life	To gain from suppliers their specialist expertise and skills	Work jointly with suppliers to increase value in supply chain	Improve total understanding Mutual network development
Supply Mechanism:	Volume leverage	Cost leverage	Total service leverage Benchmarking Supplier development	Leverage through co-operation	Network leverage
Supply Structure:	Multi-supply Multi-relationship	Multi-supply Multi-relationship	Fewer suppliers	Single/few key suppliers	Network of key single supplier
Strategic Approach:	Tactical	Tactical	Moving from tactical to strategic	Strategic	Strategic
Why Fails:	Focus on price not cost	Focus on cost not on quality and service	Resistance or failure to share relevant information with suppliers Focus on competition not co-operation	Focus on co-operation not involvement	Too expensive Need high level of trust/ dependency
Key Issues:	Low skills Low information Low level decision making	Relatively low skilled Information-based	Less purchasing but greater 'management' skills required Greater information flow between firms	High level of information flow between firms High level of commitment	Highly skilled Complete information openness High level/complex decision making
Network Structure:	Buyer-competitive	Buyer-selected suppliers	Buyer and first and second tier suppliers	Supply chain	Network of relationships

Table 7.4 Transition positioning matrix

Stages of excellence	Stage 1	Stage 2	Stage 3	Stage 4	Stage 5
Relationship Type:	Adversarial	Distant	Involved	Committed	Trust
Performance Measures:	Basic measurements based on price differences from year before	1 Process activity mapping 2 Production variety matrix 3 Decision point analysis 4 Cost transparency	1 Communications analysis 2 Supplier development matrix 3 Quality function deployment	1 Supply chain response matrix 2 Quality filter mapping 3 Performance measurement of purchasing	1 Value stream mapping 2 Advanced communications analysis
Purchasing's Organization Perception:	Passive	*Supportive*	*Independent*	*Integrative*	*Differentiator*

Table 7.4 continued

Application of the transition model

In designing the model three clear implementation stages, were identified, Assessment, Strategy development and Benchmarking, which are shown in Table 7.5.

Our research clearly showed that a generic benchmarking approach for the purchasing function would have been impossible. We found that the level of strategic focus was contingent upon the types of goods or services being purchased, i.e. commodity versus specialized; and the relationship strategy being followed, i.e. traditional versus collaborative. Therefore, in order for firms to be able to focus on strategic development they must first assess the types of goods that they purchase.

This can be achieved by using the Kraljic matrix (1983), which positions against value/cost and market exposure. Each of these quadrants will require a level of strategic focus. For example, 'Tactical Acquisition' will need a stage 1 level of maturity, whereas 'Strategic Critical', will require stage 4 or 5 in our five-stage transition model. The various quadrants and stages are mapped (see Figure 7.8).

Stage 1: Assessment

Stage 1 requires an assessment of the current resource capabilities and the strategic profile of the purchasing function within the organization against the commodity or service grouping. The purchasing function will need systematically to examine each of the assessment criteria and position themselves against them. This process will produce a profile effect, as shown in the example in Figure 7.9.

The respondents from this company said that they believed, according to the Kraljic matrix, that the IT purchasing activity would be positioned in the bottom right quadrant, with a low

Stage	Purpose	Description
1	Assessment	The purchasing organization should benchmark where it currently sees itself against the characteristics and criteria listed within the model
2	Strategy Development	Purchasing should consider where it wants to be and examine the gaps in its approach *vis-à-vis* what the model is telling them. They should then develop a strategy to take the function forward
3	Benchmarking	The final stage is to use the model to review current progress and see how the function is developing

Table 7.5
Stages of implementation of the transition model

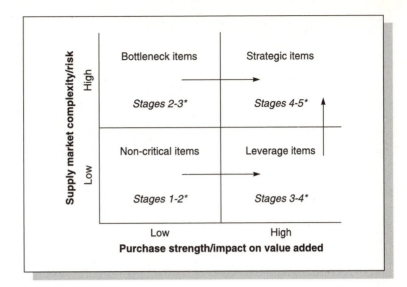

Figure 7.8
Strategic positioning
matrix: purchase portfolio
strategic deconstruction
(*from the transition model)
(after Kraljic 1983)

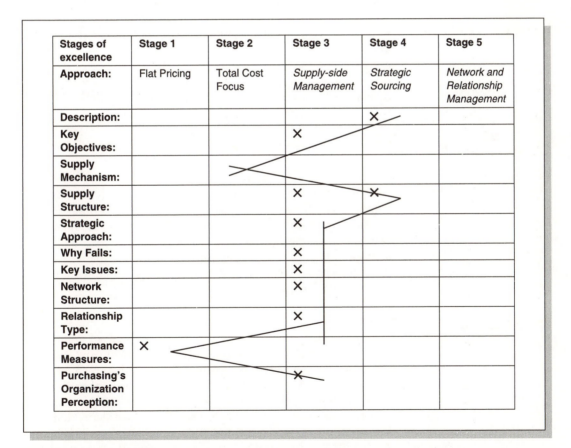

Stages of excellence	Stage 1	Stage 2	Stage 3	Stage 4	Stage 5
Approach:	Flat Pricing	Total Cost Focus	*Supply-side Management*	*Strategic Sourcing*	*Network and Relationship Management*
Description:				X	
Key Objectives:			X		
Supply Mechanism:					
Supply Structure:			X	X	
Strategic Approach:			X		
Why Fails:			X		
Key Issues:			X		
Network Structure:			X		
Relationship Type:			X		
Performance Measures:	X				
Purchasing's Organization Perception:			X		

Figure 7.9 Example of purchasing profile for IT purchasing at a UK pharmaceutical company

145

supply market complexity but a high impact on value added. Therefore, they should be aiming for a focus of stage 3 moving to stage 4. The majority of factors were located in stage 3 with notable exceptions, supply mechanism which was located in stage 2 and performance measurement which was located in stage 1. The profile gave the respondents a sense that the purchasing of IT had to be changed and adapted to reach the required level. Also, it was agreed that stage 4 would be the optimal level to be reached and those factors which were situated in stage 3 could be improved upon in order to reach the stage where IT products and services would be strategically sourced.

Stage 2: Strategy development

The purchasing function needs to understand the overall goals and objectives of the organization, which can then be fed into the overall supply strategy. The strategy is then broken down into the various sourcing groups within the Kraljic matrix. For example, if the overall view of the purchasing activity is of a strategic sourcing focus, the factors which are not stage 3 or above need to be improved. There has to be a clear strategy, with resources allocated against the factor that needs the most attention. In the case of the pharmaceutical company, it was decided that performance measurement was in need of the most improvement, therefore the management of this activity could deal with it effectively and did not waste time and energy on the factors that had achieved the desired level.

Stage 3: Benchmarking

The tool that was developed had to be uniform enough to enable the benchmarking of all activities within the purchasing department. This enables managers to focus their attention on the activities that are out of alignment with the strategic focus and provides a method for reaching a desired state for each of the activities. It could also provide a tool for persuading senior management of more efficient allocation of resources where it was needed most.

Conclusion

This chapter has discussed the strategic evolution from purchasing to strategic supply management. Whilst it is possible to give an overall strategic viewpoint, it is vital to remember that this is dependent upon the product or service being purchased. Although the current trend is towards increased dependency on fewer suppliers, which implies that sourcing groups (delegated sourcing) will tend towards a strategic role, it was found that certain purchasing activities will never be perceived as strategic.

Activities which have low added value and have low market uncertainty would therefore be better off competitively supplied as time would be wasted on the management and building of closer supplier relationships.

Positioning purchasing on the 'transition model' provided motivation for change, as was shown in Figure 7.9. This type of benchmarking creates a tool for managers to improve the effectiveness of purchasing activities. This leads to the improvement of the overall focus of the purchasing department and also can improve the organization's perception of the function. Once activities have been positioned and assessed against the 'transition model,' managers are then able to allocate time and resources most effectively to the activities under his/her control.

The use of the 'transition model' allows purchasing managers to understand clearly how the management of the purchasing activities needs to be changed, how resources can be distributed most effectively and can adjust the profile of the department within the organization.

References

Browning J.S., Zabriskie N.B. *et al.* (1983) Strategic purchasing planning. *Journal of Purchasing and Material Management*, 19 (1), pp. 591–605

Burt D. and Doyle M. (1994) *The American Keiretsu: A Strategic Weapon for Global Competitiveness*. Homewood, IL: Richard D. Irwin.

Burt D. and Soukup W.R. (1985) Purchasing's role in new product development. *Harvard Business Review*, Sept–Oct, pp. 90–6.

Caddick J.R. and Dale B.G. (1987) The determination of purchasing objectives and strategies: some key influences. *International Journal of Physical Distribution and Materials Management*, 17 (3), pp. 5–16.

Cousins P. (1992) Purchasing: a professional approach. *Purchasing and Supply Management* September, pp. 20–3.

Cousins P.D. (1998) *The Snake and the Old Women: A Study of Inter-Firm Relationships*. World-Wide Purchasing Symposium, London, UK, Chartered Institute of Purchasing and Supply.

Cousins, P.D. (1999) An investigation into supply base restructuring. *European Journal of Purchasing and Supply Management*, Summer.

Cousins, P.D. (1999) *Strategic Supply: Report on Trends and Developments in Supply Management*. Bath, University of Bath, pp. 1–63.

Cousins, P.D. (1999) Supply base rationalisation: myth or reality. *European Journal of Purchasing and Supply Management* 5 (1).

Cousins P. and Spekman R. (2000) Strategic Supply and the Management of Inter- and Intra-organisational Relationships. IMP Conference.

Ellram, L. (1994) A taxonomy of total cost of ownership. *Journal of Business Logistics*, 15 (1), pp. 171–91.

Ellram L. and Carr A. (1994) Strategic purchasing: a history and review of the literature. *International Journal and Purchasing Materials Management*, Spring, pp. 10–19.

Farmer D. (1973) The impact of supply markets on corporate planning. *Long Range Planning*, 5 (1), pp. 10–15.

Ford D. (ed.) (1990) *Understanding Business Markets*. London, Academic Press.

Håkansson, H. (ed.)/IMP Group (1982) *International Marketing and Purchasing of Industrial Goods: An Interaction Approach*. Chichester: John Wiley & Sons.

Harland C., Lamming R. *et al.* (1999) Developing the concept of supply strategy. *International Journal of Operations and Production Management* 19 (7), pp. 650–73.

Hines P. (1994) *Creating World Class Suppliers: Unlocking Mutual Competitive Advantage*. London: Pitman.

Kearney A.T. (1999) Report on the Strategic Sourcing Market Place. White Paper.

Kraljic P. (1983) Purchasing must become supply management. *Havard Business Review*, Sept–Oct, pp. 109–17.

Landeros R. and Monczki R.M. (1989) D0 operative buyer/seller relationships and a firm's competitive position. *Journal of Purchasing and Materials Management*, Fall, pp. 9–19.

Lopez K.C. (1993) Breaking new frontiers, Video.

MacBeth D. and Ferguson N. (1994) *Partnership Sourcing: An Integrated Supply Chain Approach*. London: Pitman.

Nishiguchi, T. (1994) *Strategic Industrial Sourcing: The Japanese Advantage*. Oxford: Oxford University Press.

Quinn J.B., Mintzberg H. and James M. (1988) *The Strategy Process: Concepts, Contexts*. Englewood Cliffs, NJ: Prentice Hall.

Reck R. and Long B. (1988) Purchasing: a competitive weapon. *Journal of Purchasing and Materials Management*, Fall.

Saunders M. (1994) *Strategic Purchasing and Supply Chain Management*. London: Pitman.

Spekman R. (1989) A strategic approach to procurement planning. *Journal of Purchasing and Materials Management*, Spring.

Syson R. (1992) *Improving Purchase Performance*. London: Pitman.

Questions

1. Why has purchasing become strategic?

2. Define what you understand to be 'strategic supply management'.

3. What problems might a Purchasing Director face when trying to develop his or her department from a clerical to a strategically focused organization?

4. How would you go about developing a strategic plan for re-engineering purchasing within an organization?

Logistics and information management

Denis Towill

Key objectives

- To describe how effective logistics integrate material flow, information flow and the flow of orders throughout the supply chain

- To illustrate how the underlying principles have been applied to such diverse supply chains as BhS, Domino's Pizza and the 'Warren Buckley' Hotel

- To show that a recommended route to customer satisfaction at reasonable cost is via just-in-time (JIT) logistics. This is targeted at delivery of the right products, available at the right time, at the right price and of the right quality. Such an outcome retains existing customers and also attracts new ones

- 'Best practice' supply chain logistics and requirements for E-shopping are further discussed in the Peapod case study which appears in Part 3 of the book (Perspective 10)

Introduction

A supply chain consists of a number of echelons (business units) operating sequentially. A simple supply chain can consist of just four echelons (raw materials supplier; manufacturer; distributor; retailer) and thus on to the end customer. *Typically there will be many more echelons or levels* (i.e. a number of discrete businesses each adding value during their specialist activities) and at each echelon there are usually a variety of businesses operating in parallel with each other e.g. multiple sourcing, multiple manufacturers and multiple customers. It is customary to refer to various businesses as supply chain 'players'. Partnering is an example of a particular supply chain philosophy in which the players regard effective supply chain management as a team activity in which the whole is bigger than the sum of the parts. Thus, the acceptance by all parties of the present day axiom that it is supply chains that compete, and not individual businesses (Christopher 1997).

As shown in Figure 8.1, material flows downstream and orders traditionally flow upstream from echelon to echelon. Hence the frequent reference to the supply chain as a pipeline (Farmer and Van Amstel 1991). Depending on the type of supply chain, goods may be stored at any combination of these echelons. Note that our definition of supply chain applies right across the business spectrum, ranging from global enterprises down to a number of related sequential activities undertaken under one roof but covering a number of independent cost centres. So proposals for improving supply chain performance based on material flow control are equally applicable to internal re-engineering as much as to global networking. Streamlined flow enables seamless operation of the supply chain. *Here 'seamless' is defined as a supply chain in which all 'players' think and act as one (Towill, 1997a) and which is a necessary condition for agile, i.e. 'nimble' supply.*

Each echelon within a supply chain embraces the following constituents:

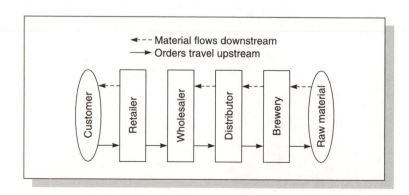

Figure 8.1
Flows within a simple
supply chain

1. *perceived demand for products,* which may be firm customer orders already placed or just sales department forecasts of what might happen;

2. *at least one 'production' or added value process* which the customer is prepared to pay for;

3. *information on current performance,* which may be 'stale' or alternatively 'distorted' or both;

4. *'disturbances'* affecting performance and due to machine/equipment/transport breakdowns etc;

5. *'interference'* between products in different supply chains competing for the same resources and leading to queuing and/or non-delivery;

6. *decision points* where information on material flow, orders and stock levels is brought together and acted upon;

7. *transmission lags (or lead times),* which occur for both material flow and information flow;

8. *decision rules* (based on company procedures) for changing stock levels, placing new orders, etc., in the light of available internal and external information and forecasting mechanisms.

The potentially complex operation of supply chains implied above is made worse because there is uncertainty associated with perceived demand, with the quality of information and with the time associated with the many transmission lags (both for material flow and information flow). As we shall see later, there are enormous benefits to be obtained by improving information and material flow throughout the supply chain. Both flows are much enhanced via time compression of value added, i.e. essential activities and the total elimination of non-value added activities (Towill 1996). Process flow charting is essential in enabling time

Elemental supply chain process	Cycle time Traditional operation	Best practice target	Achievable via EDI transfer
Communicate order, retailer to supplier	3 ± 2 days	1 day	0 days
Supplier processing of order	2 ± 1 day	1 day	0 days
Order picking (or production)	5 ± 4 days	1 day	1 day
Transport goods to retailer	3 ± 2 days	1 day	1 day
Retailer goods-in receiving	2 ± 1 day	1 day	0 days
Total order cycle time (place order to goods being available)	15 ± 10 days	5 days	2 days

Table 8. 1 Total order cycle times in the retail sector

compression. Johansson *et al.* (1993) contains a number of detailed examples. Time compression dramatically reduces uncertainty; typically halving the forecasting horizon reducing the forecasting error by a factor of four. However, these improved forecasts must additionally be made transparent and transmitted without distortion or delay throughout the supply chain, hence the importance of utilizing Electronic Data Interchange (EDI) (Mason-Jones and Towill 1997).

Supply chain logistics

Logistics is all about managing the flow of materials and information from source to customer across the entire range of materials-handling and movement functions and throughout an organization and its supply channels (Hughes *et al.* 1998). Unfortunately, there is an enormous gap between best practice and the average performers in this area, as typified by the data in Table 8.1. For example, the mean total order cycle time is 15 days but there is a minimum of 5 days if everything is done on time and consistently (Stock and Lambert 1987).

Also shown in the table are the current targets achievable by the use of EDI and JIT logistics. Thus via EDI the communication to the supplier plus the processing of the order can be undertaken instantaneously. Furthermore, both order picking and order transportation to the retailer can be undertaken within a one-day time slot.

Finally, JIT logistics enable us to deliver straight to retailers shelves, thus eliminating the goods-inward receiving process. Hence by good supply chain re-engineering the inconsistent 15 days total cycle time has been reduced to a consistent 2-day cycle.

In many companies there is still a need to shift from a warehousing approach centred around storage, to a much greater emphasis on managing and accelerating material flow. This forces the necessary focus on customer responsiveness, speed of operation and streamlining the total process. Indeed, it can prompt a complete redefinition of the supply chain so that the needs of the end-customer are made transparent throughout the chain.

It is manifest therefore that the concept of integration of logistics across entire regions is rapidly taking hold. This includes determining the optimum number and location of warehouses, the design of warehouse handling systems for rapid picking of orders and an intelligent policy on where and how much inventory is to be carried. Not enough items in stock means turning custom away; too much stock means holding costs are incurred and wastage and write-offs occur all too frequently.

An example of a best practice supply chain is Campbells Soups, as shown below.

Case study – Campbells Soups

Background to Campbell operations

The Campbell Soup Company is a household word for brands that astute advertising persuades customers they cannot do without. The present product range includes much more than the original soups, with numerous items such as vegetable juice, frozen dinners, pickles, chocolates, bakery goods and canned pastas. An extensive management audit survey showed that on-time delivery was already at 98% but this simple statistic masked ineffectiveness in the supply chain. Fortunately the audit additionally identified the opportunity to make major improvements to the distribution system. These enhancements were aimed at reducing paperwork, preventing damage to goods and helping many customers save money by ordering products directly from a manufacturing plant, rather than through a multi-tiered procurement process. Prior to the changes, the company was awash with paperwork generated by dealing with more than 300 carriers, servicing 24 autonomous shipping locations, adding up to over 197 000 shipments per year. The operation was so outdated that to check on the status of a delivery, people at each manufacturing plant would have to call each individual customer. But communications within this vast network were so unwieldy that on-time deliveries suffered badly when third-party trucks broke down or drivers failed to secure a delivery time window. Hence the need for streamlining the material flow system and making it transparent to all 'players' in the system resulting in a supply chain reckoned by *Andersen* Consulting as typical 'best practice'.

Action programmes undertaken to streamline the supply chain

Following the operations audit the company initiated numerous improvements in its distribution system which may be grouped under the following six major programme areas:

- *Alignment of delivery strategies.* Orders used to originate in all sales regions yet transportation was managed at each of the manufacturing plants. Furthermore the supply chain was unnecessarily complicated because the associated tasks of cash control and credit collection were done back at headquarters. Since the establishment of a centralized customer service centre each customer now works with a specified contact person responsible for 'one-stop shopping'. Using the new system, a customer can check on the status of an order, change an order, or reschedule a delivery time by making just a single telephone call to their nominated contact.

- *Integration of delivery operations.* Using electronic transmission, the central customer service centre monitors the progress of goods from distribution points to the final destination. This system avoids 'dead time', both at the point of origin and at the destination when the schedule for loading and unloading trucks was liable to be interrupted. Rather than loading a truck at 9.00 a.m., waiting several hours and then driving it away at 4.00 p.m., the new system utilizes paperless EDI technology to ensure that the shipping department will begin loading precisely on schedule with the truck's departure, hence eliminating such dead time and associated costly delays. The system then continues to track that particular shipment and reports any surpluses, shortages and damages observed at the customer's unloading site. By noting any damaged or unfulfilled orders and automatically taking compensatory action the system creates a streamlined and efficient network for integrating the delivery process with customers.

- *Core carrier concept.* Statistical process control (SPC) is employed continuously to maintain top performance from this already highly efficient delivery system.

A turn-key four-module product delivery management system, purchased from Westinghouse, streamlines the process from the receipt of order right through to the choice of carriers. If a truck is only partially full, the system looks for other orders to complete the load. Then it selects the best carrier in terms of overall costs, service, equipment and supply. The new system, first introduced in January 1997, has reduced costs at the pilot site by 16% and is now fully integrated throughout the organization. The consequent route streamlining has reduced the number of carriers needed to support the system.

- *Pallet standardization programme.* With the old distribution system, goods sometimes arrived in poor condition at customers' warehouses. This was traced back to pallets not being standardized, or not being of a sufficient build standard. To solve this problem a third party rental company was contracted to provide standardized pallets measuring 48 by 40 by 5 inches which would then be used for all deliveries. This programme resulted in more efficient arrangement of pallets on trucks, reduced damage to goods and increased the possible payload on each truck.

- *Continuous Replenishment Programme* To ensure continual integration of its vast delivery system, Campbell logistics managers now meet regularly with logistics experts from customers' sites. Working alongside salespeople, these teams co-ordinate every step of the delivery process, from taking orders to issuing invoices. Campbell's began its version of a Continuous Replenishment Programme in 1992 whereby the company takes over the ordering process for its major customers and thereby becomes responsible for keeping their shelves full. Today, approximately 20% of Campbell's total volume is handled by the continuous product replenishment system, thus avoiding delays, unnecessary paperwork and damaged goods.

- *Direct plant shipping programme.* This allows the company to further reduce manufacturing costs by concentrating production on one or more items at a specific plant. Under normal conditions, products are shipped to a distribution centre, then reloaded for shipment to customers. This is a process which costs money but adds no value to the product. With direct plant shipping, however, the company can offer its customers reduced costs if they buy directly from the manufacturing plant itself. Hence by bypassing the distribution centre and thus saving time and money, the company shares those savings with its customers, thus benefiting several 'players' in the chain.

Observations on the re-engineered Campbell supply chain

This case study clearly demonstrates application of the five well-established supply chain principles which enable streamlined material flow. These are synchronization of events; information transparency; cycle time reduction; choice of appropriate DSS; and finally echelon elimination/interface management. So although most customers think of Campbell's as a company famous for its stable, traditional products, many are unaware of the vast changes that have recently occurred behind the scenes. The familiar labels are still in place, but how those cans get to the shelves of the local supermarket is no longer simply a matter of providing trucks and issuing purchase orders. Electronic commerce has streamlined Campbell's delivery chain, creating a seamless communication system with customers. This eliminates delays and provides information transparency throughout the system. Products are pulled through the distribution chain via a synchronized logistics system incorporating Continuous Replenishment DSS concepts (sometimes called Vendor Managed Inventory). Here Campbell's are directly responsible for keeping the supermarket shelves topped up, thus cutting out a layer in both information and material flow channels.

(*Source:* Author based on T. Hiebeler, T.B. Kelly and C. Ketteman (1998) *Best Practices: Building Your Business with Customer-Focused Solutions*, Simon and Schuster, New York; plus D.R. Towill and P. McCullen (1999) The impact of an agile manufacturing programme on supply chain dynamics, *International Journal of Logistics Management*, 10 (1), pp. 83–96)

Market qualifiers and market winners

What makes one supply chain more effective than another? To answer this question we need to consider the factors that affect the customer's decision to use *our* supply chain in preference to our competitors. Five key performance indicators related to customer choice are as follows:

- Cost (which can be purchase price, or in some cases total ownership costs).

- Quality (the ability of the product to meet the expectations of the purchaser).

- Lead time (how long must we wait to acquire the product).

- Service level (how consistently is the lead time target met).

- Stock turns (how many times a year do we rotate our stock).

Whilst all of these indicators are important, at any given moment they are *not* equally important. To illustrate the point Terry Hill (1993) has introduced the concept of 'market qualifiers' and 'market winners'. He argues that for a given type of supply chain, only one of our five attributes will be the instant account market winner. However, the other four indicators are market qualifiers which require us to meet stringent standards in order to be considered 'in the race'. If the product is a commodity, i.e. corn flakes, then cost will be the market winner, always provided adequate standards are achieved in the other four criteria (who wants corn flakes which have been around for months?).

It is part of the competitive nature of supply chain logistics that the market winner/market qualifier scenario is dynamic and continually changing. Hence this year's market qualifier may become next year's market winner (Johansson *et al.* 1993).

For example, in 1970 Japanese TV manufacturers exploited quality as the market winner and even commanded a price premium whilst increasing market penetration. By the time the competition had improved their quality some years later, Japanese producers, aided partly by economies of scale, could retaliate by reducing prices and turning this to their advantage as the new market winner.

It is important to emphasize that nothing is gained (and much may be lost) by improving one performance metric at the expense of another. We must be at least as good as the competition with the market qualifiers and be better than them with the market winners.

Case study – the 'Warren Buckley' Hotel

Background

Just-in-time (JIT) logistics is a technique that can be profitably applied to the food and drinks supply chain. This case study is concerned with the provision of alcoholic and related beverages to the restaurant and bar complex within a medium-sized London establishment with the pseudonym Warren Buckley Hotel. The initial problems identified during an analysis of material flow included excessive stock, obsolescent stock and stock-outs. Hence, despite the average stock being 108 days of sales, the percentage of items ordered from the cellar, but not delivered to the cocktail bar, due to being out-of-stock, was as high as 17% and rarely dropped below 10%. Hence we have a classic logistics problem in that carrying large stocks does not in itself offer any guarantee of satisfying customer need. The total cost resulting from such poor logistics is considerable and includes lost revenue, stock carrying costs, wastage, write-offs and storage costs.

Actions

To help stay competitive, the hotel introduced JIT logistics to the acquisition and control of drinks items. This application has to be seen against a market sector background of a low degree of technology, low levels of investment, both in materials and human resource training, and the expectancy of quick and sustainable results. Hence the need for the implementation of simple robust solutions to the material flow problem. Central to the concept of lean logistics is the matching of supply to customer demand simultaneously with reducing storage costs and space. To achieve this twin objective it is essential to be able to order replenishments frequently and to receive small quantities. This is in line with the definition of JIT according to Schonberger (1990), who likens it to the behaviour of the water beetle, i.e. 'travel frequently carrying small loads'. A supplier specification was thus drawn up by Warren Buckley seeking vendor capability to deliver spirits, wines and fortified wines and minerals five or six times per week and beer three times per week. Also to supply these goods at a price premium no greater than +5%.

An important condition was laid down that the successful suppliers should be prepared to enter into meaningful partnership arrangements necessary to enable seamless operations. The two selected suppliers then became part of the hotel team, attending JIT familiarization and related training sessions. This included exposure to the new EPoS system and an understanding that suppliers are responsible for both quality and quantity conformance, in maintaining agreed minimum stock levels, for all items, as an integral part of the Vendor Managed Inventory (VMI) agreement. Typical benefits to Warren Buckley include reduction in total stock holding from 108 days to approximately 22 days plus redeployment of saved storage space, reduction in paperwork and saving of staff time. In the first six months of operation of the new JIT logistics system, average unfilled cocktail bar orders to the cellar of less than 2% were recorded. This is a reduction of over 8:1 following JIT installation and it is also worth noting that in three months out of the six there were zero stock-outs. So the hotel has engineered a solution incorporating the best of many worlds, including stock-turns improved by 5:1 plus better use of all resources.

Observations

This is an excellent example of JIT application in the service sector. An essential feature of the method is frequent deliveries essential to maintain minimum stock levels. The latter are selected on the basis of usage of individual stock holding units (SKUs) and not on global averages. Implementation of EPoS also means that both stock and usage data may be rapidly updated and used as the basis of VMI with the associated supplier responsibility for keeping shelves full.

Successful application of JIT depends on identifying and attacking fundamental problems aimed at elimination of any form of waste including duplicate activities (Scott and Westbrook 1991). In the hotel sector the JIT system needs to be as simple as possible, with proper involvement and training of staff encouraged ('empowered') to control their own area and take responsibility to solve problems as they arise.

(*Source:* Author based on G.L. Barlow (1995) 'JIT Implementation within a Service Industry: A Case Study', Proceedings of the 2nd International Symposium on Logistics, Nottingham, 1995, pp. 197–207)

Modern material flow systems

In logistics circles a number of approaches embracing ideas on lean production and JIT delivery (Womack and Jones 1996) have been well publicized and associated with particular market sectors and/or management consultants. These approaches, namely Quick Response (QR), Efficient Consumer Response (ECR), Vender Managed Inventory (VMI) and Continuous Replenishment Programme (CRP) are covered in more detail in the glossary.

There are a number of important supply chain design principles running through the foregoing initiatives. They have been confirmed by theoretical analyses, simulation experiments and industrial case studies covering various market sectors (Towill 1997b). All of these simulation experiments were based on synchronous control, i.e. constant 'time buckets' for decision making, since this had already been shown to reduce 'interference' between various value streams competing for the same resources. Hence the synchronization principle is a key enabler in modern logistics. The remaining principles of total cycle time compression, echelon elimination, information transparency and use of appropriate simple robust decision support systems (DSS) have been evaluated on a wide range of supply chain models so can be recommended with confidence (Wikner *et al.* 1991).

Setting stock levels in the supply chain

The requirement here is to make sure that we have enough stock within the supply chain to satisfy customer need but not so much that we will lose on the cost downside due to holding costs, damage and obsolescence. The fundamental equation for setting stock levels is:

Target stock level = Safety stock + Buffer stock

(a) where **safety stock** is selected to cope with any problems on the supply side of our operations. It is how much we feel we need to keep in stock in case our supplies do not arrive on time, or are the wrong goods, or are faulty. This is usually expressed as (**cover** × **average usage**), where the cover factor is related to the acquisition lead-time. So reducing the latter is highly beneficial in minimizing stock levels.

(b) where **buffer stock** is required to cope with unexpected variation in the demand side of our operations. It usually includes a multiple of the forecast error so as to protect us against unforeseeable fluctuations. For example, if the forecast errors form a bell-shaped distribution, then setting the buffer stock at (**Average usage** + k × **Forecast error**) where $k = 2$ will result in stock-outs occurring on about two occasions in a hundred. Increasing k will reduce the chance of stock-outs still further; $k = 3$ decreases the chance of stock-out to one in a thousand.

To lower our stock levels we need to look at the key drivers of Equation 1 in turn. These are the acquisition lead time and the forecasting error. As we shall see, the time span over which we operate is a dominant force in both cases.

Acquisition lead time has many component parts. These include the time taken to make the decision, the time taken to transmit the order, the time taken to pick or produce the goods, the time taken to physically deliver the goods, plus any checking time.

Forecast errors depend on many factors including our knowledge of special events, seasonality, the weather and the state of the 'feel good' factor. However a key determinant is the time horizon over which the forecast is made. As a rule of thumb, forecast errors increase as the square of the time interval. So, if we need to look ahead for a two-week period, the forecast error may be as high as four times the one-week ahead forecast error. So, again, reducing time span is highly beneficial to the smooth running of the business.

In recent years it has become increasingly recognized that achieving the best balance between stock holding costs and customer service level is an important factor in business competitiveness. So much so, that when comparing businesses, 'stock turnover' is now commonly benchmarked as a key performance indicator. Accountants use complicated formulae to calculate stock turnover. A simple estimator is the annual usage divided by average stock level. Hence if an item has a usage rate valued at £K150 p.a. and the average stock level is valued at £K5, then our stockturn will be 30 times p.a. The consensus view is that if we can increase the stockturns, whilst at least preserving our competitiveness in other areas, then our business performance is improving. A consequence of this belief is the move towards stockless operations, which will now be explored.

Moving towards stockless operation (or Minimum Reasonable Inventory, the latter title more clearly retains the notion of still serving the customer: Grunwald and Fortuin 1992). All the available evidence suggests that 'time compression' is a major lever in reducing stocks. The objective is to remove the necessity of storing goods 'just-in-case' by moving to 'just-in-time' operations. For example, by using EPoS data we can download information for automatic decision making and order placements so that this process is literally undertaken at the speed of light. Automatic stock picking can also further reduce the acquisition lead time, setting up local distribution centres reduces the transport time and production engineering expertise is used to compress manufacturing lead times and reduce minimum batch sizes, preferably to one. The overall aim is to be able to move small quantities reliably, quickly and frequently, thus allowing us to operate in narrow time slots, which in turn enable us to avoid queues and to reduce both safety stocks and buffer stocks.

Deciding how much to order

To place an order to replenish our stocks the following general formula is used:

Orders placed on our suppliers =
Constant + Forecast usage + Fraction of stock deficit
– Fraction of orders in pipeline

If we make orders equal to a constant (usually average usage) and ignore the other terms, we are operating in the **level scheduling** mode (Suzaki 1987). This buffers the production or delivery process from demand volatility and requires more or less constant capacity. However, if the usage varies by more than about ± 10% this rule can easily cause the system to break down either by generating excess stocks (if demand dries up) or causing stockouts (if sales are on the up). Another simple formula is to make orders equal to most recent usage. This is termed **passing on orders** mode. But this has the twin disadvantages of requiring high capacity flexibility and short lead times if we similarly wish to avoid stockouts and lost business. Hence the compromise modification to Equation 2 which takes into account any current stock deficit (or surplus) and any current orders in the pipeline (orders placed but goods still in transit). The object here is to balance stock levels against fluctuations in capacity so as to give good service at least total cost.

This is best done by making the fractional components of Equation 2 a function of average lead time. For example, if the orders are placed daily and the acquisition lead time is 3 days, then a typical 'good' set of parameters for this purpose would be stock deficit fraction = 1/3; orders in pipeline fraction = 1/6; and forecast usage is actual demand exponentially smoothed over 6 days (Mason-Jones *et al.* 1997). (The constant term would then be set at zero.)

The stock deficit in Equation 2 is the difference between the target stock level and goods actually in store. Hence, the need for accurate and fast stock monitoring, via satellite communication if necessary. It is important to note that the algorithmic (computer software) form of Equation 2 is modified depending on the particular SKU, i.e. the individual item in question. The ordering rule is selected according to the shelf life, acquisition lead time, value and substitutability of the item. For example will the customer accept an alternative soft drink or an alternative whisky? It is the subject of a special promotional campaign, or is it shortly to be replaced by a new product? Can we get emergency supplies if necessary? Is it a critical item where a stock-out can lose us that particular customer permanently? Is it vintage wine or 'plonk' that needs a rapid turnover? So by answering these questions intelligently we would expect our SKUs to be categorized according to their marketing characteristics. The computer software used is properly called a Decision Support System (DSS). This is because it advises the manager on what should be ordered, but he/she normally has the authority to override the numbers on the basis of local knowledge. Under these circumstances they must perform at least as well as the DSS! Unfortunately many managers do not, as the MIT Beer Game ably demonstrates (Dornier *et al.* 1998).

Exchanging information for supply chain inventory

Supply chain management is ultimately about meeting customer demand as effectively as possible. Consequently, communicating end customer demand throughout the chain is critical (Mason-Jones and Towill 1997; Charaton 1999). Typically, demand is communicated in two ways, via forecasts and via firm purchases. Both start with sales data, but forecasts mask true demand because of judgements on the future, projected sales targets and current inventory. If each echelon in the chain similarly distorts the picture of end-customer behaviour, the consequence will be that upstream suppliers are subject to an amplified demand pattern, or 'bullwhip effect' (Fransoo and Wouters 2000). This is a very costly phenomenon, leading to cyclical over- and under-stocking and wild swings in capacity requirements. Thus ± 10% changes in the marketplace can become ± 50% at the factory.

Best practice is to simplify the flow of orders and make the information transparent throughout the chain (Mason-Jones and Towill, 1997; Charaton 1999). One recommended procedure is for orders placed on a supplier to be clearly indicated as to which are needed to satisfy end-purchase firm demand (i.e. the Passing Orders On element) and those which are required to build-up depleted stocks (Wikner *et al.* 1991). This information sharing means that the bullwhip effect is much reduced provided only one 'player' takes responsibility for controlling orders for buffer stock. Note that information sharing requires both stock and goods-in-transit to be continuously monitored if full benefit is to be obtained.

As an example of the exchange of information for inventory consider the case of the UK retailer, BhS. They have worked continuously to refine their replenishment systems to the point where the effective use of information has all but eliminated the need to hold inventory (Christopher 1997). BhS decided to concentrate on its core competencies of buying and selling, outsourcing all other aspects of its operations to specialist contractors. With their help BhS went on to overhaul its stock management systems and hence embrace the principles of Quick Response. A radical rework of the retailer's supply chain followed, leading to the abandonment of over half of its 800 suppliers. Only those that were willing and able to adapt to the demanding requirement of a long term retailer–supplier relationship were retained. An upgraded EPoS system and improved co-ordination of the buying function has led to a more coherent and harmonious product range. Almost all stock is now held by suppliers. EDI links give BhS's vendors access to data on how their own lines are selling in the stores, allowing them to detect emerging sales trends and anticipate replenishment orders. Goods are now prepared and ready to ship in JIT mode by the time BhS pulls them through the pipeline.

A single specialist contractor, Exel Logistics, has been appointed to handle the distribution of all of BhS's 8000 non-food and 350 food lines. Exel transports the merchandise – ready bar-coded for its final destination – from suppliers to a single dedicated warehouse at Atherstone, Warwickshire, where it is sorted and despatched within 24 hours to BhS's UK stores. The daily deliveries arrive at the shops between 6am and 10am each morning, just in time to meet the lunch-time shopping rush. Thus by re-engineering the supply chain and enabling information to flow upstream, inventory has been considerably reduced. It is an excellent example of the improvement in performance made possible by the adoption of the seamless supply chain concept via time compression and transparency of information flow (Mason-Jones and Towill 1997). In five years BhS's replenishment cycles have been reduced to the point where 60% of all orders arrive the next day and the full 100% are released within 48 hours. Furthermore the daily deliveries have reduced storage space requirements on BhS retail sites from 20% to 10% which leads to much more effective use of resources via larger sales areas.

Case study – Domino's pizza High Street franchise

Background

Domino's are a leading pizza supplier in which the high-street outlets operate on the franchise system. The supply chain has three main echelons; the fast food outlets, the Domino Distribution Business (Commissary in the UK) and the ingredient suppliers including farmers, producers, etc. At the Commissary level the function is to supply on a regular 'milk-round' basis everything needed by the franchise. Each Commissary distribution centre has a private fleet of trucks and is the recommended supply and support channel to the outlets for all its services. This includes provision of best store equipment, delivery of fresh, ready-to-use dough and best ingredients and installation of the individual store management and order software. The chain is not complex in terms of numbers of SKUs. Also the outlets are well known, accessible and the distribution entres (DCs) are relatively small. The complexity arises from the high-velocity, high volume of orders that need processing, the acquisition of goods, routing of trucks and picking and delivering items to the outlets.

Currently over 98% of orders placed on Commissary are met 100% correct, an important statistic when a stock-out of key items can temporarily close the outlet. In practice this latter situation would be addressed by sending a member of outlet staff to Commissary to make an emergency collection.

Actions

Pizza outlets have to cope with highly variable demand patterns according to both hour of the day and day of the week typically by factors of three to one in each case. Hence the maximum hourly throughput can be of the order of nine times the minimum off-peak sales. These two factors mean that available capacity is controlled by adjusting the number of operatives on duty at any particular time. The daily variation in demand means that considerable care must

be taken to achieve the best balance between having sufficient perishable items available and wastage due to ingredients passing their use-by date. Fortunately there are distinctive patterns describing day-to-day variations. Hence the outlet can make use of standard computer software to suggest re-order quantities needed to provide sufficient top-up of individual stocks. The recommended orders can then be fine-tuned by the local manager in the light of extraneous circumstances such as changes in the weather, festival days, pop concerts etc. The immediate entering of individual sales onto the PC and logged according to detailed pizza specification, makes materials management in the outlet transparent.

A typical high street outlet will need about 60 SKUs of which about 80% relate directly to pizzas, about 10% to other direct sales items, such as soft drinks, and about 10% to non-consumable stocks, such as packaging etc. The useful shelf-life of the SKUs vary widely. Both dough and vegetables must be used within days, cheeses within weeks, but tinned sauces may last for months. Also, goods that have lengthy shelf life when unopened must be used quickly once the seal is broken. All SKUs are delivered in standard containers with trays used wherever possible to simplify handling and stacking. With just 60 items, manual stocktaking is possible and is undertaken every evening. The information is fed into the PC and is taken into account when the DSS recommends order quantities. It is also used to monitor the current utilization of ingredients. Orders to Commissary are placed during the late evening and will be delivered about 36 hours later. Since dough has a shelf-life in total of 5 days, including the first two days after manufacture when it is unusable, and deliveries are only made every 2/3 days, maintaining optimum stock levels is very much a juggling act. To aid the local manager, the facility does exist to make emergency collections by sending a van to Commissary HQ, or to another franchise-holder, who has spare stock. However, the operating principle over the 4-day cycle is clear: the local manager expects to satisfy demand for days 1–2 from existing stock: and orders on day 0 for a delivery on day 2 which is sufficient to cover forecast demand for days 3–4.

Observations

Domino regard their franchisees as principal stakeholders and aim to provide the best return to them via striking a balance between value added service and least-cost distribution. This in turn provides the franchisees with the opportunity to provide excellent service from their outlets. A major feature of the Domino supply chain is the standardization of the product, the standardization of operating procedures and the standardization and frequency of SKU deliveries.

By providing good training and support, including computer software, coupled with simplified material flow, the local manager can concentrate on matching pizza supply to local demand. This includes taking responsibility for the recruitment, training and performance of operatives and delivery personnel.

(*Source:* Author based on J.D. Krasner and M. Soignet (1999) Strategic vision drives Domino's pizza distribution, *Logistics Management Homeplace/Manufacturing Marketplace*, May 1999)

Conclusions

We have seen that in every kind of supply chain there is a need to totally integrate material flow and information flow. Also the effectiveness of the supply chain is greatly increased if the speed of material flow can be increased. One measure of this is the number of stockturns per annum. The way to achieve this is to compress time in the necessary value added activities and to eliminate wherever possible the non-value added activities from the chain. As the 'Warren Buckley' case study shows, there are occasions when better control of supplies justifies payment of a small cost premium. The result is greatly increased material flow, more reliable deliveries, better customer service and more effective use of space.

Flow synchronization, transparency of information and usage of simple DSS are a feature of Domino's pizzas. Here the franchise is provided with an effective supply chain infrastructure but is very much left to control operations in the light of local knowledge. BhS are a good example of supplier integration and show that speeding up material flow coupled with information transparency very much reduces the need to carry inventory. Finally, modern logistics requires the removal of redundant processes wherever possible. Thus VMI, as incorporated within the 'best practice' Campbells Soups supply chain, eliminates an information handling delay, via sales data transparency, demand distortion is avoided thus improving quality of decision-making. Furthermore such agile logistics is imperative in enabling E-shopping, as explained by the Peapod example described in Part 3 of the book.

References

Charaton A. (1999) Retail supply chain integration, in Donald Walters (ed.), *Global Logistics and Distribution Planning Strategies for Management*, London: CRC Press/Kogan-Page.

Christopher M. (1997) *Marketing Logistics*. Oxford: Butterworth–Heinemann.

Dornier P-P. Ernst R., Fender M. and Kourvelis P. (1998) *Global Operations and Logistics*. New York: John Wiley and Sons.

Farmer D. and Van Amstel R.P. (1991) *Effective Pipeline Management – How to Manage Integrated Logistics*. London: Gower Press.

Fransoo, J.C. and Wouters, M.J.F. (2000) Measuring the bullwhip effect in the supply chain. *SCM Journal*, 5 (2), pp. 78–89.

Grunwald H.T. and Fortuin L. (1992) Many steps towards zero inventory. *European Journal of Operations Research*, 59, pp. 359–69.

Hill T. (1993) *Manufacturing Strategy: Text and Cases*, 2nd edn. London: Macmillan Press.

Hughes J., Ralf M. and Michels W. (1998) *Transform Your Supply Chain in Releasing Value in Business*. London: International Business Press.

Johansson H.J., McHugh P., Pendlebury A.J. and Wheeler W.A. (1993) *Business Process Reengineering: Breakpoint Strategies for Market Dominance*. Chichester: John Wiley and Sons.

Mason-Jones R. and Towill D.R. (1997) Information enrichment: designing the supply chain for competitive advantage. *SCM Journal*, 2 (4), pp. 137–48.

Mason-Jones R., Towill D.R. and Naim M.M. (1997) The impact of pipeline control on supply chain dynamics. *International Journal of Logistics Management*, 8, pp. 47–62.

Schonberger R.J. (1990) *Building a Chain of Customers*. New York: The Free Press.

Scott C. and Westbrook R. (1991) New strategic tools for supply chain management. *International Journal of Physical Distribution and Logistics Management*, 21 (1), pp. 23–33.

Stock J.R. and Lambert D.M. (1987) *Strategic Logistics Management*, 2nd edn. Homewood, IL: Irwin.

Suzaki K. (1987) *The New Manufacturing Challenge*. New York: The Free Press.

Towill D.R. (1997a) The seamless supply chain – the predators' strategic advantage. *International Journal of Technical Management*, 13 (1), pp. 37–56.

Towill D.R. (1997b) Forridge – principles of good practice in material flow. *International Journal of Production Planning and Control*, 8 (7), pp. 622–32.

Towill D.R. (1996) Time compression and supply chain management – a guided tour. *SCM Journal*, 1 (1), pp. 15–27.

Wikner J., Towill D.R. and Naim M.M. (1991) Smoothing supply chain dynamics. *International Journal of Production Economics*, 22, pp. 231–48.

Womack J.P. and Jones D.T. (1996) *Lean Thinking*. New York: Simon and Schuster.

Questions

1. Discuss the five performance criteria usually used to measure supply chain effectiveness. Explain how at any time, one of these criteria is the market winner, whilst the other four are important market qualifiers. Why is it that this year's market qualifier may become next year's market winner? Illustrate your arguments by reference to a real-world supply chain in which there have been three different market winner attributes covering competition over the past decade.

2. Time is money! This old adage is highly applicable to supply chain logistics. Discuss the many ways in which Total Cycle Time Compression can improve business profitability. How would you investigate the opportunities present for time compression in a supply chain delivering pre-packed meals to the marketplace?

3. How far can we go in eliminating stock throughout the supply chain? Explain carefully how our stockturns may be improved via (a) time compression, (b) information transparency (c) order synchronization (d) using simple robust DSS. What are the dangers inherent in trying to operate a completely stockless supply chain?

Relationship marketing

Terry Robinson

Key objectives

- To trace the development of the concept called 'relationship marketing'

- To attempt to define relationship marketing and to summarize the key criticisms of the transactional four Ps approach to marketing

- To examine the concept of the primacy of the customer

- To outline the key models of relationship marketing

- To attempt to devise a general framework for the understanding of relationship marketing

- To contrast the key elements of the transactional approach to marketing with relationship marketing

- To outline the key stages in the relationship

Introduction

The development of relationship marketing

Although marketing practices can be traced back as far as 7000 BC (Carratu 1987), marketing as a distinct discipline originated from economic thought around the beginning of the last century. As the discipline gained momentum and developed through the first three-quarters of the twentieth century, the primary focus was on transactions and exchange (Sheth and Parvatiyar 1995). The traditional view of marketing expressed in most textbooks today focuses around the marketing mix concept and the four Ps of price, product, place and promotion. This concept was first introduced into the marketing literature by Neil Borden in the 1950s although many organizations had been using elements of his marketing mix for many years (Grönroos 1994). It quickly developed into an almost unchallenged basic model of marketing, so much so it totally overpowered previous models and approaches (Grönroos 1994).

Criticisms of the four Ps approach to marketing

Its theoretical basis

The development of the four Ps as a general marketing theory stems from lists of marketing functions from the functional school of marketing (McGarry 1950), largely developed under the influence of micro economic theory. However, Grönroos (1994) believes that the usefulness of the four Ps as a general marketing theory for practical purposes is highly questionable as the link between micro-economic theory and the marketing mix has diminished over time. He suggests that the marketing mix has become just a list of Ps without theoretical roots. It is not just the theoretical links that have diminished, but so have elements of the original marketing mix. The four Ps represent a significant oversimplification of Borden's original concept (Borden 1964), which was a list of 12 elements and not intended to be a definition at all.

Grönroos (1994) suggested that a paradigm such as the marketing mix should be well founded by theoretical deduction and empirical research. He argued that the four Ps and the whole marketing mix management paradigm is theoretically based on a loose foundation.

Gummesson (1987) called for the old marketing concept to be replaced, stating that, although it may be rich in research and data, it is poor in theory. The theories and models that constitute the present concept are too limited in scope, exaggerating some aspects, namely advertising and competition and suppressing other aspects, such as interrelationships and co-operation.

Its generalizability

The four Ps model of marketing can be criticized for its suitability across all fields of marketing including consumer, industrial and services markets. It is primarily built on research in the area of packaged consumer goods and consumer durables. The marketing theories developed for consumer goods marketing emanate almost exclusively from the United States and are based on unique conditions there, among them a huge domestic market, extensive media coverage by commercial television, radio and press and a large number of competitive distribution solutions (Gummesson 1987; Grönroos 1994).

Gummesson (1987) suggested that the application of the marketing mix concept to areas other than consumer goods can be destructive, as it fails to recognize the unique features of, for example, services marketing and industrial marketing. Ford (1990) and the IMP Group have a similar view; they criticize the four Ps approach for trying to transfer its analysis to industrial markets, where the only differences between approaches occur through greater emphasis on the sales force than on advertising and the occasional inclusion of a service function.

Furthermore, companies are seldom in a single category of goods; they tend to be hybrids of consumer, services and indus-trial goods. Gummesson (1996a) acknowledges that the theories around the four Ps approach hold a lot of important messages and knowledge for the issues to which they are appropriate. The four Ps are appropriate for the marketing of consumer durables where the concept originated, however they cannot claim to be applicable to services and industrial goods. Gummesson (1996a) believes they have thus contributed to moulding an 'unreal reality'.

Its orientation

This is based on the belief (Grönroos 1989, 1990, 1994, 1996) that the marketing mix and its four Ps approach constitutes a production-orientated definition of marketing and not a market-orientated or customer-orientated view. The simplicity of the marketing mix has made marketing seem too easy to handle and delegate, resulting in the creation of marketing departments. The separation of marketing departments from the other activities of the firm may be a trigger that makes everyone else lose what-ever interest in customers they may have had. This may lead to the elimination of Gummesson's (1987) 'part-time marketers' that are often essential in influencing customer purchases.

Its transactional basis

The present model of marketing has evolved during the advent of mass production, the emergence of middlemen and the sepa-ration of the producer from the consumer, all of which have led to a transactional focus of marketing (Sheth and Parvatiyar 1995). This model of marketing suggests that the marketer makes deci-sions about the marketing mix variables on a single transaction basis with customers who are normally characterized as an anonymous mass. This approach, centring on the marketing mix, is called transaction marketing, where the seller is active and the buyer is passive (Grönroos 1991). The IMP group have viewed this approach as inappropriate in industrial marketing where the roles of seller and buyer may vary between passive and active.

What is relationship marketing?

Some definitions of relationship marketing?

Over the past 20 years a contrasting approach to marketing has emerged based on the development of long term, interactive relationships with customers and other parties such as suppliers, distributors and financial institutions. Given the title of 'relationship marketing', it has developed an increasing body of literature by authors from both Europe and North America.

Although, in the literature to date, there is no agreement as to a single definition of relationship marketing, most definitions have many common denominators (Grönroos 1996). Arguably no definition of relationship marketing will ever be precise – it cannot be, because social phenomena are not in themselves precise (Gummesson 1993, 1996b). Since markets are dynamic, definitions of relationship marketing will constantly evolve as we develop our understanding of them. However, there is enough consistency between alternative definitions of relationship marketing to help us understand the phenomena. Gummesson (1996b) has expressed that:

> I don't perceive my 'definition' of relationship marketing (is marketing seen as relationships, networks and interaction) as a description. It is a perspective or a short-listing of the core variables that have emerged out of real world studies and those theories that have so far given theoretical contributions to the current efforts of identifying the content of relationship marketing. These core variables provide a focus for our search for a meaningful content of relationship marketing, unfortunately not a precise one, but one that captures the essence of relationship marketing enough to guide a reader into the subject.

The primacy of the customer

Customer primacy is at the very heart of marketing itself. The concept of customer satisfaction is present in all definitions of marketing but relationship marketing takes customer primacy to even greater levels of importance. Customer profitability is the very basis of relationship marketing insofar as profits are seen not to be derived from products but from customers. It is retained customers that are inevitably the most profitable.

Customer profitability is not the result of a single transaction, nor even the result of multiple transactions. Profitability is the result of sustained transactions, over time, within the framework of a relationship. Thus we can begin to see what is often termed as the 'lifetime value' of a customer, that is how much does a customer spend with a supplier over a period of 10, 20 or 30 years.

The relationship marketing concept has become of even greater significance in the millennium world of electronic commerce through the Internet. Opportunities for customers to defect are now even more available and when these opportunities are combined with a profit break-even point, that only comes about after numerous purchase episodes, then the management of the relationship assumes even greater levels of importance. Whereas the customer has always assumed primacy in the mind of the marketer, it assumes even greater primacy in the mind of the relationship marketer.

The customer primacy issue is not confined to relationships along the supply chain. As more and more businesses subject their various divisions and departments to a competitive process and internal business is no longer deemed to be a right, the concept of internal marketing and internal relationships comes to the forefront of thinking. In reality, supply chain relationships are now often as much internal as external to the firm and, over time, the distinction that is often made between internal and external customers may erode.

Nor is customer primacy confined to the supply chain, internal or external. The management of relationships with the external environment assumes greater significance as the firm's 'publics' – its geographic neighbours, its adversarial pressure groups, its local, national and supra-national governments – become better informed through electronic communication. Thus external relationship management becomes even more complex as the firm's publics become more powerful.

Some key relationship marketing theories

Despite the many definitions of relationship marketing, the current literature referring to relationship marketing frameworks remains fragmented. It is lacking in the convergence of ideas and theory generation. Gummesson (1996a) believes that:

> Much of what is currently written about relationship marketing is theory-less, a stack of fragmented philosophies and observations which do not converge in the direction of an emerging theory. Efforts to contribute to theory are found in Christopher, Payne and Ballantyne (1991) (other work that has contributed to this view include Millman 1993, Christopher, Payne and Ballantyne

1994, Cravens and Piercy 1994, Payne *et al.* 1995 and Peck 1996); in Kotler (1992); and in Hunt and Morgan (1994). (Gummesson 1996a)

In addition to the above authors highlighted by Gummesson, the recent work of Doyle (1995) and Gummesson's (1996a, 1996c) 30 Rs have arguably provided a contribution to relationship marketing theory.

While traditionally marketing has been seen from the perspective of managing relationships with customers, the theories of relationship marketing put forward by Christopher, Payne and Ballantyne (1991, 1994), Kotler (1992), Millman (1993), Hunt and Morgan (1994), Doyle (1995), (Peck 1996) and Gummesson (1996c) view the management of customer relationships as only part of relationship marketing. Their theories take a broader view of marketing. They suggest that, in addition to formulating marketing activities directly at customers, a company should consider a range of parties including suppliers, internal customers, institutions and intermediaries. These theories are thus redefining the scope and nature of relationship marketing.

This section now examines some of the key theories of relationship marketing.

The six markets model

The six markets model consists of six role-related domains or 'markets' each representing dimensions of relationship marketing and involving relationships with a number of parties – organizations or individuals – who can potentially contribute, directly or indirectly, to an organization's marketing effectiveness (Peck 1996). In its first inception, the six markets model of Christopher, Payne and Ballantyne (1991), centred on the 'internal market'. Peck (1996) explains that the six markets model configuration with the internal market as the centre (see Figure 9.1), emphasizes internal marketing's role as an integrator and facilitator, supporting the management of relationships with parties within other 'markets'. However, placing 'internal markets' at the centre of relationship marketing moves the emphasis away from the main issue in marketing – the 'customer'.

This has led to a reshuffling of the six markets model, placing the 'customer' at the centre of the model. Later versions of the model by Millman (1993), Payne *et al.* (1995) and Peck (1996) (Figure 9.3) have all placed customers rather than the focal organization at the centre of the six markets model. In fact, Christopher, Payne and Ballantyne have subsequently incorporated a customer focus into the paperback edition of their 1994 book entitled *Relationship Marketing: Bring Quality, Customer Service and Marketing Together* (see Figure 9.2).

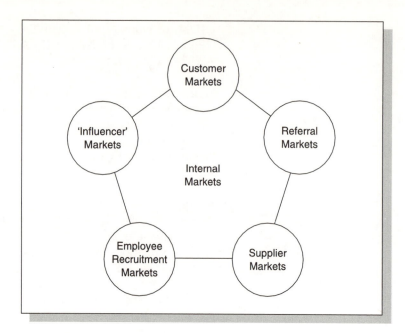

Figure 9.1
Six markets model
(Christopher *et al.* 1991)

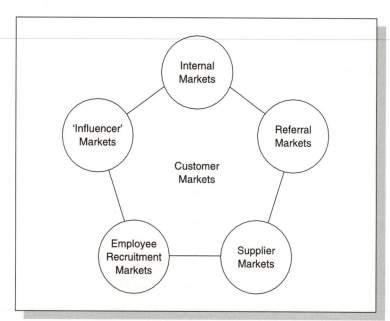

Figure 9.2
Six markets model
(Christopher *et al.* 1994)

Since its reshuffle, the six markets model has been revised again, by Peck (1996). Peck (1996) highlights three aspects of the model that she believes would benefit from further consideration. First, its current treatment of the 'customer market' does not adequately distinguish between intermediaries as customers and end users as customers. Secondly, it is limited in scope. According to Peck (1996) the Christopher, Payne and Ballantyne

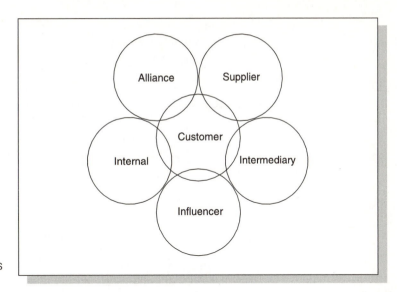

Figure 9.3
A redrafting of the six markets
models (Peck 1996)

(1994) version of the six markets model makes inadequate provision for some of the more sophisticated forms of strategic alliance. That is those alliances that go beyond the realms of 'supplier' relationships – including joint development of projects between competitors and equity sharing joint ventures (Cravens and Piercy 1994).

Thirdly, the model aims to provide a strategic overview of relationship marketing, yet it encompasses tactical rather than strategic elements to 'recruitment' and 'referral' markets. Peck (1996) argues that although these are both important opportunities they should be referred to on a tactical rather than strategic level. She addressed these limitations in her redrafting of the six markets model in Figure 9.3.

It is essential that academics and practitioners realize the purpose of the six markets model. It provides the basis of a simple framework to convey the complex reality of relationship marketing. Unlike Gummesson's (1996c) 30Rs approach, it does not attempt a detailed identification of individual relationship forms or parties. Peck (1996) argued that these are time- and situation-specific. The model aims to provide a strategic overview of relationship marketing's scope, nature and purpose.

Relational exchanges in relationship marketing

Morgan and Hunt (1994) define the scope of relationship marketing through their 'relational exchange' approach to relationship marketing. They make a positive distinction between relational exchange (relationship marketing) which 'traces to previous agreements [and] . . . is longer in duration, reflecting an ongoing process' (Dwyer, Schurr and Oh 1987) in contrast to discrete transactions (transactional marketing) which have a 'distinct beginning, short duration and sharp ending by performance'.

In their conceptualization of relationship marketing, Morgan and Hunt (1994) place the focal firm at the centre of relational exchanges. They identify four categories of relational exchange that occur with the firm. These are supplier, lateral, internal and buyer partnerships. In addition, Morgan and Hunt (1994) have broken down their conceptualization of relationship marketing further, identifying ten specific types of relationships. The above are shown in Figure 9.4.

The core firm and its partnerships

Doyle (1995) suggested a general framework for relationship marketing which integrates what he believes are the key concepts in relationship marketing; core capabilities, strategic intent and value creation. Doyle's model describes four types of networks. The first two types of network relationships are 'supplier partnerships' and 'customer relationships', which together comprise the firm's supply chain. These include relationships with suppliers of raw materials, components, services, final customers and channel

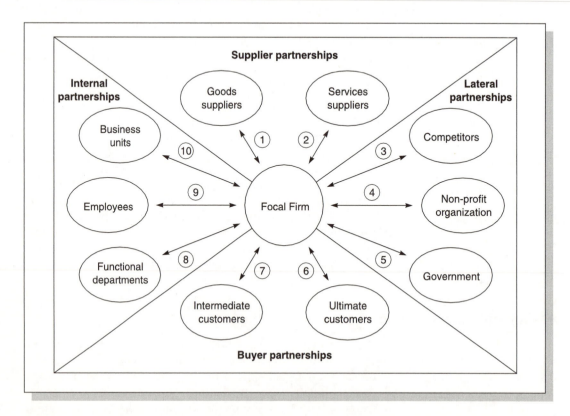

Figure 9.4 The relational exchanges in relationship marketing (Morgan and Hunt 1994)

partners. There are two types of relationships that Doyle (1995) suggests occur outside the supply chain; these are 'external partnerships' and 'internal partnerships'. External partnerships occur with competitors, governments and through strategic alliances. Internal partnerships occur with stakeholders including employees, functional departments and other SBUs within an organization. Doyle's framework is shown in Figure 9.5.

The 30Rs approach to relationship marketing

At the core of Gummesson's (1996a, 1996c, 1996d) 30Rs approach to relationship marketing is the identification of 30 tangible relationships that he claims exist in businesses and other organizations.

Gummesson's (1996c) 30 relationships are grouped into four categories of relationships: classic market relationships; special market relationships; mega relationships; and nano relationships. Gummesson (1996c) describes the first two categories as market relationships. These are relationships between suppliers, customers, competitors and others who operate in the market. He believes that they constitute the basis for marketing; they are externally orientated and apply to the market proper.

Some relationships are concerned with both consumers and other organizations, while others focus on either consumers or

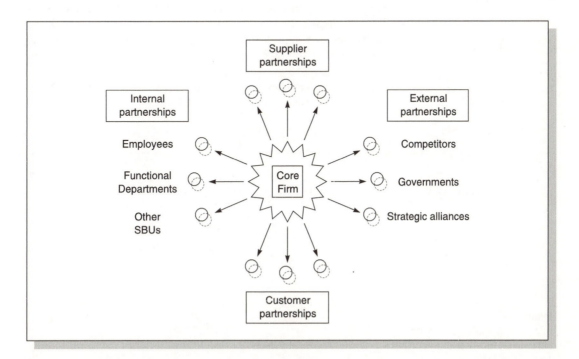

Figure 9.5 The core firm and its partnerships (Doyle 1995)

they are interorganizational relationships. The latter two categories are non-market relationships that indirectly influence the efficiency of the market relationships.

Figure 6 shows how Gummesson's relationships are connected and the dependencies that should be considered when a company organizes its marketing. In Figure 9.6 the special market relationships and classic market relationships constitute the market relationships.

The inner and outer sections represent the non-market relationships. Gummesson (1996c) suggests that the nano relationships are the nucleus and together with mega relationships they constitute the necessary conditions for the market relationships.

The argument for the 30Rs approach is that 'the philosophy of relationship marketing has to be converted into more tangible and systematically defined relationships that can become part of a company's marketing planning' (Gummesson 1993). In this approach, the identification of individual relationship forms is not only based on specific parties, it also takes into account the content, form and conduct of relationships, which makes Gummesson's approach unique. However, Peck (1996) argues that a detailed identification of individual relationship forms or parties is not possible, as they are time- and situation-specific.

A criticism made by Grönroos (1994) regarding the marketing mix is that 'a list never includes all relevant elements, it does not fit every situation and it becomes obsolete'. It is questionable whether Gummesson's list of 30 relationships includes all relevant elements, whether it fits every situation and whether it will become obsolete. In Gummesson's (1996c) defence he does not claim that the 30Rs are the 'final classification'. Welcoming further research, he argues for the identification of more relationships, the condensing of them into fewer classifications, or the finding of more pertinent classifications.

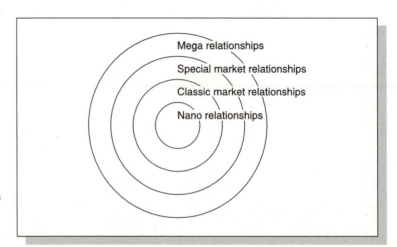

Figure 9.6
Connections and dependencies between Gummesson's 30Rs (adapted from Gummesson 1996c)

In fairness, Gummesson's 30Rs approach provides management with a list of relationship forms that can aid managerial decision-making. It brings forward several forms of relationships to which managers can relate. It must be borne in mind that it is not a definitive list of relationship forms but provides a useful insight into relationship marketing's nature and scope.

A general framework for relationship marketing

The new theories of relationship marketing discussed have some interesting similarities. They acknowledge four main categories of relationships in which a firm is involved. First, a firm has relationships with its customers; called 'customer markets' in Christopher, Payne and Ballantyne's (1994) and Millman's (1993) versions of the six markets model and simply 'customers' in Peck's 1996 version; called 'buyer partnerships' in Hunt and Morgan's work; called 'customer partnerships' in Doyle's framework; is part of the 'immediate environment' in Kotler's (1992) total marketing approach and; is closely related to Gummesson's 'classic market relationships' in the 30Rs approach.

Secondly, a firm has relationships with its suppliers, and again there are similarities between the authors' frameworks. Christopher, Payne and Ballantyne (1994) and Millman's (1993) versions of the six markets model have 'supplier markets', while Peck has 'suppliers'; in both Doyle's and Hunt and Morgan's frameworks they have 'supplier partnerships'; suppliers are part of Kotler's (1992) 'immediate environment' and are closely related to Gummesson's 'special market relationships'. Both customer and supplier relationships are within the supply chain (Doyle 1995) or are what Gummesson (1996c) calls market relationships and Kotler (1992) calls the 'immediate environment'.

Thirdly, a firm has external relationships, relationships with parties outside the supply chain (Doyle 1996) or what Gummesson (1996c) describes as non-market relationships. The six markets model has three categories of external relationships: Christopher, Payne and Ballantyne (1994) and Millman's (1993) have 'influence markets', 'referral markets' and 'employee markets' ('recruitment market' in Millman's case) while Peck differs again with 'alliance', 'influencer' and 'intermediary'. External relationships are part of Kotler's (1992) 'macroenvironment' and called 'lateral partnerships', 'external partnerships' and 'mega relationships' in Hunt and Morgan's (1994), Doyle's (1995) and Gummesson's (1996c) frameworks, respectively.

Finally, a firm has internal relationships, relationships within its employee groups, departments and SBUs. Christopher, Payne and Ballantyne (1994) and Millman (1993) have 'internal markets' while Peck has just 'internal'. Kotler (1992) includes relationships with employees in his approach. Hunt and Morgan (1994) and Doyle (1995) both look at 'internal partnerships' and

Gummesson's (1996) frameworks includes 'nano relationships'. Internal relationships are also outside the supply chain (Doyle 1996) or are what Gummesson (1996c) describes as non-market relationships. Non-market relationships (external and internal) are believed to indirectly influence the supply chain/market relationships (Doyle 1995; Gummesson 1996c; Peck 1996).

This comparison of the frameworks developed by each of the authors above can be summarized in tabular form and this is shown in Table 9.1 below.

It can be seen that the theories and ideas for a relationship marketing framework appear to be converging towards some consensus and thus a general theory of relationship marketing. The four categories of relationships that have emerged from the literature that either directly or indirectly influence the success of a firm are:

- Customer relationships

- Supplier relationships

- External relationships

- Internal relationships.

Transactional versus relationship marketing

The relationship marketing approach is concerned with interaction, collaboration, customer service, processes and quality rather than just simply price, place, promotion and the product. The foci of these two approaches are summarized in Table 9.2 below (adapted from Christopher et al. 1994).

It is in the context of this comparison that the essential link between relationship marketing and quality management can be seen. Strong buyer–supplier relationships are an essential prerequisite for such systems as total quality management and just in time. Quite simply, they would be virtually impossible to operate in a totally transactional approach.

Stages in the relationship

The stages that a relationship passes through can be viewed from two similar perspectives. Ford (1990) suggests that a relationship goes through a series of five stages:

- The pre-relationships stage

- The early stage

- The development stage

- The long term stage

- The final stage.

Author/relationship categories	Christopher, Payne and Ballantyne (1991 and 1994)[a]	Kotler (1992)	Millman (1993)[a]	Morgan and Hunt (1994)	Doyle (1995) 'The firm and its partnerships'	Peck (1996)[a]	Gummesson (1996c) 'The 30Rs approach to relationship marketing'
Customer relationships	Customer markets	Immediate environment	Customer markets	Buyer partnerships	Customer partnerships	Customer	Classic market relationships
Supplier relationships	Supplier markets		Supplier markets	Supplier partnerships	Supplier partnerships	Suppliers	Special market relationships
External relationships	'Influence' markets	Macro-environment	Influence markets	Lateral partnerships	External partnerships	Alliance	Mega relationships
	Referral markets		Referral markets			Influencer	
	Employee (recruitment) markets		Recruitment markets			Intermediary	
Internal relationships	Internal markets		Internal markets	Internal partnerships	Internal partnerships	Internal	Nano relationships

[a]These are all variations of the Christopher, Payne and Ballantyne (1991, 1994) six markets model

Table 9.1 A comparison of approaches/frameworks which define the scope of relationship marketing

Transactional marketing	Relationship marketing
Focus on a single sale	Focus on customer retention
Orientation on product features	Orientation on product benefits
Short time scale	Long time scale
Little emphasis on customer service	High customer service emphasis
Limited customer commitment	High customer commitment
Moderate customer contact	High customer contact
Quality is primarily the concern of production	Quality the concern of all
Orders tend to be placed on a volume basis	Orders tend to be placed on a time basis

Source: Adapted from Christopher *et al.* 1994

Table 9.2 Transactional versus relationship marketing

As the relationship passes from the initial stages of 'courtship' to the final stage of 'institutionalization', the experience of the parties increases along with levels of trust, commitment and promise. There is a parallel reduction in the levels of uncertainty, 'distance' in terms of social, geographical, time and technological factors.

A similar perspective on the stages of the relationship is provided by Payne (2000) with his 'relationship ladder'. This is essentially a series of six stages of customer loyalty as follows:

- Prospect

- Customer

- Client

- Supporter

- Advocate

- Partner.

The early stages have an emphasis on new customers, e.g. customer *catching*, whereas the later stages emphasize the development and enhancement of relationships, e.g. customer *keeping*.

Conclusion

This chapter has traced the development of what is known as relationship marketing and how it challenges the previously almost unassailable four Ps view of marketing developed since the 1950s. Relationships between the firm, its suppliers (internal and external) and its public are becoming increasingly less adversarial as *all* parties derive benefits. It is the mutual benefit of the parties that provide the environment for relationships to flourish. All parties increasingly become mutually *inter*dependent as exit barriers induce costs and diseconomies. The more complex the relationships then the more complex they are to disentangle.

As the importance of relationship marketing and relationship management becomes paramount with the concept of lifetime value becoming more and more understood, it is becoming clear that relationship marketing, which is increasingly developing its own theoretical constructs, is here to stay and will eventually supersede many of the historical theories of the marketing concept.

Nevertheless, relationship marketing is founded on the very bedrock of marketing itself – namely the primacy of the customer. Perhaps in traditional marketing the *customer is king*: in relationship marketing *the customer is God.*

The following (fictional) case study of 'Manse Foods' emphasizes the importance of establishing and developing sound relationships with the customer base.

Case study: Manse Foods plc

Manse Foods plc is a large dairy products division of a major European food processing company. Manse's parent company Cowlersley Brands plc is domiciled in the UK where it is listed on the UK stock exchange. Cowlersley Brands has a worldwide turnover in excess of £600 million with the UK and Central and Western Europe accounting for some 73% of turnover. Manse, with a turnover of some £200 million, is a major player in the dairy products market producing products in various forms for sale to food processors for use in both consumer and catering market dairy products.

The vast majority of Manse's assets are based in Europe with processing plants in the UK, France, Germany, Spain, Italy, Austria, Denmark, Finland and the Netherlands. In addition it operates in a series of joint ventures with local dairy foods processors in the USA, Canada, Brazil and South Africa. Manse has customer relationships in most Central and Western European countries and it services its markets from the countries listed above. For example, Portugal is serviced from Spain, Czech Republic, Slovakia and Hungary from Austria, Poland from Germany, Norway from Denmark and so on.

The operations of Manse Foods are highly integrated and controlled in most cases from a large corporate headquarters in the UK.

Manse operates on a very autonomous basis from its parent company.

Manse Foods believes that focusing on customer needs is a crucial part of its business so much so that it is a matter of policy to forge stronger and closer relationships. Manse has been monitoring its interaction with its customers as part of the company's customer process improvement scheme and it classifies its customers into three types namely:

- key customers

- regular customers

- spot customers.

Key customers are the most important, followed by regular customers, with spot customers (typically serviced by telesales) having the least importance. Such a classification illustrates a continuum between relationship marketing for the key customers and transactional marketing for the spot customers, the regular customers being positioned as some kind of hybrid of the two approaches. All key customers for Europe are dealt with from the corporate headquarters in the UK. Outside of Europe all customers are dealt with by the joint venture companies in various parts of the world.

The exception to this is where there is a global customer relationship, that crosses all international boundaries, and thus, those customers are effectively serviced from the UK corporate headquarters for strategic customer decisions.

Regular customers are serviced either from the UK headquarters or from the operating division in each of the European countries where Manse operates. Spot customers are serviced locally in each European country, often through a national telesales operation.

The main characteristics of each of these types is shown in Figure 9.7.

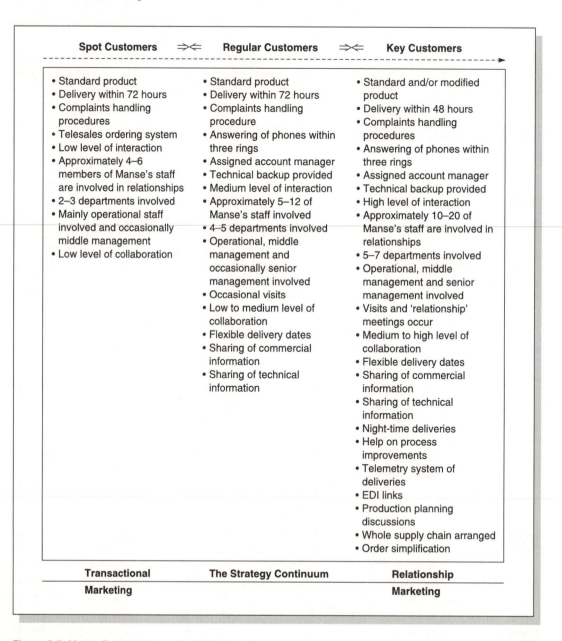

Spot Customers ⇒⇐	Regular Customers ⇒⇐	Key Customers
• Standard product	• Standard product	• Standard and/or modified product
• Delivery within 72 hours	• Delivery within 72 hours	• Delivery within 48 hours
• Complaints handling procedures	• Complaints handling procedure	• Complaints handling procedures
• Telesales ordering system	• Answering of phones within three rings	• Answering of phones within three rings
• Low level of interaction	• Assigned account manager	• Assigned account manager
• Approximately 4–6 members of Manse's staff are involved in relationships	• Technical backup provided	• Technical backup provided
• 2–3 departments involved	• Medium level of interaction	• High level of interaction
• Mainly operational staff involved and occasionally middle management	• Approximately 5–12 of Manse's staff involved	• Approximately 10–20 of Manse's staff are involved in relationships
• Low level of collaboration	• 4–5 departments involved	• 5–7 departments involved
	• Operational, middle management and occasionally senior management involved	• Operational, middle management and senior management involved
	• Occasional visits	• Visits and 'relationship' meetings occur
	• Low to medium level of collaboration	• Medium to high level of collaboration
	• Flexible delivery dates	• Flexible delivery dates
	• Sharing of commercial information	• Sharing of commercial information
	• Sharing of technical information	• Sharing of technical information
		• Night-time deliveries
		• Help on process improvements
		• Telemetry system of deliveries
		• EDI links
		• Production planning discussions
		• Whole supply chain arranged
		• Order simplification

Transactional	The Strategy Continuum	Relationship
Marketing		Marketing

Figure 9.7 Manse Foods' three main customer types

To illustrate the differences in the interaction between departments and customers, Figures 9.8 to 9.10 show the mapping out of the relationships according to the customer type in Figure 9.7 with key customers being involved in the highest levels of interaction and spot customers involved in the lowest.

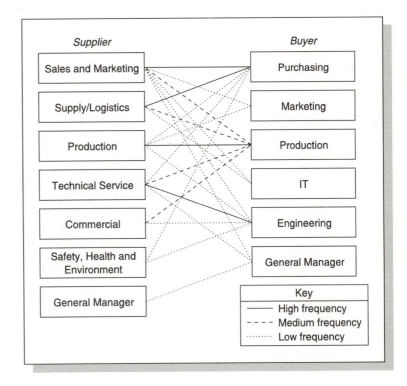

Figure 9.8
Buyer–supplier interaction. Manse Foods and Customer One (a key customer accounting for £24m of Manse's sales)

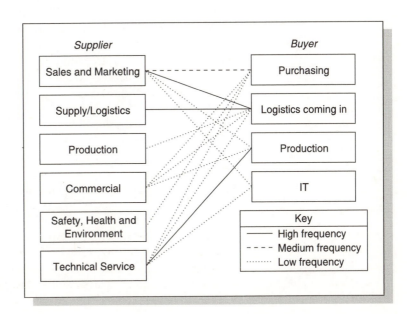

Figure 9.9 Customer Two: regular customer accounting for £1m of Manse's sales

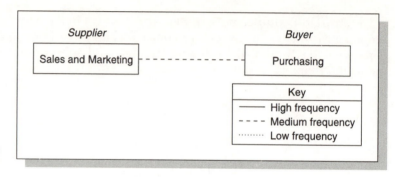

Figure 9.10
Telesales customer accounting
for £8–30K of Manse's sales

References

Borden, N.H. (1964) The concept of the marketing mix. *Journal of Advertising Research*, June, pp. 2–7.

Carratu, V. (1987) Commercial counterfeiting. In J. Murphy (eds), *Branding: A Key Marketing Tool*. London: Macmillan.

Christopher M., Payne A. and Ballantyne D. (1991) *Relationship Marketing*. Oxford: Butterworth–Heinemann.

Christopher M., Payne A. and Ballantyne D. (1994) *Relationship Marketing*. Oxford: Butterworth–Heinemann.

Cravens D.W. and Piercy N.F. (1994) Relationships marketing and collaborative networks in service organizations. *International Journal of Service Industry Management*, 5 (5), pp. 39–53.

Doyle, P. (1995) Marketing in the New Millennium. *European Journal of Marketing*, 29 (13), pp. 23–41.

Dwyer F.R., Schurr P.H. and Oh S. (1987) Developing buyer–seller relationships. *Journal of Marketing*, 51 (April), pp. 11–27.

Ford D.F. (1990) *Understanding Business Markets: Interaction, Relationship and Networks, for the Industrial Marketing and Purchasing Group*. London: Dryden Press.

Grönroos C. (1989) Defining marketing: a market-orientated approach. *Journal of Marketing*, 23 (1), pp. 52–60.

Grönroos C. (1990) *Service Management and Marketing. Managing the Moments of Truth in Service Competition*. Lexington, MA: Free Press/Lexington Books.

Grönroos C. (1991) The marketing strategy continuum: towards a marketing concept for the 1990s. *Management Decision*, 29 (1), pp. 7–13.

Grönroos C. (1994) From marketing mix to relationship marketing: towards a paradigm shift in marketing. *Asia-Australia Marketing Journal*, 2 (1).

Grönroos C. (1996) Relationship marketing: strategic and tactical implications. *Management Decision*, 34 (3), pp. 5–14.

Gummesson E. (1987) The new marketing: developing long term interactive relationships. *Long Range Planning*, 20 (4), pp. 10–20.

Gummesson, E. (1993) *Quality Management in Service Organizations*. New York: International Service Quality Association (ISQA) and St John's University, p. 233–4.

Gummesson E. (1996a) Why relationship marketing is a paradigm shift: some conclusion from the 30R approach. Presented at the 1st Management and Decision Internet Conference on Relationship Marketing, MCB Publishing.

Gummesson E. (1996b) Comments and Discussion. 1st Management and Decision Internet Conference on Relationship Marketing, MCB Publishing.

Gummesson E. (1996c) Relationship marketing: from 4Ps to 30Rs. Preliminary translation from the English adaptation of *Relationsmarknadsföring: Från 4P till 30R*, Malmö: Liber-Hermods, first published in Swedish in June 1995.

Gummesson E. (1996d) Relationship marketing and imaginary organizations: a synthesis. *European Journal of Marketing*, 30 (2), p. 31–44.

McGarry E.D. (1950) Some functions of marketing reconsidered. In Coc R. and Alderson W. (eds), *Theory of Marketing*, Homewood, IL: Richard D. Irwin, pp. 263–79.

Millman, A.F. (1993) The emerging concept of relationship marketing. Proceedings from the 9th Annual IMP Conference, Bath, 23–25 September.

Morgan R.D. and Hunt S.D. (1994) The commitment–trust theory of relationship marketing. *Journal of Marketing*, 58 (July), pp. 20–38.

Hunt S.D. and Morgan R.M. (1994) Relationship marketing in the era of network competition. *Marketing Management*, 5 (5), pp. 18–28.

Kotler P. (1992) It's time for total marketing. *Business Week*, Advance Executive Brief, vol. 2.

Payne A., Christopher M., Clark M. and Peck H. (eds) (1995) *Relationship Marketing for Competitive Advantage: Winning and Keeping Customers*. Oxford: Butterworth–Heinemann.

Payne A. (2000) Customer retention. In Cranfield School of Management, *Marketing Management: A Relationship Marketing Perspective*. London: Macmillan.

Peck H. (1996) Towards a framework for relationship marketing – the six markets model revisited and revised. Marketing Education Group Conference (MEG), University of Strathclyde, 8–12 July.

Sheth J.N and Parvatiyar A. (1995) The evolution of relationship marketing. *International Business Review*, 4 (4), pp. 397–418.

Activities

1. Select a product or service that you regularly purchase, i.e. groceries, takeaway meals, petrol, drinks in a pub. Make a calculation of your annual spend on these products or services and for how many years you are likely to continue this purchasing pattern. What then is the 'lifetime value' of your custom with your supplier of these goods or services?

2. Select an organization and its major supplier. How many different relationships do you think you can identify in the overall buyer–supplier relationship. Identify those that are the strongest and those that are the weakest.

3. Select an organization and map out all the relationships that it has with its various 'publics'. How can the organization try to retain a positive relationship with those publics?

Questions

1. Take any of the theories of relationship marketing in this chapter. Examine how this theory might work in an organization of your choice.

2. Discuss the key differences between transactional and relationship marketing in any company of your choice.

3. How do the various stages in a buyer-supplier relationship of your choice evolve? State those features of the relationship that increase and decrease as the relationship develops.

Human resource management in the extended organization

Lynette Harris

Key objectives

- To develop an understanding of alternative approaches to strategic human resource management

- To examine the dominance of flexibility in organizational human resourcing strategies as

    (a) a means of managing in a context of uncertainty, and

    (b) the pursuit of a dual human resourcing strategy through externalizing functions and services

- To explore issues of employee commitment, development and rewarding employee contribution in supply chains

- To consider the impact of external influences, such as the political and economic context of the organization and, the degree of regulation on human resourcing practices

- To examine the factors that can influence human resourcing strategies in supply chain situations

Introduction

Of all organizational strategies human resource management is the most likely to be characterized by tensions and paradoxes in its application. This can be particularly evident in organizational initiatives designed to obtain greater flexibility through the use of external sources to supply services or goods, rather, than provide these through a directly employed workforce. What may make good commercial sense frequently challenges contemporary management thinking. For example, an employer engaged in a supply relationship can be driven more by customer demands to keep costs down than the need to develop positive employment relationships through a proper recognition and reward of employee contribution.

The recession of the early 1980s led to pressures to reduce overheads and a closer examination of personnel management's specialist contribution to the business (Guest 1982; Tyson and Fell 1986). The concept of human resource management (HRM), originating in the United States (Beer *et al.* 1984), claimed to offer an approach to the employment relationship that was radically different from traditional personnel management. It is claimed that the distinction between traditional personnel management and HRM to lay in the latter's strategic intent. Fundamental to the new thinking was the emphasis on a greater integration of human resource policies with wider business objectives and between different human resourcing practices.

Due to a climate of economic uncertainty and increasing competition, the trend since the 1980s has been for HR policies to focus on adaptability and responsiveness to change rather than stability and continuity (Blyton and Turnbull 1992). This shifted the focus away from the large internal labour markets that had developed within organizations, which offered long term job security with prospects for career advancement to a directly employed workforce. To manage this uncertainty employers increasingly aimed for lean and responsive organizational forms (Kinnie *et al.* 1999), through a variety of employment contracts, other than full-time permanent positions or, by using alternative external sources for supplying services.

Encouraged by a management philosophy of 'getting back to basics', identified as an essential ingredient by Peters and Waterman for excellence in company performance (1982), many organizations reviewed their activities with the aim of returning to their core competencies. This supported an increased use of contracting out arrangements leading to the growth of the 'extended organization', which Colling observes (2000) has been one of the most significant and enduring outcomes of the shift in balance to the dominance of the market economy in the 1980s. Such extended organizational relationships focus attention on human resourcing practices in terms of their ability to provide the 'skills and behavioural flexibility necessary to support tighter integration' (Scarborough 1999).

This chapter will explore the operational context for strategic human resource management and identify some of challenges and constraints that exist in the development of positive and progressive HR practices in supply chain management.

Alternative approaches to human resource management

David Guest in a series of influential articles (1987, 1989, 1991) defined HRM essentially as having four key policy aims. These were identified as its strategic integration with business objectives, high quality, high employee commitment and flexibility. In the 1980s, political, technological and demographic changes in the operating environment led to strategic human resourcing responses being frequently focused on the last of these four goals – increased flexibility. The drivers for more flexible approaches to the structure of work have stemmed from:

- Economic pressures in an increasingly competitive and volatile market.

- Uncertainty about demand, leading to uncertainty about labour requirements.

- The demands of new technologies.

- A changing work force and new working patterns.

The difficulty in any analysis of flexibility, however, lies in identifying exactly what we mean by it. Atkinson's (1985) proposed model of the 'flexible firm' depicts three sorts of flexibility to meet varying levels of demand. These are *functional flexibility*, through developing and utilizing the skills of the core workforce, *numerical flexibility*, achieved by adjusting the numbers of the directly employed, and, *financial flexibility*, also known as distancing, based on paying a fee rather than a wage through arrangements such as outsourcing and the use of subcontracting. A fourth form of flexibility, not present in Atkinson's model, is *'temporal' flexibility*, which is concerned with *when* work is carried out, evident in the growth of alternative shift patterns and annual hours contracts designed to accommodate 'peaks and troughs' in demand.

As already identified, the use of sub-contracting, strategic outsourcing, supply chain regimes and joint ventures has proliferated in recent years (Mabey *et al.* 1998), in both the UK's private and public sector. The 1998 Workplace Employee Relations Survey (WERS) reported that 90% of employers contract out one or more services and a quarter of all employers reported a growing use of sub-contracting (Cully *et al.* 1998). The type of contractual relationship that is adopted will influence approaches to employment practices (Felstead 1993). Colling (2000) suggests that at one end of the spectrum is an emphasis on competition between providers and a scrutiny of contractual terms which will tend to lead to low trust and distanced relationships, at the other are 'engaged' relationships where greater security is built into the contract. For Beaumont *et al.* (1996) such relationships are likely to be characterized by some element of mutual dependency with opportunities to take a longer term approach to human resourcing considerations (for further discussion see section on employee commitment).

The extremes of these two approaches highlight one of the tensions that exist within human resource management, described by Storey (1992) as the 'hard and soft versions' of HRM. The stereotype of the 'hard' or instrumental approach is of a rational outcome model driven by a business strategy of obtaining competitive advantage through labour cost minimization. In contrast the 'soft' or humanistic approach embraces the concept of mutuality and is based on developing reciprocal relationships through the strategic management of people, but not necessarily at their expense. Inherent in this second approach is the development of 'a highly committed and capable workforce, using an integrated array of cultural, structural and personnel techniques' (Storey 1995). This requires 'a distinctive approach to human resource management' described by Wood and Albanese (1995) as 'high commitment management' with the following basic characteristics:

- all managers are concerned with human resourcing issues;

- human resourcing issues are central in all strategic decision making;

- a strong culture which encourages employees to be highly committed to the organization and to continuous improvement;

- a focus on high trust, team working and willing co-operation;

- an emphasis on employee development and continually developing skills to achieve both personal growth and task flexibility.

(Adapted from Watson 1999.)

In practice, the evidence is that differences in management style and approaches to human resourcing between one organization and another are shaped by such factors as size, the nature and availability of labour, its employee relations' traditions and the presence, or otherwise, of a trade union (Gratton *et al.*1999). It will be argued that in a supply chain these internal differences become even more significant. The impact of the prevailing external business environment on the nature and growth of operational networks, and their employment practices, should not be overlooked or underestimated.

HRM and its external context

The economic, political and social environment are a major influence on the way outsourcing relationships are approached and developed. The change of direction in the UK's political and regulatory framework since 1997 will arguably create a climate more conducive to the development of positive approaches to HR issues in supply chain relationships than previously existed.

The regulatory framework

HR practices are heavily influenced by levels of employment regulation (Harris 1999) and we are currently experiencing a shift to increased employment rights. Until recently UK businesses enjoyed relative freedoms in their 'hiring and firing' practices compared to their European counterparts (Grubb and Wells 1993). Employers, regardless of the size of their workforce, are having to re-examine their existing employment processes to take account of changes in employment law. There continues to be an 'incoming tide' (Ewing 1993) of provisions from EC law which has advanced the employment protection legislation of the 1970s and is supported by the present government's commitment to the provision of minimum employment standards (Gennard 1998).

Since October 1998 there has been legislation to regulate working hours, the introduction of a national minimum wage and the Employment Relations Act 1999 (ERA), which introduced a wide range of new individual and collective rights. More legislation is on its way and, from October 2000, UK courts and tribunals must take into account decisions of the European Court of Human Rights or the Commission of Human Rights. Other substantial changes are taking place which will have an impact on HR standards and practices. For example, the replacement of compulsory competitive tendering by 'Best Value' in local government will broaden measures of effectiveness away from just measuring the costs of providing a service.

If UK employers operating in a deregulated labour market demonstrated little innovation in their use of flexible working practices, (Brewster 1998) increased levels of employment law could be the catalyst for more imaginative approaches to work force flexibility. The dominance of 'numerical flexibility' as a cost minimization strategy for coping with uncertainty becomes less attractive when it is more difficult and potentially expensive to dismiss employees. One possible outcome is a greater value being placed on functional flexibility, leading to longer term human resourcing strategies, concerned with developing the skills of the existing workforce. Imposing minimum standards through the law is, however, only part of the solution in developing progressive HR standards. Imposing statutory requirements can all too easily result in compliance rather than real commitment with the minimum becoming the norm.

The legal framework needs to be actively supported by employer led initiatives such as the Race for Equality Campaign described in the following illustration.

Case study – setting standards for equality of opportunity

The Chair of the Better Regulation Task Force's anti-discrimination board has reported that the Race for Opportunity (RfO) campaign is the least supported of the Business in the Community initiatives. The aim of the RfO is to develop more proactive measures which would include the creation of an equal opportunities kite mark for firms supply chains, a change in IIP requirements and more proactive encouragement from the Treasury.

Four High Street banks and six other large employers including British Telecom (BT), Littlewoods, Sainsbury and Granada have recently announced programmes to tackle racism under the RfO banner. These embrace community relations initiatives, secondments and senior management attitude training. At the launch of these initiatives the Chairman of the Granada Group issued a strong warning against corporate back slapping as only 140 firms had so far signed up for the campaign which just wasn't enough. He observed that 'for many employers tackling discrimination was a bit like going on a diet – they are all very keen to start but not this week.'

(*Source:* News and Analysis, *People Management*, 16 September 1999)

Changes in employment

Greater innovation in approaches to human resourcing will also be driven by changes in the nature of work, the composition of the workforce, new patterns of participation and the ongoing shift of jobs from the manufacturing to the service sector. The service sector now provides 75% of all jobs in the UK compared to less than 17% in manufacturing.

The sector is also the second largest employer of female labour, with women making up 54% of its workforce (LMST 2000). This gender balance and the prevalence of part time working is accompanied by the largest proportion of workplaces with low pay and some of the lowest reported levels of productivity (Cully *et al.* 1998). It was anticipated that the introduction of the minimum wage in April 1999 would have the greatest impact on hotel and catering establishments and this was borne out by recent research undertaken by the author into the impact of employment regulation on SMEs. In an analysis of the nature of enquiries of 200 firms to an ACAS public enquiry point in June 1999, 90% enquiries concerning the minimum wage came from firms employing between 25 to 49 employees in the hotel and catering industry (Harris 2000).

Suppliers to larger companies are frequently smaller companies who have become increasingly important as a source of employment opportunities in the UK (Storey 1994). Firms employing 50 employees or less now provide 45% of non-government employment (LMQR 1999). The approach to human resource management in these SMEs tends to be very different from those of their larger customers. Research evidence indicates that SMEs are characterized by their preference for informality (Matlay 1999) and a 'reactive' model (Lane 1994) in dealing with employment issues. It is argued that the sustainability of this approach is challenged by the increase in regulation, but smaller firms face particular challenges in interpreting and applying employment legislation without internal HR expertise.

In conclusion, across the private and public sector, the extended organization looks set to increase but it is argued that a changing regulatory framework will reinforce the importance of seeking the means of securing longer term employee capability and commitment in supplier arrangements.

The quest for employee commitment

Promoting the link between organizational performance and employee commitment is a key concept in the literature on human resource management (Walton 1985; Guest 1987). At the heart of strategic HRM is the notion that to be successful there must be a climate where employees can positively identify with the goals of the organization.

Wood's study (1995) of employment practices suggests that a distinction can be made between the commitment and the performance management approach. The first of these focuses on progression, training and development and internal forms of flexibility which Hendry observes (1995) is similar to the traditional 'internal labour market', although lower on job security. By comparison, the performance management approach is dominated by the concept of increasing commitment bought through financial incentives linked to measurable outcomes and an emphasis on achieving high performance tied into the strategic objectives of the organization.

There is frequently a visible lack of congruence between employment practices, which use the language of development, yet apply hard measures when it comes to the allocation of rewards. This can erode rather than improve levels of commitment. In supply chain relationships where customer demands limit suppliers' internal organizational autonomy, the problems of meeting the expectations of the work force can be particularly acute. This is illustrated in the following, fictional, case study of a pay dispute at one large food distribution company.

Case study – the pay dispute at Friesco TGM Ltd

Friesco TGM Ltd is part of the TGM Group and has provided a distribution service for chilled and ambient food to a very large and well respected food retailer, Gilbertsons, for over 20 years. It employs some 1400 people, mainly as drivers, warehouse operatives and operational administration. The T&GWU has full recognition rights with Friesco and there is a joint agreement on pay and conditions covering all hourly paid and salaried staff. Industrial relations within the company had traditionally been very good with highly co-operative working relationships between management and employees. Eighteen months ago the Friesco contract with Gilbertsons changed from a cost plus management fee arrangement to a fixed price arrangement which is periodically renegotiated. Due to increasing competition in food retailing the customer has become increasingly concerned with seeking value for money and has unfavourably compared its distribution costs with those of its major competitors. As a result the present 3-year contract with Gilbertsons was agreed on the basis that Friesco's distribution costs would be cut by 10% for every pound of sales by the end of the contract period.

The new contract had considerable implications for staffing levels and working arrangements at Friesco which resulted in a series of cost cutting initiatives and discussions on new methods of working with the trade union since the new contract was introduced. As well as reaching a new agreement on seven day work and reducing drivers' overtime payments, two depots had been closed with redundancies among managerial and support staff, although most drivers had been transferred to work from other, albeit less convenient, depots. On the grounds of the membership's considerable co-operation over changes to working practices, the union submitted a claim for a substantial pay increase from 1 April. In response the company offered a 1.5% increase in basic pay plus a lump sum of £100 to all employees who achieved the required changes for the new seven day working patterns.

The company stressed that its inability to pay more made it impossible to increase this pay offer so it was put to a ballot and rejected by 95% of the workforce. The disagreement between the parties was further inflamed by recent press reports over the level of certain executive pay remuneration packages which had included the Chief Executive of TGM Ltd and had drawn adverse comment from the Director of the Confederation of British Industry (CBI).

The union's view was that it was wrong that employees should be urged to demonstrate restraint and bear the brunt of any cost cutting exercise if company directors were not leading by example.

The company's case was that insufficient progress had been made on achieving the necessary savings, if they were to stand a chance of retaining the Gilbertsons contract, without which the future existence of Friesco was in jeopardy. Any distribution company was by its nature labour intensive and at Friesco labour costs amounted to 75% of its overall operating costs. It was, therefore, critical that any wage award was self-financing through improved productivity. Distribution and food retailing were extremely competitive and their current contract with Gilbertsons would be one that that Friesco's competitors would be very pleased to gain.

The union's reaction was to inform the company that feelings among the workforce were running so high that their intention was to ballot the workforce over taking industrial action in the form of either an overtime ban or strike action.

A useful exercise would be the examination of the key issues raised by this dispute and the identification of alternative solutions to the problems that the company and the union, are facing.

This case study illustrates the danger that suppliers can face 'the worst of all worlds' – tied into contractual performance indicators which not only limit organizational freedoms but also reinforce a focus on short term goals. This has implications for the nature of the psychological contract that exist between employer and employee. The growing literature on the psychological contract suggests that there are broadly two types of contracts (Rousseau 1996). These can be summarized as:

- relational contracts that are built on long term relationships, based on an implicit mutual commitment, in which Herriot and Pemberton (1996, p. 762) observe 'perceptions of equity and honour' become more pronounced over time;

- transactional contracts based on a purely instrumental exchange with a focus on outcomes and distributive justice.

Kessler and Undy (1996) suggest that in the process of creating 'leaner organizations' there are three particular areas of concern – the loss of jobs for life, a breakdown in degrees of loyalty from employees, due to a loss of trust in the employer's commitment to honour their side of the bargain, and a lack of employee involvement. Flatter structures erode the potential for career progression which leads to employees adjusting their expectations of a long term organizational future. This visible lack of a longer term investment in the workforce can force employees into a more transactional psychological contract with their employers.

Kinnie *et al.* (1999, p. 223) observes how the management of the employment relationship in supply firms is influenced by the actions of customers and competitors. Three key pressures are identified of 'time compression, uncertainty and continuous change'. Competing for orders and raised customer expectations can result in constant change. The organizational response to these external pressures is to reduce costs often at the expense of the terms and conditions offered to the workforce.

Figure 10.1 illustrates how this ongoing quest for 'competitive flexibility' (Grahl and Teague 1992) through controlling and reducing labour costs can result in eroding employee trust and commitment and the positive aspects of the psychological contract between employer and employee.

The alternative approach is one that Grahl and Teague identify as 'constructive flexibility', where such conflict is reduced by identifying areas of mutual benefit to increase trust and collaboration. The aim is to develop closer working to reduce the adverse consequences of maximizing external competition, on both employers and employees, at the receiving end of the process. In human resourcing terms this can involve a radical rethink of approaches to recruitment and selection, training and development, rewards and employee involvement and participation.

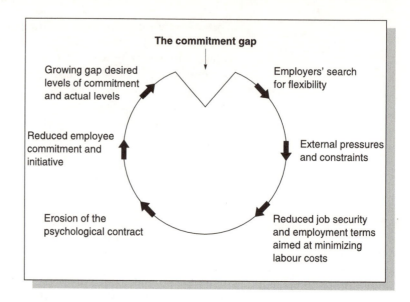

The commitment gap

Growing gap desired
levels of commitment
and actual levels

Employers' search
for flexibility

Reduced employee
commitment and
initiative

External pressures
and constraints

Erosion of the
psychological contract

Reduced job security
and employment terms
aimed at minimizing
labour costs

Figure 10.1
Competitive flexibility,
its impact on employee
commitment (Beaver and
Harris 1996)

To summarize, there are potentially real gains to be made from a highly committed workforce but to realize these individuals have to perceive that an acceptable level of reciprocity exists in the employment relationship.

Developing and sharing knowledge

The evidence in much of the literature on supplier firms, in supply chain is that the transfer of expertise is a 'one directional' process with the competences of smaller firms being absorbed by more powerful customers (Turnbull 1991; Harland 1996). Hunter *et al.* (1996) provide a more positive perspective suggesting that there could be a significant transfer of knowledge from buyer to supplier though development activities and concerns for quality and continuous improvement across the business. This is illustrated in the following example of practice at Mars Four Square division.

Case study – Mars Four Square division: mutuality in action

The Four Square division of Mars is a supplier of drinks systems. At Four Square there is a seven-step programme to develop all suppliers to be suppliers of excellence. Relevant copies of the training programme are available on the range of drinks products to suppliers with personal notes to make people aware of the formal training courses that area available. Drink Systems distributor staff are not only given technical training in servicing, fault finding and cleaning but also a lot of sales and customer care training. This is done intensively initially and then through refresher up-date courses. Distributors are also trained to help clients and consumers in the use of the product (either on Four Square's or the client's premises) and such training is included in the price of the contract from the outset. Detailed manuals, technical bulletins and newsletters supplement face to face events. Four Square also benefit by learning new techniques from their suppliers.

(*Source: People Management* September 1992, p. 29)

It is a logical step for total quality management to be applied through the extended organization and some of the issues that arise when these concerns are not addressed in supply relationship are described in the following, fictional, case study.

Case study: outsourcing the delivery service at Burneys Breweries

Burneys is a major UK brewing company that decided to outsource its beer deliveries to public houses in 1997, the main objective being to cut core business costs. The delivery service had become expensive to operate, the draymen's pay included extensive plus payments, negotiated by the union over the years, and, it was felt that this part of the company's operations could be provided, more effectively, by using an outside service provider. The majority of Burney's 280 draymen received a redundancy payment and only a small minority joined Team Services, the company that Burneys had contracted to provide their delivery service. Team Services was non-unionized, paid lower rates of pay and less in premium payments, for overtime working, than the draymen had experienced working for Burneys. Many of Burney's draymen had long service and the redundancy packages that were offered to them were not unattractive.

After a few months into the new operation Burneys had received a significant number of complaints about the new delivery service. These consisted of late deliveries, damage done to beer kegs being delivered and collected and a lower level of service generally than they had been used to when Burneys employed its own draymen. Initially these were felt to be 'teething troubles' and that the service would settle down but they persisted. Burneys spent considerable amounts of time during the 20 months of the new delivery arrangements resolving individual complaints from their customers and trying to sort out the problems with Team Services. The new delivery teams were less experienced, did not know the publicans personally or have the same loyalty to the brewery that the old draymen had. Difficulties that used to be resolved on the spot were not dealt with which added to the level of formal complaints and reported customer dissatisfaction.

The new service proved cheaper to provide and overheads had been significantly reduced, goodwill was being lost but the company's image as a first class provider to its customers was being tarnished. It was feared that certain publicans might turn to other brands. There was also a concern that Team Services were cost cutting by operating with reduced numbers on the delivery teams than the 260 employees originally proposed. As the decision to outsource the delivery service was not going to be reversed the level of service had to be dramatically improved. The problem was how to ensure the services provided by Team Services reached the standards required by Burneys.

The case study is useful in explaining key human resource issues and opens the debate about what steps Burneys could take to improve the quality of services provided by Team Services. It also raises the question of how these problems could have been avoided in the first instance.

If the core business is be properly supported new organizational forms require line management and HR specialists to recognize that training, coaching, mentoring and counselling activities have to be extended to all parties in the supply chain. Any investment in training does, however, raise questions of who should bear the costs and whether the investment will be worthwhile in terms of the potential for increased profitability. Rothwell (1992) suggests that where the benefits are mutual, for example through increased sales for the manufacturer and the retailer, then the costs should be shared. This requires close collaboration to initiate and maintain these joint activities. This may be driven by the type of issues raised in the case study or simply by legislation such as the manufacturers of food processing equipment ensuring that suppliers and retail franchises are fully conversant with food hygiene regulations.

Approaches to training and development could learn from the type of pioneering initiative recently announced by the Web, Ford, GM and Daimler Chrysler who are linking their suppliers and their products into a vast single Internet based procurement system. A company intranet or the Internet offers exciting new opportunities in training delivery and providing advice to employees across supply chains which can offer far greater flexibility and speed of access than more traditional methods.

There is insufficient scope within this chapter to discuss the idea of the learning organization which has flourished in recent years as a means of sustaining competitive advantage through human resourcing policies which promote continuous learning, teamwork, employee participation and flexibility (Edmundson and Moingeon 1996). As a concept though it has much to offer the stakeholders in supply chain relationships in terms of harnessing individual learning to support new systems for providing goods and services. It also provides real opportunities for proactive HR specialists to contribute to creative forms of development in the new organizational structures.

Conclusions

All the indications are that outsourcing will increase but to date the human resourcing complexities of supply chain management have received less attention than other aspects such as procurement and demand planning. The development of new organizational forms require HR strategies which address issues of flexibility, customer orientation, team working and knowledge management across a range of supply relationships (IPD 1998, p. 16).

For managers operating through supply relationships the transition from managing their own employees to managing through contracts is not an easy one and insufficient attention has been paid to their development needs to enable them to carry out their new role effectively. The HR specialist has much to offer in developing new approaches to employee resourcing issues in the distanced organization, although it is suggested that as outsourcing develops it is likely to be mirrored by similar changes in the provision of HR services. HR professionals will increasingly be employed themselves by outsourced providers advising a range of different account holders (McLuhan 2000, p. 33).

Intense competitive pressures on suppliers in extended organizational structures cannot only lead to increased job insecurity, the intensification of work and adversely effects levels of commitment but, also make it difficult for employers to make a credible contribution to safeguarding employee health and well-being (Burchell *et al.* 1999). One conclusion is that this can only be resolved through establishing a regulatory framework setting minimum standards and by specifying HR standards in contractual agreements, to avoid destructive forms of competition achieved at the expense of the workforce. It is argued that such measures alone will not provide a solution. They need to be supported by employer led initiatives 'championing' new and more creative human resourcing strategies which involve all the parties concerned in supply chain relationships.

References

Atkinson J. (1985) Flexibility: planning for an uncertain future. *Manpower Policy and Practice*, 1, Summer.

Beaver G. and Harris L. (1996) The hidden price of the disposable workforce. *Journal of Professional HRM*, 2, pp. 3–8.

Beaumont P., Hunter L. and Sinclair D.(1996) Customer–supplier relations and the diffusion of employee relations changes. *Employee Relations*, 18 (1), pp. 9–19.

Beer M., Spector B., Lawrence P., Mills Q. and Walton R. (1984) *Managing Human Assets*. New York: Free Press.

Blyton P. and Turnbull P. (1992) *Reassessing Human Resource Management*. London: Sage Publications.

Brewster C. (1998) Flexible working in Europe: extent, growth and the challenge for HRM. In P. Sparrow and M. Marchington (eds), *Human Resource Management: the New Agenda*. London: Financial Times/Pitman Publishing.

Burchell B., Day D., Hudson M., Ladip D., Mankelow R., Nolan J., Reed H. Wichert I. and Wilkinson, F. (1999) *Job Insecurity and Work Intensification: Flexibility and the Changing Boundaries of Work*. York: York Publishing Services.

Colling T. (2000) Personnel management in the extended organizations. In S. Bach and K. Sisson) (eds), *Personnel Management: A Comprehensive Guide to Theory and Practice*. Oxford: Blackwell, pp. 70–86.

Cully M., O'Reilly A., Millward N., Forth J., Di, G. and Bryson A. (1998) *The 1998 Workplace Employee Relations Survey*. London: DTI.

Edmundson A. and Moingeon B. (1996) When to learn and when to learn why: appropriate organizational processes as a source of competitive advantage. In A. Edmundson and B. Moingeon (eds), *Organizational Learning and Competitive Advantage*. London: Sage.

Ewing K. D. (1993) Swimming with the tide: employment protection and the implementation of European Labour Law. *Industrial Law Journal*, 22 (3).

Felstead A. (1993) *The Corporate Paradox – Power and Control in the Business Franchise*. London: Routledge.

Gennard J. (1998) Labour Government: change in employment law. *Employee Relations*, 20 (1), pp. 12–25.

Grahl J. and Teague P. (1992) Industrial relations trajectories and European human resource management. In C. Brewster and S. Tyson (eds), *International Comparisons in Human Resource Management*. London: Pitman, pp. 67–91.

Gratton L., Hope Hailey V., Stiles P. and Truss C. (1999) *Strategic Human Management*. Oxford: Oxford University Press.

Grubb D. and Wells W. (1993) Employment regulation and patterns of work in EC countries. *OECD Economic Studies*, 21, pp. 7–56.

Guest D. (1982) Has the recession really hit personnel management? *Personnel Management*, 14 (10), pp. 36–9.

Guest D. (1987) Human Resource Management and industrial relations. *Journal of Management Studies*, 24 (5), pp. 503–21.

Guest D. (1989) Personnel and HRM: can you tell the difference? *Personnel Management*, January, pp. 48–51.

Guest D. (1991) Personnel management: the end of orthodoxy? *British Journal of Industrial Relations*, 29 (2), 149–76.

Guest D. and Conway N. (1998) Fairness at work and the psychological contact. *Issues in People Management*, No. 21. London: Institute of Personnel and Development.

Harris L. (1999) Employment law and human resourcing – challenges and constraints. In J. Leopold, L. Harris and T. Watson (eds), *Strategic Human Resourcing: Principles, Perspectives and Practices in HRM*. London: Financial Times/ Pitman Publishing, pp. 265–90.

Harris L. (2000) Knowing the rules – employment regulation and smaller companies. Paper presented to the Small Business and Enterprise Development Conference, 10–11 April 2000, University of Manchester.

Harland C.M. (1996) Supply chain management relationships: chains and networks. *British Journal of Management*, 7 (Special Issue), pp. S63–S80.

Hendry C. (1995) *Human Resource Management – a Strategic Approach to Employment.* Oxford: Butterworth-Heinemann, pp. 431–3.

Herriot P. and Pemberton C. (1996) Contracting careers. *Human Relations*, 49 (6), pp. 757–87.

Hunter L., Beaumont P. and Sinclair D. (1996) A partnership route to Human Resource Management. *Journal of Management Studies*, 33 (2), pp. 235–57.

IPD (1998) *IPD Guide to Outsourcing.* London: Institute of Personnel & Development.

Kessler I. and Undy R. (1996) The new employment relationship: examining the psychological contract. *Issues in People Management*. London: IPD.

Kinnie N., Purcell J., Hutchinson S., Terry M., Collinson M. and Scarborough H. (1999) Employment relations in SMEs: market-driven or customer shaped? *Employee Relations*, 21 (3), pp. 218–35.

LMQR (Labour Market Quarterly Report) (1999) Small and medium sized enterprises: their role in the economy. *Skills and Enterprise Network Publications*, DfEE, November, 4 (99), pp. 12–16.

LMST (Labour Market and Skills Trends) (2000) *Skills and Enterprise Network.* London: DfEE Publications.

Lane D.A. (1994) People management in small and medium sized enterprises. *Issues in People Management*, No. 8. London: Institute of Personnel and Development.

Mabey C., Salaman G. and Storey J. (1998) *Human Resource Management. A Strategic Introduction.* Oxford: Blackwell.

Matlay H. (1999) Employee relations in small firms – a micro-business perspective. *Employee Relations*, 21 (3), pp. 285–95.

McLuhan R. (2000) Outsourcing skills. *Personnel Today*, Special Report, 18 April, pp. 25–33.

Peters T.J. and Waterman R.H. (1982) *In Pursuit of Excellence: Lessons from America's Best Companies.* New York: Harper and Row.

Rothwell S. (1992) Polishing up the supply chain. *Personnel Management*, September, pp. 28–32.

Rousseau D.M. (1996) *Psychological Contracts in Organizations: Understanding Written and Unwritten Agreements.* Thousand Oaks, CA: Sage.

Scarborough H. (1999) The HR implications of supply chain relationships. *Human Resource Management Journal*, 10 (1), pp. 5–16.

Storey D.J. (1994) *Understanding the Small Business Sector.* London: Routledge.

Storey J. (1992) *Developments in the Management of Human Resources.* Oxford: Blackwell.

Storey J. (ed.) (1995) *Human Resource Management: a Critical Text.* London: Routledge.

Turnbull P. (1991) Buyer–supplier relations in the UK automotive industry. In P. Blyton and J. Morris (eds), *A Flexible Future? Prospects for Employment and Organization.* New York: De Gruyter.

Tyson S. and Fell A. (1986) *Evaluating the Personnel Function.* London: Hutchinson.

Walton R.E. (1985) From control to commitment in the workplace. *Harvard Business Review,* March–April, pp. 77–94.

Watson T.J. (1999) Human resourcing strategies. Choice, chance and circumstances. In J. Leopold, L. Harris and T. Watson (eds), *Strategic Human Resourcing: Principles, Perspectives and Practices in HRM.* London: Financial Times/Pitman Publishing, pp. 17–37.

Wood S. (1995) The Four Pillars of HRM: are they connected? *Human Resource Management Journal,* 5 (5), pp. 53–8.

Wood S. and Albanese M. (1995) Can we speak of high commitment management on the shop floor? *Journal of Management Studies,* 32 (2), pp. 214 –47.

Activity 1

Refer back to the first case study (Setting Standards) in order to undertake the following tasks:

1. Outline the business case for integrating equal opportunities into overall business strategy.

2. Suggest ways to encourage more employers to sign up for initiatives to tackle discrimination such as the RfO campaign,

3. Identify the key issues to be reflected in the equality standards to be used as the equal opportunities 'kite mark'.

4. Suggest how the equality standards could be introduced into supply chain firms so that they became more than just a statement of intent but are translated into positive actions to tackle discrimination.

5. Propose ways in which the effectiveness of the proposed kite mark could be measured.

Activity 2

Many small suppliers to hotel and catering chains and food retailers have no internal HR expertise and insufficient resources to buy in expensive consultancy services. The need for access to specialist knowledge is, however, becoming increasingly critical both in terms of coping with changing legislation but also to promote the development of progressive HR practices and develop more innovative approaches to employment issues.

Suggest ways in which specialist HR support could be made available to smaller organizations without excessive cost but with a proper understanding of the particular challenges they face.

Questions

1. What changes in the external environment would encourage the development of more proactive approaches to the employment relationship in supply chain arrangements?

2. In what ways can a greater integration of human resourcing practices with wider business objectives be achieved in the *distanced organization*?

3. What mutual benefits are there for larger companies and their suppliers in ensuring that employees working in the supply chain are developed to increase their skills and abilities?

CHAPTER 11

Supply chains: issues in management accounting

Anthony J. Berry, John Cullen and William Seal

Key objectives

- To examine the management accounting issues posed through the development of supply chain management

- To explore holistic systemic accounting procedures designed to ensure the management of costs throughout the supply chain

- To consider current approaches to inter-firm accounting and discuss their succession for both customers and suppliers

Introduction

This chapter explores the management accounting issues posed by the development of supply chain management. It is based upon a research project undertaken by the authors in 1998 and 1999 across a range of companies in the United Kingdom.

The 'relevance of accounting debate' (Kaplan 1984) argued that the management accounting practices in use were about efficiency, but were also ensuring ineffectiveness and uncompetitiveness as they did not focus managers' attention upon how the whole cost structure could be managed. But Kaplan did point to the differences between cost management and measurement in, firstly (traditional) accounting terms; secondly, re. system optimization; and thirdly, re. strategic cost management. The development of activity based costing and target costing went some way to address the accounting cost issues.

There have been rapid changes in technology and organization of production, attention to lean production (Womack *et al.* 1990), closer supplier relationships (Lamming 1993), world class manufacturing and flexible specialization, a network of long-term relationships between customers and suppliers (Sako 1992; Akoi 1988; Okimoto 1986). The term 'supply chain management' seems to have originated in the 1980s consisting of the internal business functions of purchasing, manufacturing, sales and distribution and been externalized beyond the boundary of the firm to incorporate managing operations across organizational boundaries, an inter-firm view (Harland 1996). There are extensive definitions of these processes (for specific definitions see Glossary).

Sako (1992) identified four main theoretical approaches to the study of supply chains: (a) transaction cost economics, following Coase (1937) and Williamson (1975, 1979); (b) relational contract theory influenced by Macaulay (1963) and Macneil (1974); (c) a sociological approach to networks (Granovetter 1985; Frances and Garnsey 1996) and (d) networks as management strategies (e.g. Miles and Snow 1986; Nohria and Eccles 1992).

In the study of accounting issues in schema (a), Gietzmann (1996) argued that co-operative strategies required a re-examination of the accounting governance systems that assume arm's length transactions. These assumptions may act as a major obstacle to the formation of alliances or partnerships where information exchange is essential (Stuart and McCutcheon 1996). Success in partnerships (Mohr and Spekman 1994) requires commitment, co-ordination, trust, sharing of risks and information, comunication quality and participation and joint problem solving of disputes. Such partnerships may achieve reduction of transaction and production costs (Williamson 1975; Dyer and Ouchi 1993). Trust, while advocated by many authors (Pruitt 1981; Stuart and McCutcheon 1996) was recognized as needing time and care to build (Turnbull *et al.* 1992). Such partnerships are a considerable organizational innovation (Teece 1996) and may be a viable and advantageous route to achieving the benefits of vertical integration (Johnstone and Lawrence 1988). Much of the literature discusses the successes for both customers and suppliers in partnerships resulting in a win–win situation (Kanter

1994; Macbeth and Ferguson 1994) and joint successes (Helper and Sako 1995).

The management accounting problem

Lean production requires changes in the organization of production and the collection of cost accounting data in the customer and in the supplier (Lamming 1993). He also noted the success of Japanese suppliers and assemblers in the control of the Return on Assets (RoA) achieved by each company in a partnership and the poor quality of similar UK data. In his view 'lean accounting would provide the means for such information, upon which lean production might be based in the search for reducing costs, improving value and gaining a better understanding of the behaviour of both' (1993, p. 200).

As supply chains develop, via outsourcing and/or partnerships, lean supply arrangements (Saunders 1994) are needed as a greater part of the cost of production is entailed in the supplied goods. Saunders noted that 'costs are an important dimension of performance in supply chains and it is a factor that needs to be managed on an integrated basis' (1994 p. 213). He argued for a more proactive role for purchasing and supply management, for a more holistic and systematic approach leading to a 'total cost of supply' or 'total cost of ownership' which would by necessity need to evaluate dimensions such as the cost of assisting suppliers with negotiations, make or buy decision, product development and modification cost, a comparison of costs of home or overseas sourcing and analysis of product costs. Furthermore, he saw the need for the use of activity based costing, target costing and open book policies to aid supply chain effectiveness. The conflict between these ideas from partnership and the asset management basis of accounting was recognized by Gietzmann (1996). Some modification of the accounting governance seems to be necessary, based, argues Gietzmann, upon trust and commitment. But the adoption of Japanese supply chain and accounting practices has been found to be difficult because UK firms may be attempting to introduce the practice or the technique without the necessary attention to the governance issues (Gietzmann 1996).

The vertical integration role of accounting has also been reinforced by the common functional structures in organizations, each with their own budgets. The integration of functional operations has normally taken place in the discussions and debates in the planning and budgeting cycle. However, it has been argued that supply chains are essentially horizontal processes that require integration along the chain. The search for more effective cost models of operations was given impetus by the recognition of Cost Drivers (Porter 1985), the factors that determine the cost of an activity, e.g. economies and diseconomies of scale, learning or experience effects, pattern of capacity utilization, linkages, inter-relationships, integration, timing of market entry, discretionary policies, location and institutional (legal and regulatory) costs. These create the possibility of analysing the costs in value chain analysis and the search for competitive advantage. This new focus upon a wider array of causes of costs moves away from a condition where 'accounting systems do contain useful data, but they often get in the way of strategic cost analysis' (Porter 1985, p. 63). The inward vertical integration model of accounting ignores value created outside the firm's boundaries (Partridge and Perren 1994).

Subsequent research emphasized that the identification of cost drivers and analysing costs through the value chain, were essential components in the search for competitive advantage (Hergert and Morris 1989; Bromwich 1991; Shank and Govindarajan 1992; Partridge and Perren 1994).

Activity based analysis provided information along the chain of value adding activities within a 'total cost management' approach (Quillian 1991), which contained ABC, process value analysis and performance measurement. Further, Quillian noted that such an approach 'can act as a catalyst for integrating isolated logistics functions, leading to substantial improvements in costs, cycle times, inventories and levels of customer service.' (p. 9). Complementing this supplier study, Lere and Saraph (1995) examined the supply issues from the purchaser's perspective, noting how ABC can be used as a basis for price negotiation and as a means of exploring with suppliers as to how they have arrived at a price.

Their model was designed to identify the costs triggered by purchasing parameters such as product design specification, lot size, delivery schedule, shipments, number of design changes, level of documentation, inspection, allocation of overhead costs and calculations of cost per unit. These two studies taken together suggested that suppliers and buyers could usefully jointly examine these issues to gain common efficiencies but it did not indicate how any savings could be shared.

For assemblers who purchase much (approaching 80% by value) of their parts the issue of supply effectiveness and efficiency is a crucial contributor to competitiveness. 'For Nissan, achieving total cost control throughout the whole supply chain has represented a critical challenge' (Carr and Ng 1995, p. 348). These authors reported that Nissan used a multi-disciplinary team approach to supply cost management. Of special note was the very limited role of accountants in these processes which were built upon value engineering and 'value analysis to continually review product costs and manufacturing process' (p. 356). The degree of openness of the books or transparency (see Lamming 1993) in practice in the study of Carr and Ng was limited, with two major suppliers showing 'a greater concern as to whether Nissan would exploit its position of power, particularly in the light of its tougher circumstances' (p. 361).

The accounting measures of performance are based either upon profitability or cost; the supply chain advocates speak mostly about costs but partnership is intended to bring benefits to all of the participants in a shared destiny. It would be necessary to at least align the performance with the shared destiny principle (Harland 1996), with some agreement as to the measures to be used (Hope and Hope 1995), perhaps extending the concept of the balanced scorecard to the problem. The balanced scorecard has four elements: customer, internal business, innovation and learning together with the financial perspective.

Much of the literature of supply chains has its origins in the study of Japanese assemblers, especially the motor industry. Whether the social structure of Japanese industry is crucial to the operation of these supply chains is unclear, but it is argued (Whitley 1994; Scott 1995) that the wider patterns of values and beliefs do shape and construct the economic arrangements of corporations and markets. Japanese and Asian cultures are viewed as having a more dependent culture than the UK and this is held to explain some aspects of inter-organizational behaviours, where 'trust' is implied but may actually be more a case of social obligation. This may not easily be applied in Anglo-Saxon contexts. The issue of dependence, power and dominance in network formation and functioning was addressed by Zheng et al. (1997) in the pharmaceutical and automotive industries, where they found that the final manufacturer was dominant; in the retail consumer goods sector the final retailer exercised considerable power while in electronic components there was no one dominant actor. Further, Castells (1996) argued that the trend to supply chains and networking does not mean that the UK is shifting to an Asian model of the corporation. 'Countries and institutions continue to shape the organizational requirements of the new economy, in an interaction between the logic of production, the changing technological base and the institutional features of the social environment. The architecture and composition of business networks being formed around the world are influenced by the national characteristics of societies where such networks are embedded' (1996, p. 194).

In the UK, as noted by Turnbull et al. (1992), there is a lack of trust (or social obligation):

> After more than ten years of price freezes, volume cuts, multiple sourcing and the like, many suppliers view the latest moves to JIT as another means by which the vehicle assemblers intend to put the squeeze on (pp. 167–8)

This expectation of power was paralleled (Frances and Garnsey 1996) by evidence that UK large food stores used accounting techniques as control mechanisms beyond their own boundaries in which suppliers lost more degrees of freedom, gave rise to barriers to entry and an increase in market power and concentration.

Trust is not such a simple concept, nor is it readily created; Sako (1992) notes three types of trust: *contractual trust*, the keeping of promises; *competence trust*, that partners have the ability to carry out the work; and *goodwill trust*, allowing more discretion and implying the possibility of more commitment. In these cases trust appears to be about the acceptance that the other will behave well and not exploit any offers.

The management accounting problem in practice?

Much of the literature of accounting in relation to supply chains was either complaining or normatively expressing requirements in relation to governance or management. We began therefore with the question: 'What was the observed contribution of management accounting to the management of supply chains. What were the explanations for that?'

We were concerned with supply chains within firms (the intra-firm case) and between firms (the inter-firm case) and we considered four ideal types of relationships between entities:

1. The *autonomous firm* in the arm's length market relationship of free buyers and sellers. This is a condition where firm A is independent from firm B – the *inter-firm* case.

2. Where the output of firm A goes directly into the production system of firm B – *serial dependence.*

3. Where firm A and firm B affect each other's behaviour, described as *reciprocal dependence.*

4. Where the behaviour of firm A and firm B is interlinked and described as *mutual dependence.*

These four ideal types in the inter-firm cases represent the process of creating a managed supply chain through three stages of transition: from autonomy to serial dependence, from serial dependence to reciprocal dependence and from reciprocal dependence to mutual dependence where full partnership exists. This latter is the idealized state of supply chains which corresponds to the 'Japanese' model.

We considered management accounting around six main elements relating to the cycle of planning and control; the costing practices; cost management; issues in supply chains; the changing role of the management accountant; and performance management.

We studied management accounting practice in the UK in relation to the development of supply chain management. The research (fully reported in Berry *et al.* 2000), was based upon 16 companies, from four sectors. From these we wrote three inter-firm cases, one at each of the stages of serial dependence, reciprocal dependence and mutual dependence. These and the other companies were interviewed using a semi-structured schedule which, together with documentation, formed the basic data collection. One key finding was that in the inter-firm cases we found that supply chains were managed link by link with some very limited understanding beyond the first link.

Case study – 'Colfood Suppliers'

Colfood (a fictitious name but the study is based on an actual company), a multi-million pound subsidiary of an international company, were very customer oriented. Hence Colfood had always been aware of the issues in managing supply. The basic processes were the provision of many goods and services flows into a convergent production process of a dozen or so parallel and related product groups. Considerable effort had been made in procurement and logistics to get smooth loadings on the plants. Inter-product differences, planning, product and plant development were the subject of a sophisticated planning effort and were resolved by hierarchic flat when internal negotiations were failing to resolve problems.

From the production plants product was shipped in cold wagons to several cold stores and thence in ever diverging streams to customers. The accountants worked a system of full absorption costing 'down to pack size', acknowledging that this involved a great measure of judgement about allocations of overhead, processing, transport and administration and sales costs.

About four years ago Colfood had been 'shaken' from their rather established professional managerial practices by the introduction of performance management. The new performance imperative was based upon considerations of profitability and based upon driving market based metrics down into the organization. Managers were rewarded with a substantial element of profitability related pay.

The company had responded by becoming both more conscious of profit, operational effectiveness, cost reduction and efficiency. Profitability had risen more than five percentage points. As it did so the managers had become more protective of their results, were less willing to bend in negotiations and were aware that for internal transfers there was a new 'zero sum game', one manager's gain was another's loss.

Now David Smith, Managing Director, was troubled by the feeling that the different pieces were not as internally coherent as they needed to be to meet the challenge of the integrated customer services offered by competitive European firms. Also the senior management team had become aware of the need to manage the costs of the whole of the chain, from the upstream supply system, via the transformation processes in the plants and including the downstream processes including the costs of usage borne by the final customers. This meant an overhaul and maybe a radical repositioning to gain the advantages of an integrated end-to-end supply chain management with mutual working with suppliers, partners and customers.

The major problem was that the profit centre managers had become accustomed to being responsible and powerful people. The new ideas threatened their independence of action and control. Change to the new ideas looked as though it would be slow and very difficult, demoralizing and costly, even if the necessity for such action was real and the benefits were there to be won.

The decision and control cycle of planning, budgeting and reporting

In virtually all of our case study companies, routine management accounting cycles remained in place despite accounting innovations. In most situations supply chains had little impact on the routine structures of financial planning, budgeting and reporting. There was a tendency to provide routine monthly reports under traditional functional responsibility headings. However, fitting with the stages of development model, there were new horizontal integration processes created *alongside* the vertical integration procedures of management accounting.

In the supply chain environment the time cycles of order fulfilment were becoming much shorter and diachronic to monthly and annual cycles of management accounting. There was evidence of the attention directing elements of management accounting being by-passed by physical on-line real time observations and action taken without 'formal' cost analysis.

The changes in management accounting practice, broadly fitted to the stages of development model. Cost management for efficiency and for effectiveness was broadly changing in line with the stages of development model with more complexity as the nature of the interdependence became mutual.

Costing practices: how costs were measured

The use of standard cost was much wider than we had expected, largely to measure product profitability. It appeared that the advent of supply chain management had had no effect upon this, even with new understandings about how costs were incurred and managed. To some extent the changes in time cycles have led to standards not being used for detailed variance analysis; but analysis of cost movements was common among our companies. There was little evidence of the recognition and use of marginal and variable costs except in circumstances where the cost of a major material input so dwarfed other costs that the material cost was an estimate of variable costs. There was little evidence of the use of life cycle costing in any of the research companies.

ABM/C has been applied in the larger companies in intra-firm supply chains. The expectation that ABM/C would find a ready application in the inter-firm supply chain was not observed.

The expectation that supply chain management would lead to the use of target costing, as a key management accounting change was not borne out, except in the case of Japanese owned and influenced companies. There was no evidence of the use of throughput costing in any of the companies.

While many companies had active cost management procedures these were part of ongoing management and not an outcome of supply chain management. Of course, supply chain management itself was seen as a cost control approach which stimulated attention to the internal costs and especially to the input costs and the costs of procurement. The companies in inter-firm supply systems in this research had not formed cost models and analysis along the chains.

There was little or no evidence of the *analysis* of the benefits and costs of changing the process of managing suppliers; decisions were taken on the self evident propositions of simplification of number of suppliers and staff reductions would have positive outcomes. It was found that few companies had the accounting procedures to record and track the costs of the purchasing. Of course the central thrust of much supply chain thinking is to reduce costs and improve the reliability and quality of goods and services in shorter time cycles. The observed developments fitted those ideas.

The cost of management of suppliers was a major element in the management of the supply chain. In the inter-firm cases of serial dependence the reduction of the number of suppliers to one or two created a new mode of reciprocal dependence. It appeared that an efficiency frontier had been reached via reduction and simplification; the next stage was to build collaborative advantage.

All companies were aware of the need to manage the cost of stock holding. The use of lean production concepts to reduce cycle times and stock levels was common.

Cost management

Cost management in supply systems was moving from within the firm to include the upstream processes and inputs to the firm, embracing both production and procurement. There was scattered evidence of techniques such as horizontal information systems, *kaizen* costing, benchmarking, open book accounting (see later) and value engineering.

Considerations of efficiency • • •

Supply chain management offers the possibility of developing optimization analysis of supply chains to enable cost minimization to be managed. This requires sufficient knowledge of the marginal costs of the production processes across the chains. Only two of the intra-firm companies had the required knowledge of marginal cost and the models of the processes. As far as we could understand from the research companies, few if any of the supply chains were at capacity constraints. Where capacity was problematic it occurred where different supply chains were using the same production and distribution facilities.

Cost management was central to supply and supply chain management; especially noting (Houlihan 1984; Saunders 1994;

Lere and Saraph 1995) that as companies introduced lean manufacturing there was a tendency to purchase sub-assemblies which were described as material inputs. (The overall relationship of labour and material costs may not have changed but in relation to the final assembler it appeared to have changed.)

Considerations of system optimization ● ● ●

Management accounting procedures that were based upon a more systemic approach to cost management might have found a ready application in the inter-firm and intra-firm supply chains because they were developed as a means of moving away from simple overhead rate calculations. But there was little evidence of application of business process re-engineering (BPR), activity based management (ABM) or activity based costing (ABC). This was true for both inter- and intra-firm supply chains, probably because the supply chains in this study were not managed across organizations, they were managed link by link; with little or no consideration of the sequence of links in the chain.

Considerations of strategic decision making ● ● ●

The use of supply chain management as a strategic tool to generate a new mode of strategic integration was evident in all intra-firm cases. This was because the larger multi-national companies in our study operated across many regions and countries and markets. But that was not so in the inter-firm cases, acting as a barrier to supply chain effectiveness.

Supply chain processes

The use of 'open books' followed the stages model. In market or serial dependence the books were closed; as reciprocal dependence developed then the books were open to facilitate the chain relationships. The degree of openness should not be overstated; these were specific to particular cases and not a general invitation to access companies' accounts. In the mutual dependence cases of inter-firm chains specific attention was given to open books and in the case of construction projects there were cases of common open books. Often, open book accounting was perceived as a mechanism whereby the supplier opens its books to the customer. It was important to recognize, however, that the need to share information must be two-way and that there was therefore a need for the customer to open its books to the supplier.

The main focus of supply chain reporting had not changed; but the impact of supply chain development at each stage was leading to a consideration of the need to report along and about the chain.

The stages of supply chain development place greater demands upon the *integration of* accounting data with other information. Such integration was rarely observed, but the connection to process driven integrated information systems was visible in the developments in the multi-nationals.

This study was not primarily concerned with *Electronic Data Interchange*. However, much change was observed, with the early stages of the supply development using simple linking exchanges, such as ordering and scheduling; but at the most developed multi-national companies the use of EDI was via very complex logistics systems to which there were options to add systems for accounting.

There was little evidence of a role for management accounting in the strategic management of the supply chain except via special projects and the involvement of management accountants in the work of strategic management.

Relational contracting and the shared destiny ● ● ●

A supplier to a number of multi-national companies in the automotive sector found that their customers had diverse approaches to the management of the supply chain. These diverse approaches apparently stemmed from different understanding of 'relationship', a consequence of diverse trading experience.

Where their customers had been hard bargainers, it was likely to take many years before the company was likely to be more than sufficiently co-operative. They assumed that the approaches from the hard bargainers were another form of extracting compliance and cost reduction, or of the hard bargainers' extracting more of the profit from the system. The protestations of a new beginning were not believed. In contrast, the companies that had some understanding of collaboration were given more attention, and some sharing of productivity and product technology improvements with the customers and with parallel suppliers was developed. However this company was unwilling to open its accounting books in any great detail and certainly unwilling to enter into detailed discussions of its cost structures with any of its customers. This suited one of its customers, which had a concentration upon decremental costing rather than examining cost structure. This observation was at variance with the implications from Carr and Ng's study, with the supplier not wholly accepting the demands from the purchaser.

The evidence suggests that the advent of supply chain management and its stages has led to significant increase in organizations working for horizontal integration. The use of multi-functional teams was very common. The management accountants were becoming members of supply chain teams with managerial responsibility rather than providing just accounting advice. This was taking place in the context of 'delayering' and hence the complexity of work that a team was expected to handle was also increasing. It appears that the full development of the intra-firm supply chain could yet produce a very radical change to organizations and to the role of management accountants. The inter-firm companies were more limited in their changes but radical solutions to the problem of closer integration of the companies in supply systems cannot be ruled out.

All of this expansion in *scope for the management accountant* must also have been accomplished without diminution of the professional capability to assure the integrity of accounting systems and procedures and the ability to provide sound interpretation of the information provided.

Performance management

There was a significant impact of supply chain management on performance measurement and management. As the supply chain stages were moved along then the degree of attention given to this issue increased. The problems presented to performance management, which has been based upon the vertical hierarchy, when supply chain management becomes a day-to-day issue for managerial focus and decision becomes clearer. The challenge presented in the later stages is whether to continue with 'bolt on' additional supply chain performance measurements or radically to change the whole organization to a supply chain management principle and hence integrate with a process driven structure together with a process driven integrated information system.

Existing performance management systems could inhibit the development of supply chain ideas. The new demands of supply chain thinking, it was observed in one such intra-firm company, forced operational integration and redefined both the structures of responsibility and accountability and the required financial decision rules for transfer, thus affecting the divisional measures of performance. This had a direct impact upon managers who had become accustomed to performance-related pay based upon their divisional performance (in context of plans) leading to significant problems in introducing intra-organizational supply chain integration.

In some of the multi-national companies in our study, especially in the intra-firm cases, it was observed that there was considerable use of quasi-economic control such as Return on Investments, Return on Assets, Residual Income and its variants as a means of introducing financial market-related disciplines into the divisions by separating them; whereas supply chains sought to connect them.

This problem of change was based upon the use of management accounting and control procedures being used for short, medium and long term integration with horizontal integration being a residual problem. In the newer world of supply chain thinking the vertical integration of the management accounting and control cycle still exists for the longer term (and of course for financial reporting). However, there was evidence from two of the companies that there was an emerging shift to systems of information and control for horizontal integration for the short and medium term.

Discussion and conclusions

This study was of rapidly changing organizations in varied transitions along the stages model with a variety of other changes happening at the same time, with potential to affect each other and management accounting. The potential for a quite dramatic impact was observed to be greater in the mutually dependent modes, compared to the serial and reciprocal dependent modes.

Further, it was common for management accounting to be constructed upon the basis of the organization's structures of responsibility and accountability. Here management accounting and control was a basic procedure for vertical integration of financial behaviour. Horizontal integration was achieved via the use of transfer pricing within a corporate policy.

Our findings demonstrate that there has been little use made of the conceptual change in accounting cost models. Standard costing for products was common, with little use of variable, marginal, target costing (except where influenced by Japanese management), life cycle costing, or activity based costing, with no reported use of throughput costing. So the management accounting practices were observed to be very 'traditional' in their connection to product cost and margin calculations, stock valuation and working capital analysis.

These observations were largely indifferent to the classifications of inter- and intra-firm supply chains and to the stages of development of the supply chain. It seems that the normative ideas of Saunders (1994), with which we agree, had yet to penetrate our research companies to any substantial degree. But it was the case, for all of these companies, as Porter (1985) and Shank and Govindarajan (1992) have argued, that cost management in the context of product quality and market issues, was critical to competitive success.

In addition, there was evidence in some companies that the penetration of management accounting into the micro detail of organizational work was being pushed back up a flattening hierarchy. This occurred because the managers could use physical measures as a basis for decisions, having an understanding of the consequences for costs. The point at which physical and accounting measures were integrated was shifting in the intra-firm and to a lesser extent in the inter-firm cases into procedures for horizontal integration.

There was little or no evidence from the inter-firm cases of the impact of supply chains upon the use of management accounting for strategic management. In the intra-firm cases of mutual dependence we observed the firms to be close to the provision of an integrated logistics, procurement, production and market model with accounting data in it so as to create an on-line strategic management tool.

Horizontal information systems in the inter-firm cases (both the serial dependent and reciprocal dependent cases) were very much project based additions to extant procedures. There was no conclusive evidence of EDI being used systemically along the supply chain in (Marson and Massey 1999). This issue is explored in parallel with the accounting project, but in the intra-firm cases the development of supply chains was leading to a revolution in the use of EDI as an internal integration vehicle to permit supply chain management.

One case was specifically undertaken to explore the issue of management accounting and the *shared destiny* principle. The evidence suggested that accounting and management accounting aid the development of the alliance. It is argued in that case that accounting can and did play a constitutional role in developing the alliance, as Gietzman (1996) suggested.

There was evidence from the case studies that companies, having been through the first stage of cost management and supplier management, began to build upon their experience of managing serial dependence to move towards reciprocal dependence. The respondents, managers, purchasing managers and management accountants acknowledged that the next stage would include *relational contracting* to include a wider sharing of accounting information. However, in the more adversarial culture of the UK, the evidence suggested that this step will require some time to elapse before histories of dominance by customers would be set aside and invitations to greater collaboration would be accepted. The two companies in our study at the mutual dependence stage of inter-firm relations were engaged in relational contracting and in gain sharing.

The cutting edge: the intra-firm examples

In general the greatest impact of supply chains upon management accounting was in the intra-firm chains in the multi-national companies. These intra-firm companies had developed very sophisticated logistic models of procurement, production and distribution, including the flows in their suppliers' factories (procurement) and marketing data. However, the marketing and accounting data were not yet integrated into the supply chain. This was to be a next major step to meet the ideas of Quillian (1991).

These examples were the product of a convergence of a number of ideas and technologies, including computational technology, very complex logistics models, satellite communication technology, local access to global systems, application of systemic thinking as a mode of integration, moves towards the creation of lean manufacturing and world class manufacturing, the need for rich information for decision and control and analysis, the capacity to manage beyond the legal boundaries by modes of dominance, of serial dependence, of reciprocal dependence and of mutual dependence.

These were being brought together to produce a new process driven (systemic) integrated information system, PDIIS. However this new (if embryonic) system was introduced alongside the extant systems and does not as yet displace them. However if the organization structure is radically changed to being process driven then the older systems will have to change. In this way the new (or emerging) PDIIS systems may be embedded before the old systems are dis-embedded. They will not, it seems, replace the need for local operating information systems, but when integrated with accounting then they present the possibility of becoming a tool for strategic analysis and management. Two of the companies were close to such possibilities, with several more seeking to move in that direction, from reciprocal to mutual dependence.

This new ideal type of PDIIS represents a capability of hierarchic firms to gain flexibility and complex co-ordination. Such capability is unlikely to be attained in the inter-firm case although 'platforms' will soon be available.

In the inter-firm cases the 'supply chain' was almost always managed as a set of discrete links with little or no attention to managing the whole chain. This reflects the construct of a supply chain as an observed set of connections but not as a managed set of inter-firm behaviours. This absence of any integration of management accounting along the chain reflected the issues of ownership and asset protection. The experience of these companies in supply chains in the UK was that they were not surrendering to the image of the integrated supply chain; rather they were managing their destiny by engaging in a series of dependent relationships to their own and mutual advantage. This fits with the arguments of Scott (1995) and Castells (1996) that the economic arrangements will reflect the (changing) social structure.

In relation to governance issues, management accounting developments were central to the development of reciprocal and mutual dependence, in accordance with Gietzmann's (1996) suggestions. This process was clearly more difficult in the somewhat conflictual and autonomy-preferring Anglo-Saxon context (Turnbull *et al.* 1992), but the advent of the challenge to develop along the stages of supply chains was changing behaviour; it was possible to build contractual trust and in the cases of mutual dependence there was evidence of goodwill (Sako 1992).

Figure 11.1 summarizes the stages of development of the management accounting response to the stages of supply chains. Much of the observed practice of management accounting was rather 'traditional' and responsive to supply chains in episodic rather than systemic ways. The impact of supply chains upon management accounting practices followed the stages of development of the supply chain, which were easier to implement in the intra-firm case. The ideas and concepts of accounting informed all cost management practices in both intra- and inter-firm cases.

	FOCUS OF COST MANAGEMENT		
Business focus of supply chains	Accounting for efficiency	Economic optimization (effectiveness)	Strategic
Finance and operations	*Reduction of cost of management *Reduction of cost of supply/suppliers *Cycle time and working capital	Little reduction	None
Management of future business configurations	*as above*	• Organizational innovation • Active reconsideration of suppliers' contribution to design/development of products/services (balanced scorecard)	Little
Strategic development	*as above*	*as above*	*Intra-firm A process driven integrated system as a strategic tool *Inter-firm A virtual PDIIS but is it strategic?

Figure 11.1 Stages in development of management accounting for supply chain management

The shortening of time cycles does lead to the seeming redundancy of the *post hoc* information role of accounting, as action follows upon physical data rather than accounting data. Here the accountant as member of the team must be able to infer the impacts upon accounts and advise, on-line in real time, on desirable actions.

While management accounting practice might appear to be traditional in its routine operations, the practice of supply chain management accountants, in projects and analysis, was quite the opposite. Management accountants were key actors in the strategic management of the inter- and intra-firm supply chain. It was very clear from the three case studies that management accountants were active partners in the new management team's cultures which follow the logic of the chains as well as holding to the logics of hierarchy. In this sense the practice of accounting was not, as Porter (1985) stated, obstructing new developments.

It is possible that once the technology of process driven information systems is available to a wider audience it will come to impact upon the inter-firm case, to perhaps meet Lamming's (1993) request for lean accounting. Figure 11.1 provides a framework for describing the possible path of change of management accounting practices as process driven integrated information systems are developed. From the routines of hierarchic systems, via a series of complex and *ad hoc* projects, the technology is slowly being created for process driven integrated information systems. At the moment the existing systems, which require great expertise and support as organizations change in many ways, are being maintained and remain embedded. The possible new systems will become embedded in parallel and proved in practical use before any dis-embedding can take place. It is not that the managers and accountants are risk averse; it is that the technical and managerial utility of such new systems will require substantial robustness tests before they can take over.

Acknowledgement

The authors wish to acknowledge the financial support of the Chartered Institute of Management Accountants, the assistance of ISCAN, Sheffield and the participating companies for their help with the project from which this chapter is drawn.

References

Akoi M. (1988) *Information, Incentives and Bargaining in the Japanese Economy*. New York: Cambridge University Press.

Berry A.J., Cullen J., Seal W.B., Ahmed M. and Dunlop A. (2000) *The Consequences of Interfirm Supply Chain Management for Management Accounting*. CIMA.

Bromwich M. (1991) Accounting for strategic excellence. In *Okonomistyring OG strategic – nyeideer nye erfarinjer*. Denmark: Systime.

Carr C. and Ng J. (1995) Total cost control: Nissan and its UK supplier partnerships. *Management Accounting Research*, 6, 347–5.

Castells M. (1996) *The Rise of the Network Society*. Oxford: Blackwell.

Coase R. (1937) The nature of the firm. *Economica* 4, pp. 386–405.

DTI/Supply Chain Networks Group (1997) Supply Chain Management Attitude Survey. Report of the Supply Chain Working Group, April.

Dyer J.H. and Ouchi W.G. (1993) Japanese-style partnerships: giving companies a competitive edge. *Sloan Management Review*, Fall, pp. 51–62.

Frances J. and Garnsey E. (1996) Supermarkets and suppliers in the United Kingdom: System integration, information and control. *Accounting, Organizations and Society*, 21 (6), pp. 591–610.

Gietzmann M.B. (1996) Incomplete contracts and the make or buy decision: governance design and attainable flexibility. *Accounting, Organizations and Society*, 21 (6), pp. 611–26.

Granovetter M.S. (1985) Economic action and social structure: the problem of embeddedness. *American Journal of Sociology*, 91 (3), pp 481–510.

Harland C.M. (1996) Supply chain management: relationships, chains and networks. *British Journal of Management*, 7, Special issue, pp. s63–s80.

Helper S.R. and Sako M. (1995) Supplier relations in Japan and the United States: are they converging?, *Sloan Management Review*, Spring, pp. 77–84.

Hergert M. and Morris D. (1989) Accounting data for value chain analysis. *Strategic Management Journal*, 10, 175–88.

Hope T. and Hope J. (1995) *Transforming the Bottom Line: Managing Performance with the Real Numbers*. London: Nicholas Brealey.

Houlihan J.B. (1984) Supply Chain Management. Proceedings of the 19th International Technical Conference, BPICS, pp. 101–10.

Johnston R. and Lawrence P. R. (1988) Beyond vertical integration – the rise of the value-adding partnership. *Harvard Business Review*, July/August, pp. 94–101.

Kanter R.M. (1994) Collaborative advantage: the art of alliances. *Harvard Business Review*, July/August, pp 96–108.

Kaplan R.S. (1984) Yesterday's accounting undermines production. *Harvard Business Review*, July/August, pp 95–101.

Lamming R. (1993) *Beyond Partnership: Strategies for Innovation and Lean Supply*. New York: Prentice Hall.

Lere J. and Saraph J. (1995) Activity based costing for purchasing managers' cost and pricing determinations. *International Journal of Purchasing and Materials Management*, Fall. pp. 25–31.

Macaulay S. (1963) Non-contractual relations in business: a preliminary study. *American Sociological Review*, 28 (2), pp. 55–67.

Macbeth D.K. and Ferguson N. (1994) Partnership sourcing: an integrated supply chain approach. London: Financial Times/Pitman Publishing.

Macneil I.R. (1974) The many futures of contract. *Southern California Law Review*, 47, pp. 691–816.

Marson J. and Massey P. (1999) The strategic use of IT in the supply chain. *Journal of Financial Information Systems*, 4, pp. 1–2.

Miles R.E. and Snow C.C. (1986) Organizations: new concepts for new forms. *California Management Review*, 28 (3), pp. 62–73.

Mohr J. and Speckman R. (1994) Characteristics of partnership success: partnership attributes, communication behaviour and conflict resolution techniques. *Strategic Management Journal*, 15, pp. 135–52.

Nohria N. and Eccles R.G. (1992) *Networks and Organizations; Structure, Form and Action*. Boston: Harvard Business School Press.

Okimoto D.I. (1986) Regime characteristics of Japanese industrial policy. In Hugh Patrick (ed.), *Japan's High Technology Industries*. Seattle: University of Washington Press.

Partridge M. and Perren L. (1994) Cost analysis of the value chain: another role for strategic management accounting. *Management Accounting*, July/August, pp. 22–8.

Porter M.E. (1985) *Competitive Advantage: Creating and Sustaining Superior Performance*. New York: The Free Press.

Pruitt D.G. (1981) *Negotiation Behaviour*. New York: Academic Press.

Quillian L. (1991) Curing 'functional silo syndrome' with logistics total cost management. *CMA Magazine*, June, pp. 9–14.

Sako M. (1992) *Prices, Quality and Trust: Inter-firm Relations in Britain and Japan*. Cambridge: Cambridge University Press.

Saunders M. (1994) *Strategic Purchasing and Supply Chain Management*. London: Pitman for the Chartered Institute of Purchasing and Supply.

Scott W.R. (1995) *Institutions and Organizations*. London: Sage.

Shank J.K. and Govindararajan V. (1992) Strategic cost management and the value chain. *Journal of Cost Management*, 5 (4), pp. 5–21.

Stuart F.I. and McCutcheon D. (1996) Sustaining strategic supplier alliances. *International Journal of Operations and Production Management*, 16 (10), pp. 5–22.

Teece D. (1996) Firm organization, industrial structure and technological innovation. *Journal of Economic Behaviour and Organization*, 31, pp. 193–224.

Turnbull P., Oliver N. and Wilkinson B. (1992) Buyer–supplier relations in the UK automotive industry: strategic implications of the Japanese manufacturing model. *Strategic Management Journal*, 13, pp. 159–168.

Whitley R. (1994) *Business Systems in East Asia. Firms, Markets and Societies.* London: Macmillan.

Williamson O.E. (1970) *Corporate Control in Business Behaviour.* Englewood Cliffs, NJ: Prentice Hall.

Williamson O.E. (1973) Markets and hierarchies. *American Economic Association*, 63, p. 2.

Williamson O.E. (1975) *Markets and Hierarchies: Analysis and Antitrust Implications.* New York: Free Press–Macmillan.

Williamson O.E. (1979) Transaction – cost economics: the governance of contractual relations. *Journal of Law and Economics*, 22 (2), pp. 3–61.

Womack J.P., Jones D.T. and Roos D. (1990) *The Machine that Changed the World.* New York: Rawson Associates.

Zheng J., Harland C., Johnsen T. and Lamming R. (1997) Features of supply networks. Paper presented at the BAM Conference, London.

Questions

1. This chapter explains that the emergence of supply chain management requires a fundamental change in accounting procedures:

   (a) explain in detail the need for procedural change

   (b) provide a brief indication as to the nature of these changes.

2. What may be the challenges faced by companies in the implementation of total cost of ownership approach.

3. Explain the concept and importance of activity based analysis.

Supply Chain Perspectives

Internationalization of the Supply Chain

Internationalization of the hospitality industry

Kevin Nield

Introduction

The hospitality industry is by its very nature international. The demand for it is international and many of the companies that operate within it are international. A cursory look at demand sources shows us that part of the demand for hospitality services is derived from international tourists and international business. In a global economy it makes economic sense for the hospitality industry to be global.

The reasons for a company making the decision to operate in international markets are well documented, and amply illustrated by Teare and Olsen (1992). They identify two sets of reasons that stem from inside or outside the company and are either proactive or reactive. The proactive reasons include growth and profit motives, managerial urge, the opportunities that exist in foreign markets, agents encouragement, extension of products and unique products. These unique products and extension of products and product range, bring with them supply chain problems. Reactive reasons for internationalization include, the desire to diversify, risks and saturation of domestic markets, as was experienced by McDonald's in the USA. The McDonald's Corporation is discussed in more depth later in this perspective.

Multinational companies in the international hospitality industry

The international nature of the hospitality industry is reflected in the global nature of the major players. These players were at one time primarily American, but they now stem from across the globe. Major multinationals in accommodation include Granada (UK), Accor (France), Starwood which includes ITT Sheraton, Westin (US), New World (Hong Kong), Saison (Japan) and Movenpick (Switzerland). At the same time, we should not forget the major players in the global restaurant industry, including well-known names and brands such as McDonald's (US) and Burger King (UK). Table P1.1 gives the world's top five hotel chains.

The scale of investment in accommodation and catering services requires that substantial expenditure on land, buildings and equipment be made, e.g. the Ritz in Madrid was recently sold for a price in the region of £80 million. Investments of that magnitude may be difficult to finance, and the risks of such an investment may be thought, by many, to outweigh the benefits. Added to this, any expansion based on that magnitude of costs will be slow. These pressures have helped bring about change in the type of investment in overseas markets from direct investment to non-investment management arrangements (NIMAs) and management contracts. Where direct investment was the norm from the 1950s to the 1960s, management contracts and NIMAs account for over 90% of all multi-national involvement (Dunning and McQueen 1982)

Forms of NIMA

The most common forms of non-investment management arrangements in the international hospitality industry are the franchise and the management contract.

Chain	Hotels	Rooms
Cendant Corporation (Howard Johnson, Ramada, Travelodge Hotels Inc.) (USA)	5979	499 056
Bass Hotels and Resorts (Holiday Inn, Forum, Inter-Continental) (UK)	2738	461 434
Marriott International (USA)	1696	328 300
Choice Hotels International (USA)	3670	305 171
Accor (France)	2666	291 770

Note: Best Western has been omitted as it is a hotel consortium that seeks to operate as a brand.
Source: Adapted from *Hotels Magazine*

Table P1.1
The world's top five hotel chains

Franchises

Young *et al.* (1989) and Ellis and Williams (1995) identify two types of franchise, these are:

1. 'Product and trade name' franchise: An example of this is where Coca-Cola agrees to sell its syrup and the right to sell its trademark to independent bottlers (franchisees).

2. Business-format franchise: This involves trademarks and products but also marketing strategies, quality control, operating procedures and communication between the franchiser and the franchisee.

This latter type of franchise is most common in the hospitality industry. Examples of this type of franchise include McDonald's, Holiday Inn and KFC. The important thing about this is that each enterprise is separately owned, financed from independent sources but carry a single trading name. To the outside world they are one and the same, for example how many people realize that Holiday Inn is a franchise or know that KFC is not a chain? Just recently Forte have signed a franchise deal to manage two new hotels in Israel – Le Meridien in Tel Aviv and Le Meridien in Eilat.

International management contracts

A management contract is an agreement where one company (A) runs a hotel or other enterprise for another company (B). In this arrangement, company A, the contractor, may offer a brand image, e.g. Moat House, or Hilton and their operating standards, management systems, staff management, reservations and referral capabilities. In return for this the contractor receives new markets, reduced financial risks and, of course, profit (Eyster 1997).

Recent examples of management contracts are Hilton International, which has won its first management contract at the British Colonial Hilton, Nassau after a $50m refurbishment and 30 Thistle hotels which have been sold to Lehman Bros. The management contract has been awarded to Peel Hotels.

The advantages of non-investment management arrangements

The advantages of the arrangements that NIMAS bring are aptly illustrated in the scenario outlined below.

Scenario

1. A local company owns a hotel in Spain.

2. This company is in turn owned by a British holding company.

3. An American multi-national management contractor operates the hotel.

This relationship gives the optimum *best* use of the factors of production.

Figure P1.1 illustrates the factor that is contributed by each of the players in this scenario.

What happens next is that the UK company has a development portfolio and the American company becomes the well-known multi-national operator e.g., Sheraton or Hyatt. But it should be noted, that these types of arrangements are essentially part of the supply chain and as such impact upon the operation and in some cases, the ethics of the supply chain.

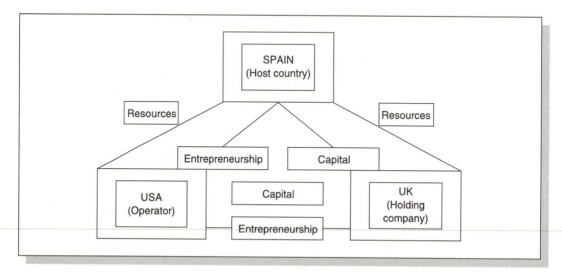

Figure P1.1 Contribution of each player in the scenario (adapted from Bull 1995)

Problems associated with internationalization

Government or legal restrictions

Quite simply there may be restrictions that mean that a franchise cannot operate in the way that it wishes to. For example McDonald's prefers to own the leases on all of its properties. This is not possible in some countries, where foreign ownership of land is not allowed. This may also have supply chain implications, e.g., there may be government restrictions on the purchase of goods.

Recruitment of suitably qualified franchisees

The problem here is that it might be necessary for franchisees to have qualifications or attributes to make the franchise a success. For example, a service culture that they simply do not possess. This is particularly true in Eastern Europe, where service may be regarded as synonymous with servility.

Lack of local funding

Franchising is potentially very expensive to the franchisee, a typical franchisee would have to pay for the cost of the restaurant and its equipment, a 'joining royalty', training costs and inventory costs. This sort of finance, and the institutions that may supply finance for franchises, are not available in many countries. This may also be the case in regard to management contracts.

Difficulty of controlling franchisees and other parties to the contract

Franchise and management contracts are legally binding agreements. A franchise package and a management contract are normally very rigid, both parties must do exactly what is stipulated in the contract. This may be easy to control in the home country, but may be extremely difficult in other countries where contract law is not the same, or where legal procedures are slow and drawn out. This may immediately have supply chain implications, e.g. where franchisees move away from prescribed suppliers.

The offerings of both the franchise and the management contractor

These may have to be re-designed to make them saleable in foreign markets. Food products that are acceptable in one country are not acceptable in another. The obvious examples are pork in Moslem countries and beef in India. However, there are other cultural considerations that will have to be taken into account and questions of national taste that may have to be considered.

Because of the problems associated with the above, it has been suggested that franchising may become more common in the later stages of market development. As was recorded in the McDonald's annual report of 1995, 47% of the restaurants that operated outside of the USA, were franchised, while only 29% were operated as company owned. The remainder were operated by affiliates (Daniels and Radeburgh 1998).

Further evidence of franchising becoming more common in the later stages of market development may be demonstrated by McDonald's entry into the UK market in the 1970s. All of the original restaurants were owned by McDonald's and of them only one traded at a profit in the early years. The reasons for this were that McDonald's wished to establish the brand and the advertising costs associated with start-up, were too high to be borne by the franchisees.

The supply chain and the international hospitality industry

It is self-evident that the hospitality industry is part of the food supply chain. How this relationship is handled will vary from company to company. At one extreme all products will be imported from prescribed supplier or suppliers, at the other extreme suppliers will be freely selected, local and imported produce will be utilized.

Daniels and Radeburgh (1998) point to the problems that McDonald's faced in setting themselves up in Moscow. After years of negotiation, a joint venture between McDonald's and Moscow City Council, was agreed. The original idea was that as far as possible, local produce should be used. Unfortunately this proved to be impossible. It had been expected that some goods would be available locally and that others would be provided as part of the national planning process. Some goods simply did not exist in Russia, e.g. the Russet Burbank potato.

The results of all of this were that McDonald's had to build and operate its own food processing plant on the outskirts of Moscow and had to provide the expertise to help Russian farmers and producers provide food stuffs of the required quality. In addition, they also had to provide transport as this was unreliable for food supplies.

Supply chain implications also come from the type of operation, e.g. many hotels are catering for foreign nationals. It is arguable, that many of the hotels on the Costas of Spain are catering for markets that are not Spanish, the result of this is that goods are imported to suit the foreign tastes. This, therefore involves problems associated with importing, such as exchange rate fluctuations, reliability of delivery and the negative impacts on the balance of payments. In the case of large concerns, some of the problems may be overcome by central buying and warehousing but this is not possible for everyone.

Other supply chain implications stem from the type of contract. As part of some franchises, the contract stipulates that foodstuffs must be supplied by the franchiser or a supplier approved by the franchiser. The result of this is that for some overseas operations, the majority of its supplies are supplied from the home country of the franchisers. The implication of this is that the supply chain is short, but the supply line is long.

The ethics of the international hospitality supply chain also need a mention. In research carried out in the Black Sea resorts of Romania, Kozak and Nield (1998) reported that many of the local food products were not to the taste of foreign tourists. The obvious solution to this dilemma was to import foodstuffs to suit foreign tastes, but this could not be done by national hotels for reasons of finance. It may be argued that this should not be considered for ethical reasons as some of the foods that were disliked by foreign nationals were in fact national dishes, and part of the cultural heritage of Romania. Supply chains within the international hospitality industry have cultural implications that should not be forgotten or overlooked.

References

Bull A. (1995) *The Economics of Travel and Tourism*, 2nd edn. London: Longman.

Daniels J.D. and Radeburgh L.H. (1998) *International Business*, 8th edn. Reading, MA: Addison Wesley.

Dunning J.H. and McQueen M. (1982) Multinational corporations in the international hotel industry. *Annals of Tourism Research*, 4, pp. 69–90.

Ellis J. and Williams D. (1995) *International Business Strategy*. London: Pitman.

Eyster J.J. (1997) Hotel management contracts in the US: 12 areas of concern. *Cornell HRQ*, 38 (3), pp. 21–33.

Kozak M. and Nield K. (1998) Importance-performance analysis and cultural perspectives in Romanian Black Sea resorts. *Anatolia*, Winter, 9 (2), pp. 99–116.

Teare R. and Olsen M. (eds) (1992) *International Hospitality Management*. London: Pitman.

Young S., Hammil J., Wheeler C. and Davies J.R. (1989) *International Market Entry and Development: Strategies and Management*. Brighton: Harvester Wheatsheaf.

Internationalization of food retailing

Nicholas Alexander

Introduction

The food distribution process has long been characterized by the international nature of food distribution channels. The movement of products from locations where the product is produced, to the location where it is required, but cannot be produced, is a fundamental of world trade and food supply systems. Traditionally, however, while the distribution system itself has been internationally based, the final commercial participant in the channel of distribution has been far from international in operation. In recent years this traditional picture has changed.

This perspective analyses the development of nationally based food retailers towards international retailing operations. A number of examples are used to explain why European food retailers have begun to contemplate non-domestic expansion and to chart through to the new millennium, the international directions that have been taken.

The growth of international food retailing

US food retailing has had an important, yet often indirect, impact on the practices adopted by food retail operations. While some US food retailers, such as Safeway, have attempted to establish international operations, their influence in international markets has primarily come from the innovations in operating practices, that have subsequently been adopted elsewhere in international markets.

In contrast, European food retailers have played, and are continuing to play, an important and direct role in the internationalization of food retailing activities. From the late 1960s, European food retailers have been increasingly constrained by the limitations of their domestic markets and began to explore the opportunities to expand within Europe and further afield. Burt (1991) has shown that the late 1960s and early 1970s witnessed a considerable growth in the international activities of food retailers based in France and Germany.

The initial period of expansion in the late 1960s and early 1970s was followed by a period of further expansion, during which market opportunities outside Europe became an important destination for European food retail investment. By 1980, 10% of US grocery retailing was in the hands of European owned retailers (Ball 1980; Seigle and Handy 1981). The attainment of 'European retailers' significant role in the distribution of food products in the US, was mainly achieved through the acquisition of existing US food chains. Important acquisitions included that of A&P (Atlantic & Pacific) in 1979 by the Tengelmann Group based in Germany, the acquisition in 1977 of Bi-Lo by Ahold the Dutch retailer and the acquisition in 1974 of Food Town Stores by the Belgian retailer Delhaize.

Structure of growth

The reasons why European food retailers began to look toward non-domestic markets, at the end of the 1960s and early 1970s, are numerous.

Although some retail organizations, such as the non-food retailers the Body Shop and Benetton, internationalized early during their commercial development, food retailers have tended to achieve considerable penetration levels within their domestic market before moving towards international activity. Thus, internationalization for food retailers is often associated with saturation of the domestic market (Alexander 1997). This saturation may take two forms:

1. Saturation as the result of market saturation: Here the retailer concerned has exploited, or nearly exploited, the opportunities available in the domestic market. For example, Tesco began international expansion on mainland Europe during the 1990s at a time when it was mopping up the last market opportunities within the UK.

2. Saturation as a result of the imposition of regulation: This regulation is often the consequence of fears expressed by independent traders, or other interested parties, who fear a reduction in local and national competition, with the removal of small enterprises from the retail structure. The Belgian and

French markets illustrate this type of development. In France the *Loi Royer* and in Belgium regulations known as the Padlock Law, restricted the development of large format food outlets from the early 1970s. Consequently, for retailers such as the French food retailer Carrefour and the Belgian retailer Delhaize, internationalization was no longer merely an option, it became an imperative.

Thus, large format food retailers have been forced out of their domestic market and into the international environment because of commercial or regulatory restrictions. In Europe, these pressures began to become significant in the 1960s. However, such pressures were exacerbated by the general economic downturn in the European market in the mid-1970s. These economic pressures further encouraged retailers to seek markets such as the US, where economic and regulatory conditions were considered more attractive and less restrictive.

The growth of a very large food distribution system in the domestic market, not only had an impact on intra-retail competition, but also on the relationships that existed within the distribution channel. The growth of retail power within the distribution system led some analysts to suggest that a new stage in the development of distribution channels had been achieved. Pommering (1979) suggested that there were three phases of development. The first stage, attributed to the 1950s, was described as a period of manufacturer domination in a context where the unsophisticated distribution system acted merely as a conduit for the flow of goods from producer to retailer. The second stage, the 1960s, was seen as a period when the consumer's role began to change as the growth in consumer choice empowered the consumer in the market. The third stage, the decade of the 1970s, with the concentration of power within the retail sector, saw retailers adopting roles previously attributed to other members of the distribution channel.

As a result of this enhanced role, retailers were in a far stronger position to develop managerial functions such as formalized marketing departments, (Piercy and Alexander 1988) and consequently consider the development of international retail operations. Food retail organizations achieved, and subsequently developed, a capacity to operate outside their domestic markets.

As Vida and Fairhurst (1998) have noted, decision maker characteristics and firm characteristics play an important role in the development of international retail operations. Thus, through increased experience of the international environment, the knowledge base within the firm and the increased commitment of resources, food retailers became more adept at dealing with the challenges of the international market.

Direction of international expansion

Some cross-border or border-hopping activity characterized the early international development of food retailing. Thus, Carrefour experimented with its innovative hypermarket format in adjacent markets in Europe. However, in many instances, European markets were not particularly attractive target markets for international expansion. In the more developed markets of Western Europe, there already existed relatively advanced food retail structures where indigenous retailers were capable of fending off the incursions of retailers from neighbouring markets.

Some international food retailers were successful in the development of less developed markets in Europe, for example on the Iberian peninsula. French retailers, such as Carrefour and Promodès, were to take the lead in these markets, and by the end of the 1980s, had established a considerable market presence in the Spanish and Portuguese markets. These French market entrants often used partnership agreements with local businesses and used fascias other than those used in the domestic market, while the expansion involved the transfer of skills and format from one market to another. This, however, was not the fundamental logic behind the initial process of food retail internationalization by European retailers outside Europe.

During the second half of the 1970s the US proved attractive to European food retailers. Before 1975, the US had seen very little external investment in its food distribution sector. By 1980, 10% of all food retail sales in the US occurred through European-owned retail operations. These sales did not occur mainly through the fascias used by European food retailers in their domestic market, although the German retailer Aldi was an exception to this general trend.

European food retailers' approach to the US retail market was fundamentally investment based. The existing fascias were retained and to a great extent so were existing management structures. Indeed, one of the lessons of this period of expansion was the role existing management are able to play in the development of acquired operations.

In the 1980s, European food retailers were faced with two fundamental options when considering international expansion. There was either the European market or there was the US. For some, diversification in the domestic market proved a third and fundamentally more attractive option. Nevertheless, a small group of ambitious retailers began to explore the possibilities of expansion within Latin America, but this was not considered an option by most of the larger European food retailers at that time.

In the 1990s, the international expansion opportunities began to change. With the collapse of political structures, in the centrally planned countries of East Europe, markets in the region offered new prospects for commercial development on the European retailers' doorstep. Although, the opportunities for expansion in East Europe did not prove as exceptional as had originally been envisaged, some market opportunities did emerge. In particular, the geographically proximate and socio-economically more developed markets of Poland, the Czech Republic and Hungary began to attract European retailers.

Also, in the early 1990s, the markets of East Asia began to attract more interest. Although, European retailers had been operating in East Asian markets for some time, these markets tended to be limited in size or culturally challenging. Hong Kong and Singapore had been the mainstay of international retail penetration within the region for a number of decades, while Japan proved a difficult trading environment. In the early 1990s, the opportunities in the region changed with the emergence of the Asian tiger economies. Suddenly, the region offered large consumer markets that were served by traditional and increasingly outmoded retail structures.

Although, the exploitation of the East Asian market was interrupted by the financial and subsequent economic crises in the region, the region has seen European food retailer expansion. By the end of the 1990s, Tesco operated 13 Lotus stores in Thailand and Ahold operated 39 Tops supermarkets in Thailand, 13 in Singapore, 7 in Indonesia and 5 in Malaysia (Retail Intelligence 1999). Likewise, Carrefour operated 19 hypermarkets in Taiwan, 7 in Thailand, 4 in South Korea, 4 in Malaysia and 3 in Hong Kong.

Latin America has increasingly proved of interest to international food retail operations as markets stabilized. Carrefour, for example has, shown considerable interest in the global region in the 1990s.

International food retailing 2000

At the beginning of the twenty-first century, the international group of food retailers is dominated by European operations. Elsewhere, food retailers have mainly remained willing to operate in the domestic market rather than explore the international opportunities available to them. For example, despite the increasing concentration of food operations in the Australian market, Australian food retailers have proved reluctant to move into potentially lucrative neighbouring markets. This is particularly surprising given the opportunities offered by markets on the Pacific Rim. Nevertheless, it is possible that recent federal government enquiries into the limited number of food retailers operating in the Australian market and their potentially damaging impact on competition, may encourage food retailers based in the market to consider international expansion.

In the US, food retailers have been generally content to remain within the domestic market. Food retailers, such as Safeway, have attempted to establish operations outside the US in the past, although these initiatives are remembered now by the fascias left behind rather than through their current influence on international food retailing. The exception to this rule is Wal-Mart with its much publicized entry into the European market through acquisitions in Germany and the UK. The company has an opportunity to become a world player in the retail food market.

The greatest influence of Wal-Mart on the market however, may not be its commercial activities, but the effect that the global development of the retailer has on the other international retailers. That is, retailers elsewhere may see the arrival or threatened arrival of Wal-Mart in the domestic market as a reason for market consolidation. The recent merger of Carrefour and Promodès is evidence of the likely response to the development of a large international US food operation. However, a particularly crucial point will have been reached when the response to such threats does not merely cause merger activity within a European market, but across European markets.

In Europe, at the end of the 1990s, the largest ten retail organizations were all retailers that had food at the core of their operation. Although many of these retailers had entered other non-food areas, in an attempt to exploit lucrative market opportunities, they were in origin all food retailers (see Table P2.1).

Internationally these retailers have major interests in the various regions of the world. They are investing in North America, in East Asian markets and markets in Latin America. They are also making investments in Europe, particularly the less developed markets of the Mediterranean and the emerging markets in Eastern Europe. One of the significant consequences of these international developments has been the emergence of a new type of food retailer – the global food retailer. Ahold is a good example of one of these.

Retailer	Market of origin	Turnover (Ecu bn)
Metro	Germany	46.6
Intermarché	France	34.5
Rewe	Germany	32.3
Promodès	France	32.3
Edeka	Germany	30.3
Tesco	UK	27.5
Carrefour	France	27.4
Tengelmann	Germany	27.1
Ahold	Netherlands	26.5
Aldi	Germany	23.7

Source: Retail Intelligence 1999

Table P2.1
Largest retailers in Europe, 1997/98

Conclusion

In the past 40 years, food retailing has moved from a nationally based competitive structure to an internationally based competitive structure. The largest food retailers in the world now have considerable international interests. Food retailers will find it increasingly difficult to compete in their domestic markets without the channel power that international operations bring.

Although European food retailers have achieved a global operating base, the food retail structure within Europe remains fractured and regionalized. In the core markets in Europe, there is still relatively little competition from food retailers based in other core markets. Thus, retail structures in France, Germany, the Netherlands and the UK have seen limited international penetration by food retailers based in these markets. Instead, firms from countries are competing for space and market share in emerging markets such as Brazil and Poland.

In Brazil, Carrefour is competing with Ahold, Auchan and Casino for market penetration. In Poland, Carrefour is competing with Ahold, Aldi, Auchan, Dohle, Intermarché, Jerinónimo Martins, Leclerc, Metro and Tesco amongst other west European food retailers.

In their domestic markets, the structure of the local market and planning regulations make it very difficult for retailers to compete with each other as they do in international markets, unless they are prepared to acquire an existing operation or engage in merger activity. Given the relative size of the organizations, the former is not easily achieved and the latter has not so far proved popular. However, with the increasingly competitive nature of the international retail market, such developments will occur as the global food retailers' attempt to secure their market position in the European marketplace. When this does occur, the power of food retailers within the distribution channel in Europe will increase considerably and further alter the balance of power within the channel between producer and retailer, to the advantage of the retailer.

References

Alexander N. (1997) *International Retailing*. Oxford: Blackwell.

Ball R. (1980) Europe's US shopping spree. *Fortune*, 1 December, pp. 82–8.

Burt S. (1991) Trends in the internationalization of grocery retailing: the European experience. *International Review of Retail, Distribution and Consumer Research*, 1 (4), pp. 487–515.

Piercy N. and Alexander N. (1988) The status quo of marketing organization in UK retailers: A neglected phenomenon of the 1980s, *The Service Industries Journal*, 8 (2), pp. 155–75.

Pommering D. (1979) Brand marketing: fresh thinking needed. *Marketing Trends*, 1, pp. 155–75.

Retail Intelligence (1999) *Retail Sans Frontieres: The Internationalisation of European Retailing.* London: Retail Intelligence.

Seigle N. and Handy C. (1981) Foreign ownership in food retailing. *National Food Review*, Winter, pp. 14–16.

Vida I. and Fairhurst A. (1998) International expansion of retail firms: a theoretical approach for future investigations. *Journal of Retail and Consumer Services*, 5 (3), pp. 143–51.

Supply Chain Perspectives

Contemporary Issues

The case of GM food

David Barling

Introduction

The large-scale introduction of GM (genetically modified) crops, mainly imported from overseas, into the food chain since 1996 has been met with strong consumer resistance in Europe. The strength of the public's reaction initially caught many by surprise, not least the large agricultural biotechnology corporations and the large food manufacturers. The force and breadth of this reaction has reverberated back along the food supply chain, creating a series of complex challenges, both to the key actors along the food supply chain and to governmental regulators (national and international) alike.

A key signal from the market has been interpreted as the need to provide the consumer with a choice between GM and non-GM foods. However, within this statement lies a range of disputed terms and definitions. Also, the establishment of a supply chain of non-GM foods has invoked a range of issues and challenges at the different points along the international food chain. The operation of a meaningful labelling regime within the European Union (EU) is also a major challenge as it is dependent on some method of verification, for which reliable and accurate detection methods are necessary. The concept of consumer choice has not stopped at the labelling of the final product. There has been a gradual, sometimes begrudging, acceptance that systems of identity preservation or segregation for non-GM and GM foods, allowing for the possibility of traceability and audit trails along the food chain, are necessary for genuine consumer choice. It has been the retailers and the food manufacturers who have taken the lead in the development of alternative supply chains to meet the consumer's desire for non-GM food.

GMOs and the food supply chain: alternative models

The established view of the entry of GMOs (genetically modified organisms) into the food chain is depicted in Figure P3.1, starting with the agricultural biotechnology companies and the development of patented GM seeds, moving along to the producer or farmer/grower until the food product reaches the consumer. However, the reaction of European consumers to the large scale entry of GM foods, has inverted the sequence of the food chain, as the large food retailers have responded to their consumers' concerns. Hence, these retailers have confirmed

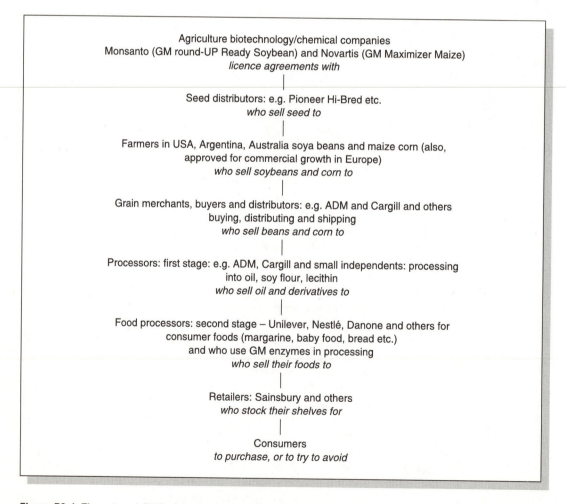

Figure P3.1 The entry of GMOs into the food chain

their key role as powerful contractors in the supply chain, as well as effectively being gatekeepers for their customers concerns (Marsden *et al.* 2000). The food retailers have sought to manage the supply chain in order to provide a non-GM supply separate from the intermingled supplies (of GM with non-GM commodities), that initially entered the food chain in 1996.

Figure P3.2 provides a different dynamic to the food chain relationship for the supply of GM/non-GM foods. In this dynamic the end user, the consumer and subsequently the retailer become key drivers. To quote Bill Wadsworth, technical director of Iceland, who pioneered the search for a non-GM soybean supply: 'The only way that any European consumer was given a choice was because we fundamentally broke the supply chain. We set up a totally unique supply chain' (House of Commons Select Committee on Science and Technology 1999). Hence, we see two alternative models of the food supply chain in existence with the latter model seeking to establish itself effectively. It was the large-scale entry of GM soybean and maize commodities into the European food chain that triggered these developments, as the next section explains.

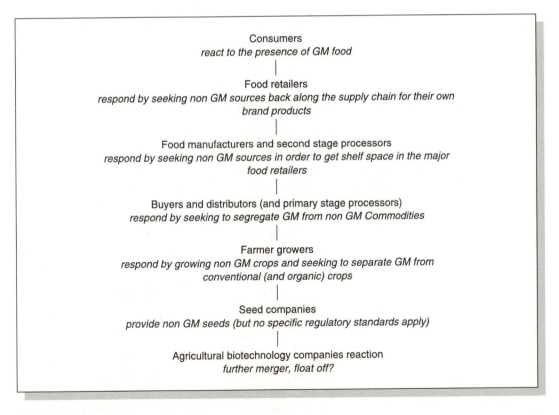

Consumers
react to the presence of GM food

|

Food retailers
respond by seeking non GM sources back along the supply chain for their own brand products

|

Food manufacturers and second stage processors
respond by seeking non GM sources in order to get shelf space in the major food retailers

|

Buyers and distributors (and primary stage processors)
respond by seeking to segregate GM from non GM Commodities

|

Farmer growers
respond by growing non GM crops and seeking to separate GM from conventional (and organic) crops

|

Seed companies
provide non GM seeds (but no specific regulatory standards apply)

|

Agricultural biotechnology companies reaction
further merger, float off?

Figure P3.2 The dynamic for the supply of non-GM foods

None the less, in attempting to realize the non-GM food chain the actors in the food chain and the regulators are faced with a number of complex challenges.

The large scale entry of GM crops into the European food supply and the market reaction

The first large scale planting of GM crops began in North America in 1996. By 1998, farmers in the large crop-growing areas of countries such as the US, Canada and Argentina grew commercially an estimated 27.8 million hectares of GM crop varieties, increasing to 39.9 million hectares in 1999 (Gene Watch UK 1999). This first generation of GM crops were cleared by their government authorities for field characteristics determined by bacterial genes, such as tolerance to the broad spectrum herbicides glyphosate and glufosinate ammonium and insect resistance due to the insertion of genes from the soil bacterium *Bacillus thuringiensis* (*Bt*).

The first GM crops were novel extensions of the agrochemical technology inputs that offered potential agronomic benefits to farmer/growers, such as reducing the number of herbicide sprays during crop cultivation and more effective immediate pest control. This first generation of GM products reflected the growing corporate concentration that was developing in the so-called 'life sciences' sectors. The 'life sciences' strategy was to bring together pharmaceuticals, biotechnology, agribusiness, food, chemicals, cosmetics and energy (e.g. ethanol) all under one corporate umbrella. The large agrochemical companies were rapidly merging and integrating in the 1990s both horizontally and vertically. For example, Aventis was formed from the merger of Hoescht (which included AgrEvo) and Rhône Poulenc. Novartis emerged from the merger of Ciba Geigy and Sandoz and Astra Zeneca was a merger of a pharmaceutical with a crop science company. In the US, Monsanto and DuPont, as well as Novartis and Astra Zeneca from Europe, were rapidly absorbing seed companies to exploit their germplasm holdings (RAFI 1999). In addition, the agricultural biotechnology corporations had entered into strategic alliances with the large agribusinesses who in turn controlled large sections of the grain commodity gathering and distribution markets in the US and for overseas export. Monsanto formed an alliance with Cargill and Novartis with Archer Daniels Midland (ADM) (Heffernan *et al.* 1999). The US agricultural biotechnology companies were estimated to have spent approximately $2000 million on research and development by 1995, while sales of agricultural biotechnology products amounted to just $100 million in that year (Robinson *et al.* 1998: 52). Hence, there was a pressing need to realize these investments with increased sales as the first large scale plantings of GM crops began. In 1996, Monsanto's Round-Up Ready soybean, containing bacterial genes for glyphosate tolerance and a marker gene resistant to the antibiotic ampicillin, received an EU marketing licence for grain importation, storage and use in agriculture. This was initially seen as a turning point for the industry, by critics and supporters alike, as it allowed for the large scale importation of GM soybean and derivatives into the European food market (Anon 1996).

It was estimated that something like 60% of foodstuffs on sale in Europe would contain GM soybean derivatives. In 1997, Novartis' Maximizer GM *Bt* maize, which included novel genes for resistance to the European corn borer and marker genes for tolerance to glufosinate and resistance to the antibiotic ampicillin, was licensed for importation and agricultural use. Subsequently, in 1998 some 15 000 hectares of *Bt* maize were grown in Spain and 1000 hectares in France (NFU 1998).

The EU's approval of the Novartis' *Bt* maize had been extremely divisive. The presence of the marker gene for resistance to the antibiotic ampicillin had lead several competent national authorities to vote against commercial approval under the regulatory directive for the deliberate release of GMOs into the environment (90/220). The national authorities were concerned that as the maize would be used for animal feed, the marker gene resistant to ampicillin might pass to the animal's gut, become activated there and cause therapeutic problems (Barling 1997). This conflict symbolized the difficulties that the regulatory regime under Directive 90/220 was experiencing, which has led to its revision.

The risk assessment boundaries under the regulation were unclear and had generally failed to take adequate account of the possible wider ecological effects of the release of GMOs, in particular with the regard to the potential impacts upon local and regional biodiversity in Europe.

Also, the agricultural impacts of particular GM crops were often ignored in the risk assessment process under the regulatory regime's procedures. Consequently, although certain GM varieties of maize and oilseed rape gained regulatory approval, under the EU process, they were subsequently denied market access in individual member states, putting further stress on the regulatory regime (Barling 2000). In June 1999 the Council of Ministers announced a *de facto* moratorium of new commercial approvals until the completion of the revision of the Directive. Also, this example highlighted the lack of legislation covering GM animal feed.

The first large scale shipment from the US of GM soybean mixed in with non modified grain reached Antwerp in 1996 where Greenpeace organized an unsuccessful attempt to prevent the unloading of the cargo. The protests did succeed in raising public awareness, notably amongst northern continental consumers, of the large scale entry of GM commodities into the

European food chain. The disquiet amongst the German public led some of the main food processors and distributors, including Unilever and Nestlé, to remove soy oil from these modified soybeans at the end of 1996 (Nottingham 1998). However they refused at this stage to remove the oil from their products in other European countries. Survey evidence through the 1990s suggested that the European public were wary of the application of GM to food, wanted clear labelling and were concerned with the environmental impacts, as well as the potential human health risks, of GM food production. Trust in the regulators was extremely low in most of Europe, in part reflecting the lack of confidence from successive food and health crises (Barling *et al.* 1999).

The publicity attached to the imports of the soybean and maize and the increased focus on the potential impacts upon biodiversity and farming practice in the European agri-environment, of herbicide- and pesticide-modified GM crops, all helped to heighten these public concerns further. The sluggish response of the regulatory process was quickly outpaced by the further response of the key commercial players in the food chain as the public voiced their disquiet as consumers.

The public discontent at the entry of these GM products into the food chain spread to other major European nations, notably in France and the UK, by the end of 1998. The public's concerned reached fever pitch in the early months of 1999, as was reflected by campaigns on the issue of GM foods by the tabloid newspapers, the *Daily Express* and the *Daily Mail*. The sensitivity of the UK market was reflected in the case of a GM tomato paste that had been launched in both the Sainsbury and Safeway supermarket chains in the UK in 1996. The launch of this product was seen as an example of good practice for a new technology product entry, with full labelling and explanatory leaflets. Initially, it outsold its non-modified alternative, which it undercut in price. However by the end of the decade the supermarkets, due to falling sales, had withdrawn the product. Sainsbury had responded to the increased media reports about GM food in early 1999 by opening a dedicated customer call line on the subject. They received 300 calls in the first four hours and reacted accordingly (House of Commons Select Committee for Agriculture 1999).

Initial calls from European food retailers and processors for the segregation of modified from non-modified soybean for the European market were met with resistance in the US by the large US grain companies and the American Soybean Association (Anon 1997). The UK frozen food retailer, Iceland, responded by leading a search for non-modified sources of soybean from Canada and Brazil for their own brand foods. Iceland also sourced non-modified soybean derivatives from the same area in Brazil. The company sought to verify their supplies using the detection methodology for GM DNA of polymerase chain reaction (PCR) technology, developed by a US company, which they then brought over to labs in the UK. However, the reliability of these detection methods was not complete, so Iceland supported them with a clear audit trail of testing through the different stages of the food chain, from the field through to the different processing and manufacturing phases (House of Commons Select Committee on Science and Technology 1999). In March 1998 they were able to announce their own brand foods as being non-GM.

The major supermarket retailers in the UK and northern Europe soon followed Iceland's lead. In March 1999, a consortium of Sainbury, Marks & Spencer, Carrefour (France), SuperQuinn (Ireland), Effelunga (Italy), Migros (Switzerland) and Delhaize (Belgium) was announced. Their intention was to create a market presence with enough buying power to ensure the maintenance of a non-GM supply chain, fully tested and audited for their own brand products (Anon 1999). The major processors also followed suit, under pressure from the retailers, as did some of the major restaurant and catering groups. A survey by Friends of the Earth found that in March 2000 most of the world's top twenty-six food manufacturers who sold in the European market had adopted non-GM policies for that market (Friends of the Earth 2000).

The US suppliers began to make more amenable responses to the question of segregation of soybean (and maize) exports to Europe and Japan by the end of decade, as they saw their share decline in these export markets. This meant the dedication of discrete grain elevators, silos and ship containers for non-GM commodities by companies like ADM. Some US farmers also began to respond to the demands of the European and Japanese market by revising their growing of GM crops. Cargill offered some growers a premium for non-GM soybean for manufacture as Japanese Tofu. The Managing Director of Cargill in the UK, speaking in late 1999, considered that for the next five years the food industry would 'remain where it is . . . i.e. that it will not receive GM ingredients' (House of Commons Select Committee on Agriculture 2000). Hence, the creation of a non-GM supply chain was international in its scope. In 1999 the regional government of the Brazilian province of Rio Grande del Suid sought to ban the growing of GM soybean, putting it in dispute with the national authorities (Bellos 1999). The following year the first futures contract for GM free grain (soybean) was announced for the Tokyo Grain Exchange (Tett 2000). The value of agricultural bi-technology within the large 'life sciences' corporations came under scrutiny. Further mergers occurred (e.g Monsanto with Pharmacia Upjohn) and the possible float of the agricultural biotechnology arms from some of these large corporations was rumoured.

In effect, a private system of regulation that was market led rapidly appeared, enabled both by the corporate concentration in different stages of the food chain (at retailing, processing and, to a lesser extent, catering) and to some extent by the improvements in detection technology. At the production and commodity distribution end of the food system corporate concentration had facilitated the development of agricultural biotechnology. Ironically, corporate concentration at the retail and food processing ends of the food system was enabling the European consumers' rejection of the technology. However, despite the rapid move to find non-GM supply chains, the search for non-GM products, especially soybeans and maize and their derivatives, faced a number of difficulties at the various stages of the food chain.

The challenges for segregation/identity preservation of non-GM food

The use of identity preservation (IP) systems for separating premium crops from the main bulk predated the growing of GM crops. However, the introduction of IP systems on such a large scale amongst crops like soybean, that were traditionally intermingled through bulk methods of collection, storage and transportation, were more challenging.

The challenges to generating a non-GM supply of, for example, soybean or maize starts with the planting and harvesting of seed on the farm. Potential problems include the possibility of the mixing of GM with non-GM seeds due to: impurity in the seed, mixing with volunteer plants already in the field, seed lying dormant in the soil seed bank and mutation in the crop emerging in later generations. Also, there is possibility of cross-pollination, raising questions of the adequacy of the separation distances between GM and non-GM crops. Mixing with seeds through harvesting, drilling and storage equipment is also a possibility. Hence strong protocols of good practice need to be adhered to by the agricultural industries (Barling 2000). In addition, care needs to be taken over segregation in animal feed, where the industry has lagged behind in developing protocols and segregation compared to the human food supply.

The subsequent move towards segregated handling systems has begun, but accidental or adventitious contamination remains a remote possibility during these stages, although safeguards were being put in place to try to avoid any intermingling beyond the farm gate during the shipment and transportation of grain. Initial claims that premiums would be added to the non-GM supplies and result in increased cost to the consumer were not realized. The final costs of segregating non-GM from GM grain within these bulk systems have yet to reach the consumer (House of Commons Select Committee on Agriculture 2000). Also, the derivatives added to the final manufactured food product are such a small percentage of that product that the impact on the final cost has been minimal. The segregation at the processing of the grain at both the primary stage (into oils, flour and other derivatives such as lecithin) and the secondary stage (insertion of oils etc. into the final manufactured product, such as margarine) intended for human consumption, has become increasingly widespread.

Finally, the presentation of the final product to the consumer via food retailers and catering outlets, has been the focus of an evolving and somewhat confusing labelling regime within the European Union (EU).

The EU labelling regime for GM food and international tensions

The prevalence of soya derivatives in processed foods highlighted the shortcomings of the EU's regulations for labelling GM foods as laid down in 90/220 and the Novel Foods and Novel Food Ingredients Regulation (258/97). The estimated 60% of foodstuffs on sale containing GM soybean derivatives would not be labelled as to their GM content. The Commission then began an incremental process of strengthening the labelling provisions relating to live GMOs and GM foods, focusing in particular on those foods with ingredients derived from GM soybean and maize. The labelling of ingredients and manufactured foods was dependent upon the detection of any GM DNA or protein in the final product.

Threshold levels for adventitious contamination were also set, at a maximum of 1% for the total food product and also for any specific ingredients therein. The emphasis was on accepting a tolerance limit for any adventitious contamination, as it was realized that such contamination remained possible at the various stages of the food chain. The threshold level was also seen as realistic given the limited ability of the technology to detect extremely low levels of GM DNA or protein presence. However, as the detection technology was seen as becoming more precise, so pressure remained for the threshold level to be reviewed and revised downwards when possible. The labelling regime has also extended to food additives. A further goal of the Commission was the introduction of a 'GM free' label, as opposed to 'non-GM'. However, the adventitious contamination and incomplete detection methodology remained obstacles to introducing a truly accurate GM free label (House of Commons Select Committee on Agriculture 2000). Certainly, to achieve such labelling a far tougher regulatory regime in terms of isolation distances for the planting of GM crops would have to be introduced and GM seed regulation would have to be in place. Neither regulatory condition exists at the time of writing (mid-way through 2000).

The extensions of the labelling regime still focused on the composition of the final product, not upon the methods of production. Systems for traceability from seed to shelf, which might force consumers to take a process based choice in their food purchase, were not regulated in the 1990s, rather they emerged from the industry initiatives explained previously. None the less, the European Commission conceded that such systems of complete traceability of food products, from seed to shelf, would be its goal and the requirements in the Common Position on the revision of 90/220 reflected this ambition (Barling 2000).

The reaction of the US regulators to the resistance of the European consumers was to seek to support the interests of the large agricultural biotechnology companies through recourse to international trade politics. The General Agreement on Trade and Tariffs (GATT) Uruguay Round agreements from 1993 had set up a rules based regime for international trade, including food and agriculture within its scope, under a newly formed World Trade Organization (WTO).

The agreement on the application of sanitary and phytosanitary (SPS) measures had given the WTO governance over disputes concerning food standards, including the power over the imposition of sanctions upon member states deemed to have broken the rules, through a disputes panel process. The advisory body on issues of safety and standards to the WTO was to be the United Nations' joint FAO/WHO body, the Codex Alimentarius Commission. A further agreement, on Technical Barriers to Trade (TBT), also included a rule prohibiting the imposition of labels on traded goods that discriminated against them on the basis of means of production. This provision offered a potential challenge through the WTO disputes procedures to the evolving European regime on labelling. The presence of these agreements loomed over the increasing divergence between the US and EU regulatory regimes on GM foods. The US employed the rhetoric of potential trade war over the transatlantic disagreement over GM foods and the Clinton Administration put diplomatic pressure on the UK government under Tony Blair to seek concessions from their European partners (Hencke and Evans 2000). The US government's official position was that labelling of GM foods was discriminatory, as there were no scientific grounds for distinguishing GM crops and foods from non-GM. The validity of this scientific position was highly contested, however, both by social interests and national governments.

Many of the key differences between the US, EU and other nations were on the subject of ongoing negotiations within Codex, including the labelling of GM foods. Early in 2000 an International Biosafety Protocol was finally agreed on the safe transfer, handling and use of any living modified organisms resulting from biotechnology, under the Convention on

Biodiversity. The conclusion was reached after extensive delays from the so called Miami Group of large scale GM commodity exporters, whose positions were co-ordinated by the US and supported by the large biotechnology industries. The agreements reached by the Protocol suggested a positive way forward to handle the international movement of GMOs. None the less, differences remained between the WTO agreements and the Protocol and the relationship between these agreements in international law remained ambiguous (Allen 2000).

Conclusions

The dynamics behind the entry of GM food onto the European market and the reaction, in turn, of the European market and the food supply chain have been outlined. The key roles of the large food retailers and the other sectors of the food chain close to the consumer, such as the food manufacturers and processors, have been identified. The drivers in the food chain are increasingly those actors placed at the consumption end rather than at the production end.

The search for a non-GM food supply became an issue of international politics, as the EU and other national and international regulators sought to balance the demands of the European public with the priorities of international trade and the economic interests of the large scale agricultural biotechnology corporations. The case of GM food or, more accurately, of non-GM food provides a vivid example of the challenges facing the management of the international food supply chain in the new millennium.

References

Allen E. (2000) Greens and free-traders join to cheer GM crop deal. *The Financial Times*, 31 January, p. 11.

Anon (1996) European Union okays use of soybean produced by biotechnology; case seen as turning point for industry. *World Food Regulation Review*, 5/12: 27

Anon (1997), Boycott begins against products containing US genetically engineered soybeans. *World Food Regulation Review*, 6 (6), pp. 22–3.

Anon (1999) Sainsbury's, M&S in 'GM-free' retailer consortium. *ENDS Report*, 290, pp. 33–4.

Barling D. (1997) Regulatory conflict and the marketing of agricultural biotechnology in the European Community. In John Stanyer and Geoff Stoker (eds), *Contemporary Political Studies 1997*. Nottingham: Political Studies Association of the United Kingdom, pp. 1040–8.

Barling D., de Vriend H., Cornelese J.A., Ekstrand B., Hecker E.F.F., Howlett J., Jensen J.H., Lang T., Mayer S., Staer K.B.

and Trop R. (1999) The social aspects of food biotechnology: a European view. *Environmental Toxicology and Pharmacology*, 7, pp. 85–93.

Barling D. (2000) GM crops, biodiversity and the European Agri-environment: regulatory lacunae and revision 2000. *European Environment*, 12 (4).

Bellos A. (1999) Brazil fights phantom menace in soya wars. *The Guardian*, Society section, 9 June, p. 4.

Buffin D. (1998) Genetic segregation: an interview with Malcolm Walker. *Pesticides News*, 40, June, pp. 6–7.

Friends of the Earth (2000) European food manufacturers shun GMOs but consumers urged to keep up the pressure. Press Release, Friends of the Earth, UK, 7 March.

Gene Watch UK (2000) GM Crops and Food: A Review of Developments in 1999. Gene Watch UK Briefing 9. Tideswell: Gene Watch UK.

Heffernan W.D., Hendrickson M. and Gronski R. (1999) Consolidation in the Food and Agriculture System. Report prepared for the National Farmers Union. Columbia: University of Missouri.

Hencke D. and Evans R. (2000) How US put pressure on Blair over GM food. *The Guardian*, 28 February, p. 8.

House of Commons Select Committee on Science and Technology (1999) Minutes of evidence: Examination of Witnesses (Questions 1–19) 3 March 1999. http//www.parliament.the-stationery-office.co.uk/pa/cm199899/cmselect/c. . ./9030303.ht. 1 April 1999.

House of Commons Select Committee on Agriculture (2000) The Segregation of Genetically Modified Foods. Third Report 199–2000. http://ww.publications.parliament.uk/pa/cm199900/cmselect/cmagric/71/7103.htm. 15 March 2000.

Marsden T., Flynn A. and Harrison M. (2000) *Consuming Interests: the Social Provision of Foods*. London: UCL Press.

NFU (1998) Written evidence of the NFU of England and Wales to the House of Lords' European Communities Committee inquiry into EC regulation of genetic modification in agriculture. London: National Farmers Union.

Nottingham S. (1998) *Eat your Genes: How Genetically Modified Food is Entering our Diet*. London: Zed Books.

RAFI (1999) The Gene Giants: Masters of the Universe? RAFI Communique March/April. http://www.rafi.org/communique/flxt/19992.html. 9 September 1999.

Robinson D.J., Davies H.V., Birch A.N.E., Wilson T., Kerby N.W., Squire G.R. and Hillman J.R. (1998) Development, Release and Regulation of GM crops. Scottish Crop Research Institute Annual Report 1997/98. Invergowrie: SCRI.

Tett G. (2000) Japan starts first GM-free futures contract. *The Financial Times*, 22 March, p. 43.

European trends in food safety: implications for the hotel sector

Tim Knowles

Context

Throughout the food supply chain, food safety is of paramount importance and successive governments have legislated to ensure this is achieved. In Europe, following more than 30 years of legislative activity, most national food laws have been harmonized at European Union (EU) level. However, a gap has emerged between legislative intention and operational good practice in hotels. Such dissonance has clear implications for the provision of safe food to the customer (Knowles 1992, 1994, 1999).

Many studies have maintained that the community's legislative programme in the foodstuffs sector has had a generally positive impact (EC Commission 1996). Yet, by contrast, Knowles (1999) has highlighted a number of criticisms of the programme in terms of unnecessarily detailed legislation; fragmentation; difficulties of adapting the legislation to innovation and problems in the day-to-day functioning of the internal market. Furthermore, recent unfortunate events, such as BSE, *E. coli* and the continuing debate over GM foods, raise doubts about the capacity of existing legislation to fulfil its public health objectives (Pennington Report 1997).

The central issue from the literature is that, in contrast to legislation in most member states, EU food law has developed very much in an *ad hoc* fashion over time (Painter 1991; O'Connor 1993; Roberts 1993; North 1996). There has been no central unifying text setting out the fundamental principles of EU food law, one that clearly defines the obligations of all concerned (WHO 1988).

Influences

Whilst this perspective focuses upon the hotel industry, the primary influence on food safety has evolved specifically from the realization of the internal market (EC Commission 1986). For the future, the development of activities in the hotel sector will also be strongly influenced by the new provisions added by the Maastricht Treaty concerning human health protection (Article 129), consumer protection (Article 129a) and the environment (Article 4 130r) (see EC Commission 1993b).

EU legislation applicable to foodstuffs has developed from the variety of legal bases set out in the treaty to serve different policy objectives. Such opacity is open to criticism since there is no coherent policy and the approach is piecemeal. The BSE crisis, which has affected red meat sales in hotel restaurants, is one example that has highlighted the need for a European food policy to mitigate the fragmentary approach of legislators (COMM 1997a, 1997b; EC Commission 1985).

Rationalization

The need for rationalization comes from the complexity, fragmentation and incoherence of EU food law, specifically in terms of the formulation of a European food policy. Certain legislative provisions are unnecessarily detailed and prescriptive and fail to take account of the development of internal control systems by the hotel industry. Duplication of legislative provisions is a case in point (EC Commission 1985). All developed countries have adopted a substantial body of legislation which seeks to guarantee that food is safe, wholesome and fit for human consumption, that commercial transactions are conducted fairly and that the necessary systems of official control and inspection are put in place.

However, in recent years, a new range of issues concerning foodstuffs has emerged, as a result of increasing scientific knowledge (e.g. genetically modified organisms, awareness of the links between nutrition and health) and as a result of the new aspirations of consumers. As the implementation of the internal market has progressed, national rules have increasingly been replaced by EU legislation. It follows that, with this transfer of decision-making, the EU must itself develop policies that both provide for a high level of protection and meet the legitimate demands and expectations of consumers. However, at the same time, the EU must also avoid legislation that imposes unnecessary burdens on the hotel industry, the costs of which, of course, would ultimately be passed on to consumers through higher prices. In essence, the central issue in developing an appropriate policy revolves around the adopted regulatory framework (Jackson 1990).

Regulatory approach and EU working procedures

The regulatory framework must be designed and implemented in a way that places primary responsibility for the production of safe and wholesome food with producers and the hotel industry. As a principle, the framework should offer the industry flexibility to design and implement appropriate internal monitoring procedures, provided that these procedures are backed up by effective official control systems. The problem for EU legislators is that both industry- and product-specific approaches offer advantages and disadvantages. An industry (horizontal) approach makes it possible to take a general overview of a particular situation and facilitates implementation, particularly for food businesses working in many sectors, including not only manufacturers, but also hotels, both small and large. A product (vertical) approach, on the other hand, makes it possible to adjust the legislation to the needs of a specific sector, particularly in cases where a more targeted approach to legislation has been judged necessary. It also makes it possible to envisage a more integrated regulatory framework that covers all facets of a particular sector.

Since a more prescriptive approach requires legislators to identify the major risk factors and the means of managing those risks, it often makes it easier for hoteliers to identify their obligations and hence facilitates the tasks of the control authorities. In this sense, prescription results in control (North 1996).

A more general approach, on the other hand, leaves industry with greater flexibility in the implementation of the legislation and is thus likely to reduce compliance costs. It is also likely to minimize the need for frequent updating of the legislation. However, it requires both hotel businesses and the control authorities to take a much more proactive role in analysing the food safety hazards presented by different activities and ensuring that effective measures may be taken to control them. Evidence from Knowles (1999) suggests that a sizeable minority have not adopted this proactive approach. The need to be proactive may present particular difficulties for small businesses in the hotel sector, (i.e., 80% in the UK and 95% in Italy), although the elaboration of industry-wide codes of practice may provide a partial solution to this problem.

It should be noted that industry- and product-specific approaches are not necessarily mutually exclusive. Indeed, empirical evidence from Knowles (1999) suggests that the industry is experiencing difficulties in adapting to a general approach and while this problematic situation does not negate such an evolving framework, stronger emphasis should be placed on training and monitoring by the authorities. In such circumstances, a balanced approach is necessary between detailed prescriptive legislation and a more general legislative approach.

In developing this theme of regulation, due to the sensitivity of the foodstuffs sector within hotels, debate has occurred upon the extent to which the use of codes of practice are appropriate, either as an alternative to regulation, or in order to supplement it. The problem here is the degree to which codes remain genuinely voluntary.

Another issue to recognize is that, at the national level, there has been an increasing employment of codes of practice, a usage that brings with it the risk of new *de facto* barriers to intra-Community trade and the free movement of goods and services within the EU. In the field of food hygiene, voluntary instruments are being used to complement the existing legislation, for instance, Article 5 of Directive 93/43/EEC (EC Commission 1993a).

It should be noted that to be fully effective, the principles of subsidiarity and legislative simplification must be applied at the *national* as well as at the *Community* level – situations contradicted by current available evidence i.e. differences in temperature control within member states. Consistency in the application of this principle is important, otherwise there will be a constant risk of fragmentation of the internal market into separate national markets. In line with the principle of subsidiarity, member states can therefore adopt more detailed legislation in order to take account of the particular situation in their countries, a good example being Denmark in relation to the issue of temperature control (Act 1973, 1993). However, so as to protect the Community interest, notably the operation of the internal market, the Commission has powers to supervise the use that member states make of this possibility.

To be effective, consultation on food safety matters should be concerned with the technical aspects of a proposal and should also involve those with socio-economic interests affected by EU legislation, e.g. hoteliers. While this consultation process does in part exist through the *Advisory Committee on Foodstuffs*, established in 1975, it is important for reasons of clarity to take steps to improve the process through, for instance, the increased use of Green Papers.

Directives versus regulations

The provisions of certain initiatives can be extremely detailed and leave little or no margin for the discretion of member states in their implementation. Examples include specific EU provisions relating to materials in contact with foodstuffs (EC Commission 1989a). In such circumstances, the use of regulation as an alternative to the directive may present several advantages:

- Enabling the uniform application of legislation throughout the internal market.

- Increasing the transparency of EU law and since member states can avoid the implementation of legislation, facilitating the rapid updating of Community legislation in order to take account of technical and scientific developments.

For these reasons, it is argued that consideration should be given to greater use of regulations in appropriate cases, both in primary and in secondary EU legislation. However, legislation that is limited in scope to the harmonization of general principles and criteria, such as legislation on the Official Control of Foodstuffs, should continue to be adopted by means of a directive (EC Commission 1989b).

Democratic deficit

Practices and procedures within the foodstuffs industry are continually evolving and, from the point of view of innovation and the competitiveness of the hotel industry, it is important that innovatory products should gain swift access to the European market. This environment of rapid change means that an ability to amend legislation quickly to take account of technical and scientific progress is of fundamental importance. From the public health perspective, it is also important to be able to adapt legislation promptly so as to take account of new risk factors that may emerge. However, the problem lies with a Community that does not possess the instruments that are necessary to respond to the growing pace of innovation and the ever-increasing range of scientific knowledge, as in the case of GM technology.

One reason for this situation is the unwillingness of the Council and Parliament to delegate to the Commission the necessary powers for the technical implementation of EU legislation. Although the Council and Parliament have entrusted significant powers to the Commission in fields such as general food hygiene, materials in contact with foodstuffs and food labelling, in other areas there has been much less delegation of authority to the Commission. For example, in the area of food additives, any amendment requires, on average, about five years to complete procedures at the EU level which increases to six or seven years, if allowance is also made for the time necessary for the adoption of national implementation measures. By contrast, in most, if not all, member states, a similar decision would be taken far more rapidly by a ministerial order, on advice from the competent national scientific advisory committee and without the need for primary legislation. It is argued that the adaptation of Community legislation to innovation and technical progress in the foodstuffs sector constitutes a serious problem, which needs to be urgently addressed.

Definitional problems

Another area to tackle in the EU foodstuffs legislation is the problem of definition. Many directives already contain a series of definitions, including those on materials and articles intended to come into contact with foodstuffs, labelling, nutrition labelling, nutrition claims, official control of foodstuffs and hygiene of foodstuffs.

However, doubts have sometimes arisen as to whether these definitions apply only to those specific pieces of legislation in which they are contained, or whether they apply more generally. To remove any further doubt, these definitions should be generally applicable to all EU legislation on foodstuffs. Furthermore, although the legislation of most member states contains a definition of 'foodstuffs', the Community does not yet have its own definition. The benefit of an EU definition is that it would ensure that all such legislation on foodstuffs would apply to the same products and substances in all member states.

A further question concerns the application of the definition of primary food production, which may be intended either for human consumption or for industrial use (e.g. potatoes, which may be consumed as food may also be used for the production of industrial starch, or chemicals used as food additives). Their inclusion within the scope of the definition would mean that producers would have to fulfil all the relevant obligations arising under EU food legislation, which may be inappropriately restrictive. However, it is obviously necessary to ensure that all substances used in food meet the requirements of Community legislation. Furthermore, the concept of 'placing on the market' is employed several times in EU food legislation, without actually being defined.

Although a definition of marketing is included in the veterinary hygiene directives, its use is not entirely suitable for the purposes of foodstuffs legislation since it excludes retail sale. Other definitions of placing on the market are included in Directive 90/220/EEC (EC Commission 1990) on the deliberate release of genetically modified organisms into the environment, but these definitions are not entirely appropriate to the foodstuffs sector.

Food hygiene

EU legislation on food hygiene and the hotel industry is an area that raises difficult questions for simplification and rationalization within the Community. For instance, foodstuffs of animal origin are covered by a series of 11 product (vertical) directives establishing specific conditions of hygiene for the categories concerned: fresh meat, poultry meat, meat products, minced meat and meat preparations, rabbit, farmed and wild game, fish, shellfish, eggs and egg products, milk and milk products and other products such as frogs legs, snails and honey. These directives set out specific regulatory requirements for various features of these products, while using a HACCP based approach for other aspects.

Alternatively, for foodstuffs not covered by these specific provisions, it is the General Directive on the Hygiene of Foodstuffs that applies (EC Commission 1993a). This directive adopts a more generalized approach to hazard management, based on the application of HACCP principles and the development of voluntary codes of good hygiene practices.

The co-existence of these two approaches opens the door to numerous criticisms of inconsistency and incoherence. Thus, Article 1(2) of the general hygiene directive requires the Commission to establish a relationship between specific hygiene rules and those of the general directive and, if necessary, to make proposals.

As a first step in this process, the Commission has launched a large-scale consultation exercise on the inter-relationship between the vertical veterinary hygiene rules, which apply to foodstuffs of animal origin. To this end, the Commission has prepared a guide to certain rules governing the production, marketing and importation of products of animal origin intended for human consumption. The guide envisages the consolidation of the provisions of 14 separate directives relating to animal and public health into a single text that would also cover the conditions of imports from third countries. Certain common principles, such as HACCP, would be extended to cover all the directives and a number of unnecessarily detailed provisions and contradictions in the texts would be eliminated.

Additionally, the Commission has launched a consultation exercise on the possibilities for simplification of the rules, with the following areas being investigated:

- The role of voluntary instruments, such as standards or codes of practice in veterinary hygiene.

- Temperature control requirements.

- The need and appropriateness of derogations (allowances) for small and medium-sized enterprises.

- The international dimension of veterinary hygiene rules.

- The role of self-control by manufacturers and the role of the public authorities.

- Authorization procedures and procedures for the approval of establishments.

Further questions have also been raised concerning the inclusion in hygiene legislation of quality or labelling provisions that are not directly related to food hygiene. Once the relationship between the specific vertical hygiene directives has been clarified, consideration must be given to the association between them and the general directive on food hygiene. In this context, it would appear appropriate to give priority to ensuring that there is a coherent and consistent body of legislation relating to food hygiene. This goal can best be achieved by the application of HACCP principles and limiting detailed prescriptive provisions to cases where they are considered essential. Nevertheless, it should be noted that there is some flexibility in the manner in which HACCP principles are conceived and applied in present legislation (HMSO 1993).

In the general hygiene directive, it was not considered necessary to lay down formal HACCP requirements regarding verification and documentation, which may be considered a significant weakness. Each food business is left with the flexibility to decide what requirements are necessary, subject to the supervision of the competent authority, thus leaving an element of discretion. By contrast, because of the nature of the foodstuffs concerned, the basic principles for 'own checks', set out in the veterinary hygiene directives, include detailed rules on keeping written records for presentation to the competent authority. This example illustrates flexibility in the design and implementation of food hygiene regulations to ensure the maintenance of a high level of protection, while keeping the regulatory burden for hotels to a minimum.

The search for consistency and coherence between the two approaches has therefore been unsuccessful. Ultimately there is no uniform system.

Weaknesses are therefore emerging in this twin track approach, since to be effective, any system of food hygiene legislation must cover the entire food chain, from primary production until the point of consumption. The general food hygiene directive covers all stages of food production and distribution *after* primary agricultural production. There is no general community legislation covering the hygiene of products of non-animal origin at the primary agricultural production stage. In the case of foodstuffs of animal origin, the primary production stage is covered by the veterinary hygiene rules. These directives cover all stages from primary production to distribution. However, retail sale in general is excluded from the scope of the veterinary hygiene rules and the general hygiene directive therefore applies. The result of this lack of coherence and consistency is confusion.

Protecting the consumer

Contained within Article 100a (3), Article 129 and Article 129a of the Treaty, there are varying requirements for the Commission to address consumer protection (EC Commission 1986).

It is argued that the establishment of a proper EU food policy that gives pride of place to consumer protection and health is an important step towards satisfying these Treaty obligations. In this spirit, the Union must provide itself with the necessary means of action, by identifying two imperatives:

- The closer involvement of the Parliament in the decision-making process (to this end the Commission should make more use of Article 100a, qualified majority voting).

- The need to give the Community greater powers in the field of health.

As far as food safety is concerned, there can be no scope for compromise. The Treaty requires the Commission to take as its basic position a high level of protection in its proposals, to ensure that public health requirements are fully integrated into its policies. This level of protection must be kept under constant review and, where necessary, it must be adjusted to take account of new information, or of a re-evaluation of existing information.

Conclusion

The argument presented here is that the root of the problem concerning the gap between legislative intention and operational good practice in hotels related to food safety lies with the law and not hotels or personnel. The views advanced are for various measures that might be taken to rationalize or simplify existing EU legislation to address the variances present within European hotels (Jukes 1991, 1993). They began with a consideration of certain aspects of the EU's working procedures, such as the choice of legal instruments and the possibility to update legislation in accordance with technical and scientific progress. They also considered the scope for improving the coherence of legislation through the introduction of common terms and definitions. All these matters are of relevance to food legislation and its implementation within the European hotel industry.

References

Act (1973) Denmark Food Act etc., Act No 310 of 6 June, translated by Leatherhead Food Research Association.

Act (1993) Denmark Act Amending the 1973 Act on Foodstuffs etc., translated by Leatherhead Food Research Association.

COMM (97) 184 (1997a) The Action Plan for the Internal Market. Brussels: EC Commission.

COMM 97 (1997b) Results of the Official Control on Foodstuffs: EU Summary of the Inspection and Sampling Statistics 1994, February. Brussels: EC Commission.

EC Commission (1985) Completion of the Internal Market: Community Legislation on Foodstuffs. Communication from the Commission to the European Parliament, COM (85) 603, Final, Luxembourg.

EC Commission (1986) Single European Act 1986. Cmnd 9758(1986). Bull EC Suppl 2/86. Brussels: EC Commission.

EC Commission (1989a) Official Control of Foodstuffs, Council Directive, 89/397/EEC, OJ No. L 186, June. Brussels: EC Commission.

EC Commission (1989b) Materials and Articles in Contact with Food – General Requirement, Council Directive 89/109/EEC, OJ No L40, February. Brussels: EC Commission.

EC Commission (1990) Nutrition Labelling of Foodstuffs, Council Directive, 90/496/EEC, OJ No L 276, October. Brussels: EC Commission.

EC Commission (1993a) The Hygiene of Foodstuffs, Council Directive, OJ No L 175/1, June. Brussels: EC Commission.

EC Commission (1993b) The Treaty on European Union. Brussels: EC Council and Commission.

EC Commission (1996) The Study of the Impact and Effectiveness of the Internal Market Programme on the Processed Foodstuffs Sector, The Sutherland Report. Brussels: EC Commission.

EC Council (1992) European Communities to the Council, Common Position Adopted by the Council with a View to the Adoption of a Directive on the Hygiene of Foodstuffs, 16 December. Brussels: EC Commission.

HMSO (1993) *Assured Safe Catering*. London: HMSO.

Jackson C. (1990) The role of the European Parliament in the control of foodstuffs legislation. *European Food Law Review*, 1 (1), pp. 53–71.

Jukes D.J. (1991) *Food Law Enforcement in the UK – Time for Change?* Doncaster: Horton Publishing.

Jukes D.J. (1993) *Food Legislation of the UK*, 3rd edn. Oxford: Butterworth-Heinemann.

Knowles T.D. (1992) Effect of the EC Law on the Hospitality Industry – Discussion Paper. Leeds Metropolitan University.

Knowles T.D. (1994) Some aspects of UK and European food legislation. *Hygiene and Nutrition in Foodservice and Catering*, 1 (1), pp. 49–62.

Knowles T.D. (1999) Attitudes towards Food Safety within selected countries of the European hotel industry. PhD thesis, two volumes, unpublished, University of Luton.

North R. (1996) *Food Safety Policy in the Hospitality Industry, Tourism and Europe* (R. Thomas ed.). London: Cassell.

O'Connor B. (1993) Free movement of foodstuffs in EC law. *European Food Law Review*, 3 (2).

Painter A.A. (1991) The origin of food products. *European Food Law Review*, 2 (4), pp. 282–90.

Pennington Report (1997) The Pennington Group: Report on the Circumstances Leading to the Outbreak of infection *E. coli* 0157 in Central Scotland: the Implications for Food Safety and the Lessons to be Learned. London: HMSO.

Roberts D. (1993) Level playing fields in Europe. *European Food Law Review*, 4 (1), pp. 32–44.

WHO (1988) *Food Safety Services*, 2nd edn. Rome: World Health Organization.

European developments in Efficient Consumer Response

Herbert Kotzab

Introduction

In 1992, Efficient Consumer Response (ECR) was presented as a powerful tool for optimizing the supply chain performance within the US grocery industry. Since then, different European approaches have been developed to transfer the basic ideas of ECR to Europe. The efforts of the European ECR initiatives are presented here, with some discussion of ECR's future directions.

What is Efficient Consumer Response?

Over the past 15 years, the grocery industry has faced many changes in business practice. There has been a major power shift from manufacturers to retailers. Retailing companies have established their own marketing and logistics approaches and both parties have been finding out how IT and co-operative management styles can help in gaining competitiveness and economic growth in an increasingly competitive marketplace.

An excellent example of this phenomenon is that of Wal-Mart Corporation's distribution strategy (Stalk, Evans and Shulman 1992). Wal-Mart has consistently made improvements to its bottom line through streamlining distribution operations to better serve its customers. Importantly, it is not only Wal-Mart's distribution policy, but also the customer focus of the implementation of the policy, throughout the retailer's operation, that has led to greater profitability for the company (Karch 1997).

Wal-Mart's partner on the manufacturers' side has been Procter and Gamble. Their partnership is seen as the benchmark within the grocery supply chain. One industry-led initiative which analysed the way in which these two companies co-operate has highlighted Wal-Mart's and Procter and Gamble's strategy as an example of Efficient Consumer Response (ECR). For Martin (1994) ECR is a strategy of 'how partners in the supply chain can best synchronize the flow of product through the distribution pipeline from point of manufacture to point of final sale'.

In a highly competitive market, where market shares can only be taken from competitors, ECR is of particular value. Co-operative distribution strategies can help to increase productivity through increased stability of volume. ECR has been defined by many parties since 1993; for example (Salmon 1993); the Joint Industry Project on Efficient Consumer Response (1995); Tietz (1995a); Tietz (1995b); Töpfer (1995); ECR Europe (1996a); ECR Europe (1997). These definitions show that in the food supply chain ECR is primarily utilized by strategic partnerships to more effectively meet customer needs.

Where Efficient Consumer Response started – the US grocery supply chain

General background

In the late 1980s and the beginning of the 1990s, a growing number of retailers and manufacturers in the US grocery industry were confronted with losses in market share and declining productivity (JIPOECR 1995). In 1992, representatives of the grocery industry founded the Efficient Consumer Response Working Group, with the goal of analysing the grocery supply chain. Companies included: the Coca-Cola Company, Crown/BBK Incorporated, Kraft General Foods, the Kroger Company, Nabisco Food Corporation, the Procter and Gamble Company, Ralston, Purina Company, Safeway Incorporated, Sales Force Companies Incorporated, Scriver Incorporated, Shaw's Supermarkets Incorporated, SUPERVALUE Incorporated and the Vons Companies.

Their interest lay in the analysis of the mass merchant channel and in particular, the major players Wal-Mart, Target and K-Mart (Browning 1997).

Kurt Salmon Associates, a US-based consulting company, were asked by the ECR Working Group to 'examine the grocery supplier/distributor/consumer value-chain to determine the cost and service improvements the industry could achieve through technological and business practice changes' (Salmon 1993). Kurt Salmon Associates were chosen due to their experience within the textile industry, where they have developed Quick Response (QR). QR is a logistics strategy, which harmonizes the replenishment of merchandise within the textile channel. Instead of focusing on the replenishment of merchandise, Salmon (1993) worked out a distribution model that also considered other business areas critical for the grocery industry: promotion, new product introduction and assortment (Tietz 1995b).

Efficient Consumer Response: improving the supply chain performance of the US grocery industry

ECR is essentially an end consumer-driven distribution system in which the production is permanently managed by the consumers' POS activities (shown in Figure P5.1). Each step of the channel concentrates on its very own core competences and reduces non-value-adding activities. A paperless information flow controls the flow of merchandise. Efficient Replenishment (ER), Efficient Store Assortment (ESA) at POS level, Efficient Promotion (EP) and Efficient Product Introduction (EPI), should ensure ultimate consumer orientation (see Table P5.1).

An optimal combination of these four areas thus leads to improvements in consumer satisfaction (Salmon 1993). The benefit of ECR was calculated by Salmon (1993) at US$30 billion. The potential saving results from a 41% total chain reduction of inventory by speeding up cycle time from an original 104 days to 61 days (see Figure P5.2).

The full implementation of ECR based on an 'everyday-low price-strategy' then reduces consumer prices by approx. 11%. Based on the different ECR strategies, the savings potential is distributed as presented in Table P5.2.

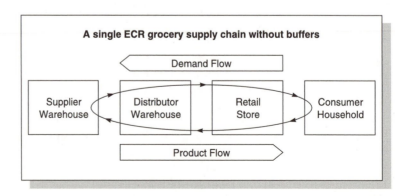

Figure P5.1
Vision of the US-ECR model (Salmon 1993)

ECR strategies	Scope of the ECR-strategies
Efficient Store Assortment (ESA)	Providing a complete, easy-to-shop, assortment of products wanted by the consumers
Efficient Replenishment (ER)	Maintaining high in-stock levels of the required assortment
Efficient Promotion (EP)	Harmonizing the promotion activities between manufacturer and retailer by communicating benefits and value
Efficient Product Introduction (EPI)	Developing and introducing new products the consumers really want by meeting their ultimate needs.

Source: Salmon 1993

Table P5.1 The four ECR strategies

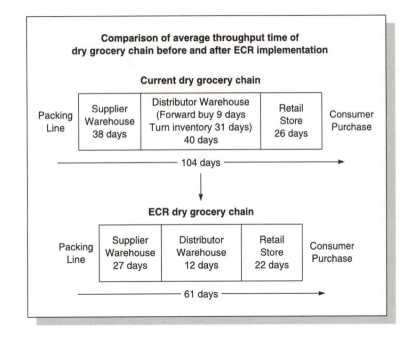

Figure P5.2
Acceleration of the throughput-time of the merchandise flow in the grocery industry (Salmon 1993)

ECR strategy	Cost savings	Financial savings	Total savings
ESA	1.3%	0.2%	1.5%
ER	2.8%	1.3%	4.1%
EP	3.5%	0.8%	4.3%
EPD	0.9%	—	0.9%
Total	8.5%	2.3%	**10.8%**

Source: Salmon 1993

Table 5.2
Savings potential in percentage of sales prices

Among these savings, Salmon (1993) differentiates between:

- Cost savings, which result from the elimination of activities and expenses.

- Financial savings, which result from reducing inventory and physical assets allow organizations to generate similar Returns on Investment from lower input levels.

The savings would be shared between manufacturers and retailers, whereby 54% of the savings will be realized by the manufacturers and 46% by the retailers (Salmon 1993).

Making ECR work in Europe

General background

ECR-Europe was founded in 1994 by leading European retailers and manufacturers (ECRE 1996a). Founding members included Albert Heijn, Birds Eye Walls, Coca-Cola Germany, Coca-Cola France, Fegro/Selgros, Henkel, ICA, Johnson and Johnson, Mars, Procter and Gamble (UK and Italy), Promodès, Tesco and Van den Bergh Foods. The organization has its principal office in Brussels, Belgium and is financially supported by the following four associations: AIM – European Brands Association, CIES – The Food Business Forum, EuroCommerce – the European representation of wholesale and retail trade, and EAN International – the international article numbering association.

The initial goal of this initiative was the development of ECR models and practices that are suitable for the European business situation. In March 1997, during the 2nd ECR-Europe Congress, the ECR-Europe-model, developed by a number of major consulting companies, was presented to the public (Kotzab 1997).

Nowadays, ECR-Europe has four focus areas (ECRE 1998):

- Promotion of national ECR initiatives.

- Initiation and financial support of ECR pilot projects.

- Publication and distribution of ECR literature documenting the progress and the results of ECR.

- Organization of the annual official ECR conferences.

ECR-Europe is led by a board, consisting of top managers from manufacturers and retailers who are actively involved in national ECR initiatives (Kalmbach 1999). ECR-Europe is a non-profit organization and is financed by the conference fees of the annually organized ECR conferences. The consultant companies, which are involved in the ECR pilot projects, do not charge the participants for their efforts.

How ECR should work for the European grocery supply chain

The ECR-Europe model is a co-operative strategy between retailer and manufacturer to fulfil consumer wishes better, faster and at less cost (ECRE 1996a). This strategic objective can be implemented by the realization of selected focus areas (shown in Figure P5.3).

This model includes a demand and a supply side representing the marketing and the physical distribution functions in the supply chain. The interaction of these focus areas leads to improvements of the overall performance, inside and outside of the companies involved. Thus, the result is a higher consumer value, which is represented in the ECR-Europe model as a function of quality, trust, variety, service, response time and price (see Equation 1)

$$\text{Consumer value} = \left(\frac{\text{Quality} \times \text{Trust} \times \text{Variety} \times \text{Service}}{\text{Response time} \times \text{Price}} \right)$$

In other words, ECR should guarantee end-users better quality, more variety and better service, but for less money, less time out of busy schedules and less complexity in the information needed to make educated choices (ECRE 2000).

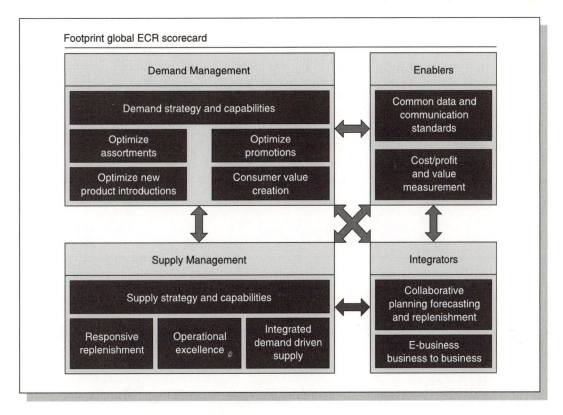

Figure P5.3 ECR-Europe focus areas (ECRE 2000)

Referring to ECRE (1996a), the improvement of the consumer value is the result of the 'new' co-operation between manufacturer and retailer in the logistic channel. Figure P5.4 tries to describe this suggested improvement.

Instead of offering consumers trade-offs between the retailers' and manufacturers' activities, both partners combine their offer to 'categories'. A 'category' is a distinct, manageable group of products/services that consumers perceive to be interrelated and/or substitutable in meeting a consumer need (ECRE 1997). The consumers then perceive categories as 'complementary information' (ECRE 1997).

The application of the ECR practices suggested in the ECR-Europe model will lead to a savings of 5.7% (based on retail prices), which is DM50 billion (ECRE 1997; Wiezorek 1997; see also Table P5.3). Inventory can be reduced by 42% and the lead time can be shortened to approx. 43 days.

Eighty-four per cent of the reductions are due to savings in the field of operative costs; the remainder results from

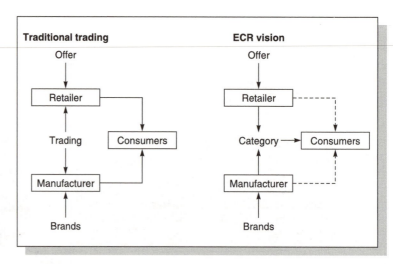

Figure P5.4
Comparison of the traditional and visionary cooperation between manufacturer and retailer in the Europen grocery industry (ECRE 1996a)

90% of the savings in the field of operative costs are made by ...		95% of the savings by reducing inventory are made by ...	
New product introduction	−17%	Optimal assortment	−10%
Efficient promotion	−16%	Continuous replenishment	−24%
Synchronized production	−13%	Crossdocking	−10%
Reliable production	−17%	Synchronized production	−40%
Integrated suppliers	−28%	Integrated suppliers	−11%

Source: Wiezorek 1997

Table P5.3 Top ECR activities to reduce logistics costs

inventory reduction. The total inventory level in the different channels is from 28 working days in the UK to 50 working days in Germany.

Differences between the ECR in the US and the ECR in Europe

The major difference between the two models lies in the potential for optimization offered by ECR-Europe. On a first sight, the European ECR model does not contribute as much value to the supply chain as does the American model. Yet while ECR in the USA tries to reduce, e.g. lead time from 104 working days to 61 working days, ECR in Europe starts from a basis of 28 to 58 (dependent on member states) working days' inventory levels within the various supply chains. For that reason, we could conclude that the logistics performance in the European grocery industry *per se* is more sophisticated than the American solutions. None the less, Europeans consider that there is room for improvement, particularly in areas other than logistics. Consequently, ECR-Europe, contrary to the US model, considers the issues facing both the supply and demand side (see ECRE 1997). The supply side includes all activities referring to the merchandise flow and is defined as category logistics. The different action areas of category logistics are described in Table P5.4.

The demand side contains all activities related to strategic management defined as Category Management (Maximow 1997). Category Management is seen as a 'retailer/supplier process of managing categories as strategic business units, producing enhanced business results by focusing on delivering consumer value' (ECRE 1997).

Category logistics-strategies	Characteristic
Efficient sourcing:	Pull instead of push
	Flow-through-systems
	Global sourcing
	Vertical integration of the value-chain
Efficient replenishment:	Short lead times
	Just-in-time-systems
	Category-useful logistics
	Best conditions
Efficient systems:	IT networks
	Data warehouses
	EDI messages
Efficient controlling:	Activity based costing
	Reporting and forecasting systems
	Real-time-controlling

Source: adapted from Maximow 1997

Table P5.4
Action areas of category logistics

Category Management is a joint retailer/supplier process that involves managing product categories as business units and customizing them on a store-by-store basis to satisfy customer needs. This approach leads to better business results by focusing on delivering consumer value. In the traditional product management approach, single products were pushed in a non-harmonized manner through the channels.

By considering a category as measurable and manageable group of products/services that consumers perceive to be interrelated and/or substitutable in meeting a consumer need, suppliers, as well as retailers, deliver customer-required solutions to the end user. Traditional approaches to characterize the offer of a retailer remained only on the product-side.

This whole business process is managed in close co-operation with retailer and supplier. It allows not only the creation of a commonly accepted language, but also the development of common goals and achievements. Instead of arguing on prices and discounts, the two involved organizations work together on the fulfilment of consumer needs. Following

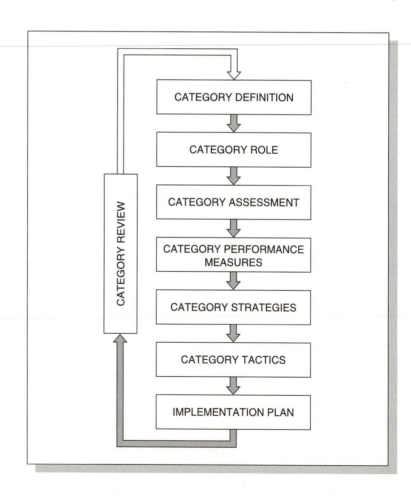

Figure P5.5
The Category Management process (ECRE 1996b)

Maximow (1997), Category Management will revolutionize the purchasing function of a company by eliminating the purchasing department.

The changing picture of ECR in Europe

Since the first introduction of ECR within the European grocery industry, ECR has changed its face (see Figure P5.6).

While in the beginning the efforts concentrated more on the supply side of ECR, the 'hard ECR work' of today focuses increasingly on the demand side of ECR. The future themes and topics for ECR in Europe are consumer oriented: they make the consumer more enthusiastic and increase the consumer's perceived value!

Conclusion

Efficient Consumer Response is the name of a co-operation oriented holistic marketing and distribution strategy in the grocery industry. ECR includes more strategies than the pure optimization of the product replenishment. Since the first introduction of ECR in Europe, ECR-Europe has established 14 national ECR initiatives (Austria, Italy, Greece, Finland, Norway, Denmark, Sweden, The Netherlands, Germany, France, UK, Spain, Switzerland and Ireland – based on ECRE 2000). The European grocery industry is known for having extremely low average margins for retailers. These margins can range between

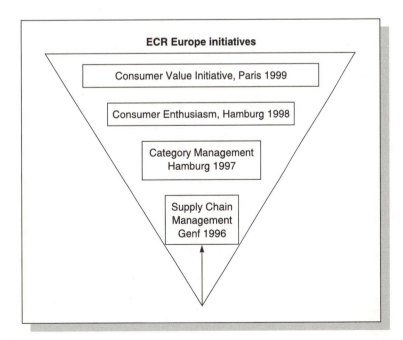

Figure P5.6
Conference themes and topics from 1996 to1999 (ECRE 1999)

−1 and +2.5% (Seth and Randall 1999; Shephson 2000). As such, with its assurance of greater efficiency in the channel, the implementation of ECR practices promises to be a powerful tool to improve the business performance within the channel (Troyer 1997). Representative results from academia and industry include:

- Fleury (1997) reported higher margins (8%), faster category turnover (27%) and greater retailer market share (12%) effects from the implementation of ECR principles within the laundry detergent category in a European country market.

- Partch (1995) noted a 50% improvement of distributors' profits by eliminating techniques like forward buying.

- Hven and de Soysa (1998) presented results from an ECR partnership between their companies, ICA and Lever Sweden. Highlights were an increase in turnover of 9%, a reduction in number of SKUs by 20%, a higher market share of 7% and higher profits of between 3% and 16%.

- Johnson & Johnson representatives disclosed two-digit turnover increases in their respective business segments (Celada and Mei 1998).

- Kotzab (1997) reported a somewhat obscure ECR example in his work with the John Menzies Publishing Company. The UK-based magazine and newspaper distributor implemented certain ECR principles during the 1990s by establishing electronic links between its distribution centres and the newspaper stands of 20 of its clients. This partnership resulted in increased sales volume of 35%, a reduction in inventory levels of 10% and increased margins of 2.1%.

ECR has started to revolutionize the way business should be done in the grocery supply chain. Indeed, ECR has initiated a lot of change, especially the business culture and the way the partners deal with each other within the grocery supply chain. The next dramatic change expected will be by combining the ideas of ECR with the future technologies, e.g. the Internet. While ECR concentrates on traditional 'bricks and mortar' distribution channels, the Internet with its dot.com shops will change the way of distribution. The first ideas have already been presented at the latest European ECR conference in Turin, Italy. With the Internet, companies do expect to combine convenience and experience, two solid factors for consumer satisfaction. But as for specific consumer interaction, facilitated by the Internet approach, new distribution models have to be established (Henley Research Centre 2000).

References

Browning C. (1997) Efficient Consumer Response: Its Lessons for Everyone. Presentation, 1997 Council of Logistics Management Annual Conference, Chicago.

Celada R. and Mei S. (1998) Category Management at Johnson & Johnson. Presentation at the 3rd Official ECR Europe Conference, Hamburg, 1–2 April 1998.

Efficient Consumer Response Europe (ECR) (1996b) Category Management Best Practices Report.

Efficient Consumer Response Europe (ECRE) (1996a) European Value Chain Analysis Study. Final Report.

Efficient Consumer Response Europe (ECRE) (1997) CEO Overview – Efficient Consumer Response.

Efficient Consumer Response Europe (ECRE) (1998) How to Create Consumer Enthusiasm – Roadmap to Growth.

Efficient Consumer Response Europe (ECRE) (1999a) Consumer Value Measurement.

Efficient Consumer Response Europe (ECRE) (2000) Welcome to Efficient Consumer Response Europe. http://www.ecrnet.org/ECR/ecr.home.

Fleury D. (1997) Best Practices Category Management – Category Tactics. Presentation at the 2nd official ECR Europe Conference, Amsterdam 13 and 14 March 1997.

Henley Research Centre (2000) Drivers and Barriers of Future Channels. Presentation at the 5th official ECR Europe Conference, Turin, 22–23 March 2000.

Hven N. and De Soysa J. (1998) Joint ECR-Europe Project Lever/ICA. Presentation at the 3rd official ECR Europe Conference, Hamburg, 1–2 April 1998.

Joint Industry Project on Efficient Consumer Response (JIPOECR) (1995) ECR Alliances. A Best Practices Model.

Kalmbach U. (1999) ECR Europe und ECR Deutschland – Ein Überblick. In Heydt A. (ed.), *Handbuch Efficient Consumer Response. Konzepte, Erfahrungen, Herausforderungen*. Munich: Vahlen, pp. 24–40.

Karch N. (1997) Trends, Opportunities and Threats in Retailing. Presentation to students at the Kellogg Graduate School of Management, Northwestern University, 7 April.

Kotzab H. (1997) *Neue Konzepte der Distributionslogistik von Handelsunternehmen*. Wiesbaden: Gabler.

Martin A. (1994) The Ultimate ECR Strategy. In Annual Conference Proceedings, Cincinatti, Ohio, 16–19 October 1994, Council of Logistics Management (ed.). Chicago: Council of Logistics Management.

Maximow J. (1997) Internationales Einkaufs- und Beschaffungsmanagement im Handel. Presentation, Internationaler Deutscher Handelskongress, Bad Homburg.

Partch K. (1995) A procedural dilemma for ECR? *Supermarket Business*, April, pp. 17–20.

Salmon K.A. (1993) *Efficent Consumer Response. Enhancing Consumer Value in the Grocery Industry.* Washington, DC: Food Marketing Institute.

Seth A. and Randall G. (1999) *The Grocers. The Rise and Fall of the Supermarket Chains.* Kogan: London/Dover.

Shephson C. (2000) 3rd Party Logistics and Relationship Management. Presentations to Students of the Copenhagen Business School Supply Chain Management Master Programme, 9 March.

Stalk G., Evans P. and Shulman L. (1992) Competing on capabilities: the new rules of corporate strategy. *Harvard Business Review*, 70 (2), pp. 57–69.

Tietz B. (1995a) Effiziente Kundenpolitik als Problem der Informationspolitik. In *Handelsforschung 1995/96. Informationsmanagement im Handel. Jahrbuch der Forschungstelle für den Handel (FfH) Berlin* (ed. V. Trommsdorff). Wiesbaden, pp. 175–186

Tietz B. (1995b) Efficient Consumer Response (ECR). *Das Wirtschaftswissenschaftliche Studium*, 23 (10), pp. 529–30.

Töpfer A. (1995) Efficient Consumer Response – Bessere Zusammenarbeit zwischen Handel und Herstellern. In *Handelsforschung 1995/96. Informationsmanagement im Handel. Jahrbuch der Forschungstelle für den Handel (FfH) Berlin* (ed. V. Trommsdorff), Wiesbaden, pp. 187–200.

Troyer C. (1997) ECR Past, Present and Future. Carrying the Learning Forward. Presentation 1997 Council of Logistics Management Annual Conference, Chicago.

Wiezorek H. (1997) Efficient Consumer Response – Koperation statt Konfrontation. In Joachim Zentes (ed.), *Marketing und Management-Transfer*, 4, pp. 2.

The marketing of seafood in New South Wales, Australia: the impact of deregulation

Rayka Presbury

Fish has been a major source of protein food since the begin-ning of history. The early civilizations were established on river systems and their cultures and populations thrived because of the abundance of food from the surrounding waters. Fish was a staple and constantly available food. The earliest Australian settlers supplemented their meagre provi-sions with fresh fish caught in the rivers and seas. The settlers ate an amazing array of fish and when they caught more than they could eat, the excess was salted and kept for later use. Turtles were caught for sweet tasting eggs and cuttlefish was used to make wonderful soup (Bannerman 1998).

The Island continent of Australia is surrounded by over 2500 species of fish. From these fish the Australian economy benefits by approximately $A9 billion through its domestic as well as export sales. More than 110 000 people are employed in this very important primary industry (Australian Seafood Industry Council 2000). Any traveller to Australia would not leave without sampling the huge variety of seafood, especially lobsters, crayfish, oysters and crabs. In fact most tourists seek Australian quality seafood as a priority in their travels. The Australian tourism industry has grown to 3 million visitors a year and with it have emerged a number of sophisticated celebrity-chef restaurants that have made Australian seafood a tourist attraction.

As the Australian food industry takes a huge leap forward from the traditional 'meat and three veg', the demand for Australian seafood is showing strong economic growth both domestically and overseas. As Australians learn of the health and nutritional value of fish, to reduce cholesterol in the blood, they demand an increasing amount of fresh seafood products. The Australian Seafood Industry Council (ASIC) reports that Australian consumers eat around 12 kg of fish and seafood per year, 9 kg of which is consumed as fresh and frozen product eaten outside the home, representing a 13% increase in consumption from 1991 to 1999. As our ageing population increases and older Australians watch their diet and cholesterol levels, this percentage is bound to increase. Only 4.9% of Australians do not eat seafood and around 36% actively seek Australian seafood (ASIC 2000). While Australians are at a middle ground in the consumption of fish, they are well behind the Pacific Island nations. However, Australia is a major exporter of fish, especially whole fresh fish to Japan, who will pay a premium price for fish caught in Australian waters.

Fresh food is the challenge of the future. The frozen and dried markets are eroding, as consumers demand a greater number of fresh food products. As this demand increases so does the challenge of delivering fresh seafood products to consumers. The success of this endeavor will require a greater co-operation among all participants in the foodservice chain, including, fisherman, wholesalers, retailers, consumers and governments.

In the 1800s selling required little skill. Settlers brought their produce to market and hoped to receive a good price. The price was determined by negotiation between individual buyers and sellers. In the 1900s fisherman sold their catch individually, either locally, or to private agents, who sold fish to retailers and the public through the central fish market in Sydney. In 1963 as a result of unco-ordinated attempts in sending fish to market and gluts and shortages of fish in New South Wales, the government stepped in and established the New South Wales Marketing Authority to control the marketing of fish.

Licences were issued to fishermen who then had to sell fish to the fisherman's co-operatives or the Sydney Fish Market. Fishermen could not sell directly to the public. Even though the majority of fish were caught in the regional coastal areas of New South Wales, the major market for fish was in Sydney. The Sydney Fish Marketing Authority for the first time was able to enforce regulations onto the suppliers (size of fish and type of fish caught), as well as regulate health control.

As well as the Sydney Fish Market, over 20 co-operatives were formed along the coast of New South Wales. The co-operatives were responsible for receiving the fish and packaging the fish to transport to Sydney. Some also ran their own retail fish shops to sell to the local community, retailers and restaurateurs. For over three decades most fish marketing in New South Wales has taken place through this system of fishermen's co-operatives and the Sydney Fish Market that operated under the Fisheries Act 1935. These regulations have prohibited fishermen from selling their catch directly to consumers or retailers. In some instances this has caused a loss of profits to the fisherman due to the cost of transport and extra costs involved with having a middle man to sell the catch, as well as lower prices being paid to fishermen as a result of monopoly pricing practices.

With the general move to deregulation as a better way of doing business in Australia, the management of the Sydney Fish Market was handed over to the fishing industry in 1994. It was evident that restricting trade was not in keeping with general thinking about government agencies and that cutting one leg in the supply chain would translate into benefits for both consumers, retailers and fisherman.

On 1 November 1999, the marketing of fish in New South Wales was deregulated. Commercial fishers are no longer required to market their catch through the Sydney Fish Market or a fishermen's co-operative. The old system has been replaced by one where wholesalers, retailers, fish shops or any persons who wishes to purchase fish direct, can do so by buying from a commercial fisher (who holds a permit) or a Registered Fish Receiver (RFR), as seen in Figure P6.1.

To become a RFR, the person or company must hold a permit issued under the Fisheries Management Act 1994. Fish receivers are assessed against criteria that look at any convictions for fish marketing offences and are required to pay an annual fee of $2500. Deregulation has also meant that anyone can get a fisherman's licence and try their luck in the fishing industry. Control of fishermen is done through normal trading law and fishermen need to follow the same regulations of health, hygiene and safety as any other business would. New South Wales Fisheries Inspectors control the issues of illegal fishing, catch size and protected species.

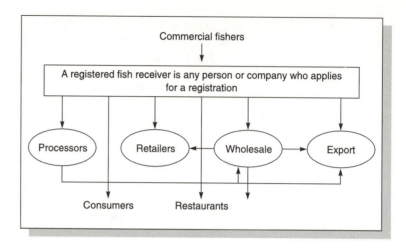

Figure P6.1
The marketing of sea food
in New South Wales

The registration of fish receivers allows for fish caught by commercial fishers to be tracked, so that data can be collected as to how much fish is caught and sold. The RFRs are required to keep records concerning the purchase and sale of all fish and to make monthly returns of those records to the NSW Fisheries Department. This system also assists in controlling black market sales and pushes operators on the black market to make their businesses legitimate.

According to the fishing industry, deregulation makes good business sense. Whilst there are certain fishing areas at risk, most are well managed and fishermen should be allowed to sell to whomsoever they choose in order to make the best deals. Deregulation will mean more fishermen selling directly to the public and to retailers. This will mean more relationship building between the supplier and the end user and much less reliance on the services of fishermen's co-operatives or the Sydney Fish Markets. The general feeling is that the fish marketing authority was not providing good service because it was a monopoly. Deregulation will create competition, which will drive improvement in the services offered, for both the fisher and the registered fish receivers.

For the marketplace this will mean a greater choice for the purchasing of fish. For example, fish shops and restaurants will be able to purchase fish from a registered fish receiver with no obligation to become permit holders. However, they will also be able apply for a permit and buy direct from any licensed commercial fisher. Whilst commercial fishers have the choice of selling their catch directly to anyone with a permit to buy, a fishermen's co-operative or through the Sydney Fish Markets.

References

Anon. (1996) The future is fresh in wholesaling. *Inside Dining*, July, p. 13.

Australian Seafood Industry Council (2000) *Facts about the Seafood Industry.*

Bannerman C. (1998) *Acquired Tastes: Celebrating Australia's Culinary History*. National Library of Australia.

Bolles S. (1996) Courting success in food. *Inside Dining*, October 1996, p. 5.

NSW State Fisheries (1986) Fisheries and Fish Marketing in New South Wales.

NSW Fisheries (1999) Discussion Paper: Fish Receivers Registration.

NSW Fisheries (1999) A Fisheries Policy Consultation Paper for Fishers.

Supply chain restructuring in economies in transition: a case study of the Hungarian dairy sector

Matthew Gorton and Ferenc Z. Guba

Introduction

Since the downfall of communist regimes in Central and Eastern Europe, one of the most widely discussed issues has been the nature and impact of the transformation process. After early optimism that transformation could be achieved quickly and relatively painlessly, it soon became apparent that the necessary changes in institutions, linkages between agents and attitudes would take considerably longer (Buckwell and Davidova 1999). This perspective presents a case study of supply chain restructuring, focusing on the Hungarian dairy sector. The dairy sector is the second most important branch of the agri-food sector in Hungary and the food industry overall makes a significant contribution to national employment, trade and income (Szabó and Tóth 1998). The next section outlines the nature of supply chains prior to transition. The following section considers the post-communist period, focusing on restructuring at the farm, processing and retail levels and the linkages between these stages. The final section concludes with a discussion of the emergence of dual food supply chains in Hungary.

Supply chains in the pre-transition period

Under communism, Hungary pursued an agri-food policy which involved three main strands: (i) collectivization and agro-industrial integration, (ii) controlled prices and margins, (iii) high border protection. The state was the dominant actor in pursuing these policies and the agricultural and food processing sectors received hefty subsidies (Szabó 1996); the provision of cheap food to the masses being perceived as a requirement for the maintenance of regime control. Prices were set according to what central planners thought reasonable and rarely reflected marginal costs.

In contrast to the sectoral division of agriculture, where co-operative production and private sector plots were important, food processing was almost entirely accomplished by state enter-prises (Csizmadia 1977) (Figure P7.1). In 1974 the private sector produced the following shares of total physical production: 62% of the potato crop, 50% of fruit, 59% of meat and bacon, 40% of poultry and 43% of milk (Elek 1980). Food processing plants were co-ordinated by industry-wide trusts. Legal barriers of entry were set in wholesaling and foreign trade so that they were controlled by specialist state companies. State processors were in practice obliged to purchase all produce offered to them by primary producers.

In the Hungarian dairy industry, until 1990, the Dairy Trust oversaw 15 state owned companies, almost all of which each had between four and six processing units. These plants were organized on a strict regional base with hardly any overlap. These state owned companies accounted for between 85 and 90% of all processing, under the control of the Dairy Trust. As such, the Trust held an almost complete monopoly on processing with hardly any competition between state owned firms. The 'competitive fringe' consisted around 30 small and rather weak co-operative processors which typically lacked sufficient capital to develop the expansion of their processing capacities, which had to be financed out of retained profits (Szabó and Tóth 1998).

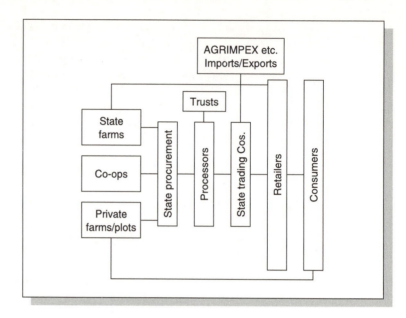

Figure P7.1
Hungarian food chains
under communism

Moreover, the Trust fought to maintain its monopolistic position by opposing the 'too-rapid expansion' of joint or co-operative enterprises (Wädekin 1982).

Despite the heavy subsidies and border protection the Communist government found it increasingly difficult to deliver high quality, cheap food to consumers. Supply chains were characterized by low productivity, high shrinkage rates and erratic deliveries. In an attempt to deal with these problems the leadership relaxed restrictions on private production and retailing (albeit within strict limits) and improved co-ordination by rationalizing the number of state enterprises. As a consequence, the number of plants in the Hungarian food industry fell from 3256 in 1960 (an average of 39 workers per industrial plant) to 2166 plants in 1973 (average of 86 workers) (Csizmadia 1977). This had a major effect on the nature of the privatization process and contemporary market structures, which are typically characterized by highly concentrated, oligopolisitc (or in a few cases, monopoly) competition.

Evolution of dairy supply chains

Restructuring has occurred at every stage of the agro-food supply chain and these trends are summarized in Figure P7.2.

Agriculture

Agricultural production in the initial post-communist era was characterized by a shrinkage in both supply and demand. Supply fell due to the cost-price squeeze, restructuring which has led to

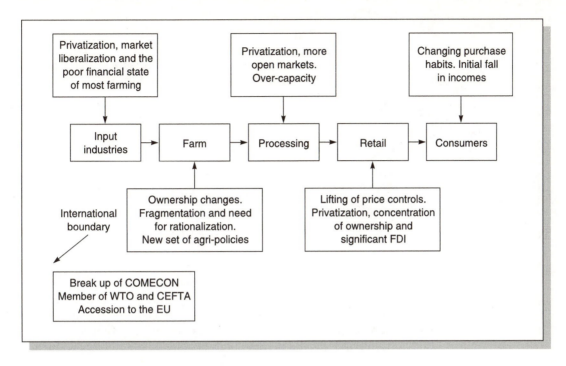

Figure P7.2 The restructuring of agro-food supply chains in Hungary

higher average costs and a decrease in real government support. Demand fell as real incomes declined and unemployment rose throughout the region. Milk production was no exception to this trend, declining by 33% between 1990 and 1997, and during the same period, the stock of milking cows decreased even more (–36%). This meant that milk production fell from 1763 million litres in 1990 to a low of 1854 million litres in 1997, with a slight recovery in 1998 and 1999 (KSH 1998/9).

Significant structural changes have occurred during transition as many state and collective farms have been split up and/or downsized as a consequence of financial troubles and bankruptcies. This has reduced the importance of these farm structures in milk production (Table P7.1). In contrast, private farms, on average, have increased their herds with some 300 family farms emerging with 20–50 cows. It is these larger private and co-operative farms which are most attractive to dairy processors, in that the quality of milk produced by these units tends to be much higher, involving lower procurement costs.

In contrast, the very small scale producers (one to two cows) have been increasingly marginalized. These producers have suffered from low payment terms, forcing them to leave the business or turn to subsistence farming and/or direct marketing by selling the milk to neighbours or small scale operations. However, a great number of elderly and poor rural people are

	1989 Share of total milk production	Average herd size	1997 Share of total milk production	Average herd size
State farms/Corporations	21.1	1300.0	27.6	948.0
Collective farms (production co-ops)	55.5	300.0	39.4	221.0
Private farms (mostly household farms of co-operative members)	23.4	1.4	33.0	8.9
Total	100.0		100.0	

Source: Data from KSH; own depiction

Table P7.1 Structural change in milk production

unwilling to give up dairy farming, even with just one or two cows, if it is their only source of revenue. It was estimated that in 1996 there were approximately 30 000 individual farmers (accounting for 15% of milk processed), in contrast to 1048 collective and corporate farms which accounted for 85% of production sent for processing.

The price paid to farmers for milk is based on milk quality. The grading system used has been in place since the early 1980s and classification is based on the physical purity of milk, its acid content, bacterial and somatic cell counts and the level of inhibitory substances (Fenyvessy and Kiss 1996). Milk is graded as extra, 1, 2 and 3 as well as ex-class. In 1996, just under 80% of all milk supplied to dairies was classified as of extra and class 1 standard (up to EU quality).

In an attempt to improve the quality of milk big price gaps between Class 1 and Class 2 milk (18% of the average price) as well as between Class 2 and Class 3 milk (15.4% of the average price), have been instigated.

The only differentials fixed centrally are those for the minimal premiums to be paid on extra protein and fat content. However, government subsidies for milk production are available to dairy companies which pay a set minimum price to producers for extra class milk although the actual level of subsidies available have varied significantly from one year to the next.

Food industry

The dairy industry is the second largest sector of the food industry, accounting for 12% of total food production. A major reform in 1990 resulted in the disappearance of the state-controlled Dairy Trust and elimination of controlled prices. The 15 state owned companies were broken down to 36 new firms. In 1997 there were 164 companies involved in dairy processing of which 103 employed less then 11 people, 47 firms employed between 11 and 300 people and 14 employed more than 300 people. All these enterprises, however, found the initial period of transformation especially tough as state subsidies were eliminated, real prices increased and incomes shrunk. As a result, the quantity of milk procured and processed by dairies dropped by over 33% between 1990 and 1997, from 2262 million to 1504 million litres (KSH 1998/9). However, dairies still procure almost 80% of total milk production with the remainder being used as fodder, or directly marketed/consumed by farmers.

In response to this sharp downturn, processors reduced their staffing levels, between 1990 and 1997 employment in the dairy processing sector falling from 19 600 to 12 400. A significant proportion of these reductions was accounted for by structural changes in the sector (acquisitions and bankruptcies). Despite these financial difficulties, by mid-1997 privatization of the industry had been completed and the share of (EU-based) foreign capital reached 60% (Table P7.2).

Foreign ownership in the dairy industry is concentrated in larger enterprises and these enterprises have sought to increase their share of the market. Between 1995 to 1999 the joint share of the four market leaders (the C4 ratio) grew from 27% to 60% through internal growth, mergers and acquisitions.

The new foreign owners have had a dramatic impact on supply chains in Hungary. The larger processors that relied on large numbers of small producers for raw milk have rationalized the number of players they deal with. More formal contractual arrangements have tended to emerge to ensure supply, reduce transaction costs or to concentrate on core competencies. Frequently dairies ensure their supplies via long term skeleton contracts with the larger milk producers, agreeing annually prices and quantities to be supplied. In a number of cases their relationships with producers have become more entwined by extending credits, handing over assets and the provision of technical advice.

Table P7.2
Share of the Hungarian dairy market controlled by non-Hungarian based firms, 1999

Company	Home country	Main subsidiaries	% share of Hungarian market
Nutricia	Netherlands	Hajdutej, Szabolcstej,	18.3
Gala Italia	Italy	Szegedtej, Gala Paszto	17.3
Danone	France	Danone Bp.	11.5
Bongrain	France	Veszpremtej, Pannontej	12.5
Parmalat	Italy	Fejertej	5.5
Total			65.1

Source: Agra Europe, 1999) p. 34; interviews

Foreign investors have developed stronger brand names and trade marks backed by significant advertising campaigns. Nationwide distribution networks have been established by firms that market fresh dairy products (Danone, Parmalat). Foreign owned processors have also been instrumental in the drive to improve the quality of raw milk produced. The processors determine quality requirements and enforce them through the procurement system. Foreign owned dairies have also introduced internal systems guaranteeing quality levels in contrast to smaller dairies which have been unable to introduce ISO systems due to lack of capital. This has limited the latter's ability to export and they will face increasing difficulties on the domestic market as Hungary adopts EU food laws as part of the process of accession.

However, accession to the EU may present problems even for the larger foreign-owned dairies. Dairy firms and plants in Hungary are still small in comparison to the EU. The largest dairy company in Hungary processed a mere 155 million litres of milk in 1995, while in the EU more than half of all milk is being processed by firms larger than this and there are fourteen European companies which are bigger than the *whole* Hungarian dairy industry (Szabó and Tóth 1998).

Retail and catering sectors

The importance of multiple retailers has grown in Hungary. This has been driven by foreign investors, the most important of which are: Metro (Switzerland), Csemege-Julius Meinl (Austria), Tesco (UK), Cora (France), Auchan (France), Tengelmann (Germany), Rowe Group (Germany), Delhaize Group (Belgium) and Spar (Austria/Netherlands). These companies account for approximately 45% of the food retail market (Gábor and Stauder 1999) and have put considerable pressure on AFEOSZ (the organization of traditional retail co-operatives in Hungary) which has a network of about 5500 small general consumer-goods outlets and other Hungarian owned firms.

Multiple retailers have sought to develop along Western lines by introducing and developing warehouse point distribution, consolidating or reducing the number of suppliers they deal with, developing own brands and concentrating on larger sized stores. The foreign owned stores primarily target wealthier segments of the population and the stratification of incomes in the population has largely removed the bottom segment of the economic pyramid from the institutional food trade channels (Fennesz-Berka 1998). In response to high taxes and lower real incomes, the black market assumes an increasing percentage of the purchases of low income families with a growth in subsistence farming and unregistered farm food sales.

In the hotel, restaurant and food service market (HRS), the biggest growth rate has been in fast food (USDA, 1999). This sector has grown through inward investment and the development of franchise networks. By June 2000, McDonald's had 73 restaurants in Hungary (mostly company owned), while other fast-food chains have sought to develop franchise led networks (Burger King, Kentucky Fried Chicken, Wendy's). With central procurement of ingredients and determination of menus, these firms largely deal with the larger, predominantly foreign owned processors and wholesalers (Kovrig 2000).

Conclusions

A considerable degree of structural change has occurred during transition. Supply chains have evolved and two distinct types of channel have emerged. First, *formal channels* have increasingly become dominated by larger producers, processors and retail chains. The linkages between larger farms and processors have become stronger, with more stringent quality requirements, complex payment terms and in some cases the provision of credit, physical assets and technical advice. These dairies in turn are dealing increasingly with centralized retail buyers. In these regards Hungarian supply channels increasingly mirror practices in Western Europe. From these channels small farms, processors and low income consumers have become increasingly marginalized. These agents are involved in much more *informal* channels, with the smallest farmers typically producing for self-consumption or sale to neighbours and small processing enterprises. These small processors have found it difficult to adjust to changing food laws or become suppliers to the multiple food retailers.

References

Agra Europe (1999) Stakes in Hungarian dairy bought by Friesland. *East European Agriculture and Food*, June, p.34.

Buckwell A. and Davidova S. (1999) *The Progress in Transformation of CEEC Agriculture and in Integration with the EU*. Ashford, Kent: Wye College, University of London.

Csizmadia E. (1977) *Socialist Agriculture in Hungary*. Budapest: Akademiai Kiado.

Elek P.S. (1980) The Hungarian experiment: in search of profitability. In R.A. Francisco, B.A. Laird and R.D. Laird (eds), *Agricultural Policies in the USSR and Eastern Europe*. Boulder, CO: Westview Press, pp. 165–84.

Fennesz-Berka A. (1998) *Annual Marketing Plan for Hungary*. Washington, DC: USDA, mimeo.

Fenyvessy J. and Kiss J. (1996) A Tiszantulon termelt tej minosege. *Elelmezesi Ipar*, 50 (3), pp. 86–9.

Gábor J. and Stauder M. (1999) A kereskedelmi láncok es az elelmiszertermelok kapcsolatának valtozasai [Change of relation between the retail chains and food producers]. AKII, Bp.

Kovig M. (2000) Golden arch-enemies. *Budapaest Business Journal*, 19 June.

KSH (1998–1999) Published and unpublished agricultural statistics, Budapest, mimeo, May.

Szabó M. (1996) A magyar tejipar versenykepesseget befolyasolo tenyezok [Facts that determine the competitivness of the Hungarian dairy industry]. Working paper, Budapest University of Economic Sciences.

Szabó M. and Tóth J. (1998) Agricultural market development and government policy in Hungary: the case of the dairy sector. Budapest

USDA (1999) *Hungary Exporter 1999*. Gain Report No. 9021.

Wädekin K-E. (1982) *Agrarian Policies in Communist Europe: a Critical Introduction*. The Hague: Martinus Nijhoff.

Supply Chain Perspectives

The Future of the Supply Chain

Future issues in European supply chain management

Michael A. Bourlakis

Introduction

Over the past decades, the concept of 'distribution management' has been replaced by 'logistics management' and lately, by 'supply chain management'. Supply chain management is nowadays of major significance to the strategic decision making activity of most companies and is a key function for food channel members, such as food retailers and manufacturers, especially when they compete in an increasingly turbulent environment.

The focus of this perspective is upon future developments in European food supply chain management. First, the externalization process of supply chain operations is discussed. The externalization of supply chain operations refers to the case where food firms utilize a specialist (logistics) firm to perform a supply chain function on their behalf. Subsequently, the internationalization process of logistics firms is analysed across European markets. In the final part, supply chain networks and the factors that will enhance supply chain network formation activities in future years are examined.

The externalization of supply chain operations in European markets

There has been a considerable shift of power within food-marketing channels, with retail firms becoming the dominant members in most European markets. It is not surprising that European food retailers command a significantly higher volume of sales, as compared to their food manufacturer counterparts. For example, Metro, the largest European food retailer in 1994, achieved a volume of European sales in that year that was at least twice the relevant sales volume for Unilever, the largest European food manufacturer (Fiddis 1997).

In the supply chain, European food retailers opted to become personally responsible for warehousing and transportation by operating their own independent warehouses (regional distribution centres) and their own fleet for transportation. Therefore, manufacturers were delivering products to retail warehouses and not to retail stores and these products were transported to retail stores by retailers' own vehicles. As a consequence, food retailers committed themselves to a substantial investment in capital for warehouses and lorries instead of investment into retail store renovation and expansion. At that particular time, the need for a specialist firm that would undertake the transportation and warehousing operations on retailers' behalf started to emerge.

Table P8.1 outlines the evolution of major logistics innovations in UK food retailing. Similar developments took place for the rest of Europe at a later stage. The table suggests that specialist logistics firms came into existence, and more specifically, companies such as Exel (UK), Hays Distribution Services (UK) and Tibbett and Britten Group (UK). As a result, food retailers and manufacturers had the option either to carry the logistics function on their own and/or to outsource – externalize – it to a specialist logistics firm. According to Dawson and Shaw (1990), externalization of operations (and supply chain operations) is more likely to replace a firm's/own account operations when no specific assets are required, many competitive specialist firms are available, when tasks are repetitive, the environment is stable and not complex and, finally, when performance outcomes for that operation can be easily and accurately assessed.

Initially, logistics firms were utilized by manufacturers and retailers in specific circumstances. Following Fernie (1989), such occasions occurred:

1. during periods of rapidly growing demand for products (e.g. Christmas) and therefore, a need for extra supply chain services;

2. for certain product categories (e.g. frozen);

3. for delivery of goods to remote geographical areas.

Period	Problem	Innovation	Consequences
1960s and 1970s	Disorderly delivery by suppliers to supermarkets and queues of vehicles led to both inefficiency and disruption	Introduction of warehouses – regional distribution centres (RDCs) to channel goods from suppliers to supermarkets operated by retailer	(1) Strict timing of supplier deliveries to RDC imposed by retailer (2) Retailer builds and operates RDC (3) Retailer operates own delivery fleet between RDC and supermarkets within its catchment area
Early 1980s	Retailers becoming too committed to operating logistics services in support of retail activity	Operation of retailer-owned RDCs and vehicle fleets to specialist logistics firms	(1) Retailer can concentrate on 'core business' of retailing (2) Retailer achieves better financial return from capital invested in supermarkets than in RDCs and vehicles
Mid-1980s	Available floorspace at retail outlets being under-used and too much floorspace used for storage	Conversion of storage floorspace at supermarkets to sales floorspace	(1) Better sales revenue potential at retail outlets (2) RDCs absorb products formerly kept in-store at supermarkets (3) Just-in-time (JIT) delivery used from RDC to replenish supermarket shelves

Source: Cooper *et al.* 1991

Table P8.1 Major logistics innovations by UK food multiple retailers

Nowadays, logistics firms are employed to a greater extent and offer a full range of services, including strategic planning, warehouse and inventory management, information systems development and other consulting services to both manufacturers and retailers. These were named 'value added services' in order to differentiate them from the traditional transportation and warehousing services offered so far. Therefore, logistics externalization encompasses a wide range of services and with Western European food manufacturers and retailers making use of logistics firms (externalization), to a considerable extent. For example, British firms externalized around 34% of their supply chain activities in 1996 (based on spending), that is the highest percentage in Europe with the lower spending taking place in Greece, where only 11% was spent on such supply chain activities (Marketline International 1997). Most surveys predict a rise in supply chain externalization across Europe (McKinnon

1999), and this is supported by the fact that supply chain externalization is in its infancy in Eastern Europe and at its 'introduction' stage in most Southern European countries.

To conclude, there is strong future potential for supply chain externalization all over Europe, especially when specialist logistics firms offer a vast range of services and there is an increasing demand for these services from other channel members.

Internationalization of logistics firms across Europe

European food manufacturers and retailers have been expanding to overseas markets (internationalization), with various market entry methods, and as a result of domestic market saturation. As a consequence, these firms have become gradually respectable players in the host markets they entered as foreign competitors. In food retailing, the French firms Carrefour and Auchan are major corporations in the Iberian peninsula (Spain and Portugal) food retail market, whilst other European food retailers such as Tesco (UK), Metro (Germany), Julius Meinl (Austria) and Spar (Netherlands) have expanded rapidly into Eastern Europe.

As a result, the growing firms' internationalization has created opportunities for a simultaneous international expansion to logistics firms as well (Fernie 1998). For example, when the British retailer Marks & Spencer entered the French market, it brought with it Exel Logistics, a major British logistics firm, to run its logistics operations as there were no suitable domestic logistics companies to accommodate the retailer for such operations (Laughlin *et al.* 1993).

Currently, there are very few, most probably none, logistics firms that are able to handle all European supply chain activities on manufacturers' and retailers' behalf. Nevertheless, logistics firms will benefit from the European Union's deregulation of markets and also from the complete harmonization of supply chain standards that will take place in the aftermath of the European Monetary Union (EMU). It is expected that full European economic and monetary integration will be followed by increased presence of logistics firms' operations (Bamford 1999). Hence, logistics firms that will be part of retailers' and manufacturers' internationalization process will be able to offer a large range of services (and 'value added services') to their client base all over Europe.

Finally, Browne and Allen (1999) argue that most users of supply chain services are increasingly demanding 'one-stop shopping'. In other words, they are in favour of dealing with one or very few logistics firms that meet their needs at both domestic and international level. The aim of the latter is to facilitate further their current internationalization process via the use of specialist logistics firms.

European food supply chain networks

Most food manufacturers and retailers used to purchase services from logistics firms on a short term basis, through a typical market transaction exchange. At a later stage, they entered into long term contracts with logistics firms as they were satisfied by their performance, although they had to spend time and resources for vetting and monitoring such performance (McKinnon 1999). This led most food companies to develop a working partnership with a few logistics firms and, gradually, a close relationship was formed based on co-operation and trust. This is the main characteristic of the network approach (Jarillo 1993), something not in line with the traditional market transaction exchange (Table P8.2).

The network approach has been applied in the food retail supply chain (Bourlakis 1998), where, under a collaborative manner, a food retailer takes the role of 'central controller' and organizes the flow of product and information among itself and logistics firms.

In the fast food sector, this approach is evident in the co-operation between the franchiser, its franchisees and its closely tied suppliers who provide raw materials and specialized equipment (Jarillo 1993). In general, food supply chain networks consist of the major channel members, like the case of Efficient Consumer Response (ECR). This movement, which was initiated in the United States in the early 1990s and commenced in Europe in 1993, is based on efficient co-operation between leading European food manufacturers and retailers with the aims of increasing savings in the food supply chain and also

Market transaction exchange	Network approach
Shorter term	Longer term
Multiple logistics firms who are played off against one another for concessions	Fewer logistics firms (maybe even one) who are treated as valued partners
Price dominates	Value added services dominate
Little dedicated investment from logistics firm	Specialized investment can be high for both partners
Firms are independent	Much sharing of every kind of information
Formal, infrequent communication	Frequent formal and informal communication
Little interaction between respective functional areas	Many functional areas may interact across the partners

Source: Bowersox *et al.* 1992

Table P8.2 Market transaction exchange and network approach

meeting the changing demands of the European grocery consumer. Since 1993, ECR has clearly changed the attitude towards relationships and has promoted a greater collaboration of channel member participants in Europe. Its success so far, indicates that it will accelerate the formation of similar food supply chain networks across Europe with food retailers, food manufacturers and logistics firms, forming the triangle of the network members.

Finally, apart from ECR, two more factors further support the network's formation:

1. the anticipated internationalization of logistics firms in Europe which will enable them to meet sufficiently food manufacturers and retailers' demands for supply chain services all over the continent; and

2. the increasing importance of information technology systems that are the major facilitators for an effective communication and co-ordination between food supply chain network members (Bowersox and Daugherty 1995), e.g. Electronic Data Interchange (EDI), which allows the transmission of data (such as product sales data, product inventory data) between the computer systems of food retailers, manufacturers and logistics firms.

Therefore, it is expected that numerous European food supply chain networks will be created in the years to come and will be supported by information technology capabilities that allow network members to respond faster and more cost-effectively to the needs of European consumers.

Conclusions

The three trends that already have engineered changes in the European food supply chain have been discussed. As far as the externalization of supply chain operations is concerned, it has been suggested that specialist logistics firms will be utilized to a larger extent in the future, especially when these firms are able to offer a full range of services. Internalization of logistics firms is another trend that is facilitated by food firms' internationalization and is expected to be intensified, following deregulation and harmonization of supply chain standards within the European Monetary Union as well as firms' preference for 'one-stop shopping'.

Finally, it is anticipated that food channel members (manufacturers, retailers and logistics firms) will become more active in network formation that will increase the welfare of European consumers in terms of lower prices accompanied by a higher quality and variety of services.

Acknowledgements

I would like to thank Dr C. Bourlakis for his helpful suggestions and Ms A. Tregear for her support during the development of this viewpoint.

References

Bamford C.G. (1999) The internationalization of logistics in the UK. In Donald Walters (ed.), *Global Logistics and Distribution Planning*. London: Kogan Page, pp. 301–13.

Bourlakis M. (1998) Transaction costs, internationalization and logistics: the case of European food retailing. *International Journal of Logistics: Research and Applications*, 1 (3), pp. 251–64.

Bowersox D.J. and Daugherty P.J. (1995) Logistics paradigms: the impact of information technology. *Journal of Business Logistics*, 16 (1), pp. 73–91.

Bowersox D.J., Daugherty P.J., Droge C.L., Germain R.N. and Rogers D.S. (1992) *Logistical Excellence: It's not Business as Usual*. Burlington, USA: Digital Press.

Browne M. and Allen J. (1999) Developments in Western European logistics strategies. In Donald Walters (ed.), *Global Logistics and Distribution Planning*. London: Kogan Page, pp. 324–42.

Cooper J., Browne M. and Peters M. (1991) *European Logistics: Markets, Management and Strategy*. Oxford: Blackwell.

Dawson J.A. and Shaw S. (1990) The changing character of retailer–supplier relationships. In John Fernie (ed.), *Retail Distribution Management*. London: Kogan Page.

Fernie J. (1989) Contract distribution in multiple retailing. *International Journal of Physical Distribution and Materials Management*, 19 (7), pp. 1–35.

Fernie J. (1998) The internationalization of the retail supply chain. In John Fernie and Leigh Sparks (eds), *Logistics and Retail Management*. London: Kogan Page, pp. 47–66.

Fiddis C. (1997) *Manufacturer Retailer Relationships in the Food and Drink Industry: Strategies and Tactics in the Battle for Power*. London: FT Retail and Consumer Publishing/Pearson Professional.

Jarillo J.C. (1993) *Strategic Networks: Creating the Borderless Organization*. Oxford: Butterworth–Heinemann.

Laughlin K.A., Cooper J. and Cabocel E. (1993) *Reconfiguring European Logistics Systems*. Oak Brook: Council of Logistics Management.

Marketline International (1997) EU Logistics. London: Marketline International.

McKinnon A.C. (1999) The outsourcing of logistical activities. In Donald Walters (ed.), *Global Logistics and Distribution Planning*. London: Kogan Page, pp. 214–39.

The future of the food supply chain: a perspective looking up the chain

Sean Beer

Introduction

The food supply chain will be governed by three key issues in the future. These are globalization, consolidation and power, each of which is considered in this perspective. These issues give rise to a whole series of ethical considerations which, depending on the position that is adopted, could be regarded as either positive or negative.

Globalization and integration

Globalization transcends all areas of society. The growth of the Internet and the concept of the global village fuel the idea that the world is shrinking. In the future the development of a global economy will continue, which, in terms of the food industry, will be characterized by consolidation, i.e. the evolution of fewer and larger companies. This trend will occur in all areas of the food chain. Within the grocery industry the concept of concentration is well documented (e.g. Bates and Whittinton 1997; Jørgensen 1997, Jørgensen 1999), while a similar trend is evident in the catering industry.

Jørgensen (1999) maintains that the concentration in the food retail sector will result in a concentration of food suppliers and that this will counterbalance power in the chain. While concentration of suppliers is certain, whether this will affect the power balance is debatable, given the existing power of the retailers. These companies will control an ever increasingly integrated supply chain, which will produce substantial economic advantages for them. Typical benefits from integrating the supply chain in non-food systems have been indicated by Gould (1998). These are:

- 16%–18% improvement in delivery performance

- 25%–60% improvement in inventory reduction

- 30%–50% improvement in fulfilment cycle time

- 25%–80% improvement in forecast accuracy

- 10%–16% improvement in overall productivity

- 25%–50% improvement in supply-chain costs

- 20%–30% improvement in fill rates

- 10%–20% improvement in capacity realization

Application of these principles would obviously have benefits for the food supply chain, although the application of such figures as those put forward by Gould (1998) to the food industry really needs examination (Poole 1997). Questions arise with regard to who this will benefit the most – producers, retailers or consumers; and the question as to whether these principles can be applied to a product such as a lettuce, with a limited shelf life, or a beef animal that takes two years to produce, is worthy of investigation.

With regard to the European Union, it is probable that there will be a total redevelopment of the agriculture and food industry based on fewer, larger farms and firms. Changes in agriculture will result in the development of a new landscape based on three geographical areas (J.R. Edwards 1999, personal communication):

- Intensive agricultural production areas producing food at world prices. This will be hampered unless regulations on animal welfare and the environment are relaxed, which is unlikely and undesirable, or restrictions are put on the way in which imports are produced.

- Areas characterized by extensive production and environmental/heritage support, where farmers are supported for producing goods other than food and fibre.

- Areas of diversified agriculture near to conurbations.

The concern about large farms is obviously a key issue in this debate. In the United States there are dairy units with thousands of cows and beef finishing feedlots with tens of thousands of animals produced per year. This is occurring at a time when society is starting to question the ethics of large scale factory farming, for example, with regard to the intensive husbandry of poultry. It is ironic therefore, that other areas of food production are being forced down the intensive route. One could, however, consider that this merely reflects a food culture that is obsessed with cheap food irrespective of quality.

Increasingly around the world, producer countries will add value to food products before exporting them. Food retailers in importing countries may fund some of this. If you can import the lettuce why not the sandwich? There will be a need for very highly developed quality assurance, involving high tech solutions such as genetic fingerprinting to maintain product authenticity. This could give rise to some very interesting alliances. If a British farming co-operative was to bid for a contract to supply chicken, for example, and could not fulfil the order, why should it not outsource the supply to another producer in another country and take a reduced percentage on the outsourced component of the deal? They may even lose money on the outsourced component simply to secure a large order where they will make money on their own share. In this way companies may move from being commodity suppliers to international food businesses, particularly as they move to add value. For many in the food industry these are revolutionary ideas.

Will this give rise to greater choice for consumers? Again this is debatable. Greater regulation appears to be 'limiting' home production, especially small scale production, giving rise to greater use of large scale, factory farming and associated declines in culture, heritage and environment. The decline in small abattoirs in the UK is an example of this. Changing the regulations about meat inspection is proving too expensive for many small slaughterhouses. Closure results in animals having to travel further for slaughter, and many small scale specialist food producers, using rare breeds or farming organically, may find their production systems compromised.

In some ways this represents the destruction of food culture, with the development of 'cyber food' and a new pseudo food culture where the whole world ends up eating the same food. This has become known as the 'McDonaldization' of food society (see also Ritzer 1993, 1996; and Germov and Williams 1999). How far will this process continue?

Alternatively, this could be viewed from a different perspective. All industries have to move on. The modern food industry has succeeded in providing high quality, cheap food to the masses. Again, there are debates about whether the food is of better quality and whether it is cheap. Certainly people in the developed world seem well fed, perhaps even too well, given the high levels of obesity found in modern society. Yet today 24 000 people will die across the world through starvation and starvation-related disease. Many people in developing countries look in disbelief at our supermarkets and the food they contain. So may be we have not got it completely right. Whether the proposed developments in the food chain will help them or the shareholders of the multi-national companies that control the food industry is another question.

There are a whole series of other issues facing the food supply industry in the UK that will influence its ability to respond to future developments. There are continuing arguments about level playing fields. It is debatable whether consumers are eating imported food in the UK that is produced using techniques that might be considered illegal in this country. For any country, discrimination against its home industry needs to be addressed in the global food chain, if indigenous industries are to be maintained. Failure to address such issues will result in the exportation of jobs and associated social deprivation.

Power

This whole process is really about consolidation and power. The situation at present is one of oligopoly with regard to food retailers, i.e. there are a large number of food producers, few suppliers and many consumers. In many ways this is the classical 'figure of eight' syndrome, with retailers controlling the narrow part of the chain, as Figure P9.1 shows.

The key question is how this situation will develop in the future. It could be argued that there are two levels here. Within

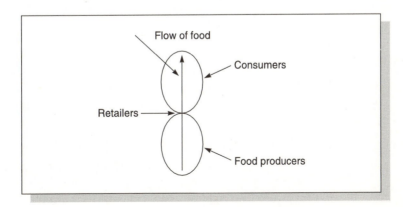

Figure P9.1
The power base of the food supply chain

the UK there is a process of consolidation, but this could be offset by the process of globalization opening up new players in the industry. However, the global industry is simultaneously consolidating and so the process continues. One often-neglected player in this is the catering industry. Evidence indicates that more and more food is being consumed outside the home. Indeed, allegedly some new homes in larger cities are now being built without kitchens! Food retailers are often heavily criticized for problems in the food chain. Caterers are in many ways less accountable than retailers in that meals do not have to be labelled with regard to their origin. Regulations with regard to declarations about the presence or otherwise of genetically modified organisms are stepping in this direction. More will come. As will the Internet. The implications of new technology are second only to those of biotechnology. In the future more of us will be ordering our food on-line for it to be delivered to our special secure wall refrigerators. Or possibly our smart fridges will order them for us. The question is not *if* it will happen, but to what extent and how quickly; and also how will this affect the whole of the supply chain? Again, there are two dimensions to this: not only will it allow large retailers to sell direct to homes but also, via the mail, specialist food producers, who were previously reliant on limited direct sales.

Conclusions

This perspective emphasizes that the processes of consolidation and integration will dominate the future of the food supply chain. The background to this is a continuing conflict between consumer inspired regulation and a cheap food culture. This conflict will have a direct effect on the home based food supply chain giving rise to more jobs being exported to less regulated countries with cheaper factors of production. The UK industry will need to come to terms with this and innovate to survive. Producing generic products is no longer a real option. Some businesses may develop niche markets for products. Ten per cent of the population may well spend an extra 10% on products with an alternative quality dimension associated with fair trade, culture, the environment or animal welfare, for example. The remainder will buy the cheapest options. Whether one thinks the future of the food supply chain is bright may depend on whether one belongs to the 10% or the 90%.

References

Bates K. and Whittinton M. (1997) Intense competition, revised strategies and financial performance in the UK food retailing sector. In J. Nilsson and G. Van Dijk (eds), *Strategies and Structures in the Agro-Food Industries*. Assen: Van Gorcum.

Germov J. and Williams L. (1999) *A Sociology of Food and Nutrition. The Social Appetite*. Oxford: Oxford University Press.

Gould L. (1998) Rethinking supply chains. *Managing Automation* 13 (32), pp. 35–46.

Jørgensen N. (1997) Quality certification is a key success factor in international marketing of food products. In J. Nilsson and G. Van Dijk (eds), *Strategies and Structures in the Agro-Food Industries*. Assen: Van Gorcum.

Jørgensen N. (1999) The Future Structure of Grocery Retailing in Western Europe. In Proceedings of the 10th International Conference on Research in the Distributive Trades, Institute for Retail Studies, University of Sterling, pp. 623–30.

Poole N.D. (1997) Changes in the European food industry: a research agenda for marketing economists. *Journal of International Food and Agribusiness Marketing*, 9 (1), pp. 1–17.

Ritzer G. (1993) *The McDonaldization of Society*. Newbury Park, CA: Pine Forge Press.

Ritzer G. (1996) *The McDonaldization of Society*, rev. edn. Newbury Park, CA: Pine Forge Press.

E-shopping: the Peapod grocery experience

Denis Towill

Introduction: a vision of the new world of E-shopping

One vision of the future envisages an end to pushing heavy shopping carts up and down the aisles, loading up with the weekly groceries, dragging tired and reluctant children behind, waiting in line at the checkout, unloading into the boot of the car, driving home amid heavy traffic, unloading from the car again and reloading into kitchen cupboards or the fridge–freezer. The shopping chores of the future will all be done electronically. The standard weekly food and household order will be set up with a local home delivery company. E-mail, a phone call or fax quoting a reference number will automatically trigger a reorder to be delivered at a pre-agreed time. Specials for the week will be added by ticking off the electronic order form. Payment will automatically be deducted from the bank account through a secure encrypted payment network. The frustrations of shopping for staple and basic items will be a thing of the past. So, how are retailers meeting these new challenges? One company at the vanguard of E-shopping is Peapod, whose operations are described here.

Peapod approach to E-shopping

In E-shopping there seem to be as many ways to manage the supply chain as there are online grocers. Peapod have specifically designed their supply chain to maximize flexibility for the customers, who select day and time of delivery. If orders are placed by 4p.m. on Monday, delivery can be arranged between 7a.m. and 1p.m. on Tuesday. Orders placed by midnight on Monday can be delivered between 4p.m. and 10p.m. on Tuesday. Customers may also nominate to receive groceries for delivery within the next seven days. To achieve cost-effective delivery coupled with flexibility, Peapod logistics and marketing act as a seamless supply chain, i.e. 'to think and act as one'. So once a customer link has been established, marketing cultivates the neighbourhood in the expectancy of building up the client base. Hence the delivery routes will become more dense, thus increasing capacity and making the drops more cost-effective. This process is further enhanced by drop-offs at homes, car parks and central pick-up points, including retail stores or even church halls.

E-shopping logistics

E-shopping logistics differs from traditional operations in three important ways: quantities, timing and demand management. In terms of quantities, single item picking is required by dot.com companies, which means an operator scans an SKU, not a pallet. As items are not protected by boxes, greater care must be taken when handling. Timing pressures mean that previously acceptable shipment times of 24–72 hours must be reduced to 12 hours and to meet a specific time window selected by the customer. This constrains the routeing flexibility and puts extra pressure on van drivers to meet deadlines. Finally, rapidly changing demand patterns place tremendous pressure on corporate resources. Frequently, the setting up of a website business leads to substantial orders being placed which cannot be fulfilled within the expectancy time frame of the customer. So costs rise trying to satisfy demand but business is irrevocably lost due to poor delivery performance.

Use of specialist E-centres

Over the past 10 years Peapod has experienced substantial growth. Until 1998 operations were essentially based on mirroring consumer behaviour experienced in supermarkets. Hence individual customer orders were 'picked' in separate areas of Peapod supermarkets just as the individual customer would. Peapod employed a replenishment manager responsible for stock control, plus the pickers who made up the orders. This old operations model had low fixed costs and flexibility to expand, low inventory and no facilities management issues to resolve. The new operations model has required a novel approach to inventory control, warehousing, order fulfilment, route planning and scheduling. It is firmly based on the concept of Peapod being a fulfilment and distribution business, developed specifically to satisfy customer demand within the 12-hour lead time and definitely not an adapted shopping business. Deliveries are made seven days a week, are ordered on www.peapod.com and typically consist of around 40 to 50 items collectively valued at around £80 per transaction. There is usually a mix of dry, refrigerated and frozen products.

E-centre operations

Consumers are fussy about their groceries. So the Peapod picker acts as eyes, nose and hands in the setting of perishable product quality standards. If the customer is dissatisfied via poor quality, they are also unhappy if a product ordered is not delivered as requested. Out-of-stocks are therefore completely unacceptable, especially since just one SKU short in the order can ruin the complete delivery. To minimize stockouts, Peapod are moving to a distribution operations model incorporating stand-alone centres dedicated to E-shopping with separate inventory and replenishment systems. Hence supermarkets and E-centres are no longer competing for the same stock. The E-centre takes responsibility for its own ordering, receiving, stocking and replenishment based on their customer SKU usage, which may be quite different from supermarket consumption. The E-centre also determines from sales patterns which products are not moving quickly and should therefore be discontinued from being offered by the Peapod marketing facility.

Further E-shopping time compression

Peapod are aggressively working to reduce the delivery lead time still further, since they firmly believe this is the next market winner and want to be first in the frame. Tools used to achieve this goal includes best-of-class routing software, which incorporates maps and travel time to determine how many stops each vehicle can make the next day. Sophisticated website technology applies airline reservation principles to consumer-direct delivery and supply to minimize transportation costs. This is achieved whilst meeting the target time window and levelling orders across days and shifts. The output from the route-planning software creates a route and stop number for the driver plus point-to-point directions and time standards for each drop. To support this delivery activity and improve the 'picking' process considerable thought is given to the design and layout of the distribution centre, designed to maximize performance of the pickers. This is distinct from store layout, which is targeted at merchandising to consumers. Consequently, Pareto analysis is used on a continuing basis to organize products into A–B–C categories based on frequency of ordering.

Likely future developments

The purpose of Peapod E-shopping is to create and keep a customer. To do that they feel they must do the things that will make people want to do business with them by providing value-added services that will reduce the consumer's overall cost, increase the consumer's productivity and make the consumer's job of buying groceries easier. Groceries are the cornerstone of Peapod's business, but they are just the beginning. Some day in the future Peapod may offer one-stop or no-stop shopping for a wide range of products including groceries, pharmacy products, pet supplies, toys, stationery and so on. They aim to be the company that delivers to the household between two and three times *every* month. If Peapod decide to move into this particular marketplace and handle these other products, it would essentially be through partnerships and using cross-docking arrangements. Service and product go hand in hand; continual improvements in warehousing and distribution are a key ongoing element of Peapod business strategy.

Acknowledgements

The viewpoint has been developed based on J.A. Caltagirone (2000) Peapod's virtual supermarket, *Supply Chain Management Review*, March–April, pp. 44–50; J. Holström, K. Tanskanen, V. Kämäräinen (1999) Redesigning the supply chain for Internet shopping – bringing EC to the household, Proceedings, 1999 LRN Conference, Newcastle, pp. 261–7; and M. de Kare-Silver (2000) *E-Shock 2000*. London: Macmillan Business Books.

Changes in supply chain structure: the impact of expanding consumer choice

Stephen Allen

Introduction

The period from the 1960s to the present day has been a time of considerable change, which has had a significant impact on the supply chain within the food sector (Shutt and Clark 1995; IGD 2000a). This change has been led by the rise of the big multiples, their commitment to convenience, quality and speed in a one-stop shop environment (IGD 2000a) and their keen interest in the reduction of product costs, cost cutting strategies and central distribution systems.

These trends have proved to be largely incompatible with traditional food sectors such as fresh produce wholesaling. It is evident, that less than 10% of the retail food market (Mintel 1999a) will be available to the wholesale markets, as the multiples expand through convenience retailing. There is clear evidence that 80% of produce sourced to retailing and even catering will be from the top five global food manufacturers or processors (Hughes 2000). This will result in the continued decline of regional and national suppliers and may affect the range of produce available to the consumer, e.g. species of apples. Yet at variance with this trend, consumers are increasingly concerned with produce choice and the provenance of food they consume. In addition, farmers, horticulturalists and the wholesale sector are looking for alternative customers to the major supermarkets. These trends appear to be resulting in the emergence of an alternative supplementary food supply chain.

The state of play within the supply chain

The continued consolidation of suppliers and retailers within the food sector has led to the decline in the numbers of wholesalers, abattoirs and other traditional food suppliers (Mintel 1999a). The emerging strategies of Category Management, in which essentially one supplier is promoted, has led to further de-listing of, in some cases, companies of corporate status (Fyffe) (Nicholson 1998).

In Category Management a single supplier takes the lead and thus administrative burden of organizing the supply of product types to the retailer. They select 'appropriate' products from portfolios of sister companies. In theory, the benefits of Category Management are gained through the marriage of skills and knowledge of major retailers and suppliers. Suppliers to the sector have specific information on consumer consumption trends whilst retailers provide information regarding the type of person who shops at their stores (Anon 1997b). However, in reality Category Management could be said (Anon 1999) to offer the retailer the opportunity to reduce the cost burden of managing the supply chain still further. In conjunction with ECR, Category Management enables the retailer to pass the cost of managing supplies and the supply base further down the supply chain. Companies who formally supplied the retail sector are therefore required to fit into the new role of sub-contractor, the preferred Category Management supplier. The rise of systems based on the criteria of price will continue to be of detriment to the UK agricultural, horticultural, processing, wholesale and retail sectors.

Unwillingness of suppliers to accept the terms and conditions of uncertainty placed upon them by the category leaders, even as a preferred Category Management supplier, could lead to a change in the future structure of the food chain. Ultimately this could result in the emergence of an alternative supply chain (Younger 1998; Hughes 2000).

In its simplest form this will be the redirecting of the business into new markets and the targeting of new customer groups. It is likely that wholesalers will cease supplying the multiple retail sector and focus more on the fast growing foodservice market (IGD 1998). This in itself is not radical; any business taking a strategic view would re-evaluate their customer base.

Yet a change in customer base and decisions to not supply to retail multiples may result in a chain of events that will in effect change the food supply chain and the structure of the national food economy. This is particularly significant for the local and regional supply chains. Those companies who obtain preferred category status, otherwise known as Category Captains (Anon 1997a) will be of national/international standing. Local and regional supply chains will be hardest hit by the de-listing exercise (Nicholson 1998), thus causing local suppliers to identify alternative markets and concentrate more upon the foodservice sector.

In this event there may be still a role for wholesaling within the supply chain. The wholesaling sector could emerge as either an intermediary, or in instances in which flexible delivery of fresh produce to local outlets is required. This is of particular significance for the catering/eat out market where the nature of the product, the location and size of outlets means that caterers need flexibility from their suppliers. The continued existence and sustained growth of the wholesale market may be through recognizing the key opportunities presented by catering and food service markets.

The fickle consumer and their changing desires – diametric scenarios

Yet it is here we are met with a paradox. Time-poor, money-rich consumers (Beard et al. 1999) have sought more efficient ways of purchasing, moving to weekly shopping expeditions. Their increased affluence has led to consumers demanding seasonal 'luxury' food, i.e. strawberries, all the year round. These consumer demands have at least in part contributed to the development of the current structure of the food sector. Whilst supermarkets are said to have increased choice (Dawson 2000; Wroe 2000), their strategies have led to a real lack of product range and lack of individuality of their product offer (Wroe 2000).

Recent findings (Mintel 1999b) demonstrate changes in consumer needs. The average number of shopping expeditions per week has increased (Mintel 1999b). Consumers are looking for meals ready for consumption, i.e. meal solutions, home meal replacement, and meals out of the home on the one hand, whilst on the other they have become more aware of the environmental and health implications of food provenance (Tregear et al. 1994), resulting in the growth in organic food and the popularity of farmers' markets.

Consumers are also apparently aware of the impact on local communities of the major multiples. SAVE, Sainsbury's scheme of providing Sainsbury products to rural community shops, was a response to the consumer's attitude to the impact of super-markets on the rural commercial infrastructure.

Local economies and the supply base

In the 1980s (Cannon 1986), the development of a global supply chain was considered to be a mechanism by which food could be delivered more efficiently to a post-industrial society. At this stage little attention was paid to the impact of this strategy on regional economies. More recently, there has been consider-able concern as to the ability of the biggest retailers to 'enter new areas and lay waste to existing retailers' (Lang 1994). Lang's concern related to the inaccessibility of food for the non-car-bound consumer, others (Westlake 1993; Ellaway and Macintyre 2000) talk about the increasing division between the rich and poor and the higher price paid by consumers who have no access to private transport. In some circles, areas that have suffered from the decline in local retailers are described as food deserts (Gannaway 1999).

There is, however, a further concern. Calculations have been made as to the respective multiplier effect of local retailers as against multiple retailers (Macdonald and Swales 1991). Such research clearly indicates that whilst multiples generate jobs, the actual jobs created do not offset the number of jobs lost through the failure of local businesses. Such failures are not isolated to the retail sector but span a whole series of other service sectors (DETR 1998).

In addition, greater levels of revenue are leaked from an area within a food supply structure dominated by public limited companies than through their traditional counterparts (Harris 1997). This is particularly evident in rural areas. It is suggested that the SME, including those within the food sector, have an important role in sustainable economic growth (Marsden 1995).

The alternative supply structure – a dual system or a new era?

Drawing from recent consultancy work within the food sector, it is evident that many SMEs within a number of regions across the UK are turning away from multiple retail supply. The recip-ient of their renewed attentions is the foodservice market. This may prove to be of great concern to the food retailer if the food-service market ultimately merges with or outgrows the food retail market – a development that is not beyond credibility given current trends in the United States (IGD 2000b).

Within the fresh produce sector, there are some 17 600 players (Mintel 1999a), 30% of whom are responsible for 70% of the busi-ness. The remaining players are often family owned operators with a low-level technological input who traditionally sourced the local green grocer sector. Their ability to source catering organizations such as the brewery and leisure chains will depend upon their capacity to adapt operating procedures to meet the criteria demanded of reliability, flexibility, consistency and volume. The central purchasing departments are increasingly looking for single suppliers, yet catering organization operate extensively in small local outlets. A national distribution or regional distribution centre due to the minimum order cost structures may not effectively meet single deliveries.

The solution would appear to be the development of integrated partnerships between fellow market traders both within and across product ranges. The pulling together of resources, product ranges and market information, would facilitate the introduction of:

1. A physical distribution system matching the requirements of the customer base.

2. An IT system which would facilitate flexible deliveries and reduce supply chain costs.

3. A multi-product delivery structure.

In some cases there may be a need for numerous supply tiers to the ultimate customer, resulting in a dynamic sub-contracting culture. The development of such initiatives, particularly within the food sector, cannot be described as widespread. In the case study below we can gain an insight into how this might look.

Case study – Sheffield Wholesale Market food supply chain project

This case study considers the impact of globalization and polarization on the local fresh produce supply chain within Sheffield and its wholesale market.

Sheffield Wholesale Market opened in 1961. At that time there were numerous fresh produce businesses operating within the market. Since then the number of businesses has declined continuously; in 1984 alone, 31 went out of business (Shaw *et al.* 1994). There are currently 16 surviving businesses, although turnover remains at 1984 figures of £50m.

Due to their concern for the future survival of the market, the local authority commissioned a study, the purpose of which was to review the future of the wholesale market and decide on the most advantageous strategic option.

The need for change
The subsequent report (PKF World-wide 2297 RF Sheffield Parkway Wholesale Market, 14 July 1997) set down the following options:

• Do nothing.

• Develop a food industry park.

• Develop alternative uses, which would best fulfil the council's objectives and most economic use of the council's land asset.

The council's ultimate decision was to sell off the land asset that was home to the wholesale market to a private developer, encouraging the developer to re-provide the wholesale market as part of its own industrial redevelopment plans. Given this action, there was concern for the market's continued existence and also concern for the following issues:

- Support for the traditional wholesale businesses and services to the local retailers within the city.
- Support for the retail markets produce supply.
- Support for policies relating to a 'Healthy Sheffield' and access to fresh produce by lower income social groups.
- The cost of missed opportunity in providing a leading regional food distribution park.

Beginnings of the change process

As these issues were evolving, a parallel piece of work was taking place, examining the food chain and future developments within the food sector, particularly the declining wholesale market sector. This independent work, led by Stephen Allen of Optimal Consulting combined with research into the relationship between wholesalers and independent caterers (Eastham 1998, 1999), acted as a catalyst for the development of a supply chain project to bring about change in and modernization of the practices of the Sheffield Wholesale Market businesses.

An evolving project

In the early stages a partnership was established between the private sector developer and the local authority. This was seen as the best way of ensuring continuity of business within the wholesale market and facilitating the redevelopment of the buildings whilst simultaneously fulfilling the needs of the local retailers, retail markets and other users within the food supply chain.

This led to the modernization programme of the fresh produce wholesaling sector in Sheffield Wholesale Markets, which included a physical regeneration of the wholesale market site and a complete

overhaul of operating procedures of resident wholesalers on the basis of supply chain management principles.

The project

A strategy for evolving an effective programme across 42 businesses in the market was established. This recognized three distinct groups:

Group 1: defined as lead or primary wholesale businesses having direct customer and supplier relationships, good operational management and an organization and structure – turnover at a minimum of £1 million.

Group 2: defined as secondary wholesale businesses in the majority serving as sub-contractors to the lead wholesaler and having predominantly customer and supplier relationships within the wholesale market itself.

Group 3: defined as secondary wholesale business. Primarily involved in the function of

(a) inter-trade, i.e. selling exclusively to other businesses within the wholesale market or

(b) speciality produce and related multi-product delivery requirements such as dairy or bakery products.

The change management model

The change management model adopted for this project originated as a manufacturing industry supply chain initiative. The model, 'The Customer and Supplier Relationship Improvement Process' (Supply Chain Management Group, Glasgow) has been adapted and evolved into a service driven five-phase productive supply chain model where:

Phase I deals with internal business commitment to the project and structuring teams to work on activities.

Phase II deals with performance analysis of the businesses' customer and supplier relationships and determines effective future targets of either.

Phase III deals with joint internal business commitment between the project business and its chosen customers and suppliers or targeted customers and suppliers.

Phase IV deals with action orientated assessment of joint customer and supplier relationships and targeted improvements in a measured and planned way.

Phase V deals with a continuous method of progress review and action for activities and responsibilities agreed in Phase IV.

The model was further adapted to meet the specific needs of the sector and the project activity. The headline sector-specific activities of the model are described below.

The supply chain project strategy supported the following activities:

- Primary research: the decline of the wholesale markets and the supply chain.

- Diagnostic work: review of the wholesaler business position.

- Mapping the supply chain – both local and regional.

- Developing a 'Business Success Model' for regeneration of the wholesale sector.

- Building productive supply chain activity within the wholesaler business, i.e. focusing on business development style supply chains.

- Building cost saving and co-operative supply chains by recognizing and understanding common business functions.

- Developing a 'marketing concept' or 'theme' in the form of a Regional Produce Centre or Food Supplier Park.

Project group results

The project on the whole has proved extremely successful and could be a valuable model for future developments in this sector. Key improvements have included:

- The adoption of technological systems such as tele-sales, temperature control and IT systems.

- The development of delivered service to customers, which in certain cases involved sharing the investment into the multi-temperature transport.

- A more focused approach to product specialisms and a greater integration between traders as to the overall product ranges stocked within the wholesale market.

The traders have also become suppliers to a facilitating organization, which operates as a single first tier supplier to the catering sector, subcontracting the sourcing of fresh produce across regions to co-ordinated independent traders. A summary of the primary and secondary business performance improvements follows. The list is not exhaustive, nor indeed have all businesses achieved equally across all areas.

Project results: a wider perspective

The change programme continues to develop a competitive and sustainable food business environment for the wholesale market business. It has also provided a catalyst for change in the regional food chain and the development of supplier partnerships to facilitate supply to the corporate foodservice sector.

In reality, the project has instigated changes in the attitudes and developed knowledge and skills of the wholesale traders. These changes are more difficult to measure in pure quantitative terms. Sheffield wholesalers have built up a greater understanding of the strategic dimension of business operations within the current market place. They recognize:

- The need to develop a parallel local and regional supply chain alongside the centralized system instigated by the multiple retail sector.

- The market potential of the catering sector. Freshness and daily delivery systems can present attractive options to major customer groups such as the breweries and leisure chains with extensive local outlets, as single deliveries cannot be met by central distribution or regional distribution, due to the minimum order cost structures.

	Improvements

Business development activity	1 The introduction of:
	  (a) Tele-sales, delivered service, catering supplies, product preparation and packing
	  (b) The reduction of product ranges
	  (c) The extension of product ranges
	  (d) Development of niche or specialisms for smaller trader

Facilities investment	Development of: 1 Chill storage 2 IT systems 3 Quality systems and product inspection

Customer relationship	1 The generation of promotional material to:
	  (a) increase awareness
	  (b) change attitudes of non-customers
	  (c) build and retain loyalty
	2 Development of Codes of Practice to guarantee standards of hygiene, product handling and trading standards (e.g. supplier bonds)
	3 Retailer–wholesaler buying groups: bulk purchasing, advice on product and retail format, shelf layouts and promotion (thus improving information flow and commitment)
	4 Links to other retail outlets
	5 Information flow on product requirements
	6 Bonus schemes for market purchases on volume discount basis
	7 Cash and carry businesses joint development
	8 Multiple retail: specialist product and top up

Supplier relationships: growers/suppliers:	1 The establishment of stronger supplier relationships
Supplier relationships: wholesalers/ traders	1 Increased sales through collaboration with other companies on key lines 2 Adoption of an umbrella marketing organization to facilitate access to larger catering multiples 3 Shared transportation systems 4 Branded market delivery service: collaborative trader activity on transport

Table P11.1 Improvements at Sheffield Wholesale Markets

- The importance of developing a delivery service to the catering sector may facilitate their survival within the current food sector.

- The value of participating in joint activities with fellow traders to provide a broader product range.

- An appreciation of the value of the development of a subcontracting culture to facilitate market access.

- The benefits inherent in the 'local' supply chain (in comparison to Central or Regional Distribution centres) which has encouraged them to promote 'local' delivery structures.

- That in improving the frequency of deliveries and quality/availability of product, smaller supermarkets have been persuaded to return to the wholesale markets.

Conclusion: future developments

Within this case study we have illustrated a change programme in the Sheffield Wholesale Market which was designed to find alternative markets for the declining wholesale sector. In essence, this is an example as to how the markets and multiple retailers can co-exist. It is seen as a potential model of development for other wholesaler markets, particularly in the light of the gathering momentum for alternatives to multiple retailers led by both consumers and businesses alike. The project will be implemented as part of the City of Manchester regeneration programme with the lead up to the 2001 Commonwealth Games.

Perhaps the most surprising of developments has emerged from Italy, north of Verona. Dissemination of the success of the Sheffield project has brought a request to help implement a similar change management process in Italy, where again the regional food economies are suffering decline due to the impact of the fast growing large food retailers.

This could be the start of a change process that will see the large retailers forced into more local sourcing, therefore preventing the effects of globalization in the European community. Who knows, we may see one or two North Yorkshire farmers, or apple growers in Kent, surviving!

References

Anon (1997a) The danger to our SME base. *The Grocer*, 4 October, p. 37.

Anon (1997b) Teamwork. *The Grocer*, 12 July, p. 32–3.

Anon (1999) *The Grocer*, 19 June, p. 6.

Beard J. *et al.* (1999) Grocery Retailing 1999: Market Review. IGD, p. 30.

Cannon T. (1986) Marketing problems in the food chain: the issues. In B. Beharrell and I. Goulding (eds), *Marketing Problems in the Food Chain*. Sheffield City Polytechnic.

Dawson J. (2000) Viewpoint: retailer power, manufacturer power, competition and some questions of economic analysis. *International Journal of Retail and Distribution Management*, 28 (1), pp. 5–8.

DETR (1998) The Impact of Large Foodstores on Market Towns and District Centres.

Executive summary, Department of the Environment, Transport and the Regions, published 8 October 1998.

Eastham J. (1998) Is catering culture different? Issues for the development of inter-firm relationships. ICCASS, Conference, Bournemouth University.

Eastham J. (1999) *A Longitudinal Study of the Development of Inter-firm Relationships in the Fresh Produce Supply and Catering Sectors*. CHME Conference, Surrey.

Ellaway A. and Macintyre S. (2000) Shopping for food in socially contrasting locations. *British Food Journal*, 102, pp. 52–9.

Gannaway B. (1999) Desert bloom. *The Grocer*, 3 April, pp. 24–6.

Harris P. (1997) Limitations on the use of regional economic impact multipliers by practitioners: an application to the tourism industry. *Journal of Tourism Studies*, 8 (2), pp. 50–61.

Hughes D. (2000) Challenges for the fresh produce industry in the twenty-first century. Conference paper, Wye College, University of London, pp. 1–10.

IGD (1998) The Catering Wholesaler. IGD Executive Briefing, conference proceedings 11 May 1998.

IGD (2000a) The Food Project Conference, 29 March 2000.

IGD (2000b) The Future of Foodservice. Executive Briefing, conference proceedings 19 April 2000.

Lang T.(1994) Feeding the captive stomach: supermarkets, the consumer and competition policy. Paper for XIV International Home Economics and Consumer Studies Research Conference, Sheffield 21–3 July.

Macdonald R. and Swales J. (1991) The local employment impact of a hypermarket: a modified multiplier analysis incorporating the effect of lower retail prices. *Regional Studies*, 25 (2), pp. 1155–62.

Marsden T. (1995) Beyond agriculture? Regulating the new rural spaces. *Journal of Rural Studies*, 11 (3), pp. 285–96.

Mintel (1999a) *Wholesaling and Cash and Carry*. Mintel International.

Mintel (1999b) The convenience shopper. *Convenience Retailing*, April.

Nicholson A. (1998) *Sunday Telegraph*, 4 October, p. 78.

PKF Worldwide (1997) *Sheffield Parkway Wholesale Markets*. July.

Shaw S.A., Gibbs J. and Gray V. (1994) The Strathclyde Wholesale Markets Study. Main report, University of Strathclyde, October 1994.

Shutt J., Clark R. and Blanchard S. (1995) *Developing Leeds Wholesale Market for the 21st Century*. European Regional Business Development Unit, pp. 1–3.

Tregear A., Bent J.B. and McGregor M.J. (1994) The demand for organically grown produce. *British Food Journal*, 96 (4), pp. 21–25.

Westlake T. (1993) cited in A. Ellaway and S. Macintyre (2000) Shopping for food in socially contrasting locations. *British Food Journal*, 102, pp. 52–9.

Wroe M. (2000) National Don't Shop at Supermarkets Day, *Sunday Express*, 12 August, p. 33.

Younger R. (1998) New structures will be required. The FT management report: supply chain challenges of electronic shopping. *The Financial Times*, 1 December, p. 3.

Glossary

Activity based costing (ABC)

The principle of activity based costing is to analyse actual product costs by specifically identifying all those activities associated with a product, at each step in the flow of that product, through the manufacturing or service centre supply chain. In practice, this will not only identify those costs associated with the change process but all other costs, e.g. the use of technology, bottlenecks, inventory storage, material delays inspection costs etc.

Back hauling

A return load taken after the delivery has been made. Back hauling is a major development, to support the reduction of lead time and costs within the supply chain.

Business process

Can be defined as a set of activities that, taken together, produce a result of value to a customer, or add value to a product, e.g. 'serving a customer'.

Business process re-engineering

Focuses on the redesigning basic or core business processes and not organizational units. It is designed to force managers to think about the relationship between core process, resources and the capability and competence required within the process.

Buying groups

These are formed by independent wholesale operators in order to improve trading terms with suppliers and offer their members, through the power of bulk buying and significant price benefits. The main distinguishing feature compared to symbol groups is that it allows members to trade under their own name, fascia or group identity.

Category
A measurable and manageable group of products/services, that consumers perceive to be interrelated and/or substitutable (see Kotzab page 276).

Category Management
Category Management involves organizing a multi-functional team around customer orientated categories and giving these teams responsibility for the strategy, operations and performance of the category across the different functions of the business.

Centralization
In logistics terms, relates to the process of bringing products from a variety of sources to a central depot for redelivery elsewhere.

Composite distribution
This is multi-temperature distribution system, including ambient, chilled and frozen products. A composite distribution centre is a multi-temperature distribution centre, which can handle products in a variety of on-site chambers each operating at a specific temperature.

Confidential rebate
A sum of money paid by the second tier supplier to the catering organization. The sum represents the difference between the agreed price and the actual price charged through the catering supply company.

Consolidation
A trend for reducing the number of players within the market place. This is characteristic of mature markets.

Continuous Replenishment Programme (CRP)
Essentially another name for VMI (q.v.) and emphasizes the passive information sharing role of customers, leaving the EDI-enabled vendors to directly manage store inventories. Two major benefits then accrue: the cost of ordering is reduced greatly, and inventory levels may be reduced by up to 25%.

Demand management
Demand management refers to the development of a customer-focused strategy, such as, optimizing promotions and introducing new products.

E-commerce
The use of the Internet as a sales tool has offered a great opportunity for many businesses. E-commerce offers the small, medium and large business, the possibility of, on-line delivery of services

directly to the consumer, and direct marketing. All internet sites are equally accessible through the Web, thus offering all organizations an equal opportunity to compete in a global market.

E-markets
Electronic markets are where buyers are connected through a website, which functions as a network of buyers and sellers. These sites are expected to create greater efficiencies through the reduction of administration costs, greater information and to enhance supplier/buyer relationships.

Efficient Consumer Response (ECR)
ECR is a global movement in the fast moving consumer goods industry, focusing on the total supply chain, suppliers, manufacturers, wholesalers, retailers and third party service providers working closely together to fulfil the changing demands of the consumer better, faster and at less cost – working to break down barriers between trading partners. This is a broadening of the QR concept to become the basis of collaborative working in the grocery supply chain. ECR is again an umbrella term that seeks to enable superior consumer value in shorter time frames and at least cost. The key terms include: demand management, supply management and enabling technologies (Christopher 1998).

Efficient Foodservice Response (EFR)
This is the foodservice initiative parallel to ECR. It is distinctive from ECR as it more specifically reflects the needs of the hospitality sector. Initiated in the United States in 1994 by the International Foodservice Manufacturers Association and the International Foodservice Distributors Association. It is currently being heavily promoted through the IGD (Institute of Grocery Distribution) in the UK.

Electronic Data Interchange (EDI)
This is a computer to computer system which transmits information between two trading partners in the supply chain. The data is usually organized in specific standards and formats for ease of transmission and validation.

Electronic funds transfer at point of sale (EFTPoS)
As with EpoS (q.v.), information is electonically recorded. The system in addition enables automatic transfer of customer funds with card payments.

Electronic point of sale (EpoS)
This is a method of recording store sales by either scanning product bar codes at the store's tills or by inputting sales through a keyboard.

Enabling technologies
Enabling technologies covers EDI, electronic fund transfer, activity based costing, product coding and database management (Christopher 1998).

Ethics
Ethics is a branch of philosophy that investigates morality and in particular the varieties of thinking by which human conduct are guided and may be appraised. (*Fontana Dictionary of Modern Thought*)

Food miles
Food miles are used to denote the fact that little of UK food is grown locally (Food Miles campaign) and food travels great distances to the consumer. SAFE indicate that food miles come in two varieties, the mileage built up within countries as food is packaged, processed, taken to distribution centres, on to shops and finally to the consumer; and the distance between the country where food is grown and where it is eaten.

Horizontal integration
A growth strategy, which involves the acquisition of one or more competitors, or fusion of firms of similar products, in order to access new markets or maintain market share. However at times this term is used loosely (see horizontally integrated networks).

Horizontally integrated networks
This is distinctive from horizontal integration, it refers to businesses that remain independent, but combine forces in order to access new markets or maintain market share. Horizontally integrated networks materialize in a number of forms and have generated numerous models of classification. One of the simplest depicts the distinctions as 'objects of exchange', (Rosenfeld 1996) and distinguishes between 'hard' groups of firms who tangibly co-operate e.g. co-produce, and 'soft' groups of firms who share information or collaboratively solve common problems.

Just-in-time (JIT)
Just-in-time is a system which enables the movement of merchandise or part finished stock to the next point of the supply chain at the point in time it is required for use or consumption. A just-in-time system has a number of supply chain benefits: reduced inventory, increased quality, reduced lead time, reduced scrap and rework and reduced equipment downtime. In broad terms, it is also used to describe the philosophy of short lead times and low inventory levels across the supply chain.

Logistics
The organization of moving, lodging and supplying materials. This is a more general term than supply chain management. Supply chain management is one method of handling logistics.

Loi Royer
In 1973, the Loi Royer was introduced in France in order to constrain the development of stores of between 1000 m² and 1500 m² and extensions over 200 m². The law was the result of political pressure from strong small shopkeeper organizations.

Organizational theories of supply chain management
States that collaborative activities within the supply chain or supply chain networks emerged as a competitive strategy, enabling organizations to operate entrepreneurially, adapt product and services rapidly within in highly dynamic environments.

Outsourcing
In the past few years, with increased global competition, pressures to reduce costs, downsize and concentrate on core businesses, has encouraged businesses to seek outside suppliers for products or services previously provided in-house. This is known as outsourcing.

Over-riders
A prearranged sum of money paid by manufacturers to retail central purchasing departments, which is based on agreed thresholds of product volumes ordered.

Padlock Law
Belgian planning regulation of 1975 restricting the development of large stores in Belgium. It would appear that given the slow growth of large stores, this measure has been relatively successful.

PESTE (Political, Economic, Social, Technological and Environmental)
Analytical framework which enables one to evaluate holistically impacts of the environment.

Process driven integrated information systems (PDIIS)
Integrated information systems which bring together information associated with a given process from across organizational functions.

Quasi-vertical integration
See vertically integrated networks (see also Fearne p. 79).

Quick Response (QR)

The umbrella term for the information systems and the JIT logistics systems that combine, to provide the right product, in the right place, at the right time (Christopher 1998). The basic idea behind QR is that, in order to reap the advantages of time-based competition, it is necessary to develop systems that are responsive and fast.

Relational contract theory

One of a number of theories which attempts to explain why strategic alliances and supply partnerships have emerged as an area of importance. In relational contract theory, relational contracts are regulated through 'norms beyond those centred on the exchange and its immediate process'. Emergence of recurrent relational contracts results from, the recognition of dependence or interdependence, and the pervasive use of coercion given the power asymmetries between members of the supply chain.

Retailer distribution centre (RDC)

A warehouse operated on behalf of or by a retailer that serves a number of stores in a specific area with a range of product types.

Sales based order (SBO)

A system of building a store's replenishment by using EPoS sales data to produce a forecast of future stock level requirements. Shelf frills and lead times can all be included in order to generate calculations.

Social network analysis/Sociological approach to networks

One of a number of theories, which attempts to explain why strategic alliances and supply chain partnerships have emerged as an area of importance. This was borrowed from anthropological and sociological studies of communities. In essence, the theory suggests that all business interactions, all economic actions, are embedded in social relations (Granovetter 1985). The individual involved in business transactions has also a place in society and the two cannot be disassociated.

Stock keeping unit (SKU)

A uniquely identifiable line within a store. Products may have different variations, e.g. 20% extra free. Each of these variations are individual SKUs.

Strategic alliances

In the main, retail organizations which operate as one buying group, thus increasing their purchasing power and market penetration. They are an alternative to the process of concentration among the grocery retail multiples and a point of contact for multi-national manufacturers.

Supply chain
Encompasses all of those activities associated with moving goods from raw materials stage through to the end user. This includes sourcing and procurement, product design, production planning, materials handling, ordering, processing and inventory management.

Supply chain management
Seeks to break down the barriers that exist between each of the units in the supply chain in order to achieve higher levels of service and substantial savings in costs. Successful supply chain management co-ordinates and integrates all of these activities into a seamless process. It embraces the different partners in the chain. In addition to the departments within the organization, these partners include suppliers, distributors and transportation carriers, third party logistics companies and information systems providers (see Horizontally integrated networks and Vertically integrated networks).

Supply management
Supply management refers to the establishment of operational procedures, issues, such as, synchronized production, continuous replenishment, cross docking and automatic ordering.

Symbol groups
A voluntary association; formed when a wholesale firm enters into an agreement with independent or small chains of retailers. In exchange for a guarantee to purchase a certain volume of goods per week, the retailer receives: a group identity, discounts, software for computer systems, own brands and umbrella national advertising and promotional campaigns.

Total cost management approach
A means of analysing costs through the value chain, by focusing upon the cost of value adding activities across the entire chain, both internal and external to the organization. Total cost management contains three key elements: activity based costing, process value analysis and performance measurement.

Transaction costs
Transaction costs have been described as the economic equivalent of friction in a physical system. In real terms they are costs other than production costs. They may include costs of drafting contracts, costs of negotiation, set of costs, the cost of risk and, indeed, social costs.

Transaction cost economics
Advances the proposition that organizations have for their main purpose the economizing of transaction costs. Transaction cost

economics focuses on the relative cost efficiencies of internally/externally managed productive activities. This theory suggest that collaborative activities have emerged as a result of seeking reductions in transaction costs in the current dynamic economic climate.

Vendor Managed Inventory (VMI)

Under VMI the customer (say a supermarket) no longer places orders with a supplier. Instead, it shares EPoS information (q.v.) with the vendor, together with knowledge of levels of current on-hand inventory, plus advice on anticipated additional marketing activity including special promotions. The customer also indicates upper and lower stock limits. Given access to all of this information, it is then the responsibility of the vendor to maintain the customer's inventory within the specified stock bands (Christopher 1998).

Vertical integration

A growth strategy, in which an organization acquires organizations upstream i.e. suppliers/distributors or downstream, i.e. customers, in order to gain or maintain a competitive advantage. Again, this term may be used loosely.

Vertically integrated networks

This, not a generally accepted term, refers to the long-term contractual agreement between members of a supply chain, e.g. suppliers, distributors, customers. It is distinctive from vertical integration – businesses retain their independent status, but combine forces through sharing knowledge/information for the purpose of maintaining or increasing market share. It is perhaps distinctive from quasi-vertical integration as it attempts to characterize the change in forms of business activity found in supply chain management.

Win–win

A term brought into common academic usage from Game theory, which indicates the state of affairs where two parties equally benefit from a given circumstances or transaction.

References

Christopher M.M. (1998) *Logistics and Supply Chain Management.* London: Pitman.

Granovetter M. (1985) Economic action and social structure: the problem of embeddedness. *American Journal of Sociology*, 91 (3), pp. 481–510.

Rosenfeld, S.A. (1996) Does co-operation enhance competitiveness? Assessing the impacts of inter-firm collaboration. *Research Policy*, 25, (2), pp. 247–63.

Index

Index of hospitality, retail, related and other organizations and divisions

Subject index